D1601064

The Campaign to Impeach
Justice William O. Douglas

The Campaign to Impeach Justice William O. Douglas

NIXON, VIETNAM, AND

THE CONSERVATIVE ATTACK

ON JUDICIAL INDEPENDENCE

Joshua E. Kastenberg

 University Press of Kansas

Published by the University Press of Kansas (Lawrence, Kansas 66045), which was organized by the Kansas Board of Regents and is operated and funded by Emporia State University, Fort Hays State University, Kansas State University, Pittsburg State University, the University of Kansas, and Wichita State University.

Library of Congress Cataloging-in-Publication Data

Names: Kastenberg, Joshua E., 1967– author.
Title: The campaign to impeach Justice William O. Douglas : Nixon, Vietnam, and the conservative attack on judicial independence / Joshua E. Kastenberg.
Description: Lawrence : University Press of Kansas, 2019. | Includes bibliographical references and index.
Identifiers: LCCN 2019006954
  ISBN 9780700628483 (cloth : alk. paper)
  ISBN 9780700628490 (ebook)
Subjects: LCSH: Douglas, William O. (William Orville), 1898–1980—Impeachment. | Political questions and judicial power—United States. | United States—Politics and government—1969–1974.
Classification: LCC KF8745.D6 K37 2019 | DDC 347.73/2634—dc23
LC record available at https://lccn.loc.gov/2019006954.

British Library Cataloguing-in-Publication Data is available.

Printed in the United States of America

10 9 8 7 6 5 4 3 2 1

The paper used in this publication is recycled and contains 30 percent postconsumer waste. It is acid free and meets the minimum requirements of the American National Standard for Permanence of Paper for Printed Library Materials Z39.48-1992.

To my parents

CONTENTS

Foreword by Senator Fred Harris ix

Preface and Acknowledgments   xiii

1 Cold War Politics and the Court under Siege 1

2 The Rising Men, the Muckrakers of the Judiciary, and
Beleaguered Judges 27

3 Douglas, Extrajudicial Activities, and the Vietnam Conflict 69

4 Ford's Attack on Douglas Begins 111

5 The House of Representatives Responds to Ford and the
Cambodian Invasion 155

6 A Long Summer of Discord: The Senate Awaits the House 200

7 Conclusion 243

Notes 259

Bibliography 297

Index 313

Several years ago I accompanied an English friend of mine to a local court-room where she was to be sworn in as a new US citizen. While we waited for the ceremony to begin, she proudly told me that she had missed only one question on the citizenship exam. Which one? The one, she paraphrased, that asked what method could be used in the United States to get rid of an unacceptable president. Her answer? Assassination!

Not the correct answer, of course, though that *was* the only successful method—a horrible one—ever used in our country. No US president has ever been removed through the impeachment process (the correct answer, of course) after conviction by a two-thirds vote in the Senate, for treason, bribery, or other high crimes or misdemeanors, as our national Constitution provides.

Nor has any member of the US Supreme Court ever been removed through the impeachment process, no matter that our founders must have thought that the constitutional availability of the impeachment process would be an especially needed and effective check on *judicial* officials who were to serve "during good behavior"—that is, for life. (And needless to say, thank God, no such official has ever been assassinated either.)

In fact, only one US Supreme Court member in history has ever even been impeached (charged) by the House: Associate Justice Samuel Chase, appointed by President George Washington. Chase's removal from office was reportedly sought (with the support of Thomas Jefferson, incidentally) because of Chase's political views as a Federalist, but the US Senate refused to convict him.

Through the years the possibility of impeachment has thus proved to be little threat to US Supreme Court justices generally; nor has it had any discernible check or restraint on their judicial behavior or decisions. But William O. Douglas, who served as associate justice of the US Supreme Court from 1939 to 1975, is something of an exception; he was the target of a serious but ultimately unsuccessful threat of impeachment in the US House of Representatives in 1970, as well as a much less serious earlier such threat in 1953.

It has been said of Supreme Court justices that few die and none resign.

William O. Douglas did resign, as have some others, in 1975, but in no case was resignation the result of impeachment threats. Douglas only resigned from the Court, and most reluctantly, after his impairment from a stroke caused his colleagues on the Court to gently press him to do so. But he never changed his private, political, or judicial behavior.

Loved and lionized by liberals, civil libertarians, environmentalists, and antiwar activists, Douglas was hated by many conservatives, who, spearheaded by the House of Representative's Republican leader, Gerald Ford, and vigorously urged on by President Richard Nixon, tried and failed to get him impeached by the House on criticisms and charges including his lack of judicial restraint, his frequent disregard for judicial precedent, his liberal political views and outspokenness against the war in Vietnam, his problematic private life with four marriages, and his receipt of certain questionable outside income.

All these and other details of the Douglas impeachment case are carefully laid out and discussed in this excellent and devotedly researched book, well worth reading, by noted law professor Joshua Kastenberg, who by his own admission has always thought of himself as a historian trapped in a lawyer's body.

Professor Kastenberg first got involved in studying the Douglas impeachment case because of his intellectual curiosity to know more about the whys and wherefores of such a historic confrontation between two famous Americans, both of whom he generally admired. He came to feel that Gerald Ford was wrong to allow himself to be duped by Attorney General John Mitchell and President Nixon into leading the attack on Douglas; he was also wrong in using, even effectively encouraging, a kind of anti–civil rights, antiliberal unholy alliance of conservative Republicans and racist Southern Democrats in the furtherance of that attack. Kastenberg notes with some interest that Ford's career was apparently not hurt by his leading the unsuccessful anti-Douglas fight; witness the fact that Ford was thereafter appointed vice president of the United States and then became president himself when Nixon resigned.

Professor Kastenberg laments the fact that in finally refusing to impeach Douglas, the House of Representatives missed a golden opportunity to specifically reject Gerald Ford's assertion that actionable grounds for impeachment are whatever in a given case a majority of the House of Representatives say they are—and moreover by failing to clearly define what actionable impeachment grounds are.

But might it not be said that in refusing to act on the impeachment charges filed against Justice Douglas, the House of Representatives was at least in a way furthering and expanding the precedent that the US Senate had set in the old Samuel Chase impeachment case when it in effect declared what are not actionable grounds for impeachment?

The Douglas impeachment case is well worth studying—and this highly interesting book well worth reading—because the Douglas case was a prototype political attack on judicial independence. It is a kind of eerie forerunner of, say, the present-day well-financed conservative campaigns we are seeing against sitting state judges who have handed down unpopular or controversial decisions.

In addition, this important book about the Douglas impeachment case makes the reader more aware that the polarization and partisanship that today characterize so much of the Supreme Court nomination process in the US Senate did not really begin with the so-called borking of President Ronald Reagan's 1987 Supreme Court nominee, Robert Bork. Indeed, this book may cause the reader to wish even more that there was some way by which Court confirmation hearings could be turned into serious discussions and considerations of judicial philosophy, including the nominee's honest and open disclosure of his or her own.

Fred Harris
Corrales, New Mexico
March 2019

When I retired from active duty after twenty-three years of wearing a military uniform, I was lucky to be able to fulfill my paramount professional ambition: to become a university professor. I practically grew up on a university campus, and I had wanted to be a part of the scholarly life. More importantly, I wanted to help students become a part of the next generation of leaders in the law and society. I attended four different universities for undergraduate, graduate, law, and graduate law programs. I learned from outstanding professors and peers. This did not stop in my military career. I believe that as I have passed the half-century mark of life, the best contribution I can make is to help future leaders learn from our past mistakes and successes, and to do so by adding to the corpus of history that is too often drowned by shallow sloganeering and stereotyping, attendant with the thirty-second sound bite that shapes current opinions. The law school students at the University of New Mexico give me ample faith that our future will be brighter and fairer than our present.

While this book focuses on the conduct of three men in particular, and hundreds of legislators who fought for, or against, racial and gender equality, as well as grappled over the question as to whether a president's claims of national security should outweigh individual liberties, I think it is important that I comment on two of the men, and perhaps two of the legislators.

I do admire Gerald Ford; I think he was decent man, and a better president than he was initially given credit for. Decent men occasionally blunder, and this was true not only in regard to Ford's efforts against Justice William O. Douglas but also in forming a temporary alliance with bigoted lawmakers and their supporters. A temporary alliance can, after all, leave a long-term if not permanent scar against the values of equality and respect for others. I "met" Ford twice. As a captain in the US Air Force, I shook his hand in Washington, DC, and he thanked me for my service. The second time requires a longer explanation. Ford had passed away, and I had just returned from my first Iraq deployment. I took my young son to pay respects to him while he lay in state at the Capitol. I returned to my work at the Pentagon, only to be confronted with a task to respond to a complaint from a judge advocate to a United States senator who was deployed to the dangerous place of Al-Udeid

Air Base, Qatar. The young judge advocate was upset because he was unable to return from his six-month deployment on a scheduled date since the aircraft had been diverted to use in Ford's funeral. By this time I was a major and working for a major general, who probably wanted me to summarily dispose of the officer. Instead, I wrote to the officer about Ford's vast contributions to the nation, including his wartime service, and added that there were other service members waiting to return who were actually in a war zone. This is the very point in time, however, where I first became aware of Ford's campaign against Douglas.

I also admire Douglas. When I teach criminal law and criminal procedure, I try to have a former Supreme Court clerk give a guest lecture on how an issue became law. One of Douglas's former clerks summed up the justice as having an unparalleled empathy for humanity. "The Justice cared deeply for the underdog," another former clerk told me. "He cared for the person at the bottom of the heap." I believe both of these clerks fairly characterized the justice. Douglas's empathy originated in his own experience with poverty; he believed that he could protect people against threats to their health and freedom through the law. He opposed McCarthyism and predatory business practices, and he sided with civil rights litigants. He was also at times accused of being of being arrogant and difficult to get along with. In addition, his four marriages provided ample fodder for conservatives who argued that he was a man without morals, though Douglas could counter that several of his critics engaged in extramarital affairs. Like Ford, Douglas was politically minded, and as a justice, he engaged in political activities including opposing the escalation of the war in Vietnam and spearheading the creation of new national parks. Douglas was an extraordinary man with extraordinary flaws, sometimes including a lack of judicial restraint. Yet in hindsight in my opinion, he was more often on the right side of history than not.

Although I researched over a hundred legislators' papers, there are two that I think are important to mention in the preface. While this book covers quite a bit on New York Democrat Emmanuel Celler, whose mastery of legislative procedures helped enable Douglas to continue on the Court, Patsy Mink and William M. McCulloch stand out to me as a models of what legislators ought to be. Mink was a liberal Democrat from Hawaii and McCulloch a conservative Republican from Ohio. They did not agree on many issues, but they supported racial equality and opposed Nixon's efforts to politicize the judiciary. They were tough and adhered to a moral principle of keeping our government honest. A number of Douglas's opponents, however, were wedded to a belief that racial inequality provided society with an important cement to preserve order.

Researching and writing a book is a journey. Well-preserved original source materials took me back to a different time and place. Although I have had the magnificent assistance of a number of archivists who labor to preserve our collective history across the country, I have not met any group does this better and with greater joy than Jeff Flannery, Joseph Jackson, Patrick Kerwin, Bruce Kirby, Edith Sandler, and Lewis Wyman at the Library of Congress, Manuscript Division.

I also want to thank my wonderful colleagues at the University of New Mexico School of Law. This book got its start with funding approved by deans Alfred Mathewson and Sergio Pareja the summer before I joined the law faculty and I am thankful for their trust. My discussions and friendships with Maryam Ahranjani, Marsha Baum, Michael Browde, Jim Ellis, Scott England, Scott Hughes, April Land, Nathalie Martin, Ted Occhialino, Mary Pareja, Leo Romero, Carol Suzuki, Clifford Villa, Peter Winograd, Dean Kevin Washburn of the University of Iowa School of Law, and Rachel Vanlandingham at the Southwestern School of Law, all helped in getting this book finished, whether they believe it or not. Although I owe a debt to each of these faculty members, I want to make special note of my two decades of discussions with, and guidance from, Gordon Hylton, a superb University of Virginia law professor and historian who passed away a year ago. He truly helped move this project along by inspiring me to seek the undiscovered gems of legal history. Although these people are august intellects, the mistakes in this book are mine alone. Of course I also thank the editorial staff at the University Press of Kansas.

This dedication is long overdue: I mentioned that I have cleared the half-century mark. I would like to believe that I have a dozen future books to write. One never knows. On more than one occasion I have dodged an unfriendly clock. I am a professor today because I had parents who prized education and loved me. I dedicate this book to them.

1

Cold War Politics and the Court under Siege

"Gerry Ford is so dumb he can't walk and chew gum at the same time." President Lyndon B. Johnson allegedly disparaged Ford with this comment in 1965 after learning that Ford had replaced Charles Halleck as the Republican minority leader in the House of Representatives. In 1964, the Republicans lost the largest number of congressional seats since the Franklin Roosevelt–led Democratic Party sweep of 1936. Johnson's comment, if he actually made it, had little to do with Ford's appointment to the Warren Commission, although there is an irony that Johnson appointed Ford to the committee charged with investigating the assassination of President John F. Kennedy, and this service added to Ford's national standing. Rather, Johnson's opinion was a reflection of the fact that in Ford's sixteen years in Congress, he had not introduced any major bill or shepherded any significant legislation into law. While Ford had served on several important committees and was reliably conservative, he avoided taking positions that would have gained him national prominence. Yet in an intraparty insurgency, the House Republicans chose Ford over Halleck. Older Republican members of Congress who supported Halleck must have wondered why those who backed Ford believed the latter possessed the leadership abilities necessary to rebuild their party. By the beginning of 1970 they did not need to question Ford's leadership. The Republicans rebounded in the 1966 midterm elections. After a full year of Richard Nixon's presidency, Ford built a durable alliance with Southern Democrats after they abandoned their party over civil rights, and in other major matters the Republicans appeared to be in lockstep. Although the Southern alliance with Ford occurred in response to Nixon's promise of empowering state and local governments, and despite the fact that Ford had voted for the 1957 and 1964 Civil Rights acts and the 1965 Voting Rights Act, he evidenced that he had the ability to convince Southern congressmen from across the aisle that he would protect their interests.[1]

On April 15, 1970, Ford, at Nixon's behest, brazenly called for the impeachment of long-serving Supreme Court justice William O. Douglas, the nation's leading liberal judge. In response, the House of Representatives Judiciary Committee conducted a six-month-long investigation. Congressional investigations of judges have been rare. Of the thousands of federal judges who have served since 1783, fewer than seventy have been investigated for wrongdoing or incompetence. Rarer still are actual judicial impeachments. Since the nation's founding, the House of Representatives has impeached fifteen judges. The Senate, in its trial process, convicted eight of the judges of violating at least one impeachment article. The bases for impeachment ranged from a judge joining the Confederacy in the Civil War to accepting kickbacks from litigants. Only one Supreme Court justice, Samuel Chase in 1805, has been tried in the Senate, though he was acquitted.

Ford was not the first legislator to seek Douglas's impeachment. In 1966 Thomas Abernethy, a Mississippi Democrat, introduced a resolution to the House to have Douglas investigated. Three Republican legislators—Senator Strom Thurmond of South Carolina, Senator Barry Goldwater of Arizona, and Congressman Harold Royce Gross of Iowa—had previously called for Douglas's impeachment. Unlike these men, however, Ford came closest to succeeding in removing Douglas from the Court. He had more than one hundred congressmen from both parties on his side. Ford's campaign against Douglas provides a mirror into the United States' changing political and social alignments: anti–civil rights Southerners were migrating into the Republican Party, liberal Republicans were disappearing from national politics, and thousands of working-class Americans who had been part of the Democratic Party since the New Deal were aligning instead with Nixon and the Republican Party. Race was also an important facet of Ford's anti-Douglas campaign.

While a few of Ford's congressional allies had voted for the 1964 Civil Rights Act, the majority subscribed to the tenets of legalized bigotry. That is, the bulk of his Southern allies were ardent segregationists; they also opposed equal rights for women. Days before Ford called for Douglas's removal, one of his staunchest allies, Republican William Lloyd Scott of Virginia, claimed that the Post Office's zone improvement plan—the zip code—was necessary because "niggers can't read." In the midst of the impeachment investigation, Florida representative William Cramer motioned the Supreme Court to permit him to argue as a special intervener in a busing appeal. When the Court denied his motion, Cramer responded that it was Congress and not the African Americans who were discriminated against. There was a balance to Ford's racist allies. None of the women or other minority members in Congress sided with Ford. Racism was not the only problem with Ford's efforts. His efforts against Douglas demonstrated that Nixon's administration would engage in actions dangerous to the nation's constitutional institutions—and in a broader sense to American democracy.[2]

Ford claimed that Douglas was unethical, had violated several laws, and was a threat to national security. Not since the Civil War, when radical Republicans insisted that Chief Justice Roger Baldwin Taney had aided the Confederacy, had such an accusation been leveled at a Supreme Court justice. Ford's actions in this instance were not a surprise, even if they stood in contrast to Abraham Lincoln's example of not joining in a political chorus to remove a justice. Six months before his speech, Ford had informed the nation in a CBS television broadcast that his office was in the process of investigating Douglas. Two days before Ford spoke against Douglas, several newspapers, including the *Austin American,* reported that Ford had prepared to introduce an impeachment resolution against Douglas. The timing of Ford's speech is noteworthy: it occurred shortly after conservative Republicans and Southern Democrats in the Senate succeeded in driving Justice Abe Fortas from the Court after revelations that Fortas—a Douglas protégé—had lied during his 1968 chief justice confirmation hearings and had accepted money from Louis Wolfson, who had been convicted of fraud. Then in 1969 Nixon nominated Clement Haynsworth to replace Fortas, only to have the Senate vote against the confirmation. Nixon's next Court nominee, G. Harrold Carswell, also failed to garner Senate confirmation. Both Haynsworth and Carswell were Southern conservatives, and both had a history of opposing civil rights. In order to prevent Haynsworth's and Carswell's nominations, congressional liberals relied on highlighting the nominees' ethical lapses, much as conservatives had pointed out Fortas's ethical shortcomings. Ethics, or rather its lack, became a theme in Ford's campaign for a sound reason. The federal judiciary, along with several state judiciaries, was already under scrutiny as justices on the supreme courts of both Oklahoma and Illinois had been removed from office after receiving kickbacks from litigants, and a small number of federal judges were accused of the same offense.[3]

Several scholars who have studied the attempted impeachment of Douglas have concluded that Ford's action was simply born of a desire for revenge for the defeat of Haynsworth and Carswell. Most recently Laura Kalman, in her superb book on how Nixon shaped the modern Supreme Court, posited that Ford orchestrated his impeachment efforts in response to Haynsworth and Carswell. This conclusion is sensible and reflects public opinion, but it is also incomplete. One week before Ford called for Douglas's impeachment, Indiana congressman Richard Roudebush forwarded to Ford a citizens' petition demanding Douglas's impeachment. "The people of Indiana are puzzled how the United States Senate can turn down men like Judges Carswell and Haynsworth and yet allow Douglas to remain on the Court," Roudebush claimed. "My mail is running heavy in favor of Douglas's impeachment and it was about 60 to 1 in favor of Carswell." In seeking Douglas's impeachment, Ford admitted that he was irate with the Senate over Haynsworth and Carswell, but he denied that this was a reason for his call to investigate Douglas. The reasons for Ford's and Nixon's actions are multifaceted and nefarious. These include Nixon's long-term hatred of Douglas, an attempted deflection for the controversial invasion of Cambodia, and a desire to rapidly build a conservative judiciary both to reverse the social and political changes the Court had enabled in the 1950s and 1960s, and to protect Nixon's policies.[4]

The reasons for Ford's actions, other than retaliation for Haynsworth and Carswell, have been partly clouded by the status of those who were a part of the nation's political machinery. Typifying the status of Ford's supporters, on March 31, 1970—a full two weeks before Ford called for Douglas's impeachment—Senator Robert C. Byrd, a West Virginia Democrat who had opposed civil rights, demanded that if the Senate were to deny Carswell's confirmation, Douglas had to be impeached. The linkage between Carswell's defeat and Ford's actions continued after Douglas voluntarily retired from the Court. Former attorney general and Ohio Republican senator William Saxbe insisted "in retaliation and probably in a fit of pique, [and] Nixon sicced GOP House minority leader Gerald Ford on Associate Justice William O. Douglas."

Likewise, Abner Mikva, a former Democratic congressman from Illinois and later a federal judge, claimed that Ford's actions had "created a sense of gratitude in President Nixon." White House counsel John Dean has written that retaliation was Nixon's motive for encouraging Ford to act. Finally, because according to John Ehrlichman Nixon despised Douglas more than any other federal jurist, the desire to have Douglas humiliated through the impeachment process could also have been motivated by revenge.[5]

Some of Ford's congressional contemporaries concluded that he acted against Douglas for purposes other than the ones he stated. Before the House adjourned on April 15, William Edwards, a three-term Democratic congressman from San Jose, California, and Edward Koch, a freshman Democratic congressman representing Manhattan, submitted a petition signed by forty-one of their peers condemning Ford's quest to impeach Douglas. The petition's signatories included Shirley Chisolm, Thomas "Tip" O'Neill, Patsy Mink, and John Conyers Jr., each of whom went on to dynamic congressional careers. The petition's wording directly charged Ford and his congressional allies with having ulterior motives in seeking Douglas's removal. "The political and social opinions of our colleagues sponsoring this bill are different than those of Mr. Justice Douglas in the major areas of civil rights, civil liberties, and the rights of the poor and the young," the petition began. "We must therefore suggest that the issues are broader than that indicated by the sponsors." Whether Koch and Edwards knew all the reasons for Ford's action is unknown, and a search of their personal correspondence does not shed any light on why they created the petition. Yet they were correct in their allegations against Ford, and by implication Nixon.[6]

A brief timeline also highlights Nixon's anger toward Douglas and involvement in Ford's actions. In early April 1970, Attorney General John Mitchell and his assistant in charge of the Justice Department's criminal division, William Wilson, provided Ford with information on Douglas. Wilson claimed that the Justice Department possessed evidence of Douglas's ties to organized crime through Albert Parvin, a wealthy casino owner, as well as a financial relationship to Lyndon Johnson's protégé, Robert "Bobby" Baker. In 1967 Baker was convicted of tax evasion. In 1960, Parvin, with Douglas's assistance, established an academic foundation to promote democracy in Latin America, and the foundation paid Douglas a stipend of $12,000 per year. Among Douglas's peers, there was nothing suspect about the foundation, but the stipend was higher than the average income of working Americans; it was also roughly one third of a Supreme Court justice's annual income. However, other judges participated in the foundation's activities. In 1961 Justice William Brennan spoke to the foundation on the importance of promoting independent judges in South and Central America as a guarantor against dictatorship, and Chief Justice Earl Warren gave the foundation his support. Moreover, it was common for judges to receive monetary compensation for serving on nonprofit organizations. Justices Brennan and Potter Stewart, for example, received stipends for serving on nonprofit boards.[7]

In spite of the common judicial practice of serving on the boards of charitable and nonprofit organizations, days after Nixon's inauguration, Mitchell informed Senator John J. Williams, a Delaware Republican, that the Justice Department had enough evidence to prosecute Douglas based on Douglas's relationship to Parvin and alleged ties to organized crime. Mitchell encouraged Williams to demand an investigation into Douglas modeled after the Senate's Teapot Dome hearings of the 1920s, in which members of President Warren G. Harding's administration had profited from illicit sales of oil stored for the navy's use. Although Williams had a prominent role in the impeachment of Douglas, he refrained from acting on Mitchell's supposed evidence. Ford thus became one of the most likely Republicans to lead the effort against Douglas because of his leadership position and the fact that he had not vocally opposed civil rights.[8]

Wilson insisted to Ford that Douglas had violated federal law by doing legal work on behalf of Parvin. Neither Mitchell nor Wilson acted without Nixon's assent, and they did not envision that the House would actually investigate Douglas. Rather, they believed that Douglas would resign rather than face the embarrassment of an investigation. Neither Wilson nor Mitchell had read through Ford's speech against Douglas before April 15, and neither man predicted that Ford would call for a formal investigation of Douglas in the way that he did. Benton Becker, an attorney who later advised Ford during his vice presidential confirmation hearings and on the pardon of Nixon, claimed that Ford had merely called for an investigation of Douglas and not his impeachment. But a reading of Ford's speech makes it clear that he intended for the House to forward articles of impeachment to the Senate, and Becker, whose personal files on the Douglas impeachment are currently sealed from public view, also played a less than distinguished role in Ford's attempt to remove Douglas from the Court.[9]

Wilson and Clark Mollenhoff, a *Des Moines Register* reporter serving in Nixon's administration, provided the impetus for Ford to begin an anti-Douglas campaign. Five years earlier, when the *Los Angeles Times* had reported on Douglas's relationship to Parvin, only Gross and Williams voiced objections to Douglas's activities. On several occasions in the 1950s and 1960s, conservatives accused Douglas of being a communist, and twice in the 1960s congressmen demanded investigations into Douglas's morality based on his four marriages and numerous alleged extramarital affairs. None of these accusations resulted in an investigation. Wilson and Mollenhoff promised Ford that the Justice Department's files contained specific instances of Mafia payoffs to Douglas, and that Ford would be given access to these files. These claims were patently untrue and the promise of access never materialized, but Ford to his detriment relied on both men.

Although there were numerous hints that Ford was to make a move against Douglas, the events that dominated the news before his April 15 speech included massacres of ethnic Vietnamese in Cambodia; stalled peace talks between the United States and North Vietnam; the launch of the United States' third manned flight to the moon and its subsequent near disaster; and the Senate voting against Carswell. In Amman, Jordan, a large number of disaffected people attacked the US embassy, and Nixon attempted to enter into arms reduction negotiations with Soviet premier Leonid Brezhnev while simultaneously trying to gain congressional funding for the development of a domestic missile protection system known as the anti–ballistic missile defense. An Israeli airstrike in Egypt killed forty-two children, and several Czechoslovakian judges were arrested in in an ongoing communist purge after the Soviet invasion of that country two years earlier. Domestically, there was a shootout between burglary suspects and police in Newhall, California, and a threatened Teamster's Union strike. A grand jury inquest into Senator Edward "Ted" Kennedy's conduct in the death of Mary Joe Kopechne was also reported in depth. Finally, as a cultural matter, the world's most popular rock band, the Beatles, broke up. For a brief time Ford's speech and the ensuing investigation into Douglas would be reported alongside these events, often as a front-page story.

Major newspapers in the United States, such as the *New York Times,* the *Philadelphia Inquirer,* the *Chicago Tribune,* and the *Los Angeles Times,* headlined Ford's speech. So too did the English-speaking world's prominent newspapers. Australia's largest circulating newspaper, the *Sydney Morning Herald,* reported that Ford's "virulent attack launched efforts by a group of conservative Republicans and Democrats to have the Judge, noted for his liberal views, removed from the Bench." On April 17, 1970, *The Times,* Britain's largest-circulation newspaper with an unequaled international reach, informed its readers that Ford had engaged in "a conservative–liberal vendetta and there is some suspicion that he has the tacit support of the White House." The British newspaper added that Nixon's most recent nominee, Harry Blackmun, had taken part in three cases involving corporations in which he held stock while on the Court of Appeals for the Eighth Circuit, thereby conveying to its readers that Ford's efforts should be examined through a highly skeptical lens. Canada's largest newspaper, the *Toronto Globe and Mail,* likewise headlined Ford's speech in a negative light. The critical features of this reporting were not only that Ford, at Nixon's behest, had sought the removal of a justice for political reasons and in so doing threatened to undermine a constitutional institution, but also that Nixon could not be trusted in other matters.[10]

Less than two weeks after Ford spoke in the House, Nixon ordered a ground invasion of Cambodia. The North Vietnamese military used neutral Cambodian territory as a means to transport weapons and soldiers south. Military plans to send large numbers of forces to a foreign land are seldom created hours before an operation; indeed, weeks before Ford spoke against Douglas, Ford was aware that an invasion was likely. In hindsight, the invasion was predictable. Six months before it occurred, Nixon initiated a covert aerial bombing campaign, Operation Menu, against North Vietnamese military targets in Cambodia, but the bombing did not curb communist activity in that country. To opponents of the war, the 1969 aerial campaign and the April 30, 1970, invasion of Cambodia were at odds with Nixon's earlier promise not to enlarge the United States' role in the Vietnam conflict, and the 1970 invasion led to nationwide unrest. Oddly, for reasons of secrecy that became emblematic of Nixon's administration, the president did not confer with the secretary of defense, Melvin Laird, or the secretary of state, William Rodgers, about his final invasion decision in 1970, but he did consult with Henry Kissinger (his national security advisor) and Ford.[11]

Laird and Rodgers had earlier presciently warned Nixon that the widening of the war into Cambodia would lead to domestic upheaval, and news leaks about Operation Menu caused Nixon to suspect them of disloyalty. Evidencing Nixon's distrust of his two key cabinet secretaries as well as Congress as a whole, the president limited information on the pending Cambodia operation to a small, select number of legislators. To this end, he informed Richard Russell and John Stennis in the Senate, and Ford and Leslie Arends in the House. Russell and Stennis were conservative anti–civil rights Southern Democrats. Both men backed Nixon's Vietnam policies and insisted that the Supreme Court had eroded traditional values. If the Senate were to vote on impeaching Douglas, it was likely that Russell and Stennis would side with Ford. Finally, Arends was the Republican minority whip—the second-ranking Republican in the House—and had an unequaled reputation for conservatism. In spite of Nixon's calculation that the invasion would be politically acceptable to a majority of Americans, when on April 29, 1970, 32,000 US soldiers and a larger contingent of South Vietnam's military forces invaded Cambodia, not only were there large-scale antiwar demonstrations on college campuses but there was also pronounced congressional dissent against the Cambodian operation. Even as Congress debated placing historically unusual limits on Nixon's ability to use military force outside Vietnam, it also debated the veracity of Ford's allegations and Douglas's fate. And Douglas had openly skewered both Johnson's and Nixon's use of the military in Vietnam. If the Cambodian invasion failed because of public dissent at home, then Douglas would have served as a public figure to blame for stabbing the nation in the back. A similar model of blame had been used before, but in Germany in the late 1920s and early 1930s.[12]

It is also noteworthy that Ford's attack on Douglas also occurred at a time when a small number of other federal judges had been attacked for allegedly undermining national security or were being prosecuted for corruption. Ford accused Douglas of having ties to organized crime, promoting rebellion on college campuses, and intentionally weakening the national security of the United States. In an attack mirroring Fortas's relationship to Wolfson, Ford accused Parvin, a casino owner who created a foundation and disbursed scholarships, of being a bridge between communism and organized crime on the one hand, and Douglas on the other. Parvin was not merely a casino owner. He had built a business furnishing hotels, but his publicly traded com-

pany was in the midst of a Securities and Exchange Commission investigation at the time of Ford's allegations. Moreover, Parvin had paid monies to
organized crime figures in securing ownership of casinos. Ford also alleged
that Douglas had allied with pornographers and had worked to undermine
Goldwater, the 1964 Republican presidential candidate.[13]

Congressional, Political, and Social Divisions: Communism, Civil Rights, and the Court

Although Johnson was given to coarse and profane descriptions of politicians, and there is some doubt that he actually described Ford as being too
incompetent to perform basic bodily functions, Johnson had little regard for
the future president. And he was not alone in his views. In the first year of
Ford's presidency, conservative columnist George Will observed that either
Ford had been "abler" than he had been given credit for, or being president
was easier than most Americans assumed. Yet Ford had a compelling life
story. He was the child of an abusive father, and his mother had secured custody and a divorce in an era when divorce carried a stigma. Because he and
his mother left while he was an infant, he did not know his biological father
until later in life. Ford was hardly mediocre. He was a successful student athlete at the University of Michigan, and he was a Yale University Law School
graduate before joining the navy to serve in World War II. But he was also
easy to lampoon as oafish, clumsy, and intellectually limited. Although he
was a former college football player and a far better athlete than several of his
presidential peers, the public saw him as a friendly dolt who fell down airport
staircases. In contrast, Kennedy was portrayed as a physically vibrant man
despite his physical infirmities. And Ford was easy to spoof. In a Peter Sellers
movie where the fate of the United Nations is at stake, the character playing
Ford only seems interested in learning the score of a Michigan–Notre Dame
football game, while the secretary of state, Henry Kissinger, tries to educate
him on the dangers to the world. In 1975, during the first season of *Saturday
Night Live,* the comedian Chevy Chase drew howls of laughter mimicking
Ford's stumbles on golf courses and airplane ramps. However, unlike current
presidents, Ford's skin was thick enough to laugh at his own expense. With
the exception of Harry Truman, Ford was fundamentally different than his
twentieth-century predecessors. He did not expect to become president. He

was content in Congress, and his loftiest goal was to become Speaker of the House of Representatives. He was the definition of an accidental president.[14]

Ford's reputation for legislative leadership before his presidency, in contrast to Johnson's and Nixon's, was largely based on his affability. Johnson was a powerful, at times bullying, Senate majority leader who could take credit for pushing several significant bills into law, including national defense appropriations and civil rights protections. He proved to be a valuable ally to President Eisenhower when Republican legislators opposed their president's policies. He also resisted Truman's prounion efforts. Nixon's reputation as a vicious campaigner followed him into the House when he took on Alger Hiss in 1948. Much more insightful than Senator Joseph McCarthy, Nixon understood and used the power of accusation to his advantage, leading him to a Senate victory in 1950 and two years later to an eight-year vice presidential tenure under Eisenhower.[15]

Congressmen who opposed Johnson and Nixon had reason to fear both men, particularly when the congressmen came from their respective parties. As a party leader from 1953 to 1961, Johnson dispensed committee assignments according to his personal alliances. He made Senator Estes Kefauver, a Tennessee Democrat known for his televised assault on organized crime, miserable by denying him prestigious assignments. Yet in 1949 Johnson reached out to Senator Hubert Humphrey after many senators had ostracized the freshman Minnesotan over his support for civil rights, and assigned him to the prestigious Foreign Relations Committee. Nixon's attack on Hiss could scare liberal Republicans from opposing the House Un-American Activities Committee. Too young to have achieved legislative prominence in the same manner as Johnson, Nixon showed promise rather than accomplishment to an older generation of conservative Republicans. At the age of thirty-nine, Nixon became Eisenhower's running mate because senior Republican leaders such as Thomas Dewey and Herbert Brownell advised Eisenhower that Nixon was the future leader of their party. Johnson and Nixon also survived political scandals before their presidencies. As a congressman, Ford was scandal free; he was a consistent anticommunist conservative, and he did not vocally take a side in the debates over civil rights versus segregation.[16]

The removal of a federal officer such as a judge is a constitutional process. A majority of the House of Representatives must vote to forward articles of impeachment to the Senate. Before the House vote, it must conduct an investigation. By its own rules, the Judiciary Committee is assigned to conduct the investigation. If a simple majority of the House votes to forward articles of impeachment, then the Senate conducts a trial. The House appoints prosecutors—known as managers—to the Senate trial. If two thirds of the senators find that the federal officer has violated one or more of the charges, then the federal officer is removed from the government. The Senate cannot sentence the federal officer to prison or seize the officer's property. Obtaining a two-thirds Senate vote on any charge has historically proven difficult. Ironically, had Nixon not resigned, the required two-thirds vote would likely have been achieved. In 1868 President Andrew Johnson survived an impeachment trial in the Senate by one vote. In the 1998 impeachment of President William Clinton, the House voted to forward one article of impeachment charging perjury and one article of impeachment charging obstruction of justice to the Senate. But because only fifty of the one hundred senators voted guilty in the obstruction charge and forty-five voted guilty in the perjury charge, Clinton retained the presidency.

One of the reasons why Ford, and for that matter Nixon, believed that there was a chance of impeachment had to do with makeup of Congress and the relationships between various congressional factions. In 1969, in the Senate, Southern Democrats aligned with conservative Republicans to force Justice Abe Fortas from the Supreme Court under a threat of impeachment. Shortly after Fortas's departure, liberal Democrats and moderate Republicans prevented Haynsworth and Carswell from being confirmed to the Court, resulting in Southern politicians claiming the existence of an anti-Southern bias. The belief in an anti-Southern bias within the Democratic Party strengthened the bonds between conservative Republicans and Southern Democrats. Congressional reactions to the Court's decisions on civil rights and national security also highlighted internal party divisions and cross-party alliances in the legislative branch. Ford and Nixon believed that if there was some tangible proof of Douglas's malfeasance, then there were likely to be enough representatives and senators to support impeachment.[17]

It may be difficult for contemporary observers of American politics to imagine that there was a time when party affiliation was merely suggestive of a political unity, and that strong and seemingly permanent congressional alliances, particularly in the Senate, crossed party lines. But in the early 1950s, liberal Republicans who supported civil rights aligned with Northern Democrats. A small number of Midwestern conservative Republicans contributed to the passage of the 1964 Civil Rights Act, even though the Republican presidential candidate, Senator Barry Goldwater, insisted that federal civil rights enforcement was unconstitutional. Likewise, Southern Democrats who were almost uniformly anti–civil rights allied with Goldwater.[18]

A decade before the 1964 Civil Rights Act, Southern Democrats had targeted the Court after it issued a unanimous decision in *Brown v. Board of Education.* Senators Olin Johnston, a South Carolina Democrat, and James O. Eastland, a Mississippi Democrat, introduced a resolution to "discover the communistic sources of information" that served as "the inspiration for the justices' legal reasoning." In 1957 Eastland advised West Virginian Robert C. Byrd to run his Senate campaign in opposition to the Court. "No one can beat this politics, running against Warren, Brownell, and the NAACP," Eastland claimed. One year later, the Court again infuriated Southerners when it upheld the use of federal military forces to ensure that Arkansas followed the dictates of *Brown* in *Cooper v. Aaron.* Other decisions that angered Southerners included *Baker v. Carr,* in which the Court in 1962 determined that the federal courts had jurisdiction to oversee state voting apportionment systems. In other words, the federal judiciary could find that voting districts that determined the composition of state legislatures were unconstitutional when the districts excluded minority voters in comparison to white voters. In 1964 the Court determined in *Reynolds v. Sims* that in states with bicameral legislatures, each part of the legislature—that is, a house and a senate—had to be equitably apportioned. This decision resulted in a similar outcry, but now Northern conservatives who had voted for civil rights bills added their voice to Southern anger.[19]

Southern Democrats not only fought the Court but also promised to oppose judicial nominations unless there was clear evidence that the nominees were prosegregationist. For instance, after Eisenhower's nomination of Solicitor General Simon Sobeloff to the Court of Appeals for the Fourth Circuit, Senator Samuel Ervin, a North Carolina Democrat, vowed to his constituents that he would vote against the nomination because of Sobeloff's civil rights jurisprudence. Sobeloff's sin, in Ervin's judgment, was that he had filed an amicus brief in support of the NAACP in *Brown.* When a constituent referred to Sobeloff as a "Jew boy," and when John Kerr, a state senator, claimed Sobeloff was a "secretive Russian," Ervin noted that he shared their views. When

Johnson nominated Thurgood Marshall, all of the Southern senators voted against him or made their displeasure known by absenting themselves from the vote. Eastland went so far as to accuse Marshall of being a racist against whites.[20]

Civil rights was only one area where the Court came under attack. Several historians have observed that after World War II, when the Republican Party's leadership was searching for a centerpiece issue, national security became the most obvious choice. In the 1930s, Republicans opposed the New Deal; several prominent Republicans were isolationist, if not accepting of Nazi Germany, and were hostile to Britain and France. Included in this latter group were legislators who later attacked the Court for being procommunist, such as Robert Taft, John Bricker, and Styles Bridges. The threat of communism, both abroad and inside the United States, enabled a Republican resurgence and accusations of a procommunist Court continued through Nixon's administration. In 1968, Herman Schneebeli, a conservative Republican representative from Pennsylvania, sent Justice Hugo Black a petition signed by more than five hundred constituents, alleging that the Court had overly protected communism and put the country at peril. Black angrily responded that neither Schneebeli nor his constituents could be considered experts in constitutional law.[21]

Just as Southern legislators proposed laws to narrow the Court's jurisdiction over state court decisions, so too during the 1950s and 1960s was it common for conservatives from both parties to introduce bills stripping the Court of its jurisdiction over national security cases. Often these bills did not make it out of the judiciary committees, but their existence demonstrated a belief that some justices undermined national security. Powerful senators such as Indiana Republican William Jenner and Nevada Democrat Patrick McCarran championed laws to prohibit the Court from reviewing the appeals of allegedly subversive citizens, whether these appeals originated in criminal convictions or from a public schoolteacher who had been fired after being suspected of communist sympathies. In 1962, Congressman Thomas Abernethy, a Mississippi Democrat, introduced a bill to remove the Court from hearing appeals arising from the lower courts' decisions upholding the constitutionality of public school prayer. Abernethy claimed that the Court's outlawing of mandatory prayer was nothing more than an invitation to communism. Even President Eisenhower, who normally avoided publicly attacking the Court, accused it of protecting "commies." In 1966 Congressman William Dickinson, an Alabama Republican, introduced a bill requiring the Senate to reconfirm all federal judges every six years. Dickinson claimed that once enacted into law, this would be a means for the legislative branch to "get rid of bad judges." The following day, Earle Cabell, a Texas Democrat, introduced a bill to end the ability of five justices to determine that a state or federal law was unconstitutional. Instead of a simple majority, Cabell's bill would have required a two-thirds majority to make such a determination.[22]

Yet there were enough Democrats and Republicans who saw the jurisdiction-stripping bills as political acts that would undermine the judicial branch by making it subservient to the president or Congress, and they managed to defeat the bills. In 1959 Senator Wayne Morse, an Oregon Democrat who had begun his senatorial career in 1945 as a Republican, admonished conservative legislators that not only were their baseless claims against the Court false and opportunistic, but they also would weaken public confidence in the judiciary, and in turn weaken international confidence in the government. In 1966 Senator Gale McGee, a Wyoming Democrat, responded to dozens of voters who called for the removal of procommunist justices, stating that impeachment resulting from disagreements with judicial decisions was a far greater constitutional danger than the Court's decisions. Unsurprisingly, legislators from both parties who opposed jurisdictional limits on the Court, like Morse and McGee, became Douglas's staunchest allies.[23]

Party disunity was one reason Ford ultimately failed to have Douglas impeached. That is, not all of the House Republicans agreed with his actions, and several objected to the impeachment campaign as being dangerous to the Constitution. As an example of preexisting divisions within the Republican Party, one only need look to the 1952 Republican national convention. Perhaps it was inevitable that Dwight Eisenhower became the Republican presidential nominee, but the other candidates reveal significant ideological differences within the party. Robert Taft, son of former president and chief justice William Howard Taft, had long been an isolationist, to the point that he opposed the United States' involvement in the North Atlantic Treaty Organization. Taft also condemned the postwar trials against Nazi and Japanese government officials, and he supported Senator Joseph McCarthy's anticommunist crusade. (In 1951, Taft "earnestly listened" to a constituent who claimed that Douglas wanted worldwide communism, but the senator resisted making a public comment against the justice.) In contrast, Eisenhower unsurprisingly embraced the United States' active participation in alliances to contain, if not roll back, communism, and he never publicly endorsed Mc-Carthy. In the 1968 Republican presidential race, Nixon stood in the middle of a spectrum, with liberals such as Nelson Rockefeller and George Romney on one side and a John Birch–backed Governor Ronald Reagan on the other. Republican Party divisions were also pronounced in Congress. Moderates such as John Sherman Cooper of Kentucky, Hugh Scott of Virginia, Charles McCurdy Matthias of Maryland, and Margaret Chase Smith of Maine were willing to vote against Haynsworth and Carswell. Moreover, Cooper, Matthias, and Smith were open critics of Nixon's Vietnam policies.[24]

Party disunity was not limited to the Republicans. At the same time that Eisenhower was seeking the 1952 Republican nomination, the Democratic Party's inheritors of the New Deal were struggling to find unity as the leading candidates—Illinois governor Adlai Stevenson, a liberal endorsed by Eleanor Roosevelt, and Richard Russell, a long-serving anti–civil rights senator from Georgia who had successfully taken General Douglas MacArthur to task during a Senate Armed Services Committee inquiry into Truman's firing of the general during the Korean War—vied for the nomination. Four years earlier, Democratic Party voters in Louisiana, Mississippi, Alabama, and South Carolina delivered those states' Electoral College votes to Thurmond after he left the Democratic Party to run as a prosegregationist states' rights Dixiecrat. Other Southern legislators refused to campaign for Truman. Among Truman's sins was that he had integrated the military and pushed for increased civil rights enforcement.[25]

Although there were a multitude of issues other than civil rights and communism that concerned Congress, these were the most visible political matters. It was in the context of these two issues that Douglas would find himself embattled, though he was not the only justice to face conservative opprobrium. In 1952 Edward M. Pooley, the editor of the El Paso *Post-Tribune*, implored Chief Justice Frederick Vinson to remove Douglas from the Court. In addition to Douglas's well-known penchant for adultery, which led to accusations of the justice being too immoral to hold a judicial position, Pooley accused Douglas of being sympathetic to communism. Vinson initially ignored Pooley's letter, which resulted in a second demand to remove not only Douglas but also justices Stanley Reed and Felix Frankfurter after they provided mitigating evidence for Alger Hiss. After receiving Pooley's second letter, Vinson responded by acknowledging Pooley's right to his opinions, but he then disagreed that the Court strengthened communism.[26]

In 1958, when the John Birch Society formed, its leaders accused Chief Justice Earl Warren of being a communist. In January 1961 the society issued a nationwide bulletin calling for Warren's impeachment. The next month the society proclaimed, "Unless the Warren Court can be stopped from its transformation of our constitutional republic into a mobocracy and from giving aid and comfort at every turn to our Communist enemies, the country was doomed." The same year that the John Birch Society came into being, another anticommunist organization based in Arlington, Virginia, asserted in its newsletter, *Task Force*, that the Court had denied both the federal government and the states the authority to protect the nation against communism. Perhaps surprisingly, the writers of this journal lauded the supreme court of West Germany for outlawing the Communist Party, "in a refreshing and realistic appraisal of the facts underlying the communist conspiracy." By 1955 the Daughters of the American Revolution had accused the Court of permitting communism to take over the country. In 1951 the Liberty Lobby, yet another anticommunist organization, formed, and its president accused Douglas of being a communist. In 1969 the Liberty Lobby accused Douglas of accepting money from Meyer Lansky, one of the Mafia's leading financiers. In 1961 New Mexico senator Clinton Presba Anderson, one of Douglas's defenders, found himself attacked by the Liberty Lobby and another anticommunist organization, the Committee for Constitutional Government, for promoting communism by defending the Court.[27]

While the John Birch Society and the Liberty Lobby could be dismissed as fringe movements, the American Bar Association (ABA) had been since its inception in 1878 the leading organization overseeing and shaping the practice of law in the nation. In 1959 one of the ABA's committees, the Special Committee on Communist Tactics, Strategy, and Objectives, openly chastised the Court for endangering national security by linking its decisions to an alleged growth of communist activity in the United States. In other words, the committee accused the Court of enabling the Communist Party of the United States to flourish, declaring that this would result in an increase in espionage. While the ABA later clarified that it did not intend to censure the Court, its committee's actions encouraged further criticism.

Occasionally prominent state court judges turned on the Court. On April 12, 1954, Michael A. Musmanno, a Pennsylvania supreme court justice, implored the House Judiciary Committee to investigate the US Supreme Court "to ensure the justices and their clerks were not in the Communist Party's employ."[28]

In 1961 Dan Smoot, a retired FBI agent turned news commentator, accused Warren of being "a socialist who welcomed a communist takeover." Smoot went on to claim that "over one thousand learned and distinguished Americans" could testify against Warren, Black, and Douglas. At the same time an organization called the Western Pennsylvania Council for America alleged Warren, Frankfurter, Black, and Douglas were communists. Joe R. Johnson, the minister of the First Christian Church of Central City, Kentucky, in a statewide mailer, claimed that although Frankfurter had voted procommunist 77 percent of the time and Douglas had done so in 95 percent of cases, Black was "a one hundred percent ally of communism." Led by Clydene Attaway, a Southwestern organization calling itself the Arizona Mothers for Warren's Impeachment sent a petition containing more than one hundred signatures to Senator Eastland, the prosegregationist chairman of the Senate Judiciary Committee.[29]

Aside from Eastland's disgust with the Court's civil rights decisions, there was a reason that conservative voters, including those that identified with the Republican Party, sent him complaints about the Court being soft on communism. In 1962 he claimed that "the whole Supreme Court is a nest of socialists and worse," continuing with the argument that Warren had to be impeached "for punching huge ragged holes in the Constitution of the United States." This was not the first time Eastland had accused the Court of coddling communists. He was certain that there was a linkage between the Court's civil rights decisions and their alleged acceptance of communism. In 1957, after the Supreme Court determined in *Jenks v. United States* that federal prosecutors were constitutionally required to provide defendants with the identities and statements of secret informants, Eastland introduced a resolution to amend the Constitution so that all serving justices would have to be renominated every four years. Eastland was not the only legislator to react to *Jenks* by trying to alter the Constitution. On June 27, 1957, Congressman Joseph Montoya, a New Mexico Democrat, informed a former governor that he "could not remember a time in [his life] when [he] had heard such controversies," before concluding that "in every conversation these days between members of Congress, the subject is brought up over and over again."[30]

With the exception of Thurmond, Southern legislators were not willing to shed their party affiliation, even in 1968. They may have agreed with much of what Nixon advocated, such as a retreat from federal enforcement of matters that had been traditionally been left to the states before the New Deal, and they certainly embraced Nixon more than they did his opponent, Hubert Humphrey. In spite of Nixon, however, the Republican Party was still the party of Lincoln, and the party title still mattered. That is, liberal Republicans and even some of their conservative peers remained committed to civil rights. Nixon and Ford realized this and sought Southern support against Douglas. This was an important element of what became known as the Southern strategy. However, obtaining the support of Southern legislators without alienating liberal Republicans was not an easy task, particularly when the efforts to do so were transparent. In 1961 Senator Paul Douglas, an Illinois Democrat, accused his Southern Democrats of entering "an unholy alliance" with conservative Republicans. By the time Nixon had left office, numbers of liberal Republicans were in decline while the conservatives were growing in strength.[31]

Nixon was initially able to disguise his attempts to woo Southern voters. In his 1968 speech accepting his party's presidential nomination, he urged that the term "American" should be applied to all races. Because large numbers of white Southerners voted for prosegregationist George Wallace in Louisiana, Arkansas, Mississippi, Alabama, and Georgia, Nixon did not have to overtly appeal to that constituency in the general election. Moreover, because Southern legislators linked the rise of crime and social dissent with civil rights, Nixon had a chance to use the Southern strategy once he had defeated Wallace and Humphrey. This meant appointing judges who had previously supported segregation, curtailing enforcement of school desegregation, and ending other federal programs that had a civil rights component, including Johnson's antipoverty programs.[32]

In order to assess how Nixon's Southern strategy played a role in the effort to impeach Douglas, it is critical to begin with the Southern Manifesto. After the Court issued *Brown,* Thurmond wrote the first draft of a protest against the Court's determination to destroy segregation laws. Thurmond and the manifesto's other signatories claimed the Court undermined "amicable relations between the races," and they insisted that a new wave of judicial tyranny threatened constitutional relations between citizens and the federal government. If the manifesto was nothing more than a statement in opposition to both the Court and to the Eisenhower administration's enforcement of the Court's decisions, then it would have merely reflected Southern dissatisfaction with the Court's jurisprudence. But the manifesto was more than a statement of opposition. It encouraged legislators to defy the Court while they tried to legislatively overturn *Brown*. In other words, although the final draft of the manifesto took a more moderate position than Thurmond's original draft, its signatories evidenced a willingness to overtly ignore constitutional standards.[33]

Many of the Southern legislators who signed the final draft of the Southern Manifesto in 1956 remained in Congress in 1970. All of the forty-one signatories who remained in the House when Ford called for Douglas's impeachment aligned with Ford against Douglas. In the Senate, the signatory list included Eastland, Stennis, Russell, Ervin, Thurmond, Fulbright, John Sparkman, John McClellan, Allen Ellender, Russell Long, and Harry Byrd. With the exception of Fulbright and Ervin, these men were predisposed to oust Douglas from the Court if for no other reason than they had more than fifteen years of lamenting his votes, including requiring school integration, prohibiting discrimination in businesses and employment, and preventing the dilution of minority votes by mandating fair legislative districting. In the last year of Johnson's presidency, Douglas insulted Southern legislators in the midst of the Vietnam conflict by pointing out that Southern conscription boards were almost universally staffed with white men who decided whether to grant African American men exemptions from military service. To Douglas, this fact was the reason that African Americans were ordered to Vietnam in increasing numbers.[34]

Vietnam and the Impeachment Winds

It would be difficult to find an issue more divisive to the national polity in the modern era than the Vietnam conflict. From Truman through Kennedy, each administration seemed to understand that the nation would not cohesively support a long-term commitment to a war in Southeast Asia. This is why, for instance, Eisenhower did not send American military personnel to fight alongside France in that country's efforts to maintain Vietnam as a colony. Yet in spite of the knowledge that a significant number of Americans would oppose a long-term war in Vietnam, Kennedy increased the numbers of military personnel in that country. By the time Johnson became president, North Vietnam's military forces and their communist allies in the south had succeeded in pushing the South Vietnamese government into defensive military operations, and the South Vietnamese government was at continual risk of falling without American support. After reports of attempted attacks on American naval vessels in 1964, Johnson sought congressional approval for a military response. Only senators Morse and Ernest Gruening voted against the resolution. However, within a year, a small but growing number of legislators began to openly voice opposition to escalating the United States' involvement. Their number included Democrats Albert Gore of Tennessee, Eugene McCarthy of Minnesota, George McGovern of South Dakota, Joseph Clark of Pennsylvania, Robert Kennedy of New York, and Fulbright. With the exception of Kennedy, who was assassinated in 1968, and Clark, who had lost in an election that year, these senators would rally to protect Douglas.[35]

The increased ranks of legislators opposing the involvement in Vietnam reflected a growing divide in the nation where antiwar demonstrations grew in number between 1966 and 1970. Regionally, the major geographic centers of antiwar demonstrations were in the Northeast, in the upper Midwestern cities, and on the West Coast. Antiwar sentiment evolved, in a few notable instances, into revolutionary antigovernment activities. Both the antiwar movement and general dissatisfaction with the Vietnam conflict entered into the armed forces as well. From 1967 through to the withdrawal of forces from Vietnam, the military suffered internal dissension ranging from underground newspapers to open defiance of orders. In 1966 the army desertion rate was fourteen soldiers out of every thousand in uniform, but by 1970 it had grown to more than seventy soldiers per thousand. Narcotic use permeated the military as well. By the time Ford called for Douglas's impeachment, the nation was not unified, the military was in disarray, and conservatives added to their criticism of the judiciary that some of the nation's justices and judges had openly sought a US defeat in Vietnam.[36]

Lack of discipline in the military was nothing new to the United States' armed forces, which, after all, had a robust, though at the time not fully equitable, system of courts-martial and administrative processes to deal with recalcitrant service members. Even at the height of World War II there were instances in which small numbers of soldiers or sailors had refused to follow orders or participated in acts of defiance. But by 1970 there were more than 130 underground newspapers, thousands of conscientious objector applicants from already serving service members, and thousands of military reservists who sought judicial rulings to declare that their federal activation orders and eventual service in Vietnam were unconstitutional. There were also instances of fragging, a term denoting the murder of officers by enlisted men.[37]

While Truman had integrated the military two decades earlier, race relations in the military were a reflection of race relations in the country. African Americans comprised 6 percent of the armed forces in 1962 but 12 percent in 1970. This increase was largely a result of a conscription scheme that placed the nation's poorer young men at a disadvantage. In 1963 future judge Gerhard Gesell, another Douglas protégé, headed a committee chartered by Secretary of Defense Robert McNamara to examine racism in the military and concluded that a variety of factors, ranging from the attitudes and laws of communities surrounding bases in the southern United States to a shortage of African American officers, led to inequities in military service. Anger over racial disparities, just like anger over the war, permeated the military, and in an unprecedented manner, much of the internal conflict over the war was fought in the nation's federal courts.[38]

Although the majority of federal judges did not side with antiwar litigants, there were a few, including Douglas, who did. Moreover, most of the federal judges who ruled against the government avoided public appearances. This was not true for Douglas. It was, and is, not uncommon for Supreme Court justices to make speeches and participate in public events. Yet Douglas was different than his peers. An avid hiker and outdoorsman, he wrote of the importance of preserving the environment. Some of his writings and speeches on the environment drew the ire of congressmen. In 1969 Delaware's representative, Republican William Roth, complained to Earl Warren that in a speech Douglas had accused the Army Corps of Engineers for "despoiling our natural resources" while appeals against the government's environmental policies were pending on the Court's docket. In addition to environmental causes, Douglas also detailed his world travels, and in doing so expressed his geopolitical views. He had long centered his public discussions on political matters; this fed the animosity against him. For instance, on April 14, 1969, the *New York Times* reported that he had "praised campus revolutionaries" in a speech at Case Western University in Ohio, and in response, Congressman John Ashbrook, a Republican Ohioan, called for his removal.[39]

It is true that Douglas was not alone in believing the conflict in Vietnam was an unjust war fought in an unjust manner. His closest ally on the Court, Hugo Black, similarly believed that without a declaration of war, the United States should not have any forces in Vietnam. On August 22, 1967, McGovern asked that the Senate place the transcript of a speech given by Benjamin V. Cohen into the congressional record. Cohen was an influential advisor to Franklin Roosevelt and a friend to both Douglas and Black. In his speech, he cast doubts on the reasons for the US entry into the conflict in Vietnam. "The issues on which we intervened consequently were murky in origin, in fact and in law, and were colored by fears and hopes of future developments which could not be foreseen or forecast," Cohen argued. Cohen made sure to send Black a copy of the speech, and Black responded, "It is not necessary to tell you, I am sure, that our ideas about the war run much along the same lines." But Black, unlike Douglas, kept his political beliefs away from the public view. Although there would be lingering anger against Black—and for that matter Brennan and Warren—over their civil rights and national security decisions, their conduct regarding Vietnam did not serve as a basis for demanding impeachment.[40]

Douglas feared a Nixon presidency. In 1968 he wrote to New York Republican governor Nelson Rockefeller and lamented Rockefeller's decision to drop out of the presidential race: "I think you would have brought a brand new dimension to the thinking of our people." Douglas believed, like many Americans, that the liberal Rockefeller was the most likely candidate to defeat Nixon at the Republican convention. Although Nixon first directed his efforts at Fortas, who lacked candor in his congressional hearings, Douglas had cause to worry that he would be next. In November 1969 Douglas wrote to his friend Charles Horowitz, a Washington state appellate judge, "The Nixon boys have been trying to plan libelous statements with the press out here in the east." He then added that Congressman Clark MacGregor, a Minnesota Republican, was likely to introduce a bill of impeachment. Horowitz tried to calm Douglas's fears by responding that MacGregor's criticisms of Douglas were not "serious," but then presciently noted that any story regarding impeachment "emanates out of Representative Ford's headquarters."[41]

While Ford had criticized Douglas as early as 1967, Douglas did not initially take Ford any more seriously than he did the Southern legislators who demanded his removal. But after the 1968 elections there were more conservatives in the House, and there were reports of judges who had failed to recuse themselves from cases in which they had an interest in the outcome, including a judge who had served on a foundation with Douglas. After January 20, 1969, Douglas no longer had a Democrat president to support him. Whether Douglas knew it at the time, there were also ordinary citizens who had begun to ally with conservatives against him. The risks of his impeachment changed with a Nixon presidency. In 1965, when two Republican legislators called for his impeachment over his ties to Parvin, he ignored their criticisms, much as he had earlier disregarded a congressman's attempt to impeach him in 1954 after trying to grant a stay against the execution of two citizens convicted of giving atomic weapons secrets to the Soviet Union, or calls for his impeachment from Southern congressmen who claimed that his four marriages were immoral. With a growing national belief in judicial corruption, Southern anger over civil rights decisions, claims of Douglas's affinity for communism, and Douglas's own questionable conduct, the Nixon and Ford team posed the first real threat to the justice, but it also posed a threat to the efficacy of the nation's constitutional institutions.

Clash of Cultures and Constitutional Imperilment

Ford's actions against Douglas mirrored the anger that millions of Americans—Nixon's so-called silent majority—had toward the social upheaval in the country as well as the changing norms of morality, a rise in crime, urban riots, and a federal government that was easily portrayed as both uninterested in the lives of everyday working white Americans and overbearing toward them. By the time of Ford's campaign against Douglas, the justice's detractors had expanded beyond Southerners and anticommunist conservatives. Several evangelical Christian leaders demanded his removal from the Court. In 1970 the leader of the Christian Crusade of Tulsa, Oklahoma, noted, "The case against Mr. Douglas goes back many years and involves several areas where the vital interests of our national survival are at stake." Another evangelical leader accused Douglas of "supporting subversive movements."[42]

On April 23, 1970, Thurman Sensing, a Southern-based radio personality, broadcast his argument that "Justice Douglas is a man who opposes every-thing the United States stands for and expresses contempt for its way of life, who abuses those who wear the uniform of their country, and who, finally, makes a blatant, open endorsement of violence." If Sensing had been just an isolated Southerner, Douglas's supporters could have ignored him. The radioman had, after all, fought for the survival of legalized racism by equat-ing civil rights advocates to "beer hall Nazis." But in Sensing's anti-Douglas broadcast, he read an analysis from Sidney Hook, a Brooklyn law professor and civil rights advocate who had opined that Douglas had violated the stric-tures of judicial ethics. Of course, Sensing's accusations against Douglas were hardly novel. In 1951, after Douglas dissented in *Dennis v. United States*—a decision upholding the convictions of the leaders of the Communist Party of the United States—conservative journalist Fulton Lewis called Douglas's dissent "a strategic betrayal of the United States." Yet hundreds of ordinary citizens from across the United States paid for postage stamps or Western Union telegram fees and sent messages to Douglas, lauding his *Dennis* dissent and thanking him for trying to protect their liberty.[43]

Douglas was a politically active justice. College students, who demon-strated against the war and social inequities in the tens of thousands, found a champion in Douglas. His writings and speeches attacked governmental in-stitutions such as the Central Intelligence Agency (CIA), the Federal Bureau of Investigation (FBI), and the military. But he regularly acted more like a politician than a judge, and his judicial decisions often incorporated his views on the war. In *Powell v. McCormack,* a decision arising out of the House's re-fusal to seat one of its members who had been accused of corruption, Doug-las opined in a separate concurrence that it would violate the Constitution to refuse to seat an elected official who spoke against the Vietnam War. The issue in *McCormack* had nothing to do with the war. Yet Douglas felt it necessary to place this comment in his concurrence.[44]

Whether one considers Douglas a flawed hero or a disgraced justice, Ford's attack on him was both politically irresponsible and potentially damaging to the country's democratic institutions. What follows is not a biography of Douglas, Nixon, or Ford, but rather an examination of the episode in which, in the summer of 1970, a seemingly benign congressman acted at the be-

hest of a calculating and vindictive president and placed the nation's constitutional institutions at risk. As such, this book examines more than Ford's
intentions to have Douglas removed from the Court, although Ford's intentions, and by implication Nixon's, have to be front and center. Instead, this
book is a legal history of an attempted impeachment that examines the risks
that Ford and Nixon created in pursuing Douglas, and how the legislative
and judicial branches reacted to those risks as well as to public pressure. It
is also a study of how the absence of political liability in this event enabled a
sweeping Nixon reelection and a Ford presidency, and increased the politici-
zation of the federal judiciary. Finally, the character of the arguments leveled
against Douglas in 1970 reemerged in 2016. Once again there was an absence
of liability for politicians who cast aspersions on the ethnicity of judges as
well as judicial rulings that are erroneously attacked as endangering national
security.

2

The Rising Men, the Muckrakers of the Judiciary, and Beleaguered Judges

In early 1968 Senator Vance Hartke, an Indiana Democrat who supported President Johnson's Great Society, observed that the Vietnam conflict had polarized the nation to the degree that citizens criticizing the war routinely found their national loyalty attacked by prowar supporters. Hartke pointed to Richard Nixon as a warning of how the war was enabling hawkish right-wing conservatives to reemerge as a political force. Having lost California's 1962 gubernatorial election, Nixon appeared to have faded from national politics. But in 1966 he campaigned on behalf of Republican congressional aspirants and helped several of them defeat their Democratic Party opponents. Throughout the 1966 midterms, Nixon alleged that the Johnson administration was failing to protect South Vietnam and that the war's critics were emboldening communists across the world. Hartke presciently guessed that Nixon was readying himself for a presidential bid by resorting to his former methods of openly questioning his opponents' national loyalty. Before 1962 Nixon was able to win elections by demonizing his opponents and their supporters as being un-American.

In 1946 Nixon asserted that Jerry Voohis, his opponent for California's Twelfth Congressional District, supported communist-oriented unions, which enabled an election victory. Repeating his performance in California's 1950 senate election, Nixon effectively convinced the state's voters that his opponent, Helen Gahagan Douglas, aligned with communists and so-called fellow travelers. While Nixon ran a divisive campaign in 1968, he focused on the

Supreme Court and liberal lower court judges. In doing so he attacked judicial activism and derided the Court's focus on the rights of defendants and pornographers. Although Nixon did not directly criticize the Court's civil rights decisions, implicit in his support for states' rights was a promise to curb federal enforcement of civil rights.[1]

Nixon's narrow election victory over Democrat Hubert Humphrey and independent George Wallace was a remarkable recovery from his political nadir six years earlier. In addition to public dissatisfaction with Johnson's Vietnam policies, worries over domestic upheaval, and perceived failures in the Great Society, Nixon's actions during the six years made such a victory possible. At the conclusion of the 1966 midterm elections, he had allies in Congress and state governments—and most importantly an increasing number of conservative Southern Democratic legislators supported him. As he campaigned for the presidency, he promised to reverse several of the Warren Court's contentious decisions, such as *Miranda v. Arizona*, in which the Court mandated that police officers had to inform suspects of their Fifth Amendment right against self-incrimination and their right to counsel. In turn, he assured voters that he would direct the federal government to be tough on crime. He also promised a renewed effort in Vietnam and restated his commitment to reasserting traditional conservative values.[2]

Nixon's attack on the judiciary's alleged support for lawlessness was given credence by the unethical conduct of a small number of state and federal judges. In 1964 the Oklahoma Supreme Court suffered a blow to its status when two of its justices were convicted and sent to prison after accepting bribes. In 1969 two justices on the Illinois Supreme Court were forced to resign under similar circumstances. That same year a federal judge oversaw a corporate bankruptcy reorganization in Tennessee, but the judge had earned a small fortune by investing in the corporation's stock before its value inflated. To make matters worse, the corporation's founder was the judge's friend and had included the judge in the initial private stock offering. These were not the most troubling news stories for the judiciary in 1969. The Supreme Court's reputation was devastated by revelations that Justice Abe Fortas had been less than honest with the Senate during his chief justice confirmation hearings and that he had accepted a sizable payment in exchange for teaching a seminar at American University's law school. When it was discovered that Louis Wolfson, a wealthy investor who had been indicted, had funded the course,

Fortas resigned before an impeachment trial could be started against him. In the midst of these scandals, Congressman William Scherle, an Iowa Republican who would side with Ford against Douglas, wrote to Chief Justice Warren that Congress and the public "had increased doubts as to the integrity" of several judges.[3]

The Rising Men: Nixon, Ford, Burger, and the War in Southeast Asia

In his 1968 Republican convention acceptance speech, Nixon claimed that he was dedicated to civil rights, but then he insisted that "the first civil right of every American is the right to be free from domestic violence." Had Nixon stopped with this comment, it would already have been clear that he promised a tough-on-crime presidency. Nixon went further, though, and attacked the Court. To be sure, he asserted that the public had to respect the judiciary, but he then claimed that "some of our courts in their decisions have gone too far in weakening the police forces against the criminal forces in this country." Although he did not list the Court's criminal law decisions, in addition to *Miranda,* the Court had placed significant restraints on police action in other areas, including mandating prosecutors to provide the identities of informants in organized crime, espionage, and subversion trials. The Court had also limited the admissibility of evidence seized by the police without warrant, and it had enabled expanded defenses against police entrapment. Conservatives argued that these judicial decisions empowered criminals.[4]

On Monday, January 20, 1969, the greatest concern confronting Nixon was not a rise in crime or stalling economic growth—both national problems. Rather, the conflict in Vietnam was the critical issue, and although it had been significantly escalated under two successive Democratic presidencies, as a vice president and congressman he had influenced the United States' commitment in Southeast Asia. In spite of his contribution to the nation's presence in Vietnam, Nixon's eight-year absence from federal office enabled him to distance himself from the conflict. While communism was important in the 1960 election, Nixon and Kennedy focused their debates on South and Central America as well as Europe far more than on Southeast Asia. Yet Nixon, like Kennedy, knew that Vietnam could become a major focus if, for no other reason, than that the political ramifications in the United States if South Vietnam fell to the communists; it could equal those felt over the loss of China during Truman's presidency. In the four years before the 1968 election, Vietnam became one of several topics Nixon used to his advantage, and there was little political liability for him in demanding a fuller commitment to South Vietnam. In essence, if the war in Vietnam destroyed Johnson's presidency, it enabled Nixon's.[5]

In April 1964 Nixon traveled to South Vietnam, where he argued that if that country fell to the communists, it would be because the Johnson administration had failed to support its leaders. In August of that year, he published an article in *Reader's Digest* in which he insisted that more military forces were necessary to support the South Vietnamese government. Throughout 1965 Nixon accused Johnson of not doing enough to defeat communism in Vietnam. Two years later, in an article published in *Foreign Affairs,* he insisted that because the United States, as a "Pacific Power," could not indefinitely police the world, it was necessary to assure its allies—in particular Taiwan, South Korea, and Japan—that it would militarily intervene in Asia to support them. This meant defeating communism in South Vietnam.[6]

The period between Nixon's defeat in the race for California's governorship and 1968 witnessed the type of social and political upheaval that favored his return to national politics. For much of his political career, Nixon had campaigned on the need to have a cohesive society in which "traditional institutions" were protected. He generally opposed organized labor's political strength, he promised to curb federal authority, and he championed a strong military and security policy to confront communism at home and abroad. He also had the benefit of realizing that Barry Goldwater's confrontational campaign style undermined the message of conservatism. Between 1963 and 1968, not only did he cement relationships with corporate leaders but he also argued a case before the Supreme Court and traveled the world to meet with foreign heads of state. He was able to convince Goldwater's supporters that he would wisely fight for conservatism without the senator's rhetoric, and he equally convinced Republican moderates that their leader, New York governor Nelson Rockefeller, was out of step with the nation. An older white American voter could find comfort in Nixon, even if the older voter had benefited from the New Deal and postwar federal programs. Nixon appeared strong in a time of uncertainty; he also appeared to have been right all along about the dangers of communism and permissive liberalism.[7]

Examining the team that Nixon brought into the government is important for understanding the character and timing of Ford's attack against Douglas. Nixon appointed John Mitchell, his advisor and campaign chairman, as attorney general. Mitchell's corporate and municipal bond lawyer credentials presented a reasonable question as to whether he was qualified to serve as attorney general. However, his tough-on-crime policies fulfilled one of Nixon's campaign promises. Nixon also brought Henry Kissinger into the administration as his national security advisor. Kissinger had been a confidant to Rockefeller and was a leading national security scholar who had influenced prior administrations. Nixon selected William Rogers to become secretary of state and Melvin Laird as secretary of defense. Rogers had served as Eisenhower's second attorney general and was a conservative Republican. Laird was a nine-term congressman, a World War II veteran, and an ally of Gerald Ford. In 1956 Laird lobbied the Eisenhower administration to ensure that Nixon served a second term as vice president. Throughout the 1960s Laird accused Johnson of not sending enough military forces into Vietnam to defeat the communists. In 1968 Laird campaigned for Nixon throughout the primaries and in the convention. Just as Nixon excluded Laird and Rogers from the Cambodian invasion planning, neither man had any foreknowledge of Ford's April 15, 1970, call for Douglas's impeachment.[8]

Despite Nixon's hawkishness, he understood that the Vietnam conflict had an enormous social and economic cost. At the time of his presidential inauguration, there were 540,000 US service members in Vietnam, and the majority of these were drafted men. While the war had unsettled the nation, Nixon believed that most Americans would not tolerate a rapid retreat from Vietnam. After conferring with Kissinger and Laird, Nixon determined to follow what can be best described as a phased withdrawal of forces from Vietnam; during the withdrawal, the United States would equip and train the army of the Republic of Vietnam to eventually fight the Viet Cong and North Vietnamese on its own. Known as Vietnamization, the withdrawal did not prevent American military forces from taking active part in operations, and indeed there was a sizable increase in the United States' military's aerial bombing missions. As part of Vietnamization, Nixon planned for the United States to have only a nominal military presence in Vietnam by 1972, but also for the country to assure the South Vietnamese government that if the North were to invade, the United States would return in force to the South's defense.[9]

In order to achieve Vietnamization, Nixon needed support from congressmen who had become critical of the war as well as from older anticommunist
legislators because Vietnamization represented a compromise between fighting until the communists were defeated and a retreat from Vietnam. Nixon
also needed the trust and support of a majority of Americans. He knew that a
sizable minority of the nation opposed the war, and he feared that leftist radicals would stoke rebellion. On June 20, 1969, White House staff assistant Tom
Charles Huston approached J. Edgar Hoover for help targeting antiwar organizations. Nixon directed Huston to prepare a report on communist influence in the United States, and specifically to concentrate on foreign support
to domestic protest movements. Huston was also tasked with determining
whether domestic organizations that promoted leftist causes should retain
their tax-exempt status. (Shortly after Huston pursued this duty, the Internal
Revenue Service informed the Parvin Foundation of its potential loss of tax-
exempt status.) On April 15, 1970, the *Wall Street Journal* reported that Nixon
aide Clark Mollenhoff had sought the tax records of nine unelected officials,
but the commissioner of the Internal Revenue Service, Randolph Thrower,
had refused Mollenhoff access.[10]

As a result of the enormity of his project, Huston turned to the CIA and
the Defense Intelligence Agency for help. In early June 1970 Hoover, CIA
director Richard Helms, and Admiral Noel Gayler and General Donald Bennett, two senior officers in charge of naval and military intelligence, met to
coordinate their efforts to obtain information on antiwar organizations.
Within a month they forwarded a plan for increased surveillance of citizens,
CIA surveillance of American students studying abroad, and the intercep-
tion of private domestic mail. Although Hoover objected to some of the
more draconian elements in the plan and Nixon never formally approved it,
the plan's timing was not coincidental to the impeachment attempt against
Douglas, and indeed provides context for it. Another matter arose that also
gives context both the plan's shelving and the impeachment attempt. In January 1970 Christopher Pye, an army officer, publicly revealed that the military
had conducted surveillance of US citizens.[11]

In addition to domestic support, the success of Vietnamization rested on
an assumption that the war could be limited to South Vietnam, but North
Vietnam's military used Laotian and Cambodian sovereign territory to transport men and matériel to aid the Viet Cong in the South. As long as com-

munist supply lines traversed Cambodia's neutral territory, Vietnamization was difficult to achieve. Nixon approved a covert aerial bombing campaign against targets in Cambodia in 1969 and a ground invasion in 1970. Millions of Americans, including a large number of legislators, protested the bombing campaign and ground invasion. The war's opponents could turn to Douglas as an ally to try to stop the war. Douglas had already proven himself willing to cross the traditional separation-of-powers barriers and become involved in foreign policy. His judicial decisions evidenced an animosity to the nation's involvement in the conflict and a profound sympathy for the young men who were drafted into the military. For a number of reasons Nixon already despised Douglas, but with Vietnamization he had an additional desire to remove him from the Court. To do so, he turned to Gerald Ford, the Republican leader in the House of Representatives, whom he had considered as a running mate in both 1960 and 1968.[12]

By 1970 Ford was known to American voters for several reasons. In early 1964 he publicly accused Johnson of not committing enough of the nation's military to Vietnam. He also became a nationally known congressman because of Johnson. Even though he had disparaged Ford, Johnson's act of appointing him to the Warren Commission brought him to the public's attention. Ironically, Ford's selection to the commission occurred as a result of Secretary of Defense Robert McNamara's advising Johnson that Ford was nonpartisan in matters of national security. One year after the commission published its findings, Ford presented the House Republican conference report to the nation's news media in which he and his peers accused the Johnson administration of failing to protect South Vietnam against communism.[13]

In early 1965, while the House Republicans worked to rebuild their strength after an election that resulted in their numbers being reduced to 177 congressional seats, Ford challenged long-serving party leader Charles Halleck for the party's House leadership. Having served in Congress since 1935 and as party leader since 1947, Halleck believed that his leadership position was safe from an internal challenge. He was surprised to learn a group of newer Republican congressmen, including Donald Rumsfeld, Robert Griffin, Charles Goodell, Robert Dole, and Melvin Laird, planned to oust him and elevate Ford. Ford accused Halleck of continually voting no on Democratic Party bills but never offering alternatives. Halleck and the Republican minority whip, Leslie Arends, went so far as to threaten Ford with "political burial." On January, 4, 1965, Ford eked out a narrow victory in a secret ballot. But he was strongly supported by congressional Republicans in the Western states; indeed, all twenty of California's Republican representatives voted for him. The unanimity of California's Republican congressional delegation provided Ford with a false certainty that Western-state Republicans would uniformly side with him against Douglas. Only a few would openly do so, and some, such as Paul McCloskey, accused Ford of undermining the Constitution. This, however, was in the future, and as a minority leader he appeared on a weekly televised news show with his Republican Senate counterpart, Everett Dirksen, giving the public greater knowledge of him. Moreover, major newspapers such as the *New York Times* often quoted Ford as representing the Republican position in the House.[14]

Ford had a life story that lent credence to the conservatives' argument that an expansive federal government was not only unnecessary to individual success but also perhaps an impediment to it. He was born Leslie Lynch King in Omaha, Nebraska, in 1913, but after a few months, his mother, Dorothy Gardner, obtained a divorce and moved with her son to a Chicago suburb, then to Grand Rapids, Michigan. Ford's father, Leslie King, was an alcoholic prone to violence. A Nebraska judge granted Dorothy Gardner a divorce on the basis of King's "extreme cruelty." Three years later she married Gerald Rudolff Ford, a paint and varnish salesman. Although the older Gerald never formally adopted Leslie King, Leslie King grew up as Gerald Rudolff Ford Jr., and by personal choice he used the last name of Ford. Between 1916 and 1927 the Fords had three additional sons, and Gerald Ford Sr. worked to ensure that they were able to afford a college education. However, before Gerald Ford Jr. could attend college, the stock market crash and ensuing Depression led to his parents' losing their house.[15]

In high school Ford worked as a dishwasher, played football, and participated on his school's debate team. He also earned the rank of Eagle Scout before attending the University of Michigan. In later years some pundits claimed he attended Michigan on a football scholarship, but the university had no athletic scholarships in the midst of the Great Depression. Harry Kipke, Michigan's football coach, wanted Ford on the university's team and found him a hospital job. When Ford graduated in 1935 he had offers from the Green Bay Packers and the Detroit Lions. Professional football, however

enticing it may have been, would not have provided him with a livable salary. Instead of attempting a future in professional sports, Ford decided to
become a lawyer. Although his grades were far from stellar—he had gotten a
D in French and a C in English composition—he nonetheless was able to gain
admission to Yale University's law school. During his law studies he was also
assistant coach of Yale's football team. In this position he coached Robert Taft
Jr., the grandson of President William Howard Taft and later a congressman
who would support his efforts to impeach Douglas, and William Proxmire, a
future Democratic Party senator from Wisconsin who opposed the impeachment. In another early connection to Douglas, Ford studied under Professor
Fred Rodell, who would later chastise him over the impeachment effort. And
of course Douglas had taught at Yale's law school, though the two men did
not meet during Douglas's tenure.[16]

There are other aspects of Ford's early life that are noteworthy in how they
shaped his congressional career. During college he had championed isola-
tionism, and in 1939 he argued against the United States' supporting Britain
and France. The next year he campaigned for Republican Wendell Willkie's
presidential bid, but after the Japanese attack on Pearl Harbor he joined the
navy. Ford's wartime service included surviving kamikaze attacks as well assisting in saving his aircraft carrier during Typhoon Cobra, a disaster that resulted in the death of more than seven hundred sailors. When Ford returned
home he became involved in local politics, and in 1948 Michigan's Fifth Congressional District's voters elected him to Congress, where he remained until
his vice presidential appointment in 1974. In spite of ascending to a congressional leadership position, Ford was not known as a legislative giant, and before April 15, 1970, he had not sponsored any major legislative efforts. While
in Congress he served on a variety of committees, including Appropriations,
and he built his career around limiting government expenditures except on
the armed forces. Although he had once been an isolationist, he became a
staunch interventionist against communism.[17]

Nixon and Ford's intended impeachment of Douglas likely would not
have occurred in the manner it did had Earl Warren remained chief justice.
Warren had come to Douglas's defense on a prior occasion, and he despised
Nixon, making it likely the impeachment would pit a chief justice against a
president. But Warren's replacement, Warren Burger, was a longtime Nixon
ally, and he repeatedly assured Nixon that his policies in Vietnam and Cam-

bodia were legal; he also informed Nixon on Douglas's reactions to the impeachment attempt. Burger had served in the Justice Department under Eisenhower before Eisenhower placed him on the United States Court of Appeals for the District of Columbia. That court has often been called the nation's second most important court, not only because of its expansive jurisdiction in comparison to the other courts of appeal but also because of the number of appeals in which the United States was a named party were far in excess of any other appellate court. Several justices began their judicial careers on this appellate court, including Frederick Vinson, Wiley Rutledge, Antonin Scalia, Ruth Bader Ginsburg, and John Roberts. On June 9, 1969, the Senate voted to confirm Burger as chief justice by a vote of 74 to 3. Only Minnesota Democrat Eugene McCarthy, Wisconsin Democrat Gaylord Nelson, and Ohio Democrat Steven Young voted against him.[18]

Born in 1907 in Minnesota to working-class parents, Burger, like Ford, fit Nixon's model of an unprivileged self-made conservative. Burger was not an Ivy League lawyer; indeed, he was the last justice to serve on the Court who did not attend a top-ranked law school. Having graduated from the St. Paul College of Law in 1931 near the top of his class, he went to work in a midsize Minneapolis law firm. He also became an active member in Minnesota's Republican Party and campaigned for Governor Harold Stassen, a perennial presidential candidate. In 1953 Attorney General Herbert Brownell brought Burger into the Justice Department as the chief of the civil division. When Solicitor General Simon Sobeloff determined that he could not in good conscience argue the government's position in an appeal that involved the removal of a security clearance based on anonymous accusations, Burger agreed to serve as lead counsel.[19]

By the time of Burger's nomination, it was well known that he was conservative, anticommunist, tepid on civil rights, and intolerant of dissent. In 1960, in a personal letter to Harry Blackmun, his longtime friend, he called Nobel chemist Linus Pauling, British mathematician-philosopher Bertrand Russell, and Nobel physicist Albert Einstein "crackpots and communists." The three men, along with a larger number of scientists, filed suit in a federal court to prevent Secretary of Defense Neil McElroy from ordering any future testing of nuclear weapons, citing the danger of radioactive fallout to human health as the basis for the suit. The government prevailed in its argument that the scientists lacked standing for the suit and that the issue was moot because

McElroy had ordered all testing to stop. But Burger ardently believed that the scientists posed a danger to the United States. So too, he believed, did their attorney, who had defended conscientious objectors in World War II and in the Korean War.[20]

Burger had a low opinion of the Warren Court's liberals. He disagreed with Douglas, leading the Court to require a more modern insanity test; he believed that it evidenced that the Court had sided with criminals. In 1968, when he shared the first draft of his decision in *Powell v. McCormack* with Blackmun, he called Justice William Brennan's jurisprudence "glib." Burger was angered further when the Court reversed his ruling in that case. The Court's approach to dissent also infuriated him. He decried the fact that anti-war protesters were entitled to the same access to Arlington National Cemetery as all other persons. "The boys should be able to rest in peace without Sloan Coffin [*sic*] or Dr. Spock orating over their headstones," he lamented. "These birds think that one loves the war if he does not scream at everyone else on the subject."[21]

Congressional and judicial conservatives lauded Burger's appointment. Senator Robert C. Byrd, who had professed the constitutionality of segregation, proclaimed "Burger's ascension to the Court will be for the good of the country." John R. Dethmer, a Michigan supreme court justice, wrote to Blackmun that Burger's appointment was "the best news I have heard from or about the Supreme Court of the United States in recent years." Chief Judge George Register of the United States district court for the District of North Dakota wrote, "The nomination and confirmation of a man possessing such recognized professional qualifications, judicial experience, and personal integrity should help restore faith in the Supreme Court by the general public." Southern judges who had opposed civil rights, such as Robert Ainsworth on the Fifth Circuit, also expressed their satisfaction in the new chief justice.[22]

A Senator and the Muckrakers of the Judiciary

Although it was Ford who called for Douglas's impeachment, there was another Republican legislator who began the groundwork for Douglas's judicial tenure to become an issue in Congress. Elected to the Senate in 1946, John J. Williams had defined his legislative career by discovering corruption in government, and a 1964 *Los Angeles Times* article caught his attention. The article

highlighted Douglas's relationship to Albert Parvin as well as the creation of
Parvin's foundation. It did not mention that Douglas had received money
from Parvin, and it noted that Parvin had made a personal fortune by "re-
educating" the hotel industry. "From the standard uniformity of the pre-1930
era, when furnishing salesmen asked 'what do you want, light or dark wood,'
Parvin designers begin their tasks from the hotel's blueprint stage from the
size and shapes of the rooms to the finest detail of accessory colors," the *Los
Angeles Times* reported. "It is a business that has grown to $42 million last
year and has nearly 1000 employees." While the article also noted that Parvin
furnished expensive hotels in New York, Los Angeles, and Palm Springs, along
with the Playboy Club and several hotels on the Las Vegas strip, its two most
important features to Williams were that Parvin and Douglas had vacationed
together and that the foundation had not issued all of the monetary prize
awards to students that it had publicly claimed it had planned to. Williams
thus concluded that there was evidence of an improper relationship between
Douglas and the casino owner, and he began to investigate both men.[23]

Williams was an iconoclast who uncovered scandals in both Democratic
and Republican administrations. In 1950, during a Longines-Wittnauer television newscast, he rebuffed accolades for uncovering corruption in the Internal Revenue Service (IRS) and instead credited "honest agents" for having
the courage to turn in their corrupt peers. In truth, without the support of
a Senate committee (he was not on any committee investigating the IRS),
Williams was responsible for the convictions of fifty-three IRS agents who
had accepted bribes from organized crime figures. Although this scandal
proved embarrassing to the Truman administration, Williams also uncovered
corruption in Eisenhower's presidency that led to the resignation of White
House chief of staff Sherman Adams.[24]

Although Williams was a conservative Republican, he was often independent of his party's leaders, and although Nixon viewed him as an ally, Williams never considered himself as such. He was a staunch anticommunist,
but he was one of the first senators to criticize Senator Joseph McCarthy
for his reckless attacks on public servants, and he demanded that McCarthy be censured, even when Senate Majority Leader Robert Taft and other
senior Republicans defended McCarthy. Williams also supported the 1957
and 1964 Civil Rights acts and the 1965 Voting Rights Act. In addition to his
individualist approach to politics, his criticisms of Douglas earned credibility

for another reason. Throughout the 1950s and 1960s he did not join other conservative senators in attacking the Court, and he opposed efforts to restrict the Court's jurisdiction. By 1960 newspaper reporters and several of his legislative peers had given him the sobriquet "the conscience of the Senate."[25]

Robert Caro, a prominent Lyndon Johnson biographer, once revealed that Johnson considered Williams "the worst possible senator." Williams was born in 1904, raised on a farm, and later owned a poultry feed center. As World War II came to a close, he convinced Delaware's voters to elect him over a Democratic incumbent. His sole political achievement before being elected in 1946 was his service on a town council. In 1946 he campaigned against the New Deal as well as against a prominent Republican family's dynastic power. Dating to the early nineteenth century, the E. I. du Pont de Nemours Company built military ordnance factories, chemical industries, and steel mills throughout the United States. The du Ponts had intermittently exercised influence over Delaware's politics and produced two senators and one congressman, as well as a decorated Civil War admiral. Although the du Ponts were conservative Republicans, their involvement in government contracting made them inviting targets to Williams. The du Ponts backed Williams's opponent, and his victory over the wealthy family did not endear him to the Republican Party.[26]

In early 1963 Williams focused his attentions on Johnson by targeting Johnson's protégé, Robert "Bobby" Baker, a longtime Senate employee. Baker became central to Ford's claim that Douglas had consorted with organized crime, and therefore a brief note on Baker is essential to understanding the gravity of Ford's claims. Baker came to the Senate as a fourteen-year-old page in 1942. The *New York Times* reported his 1954 net worth at $11,000, but within a decade he was worth $2.5 million. To gain this fortune, Baker invested in several businesses such as vending machines and hotels. US history is replete with people who have increased their riches, but it was problematic that Baker was a civil servant. In 1962 the chief executive officer of a rival vending machine company sued him in what could be considered a garden-variety breach-of-contract suit. Because of Baker's access to legislators and defense industries, news agencies had an interest in the pending litigation.[27]

The lawsuit against Baker darkened Johnson's political future. In 1949, when Johnson first came to the Senate, he had sought Baker's advice on the habits of other senators. It was Baker who steered Johnson to become a Richard Russell protégé, and under Russell's guidance Johnson leapfrogged other Democrats to become assistant minority leader and then minority leader. In 1955, when Johnson became Senate majority leader, Baker became his secretary. Baker provided Johnson with a unique type of intelligence, including the sexual dalliances of other senators and the distribution of monies from lobbyists. In 1956 Baker opened a nightclub in Ocean City, Maryland, as well as a motel in Washington, DC, where senators and "performing women" met. That same year, with the assistance of Senator Robert Kerr, an Oklahoman Democrat and Johnson ally, Baker, a defense lobbyist, and several Las Vegas–based investors formed a vending machine company under the name Serve-U.

Through a series of illicit dealings and payoffs, Baker was able to place Serve-U's vending machines throughout defense industry factories, including North American Aviation's facilities. In 1965 the Senate Rules Committee, to Williams's anger, cleared Baker of criminal wrongdoing. Ultimately the Justice Department succumbed to Williams's badgering and took a different position than the Rules Committee. On January 5, 1966, a grand jury indicted Baker. For a brief time before the indictment, Abe Fortas defended Baker, but Baker released him as his attorney as a result of a conflict of interest. Shortly after being released, Fortas was nominated and confirmed to the Supreme Court. In 1967 Baker was convicted of fraud and tax evasion, and sentenced to prison. Johnson said little about the matter, other than denying a close association with Baker. Williams, repeating his performance after the IRS scandal, did not take credit for Baker's conviction.[28]

Vending machines were to cause difficulties for others as well, including a Nixon nominee to the Court. First invented in 1884, vending machines have a checkered history. While these machines are convenient for the hungry or thirsty consumer, their proceeds were difficult to accurately tax for several reasons. The owners could claim spoilage, the machines did not count sales in the same manner as an over-the-counter business, and efforts to enact vending taxes—while supported by labor union leaders—were usually defeated in state legislatures. By the 1940s an organization that owned hundreds of vending machines could also launder money and evade taxes in the same manner as the owners of casinos, arcades, and racetracks. Finally, the nation's largest vending machine manufacturers also built gambling machines and pinball games. Organized crime pervaded the casino and arcade industries. In the early 1950s a Senate committee headed by Estes Kefauver discovered that organized crime had included vending machines in their rackets. In late 1958 Senator John McClellan headed a similar committee and found that racketeers had controlled much of the vending machine industry in major urban centers. In 1983 the Justice Department reported that organized crime had operated 170 vending machine companies during the previous four decades.[29]

By the time Johnson became president, it was well known that Baker had tried to take part in the expansion of legal gambling in the Caribbean and had comingled his investments with those of organized crime figures, including Edward Levinson. The FBI had bugged Baker's hotel room in the Fremont Casino and listed to his conversation with Levinson. (Levinson was an investor with commercial relations to organized crime and owned the hotel and casino.) At a minimum the taped conversations evidenced that Baker was willing to conduct business with people associated with organized crime. In 1964 Parvin's corporation purchased the Fremont and hired Levinson to manage it. Thus, Douglas had a relationship with Parvin, and Parvin had a reputed Mafia man managing one of his casinos. Ford would try to present Baker as the go-between for Douglas and Parvin on one side and organized crime on the other.[30]

On October 17, 1966, Senator Williams asked Earl Warren whether Douglas's association with the Parvin Foundation had undermined the Court's integrity. The *Los Angeles Times* had once again published an article on Douglas and Parvin, but this time it was less than laudatory about either man, and the paper went so far as to suggest that Douglas had violated a canon of ethics that prohibited judges from obtaining extrajudicial employment. When Douglas objected to the *Times*'s claim that he had violated ethical norms by providing legal advice to the foundation, the *Times*'s editorial board responded that they disagreed with him. The editorial board, moreover, complimented Williams and linked Baker to Parvin and Levinson. "The Supreme Court now has before it an appeal of a tax evasion conviction by Fred Black Jr., an associate of Bobby Baker and of Edward Levinson, a $100,000-a-year employee of the Fremont Hotel," the *Times* cautioned, before informing its readers that Levinson also had a pending suit against the FBI for an invasion of privacy. The *Times* then issued a challenge, which Warren failed to adequately address and which Ford later adopted into his speech. "Other members of the Supreme Court have thus far not commented on the Douglas case, but they cannot remain silent," the article concluded. "If the justices fail, Congress must act to assure the integrity of the Court is not compromised."[31]

Warren misjudged the long-term implications of both the *Times* article and Williams's inquiry. He could have responded to the *Times* by explaining that each justice was solely responsible for deciding his own qualifications to serve on an appeal, but that there was also a formal duty for a justice to serve in his judicial capacity on each and every case. In his draft reply to Williams, Warren indicated that he knew nothing of the Parvin Foundation or Douglas's association with Parvin. Warren's draft answer was likely a matter of forgetfulness resulting from his busy schedule, but Douglas had already once invited Warren to speak to the foundation's members. Warren's memory apparently came back to him after reading a description of the foundation from Harry Ashmore, one of the foundation's founders, and a letter from Douglas on October 24, 1966. Douglas defended the foundation to Warren and noted that its purpose was to bring men between the ages of twenty-five and thirty-five to the Woodrow Wilson School at Princeton University in the hopes that once they returned to their countries in Africa, the Middle East, and Asia, "they [would] become active in the government in their countries, or in education, journalism, or some other aspect of public affairs." Douglas also reminded Warren that he had helped create a similar foundation through the University of California to educate non-English-speaking students from Latin American countries in an effort to stem the spread of communism.[32]

Williams was not satisfied with Warren's defense of Douglas and asked the ABA to investigate the latter. The association's president, William T. Gossett, was the son-in-law of Charles Evans Hughes, a former chief justice and secretary of state. Gossett was also friendly with Douglas. At first Gossett tried to find other ranking association officers to issue an opinion as to whether Douglas's connection to the Parvin Foundation violated the canons of judicial ethics. However, the association's personnel determined that there were significant individual conflicts of interest against doing so. While the association would later issue an opinion against Justice Fortas, it would not do so in regard to Douglas, and so Williams sought another avenue of redress against Douglas.[33]

Contemporaneous with the *Los Angeles Times* article on Douglas and Parvin, Williams began to receive information on the relationships between Douglas, Baker, and Parvin, from Clark Mollenhoff, a Pulitzer Prize–winning crime reporter with a Drake University law degree. Born in 1921, Mollenhoff had reported for the *Des Moines Register* from 1942—with the exception of naval service in World War II—until Nixon asked him to join the administration in early 1969. As a crime fighter Mollenhoff took on the Teamsters Union and reported on two high-profile scandals related to Lyndon Johnson. The first of the scandals involved Texas speculator Billie Sol Estes, who defrauded hundreds of farmers in ammonia and fertilizer investments. A Texas court sentenced Estes to twenty-four years in prison in 1963, but the Supreme Court overturned the conviction three years later. Mollenhoff then advanced a theory that the justices who voted to overturn Estes's conviction had received some type of payoff for doing so. Mollenhoff next focused on Baker, and provided Williams with information on Baker's criminal activities. Williams in turn shared this information with the Justice Department. In 1969 Mollenhoff targeted Douglas, apparently under the belief that Douglas had consorted with Estes and Baker. After Clement Haynsworth's nomination was defeated, Mollenhoff gave Williams information that Indiana senator Birch Bayh—an outspoken critic of Haynsworth—not only had engaged in fraudulent real estate deals but also had invested money with Parvin. Williams refused to use Mollenhoff's information on Bayh after discovering it was a fiction. Bayh's unlikely defender in this instance was Senator James O. Eastland, the chairman of the Senate Judiciary Committee. Although Eastland was livid at the Senate's treatment of Haynsworth, when Mollenhoff approached him with similar information on Bayh, he refused to participate in smearing a fellow senator.[34]

In spite of the falsity of Mollenhoff's information, he had a reputation as a conscientious reporter who had worked with both parties. During Eisenhower's first term, Mollenhoff uncovered that a subcommittee had whitewashed an investigation into the relationship between industry and federal regulatory agencies. Partly as a result of Mollenhoff's doggedness, several government officials were forced to resign from office. In 1957 he reported on the Senate's investigations into racketeering and organized labor. It was officially named the Select Committee on Improper Activities in Labor and Management, but it was referred to as the Rackets Committee, and John Little McClellan, a prosegregationist Arkansas senator, served as chairman. Under pressure from Joseph Kennedy, McClellan appointed Robert Kennedy as the committee's counsel. During the investigation Mollenhoff accused Kennedy of cowering from the unions. Yet Mollenhoff also provided Kennedy advice on how to ensure that his brother won the 1960 Democratic Party convention.[35]

Mollenhoff and Robert Kennedy developed a short-lived friendship that lasted through the Democratic Party convention in 1960. But this friendship ended in 1963 when Mollenhoff uncovered that President Kennedy, while serving in the Senate, had had a sexual dalliance with Ellen Rometsch, one of Baker's nightclub employees. Although an extramarital affair would have politically damaged the president, the fact that Rometsch was an East German national, albeit married to a West German soldier stationed at the German embassy, might have proved destructive to the presidency. Mollenhoff gave this information to the FBI. After J. Edgar Hoover rebuffed Mollenhoff, the reporter turned to Williams for help and hoped that because Williams served on the Senate Rules Committee he would be able to subpoena government officials. Although Robert Kennedy supported an investigation into Johnson, Mollenhoff's inquiries into the president ended their friendship.[36]

In 1964 Mollenhoff served as an advisor to Senator Barry Goldwater's presidential campaign. It angered Mollenhoff that Douglas had not recused himself from an appeal raised by Ralph Ginzburg after Ginzburg lost a libel case to Goldwater. Douglas had, after all, published articles in Ginzburg's magazines. Because Mollenhoff was one of the few reporters to publicly compliment Nixon in 1968, the Nixon campaign granted him a far greater degree of access than other reporters. When Nixon became president in 1969 Mollenhoff left the *Register* to serve as a special presidential counsel. Although he only lasted a year in the position before returning to the *Register,* he became a central player in the Haynsworth and Carswell defeats as well as in Ford's attempt to impeach Douglas. Indeed, it was Mollenhoff who tried to tie Baker and the criminal underworld to Douglas. But he would also take an untenable route in trying to prove the justice's relationship to organized crime by using Douglas's judicial decisions, particularly his dissents, as proof. Although Mollenhoff may not have realized Nixon's capacity to use the presidency's power to destroy political enemies when he began his job at the White House, after the House Judiciary Committee cleared Douglas of wrongdoing, he resigned from the government in disgust and returned to the *Register.* He did not, however, ever retract his claims against Douglas. In addition, there is a troubling aspect about Mollenhoff's journalistic ethics. He authored at least one news report on the investigation in which he criticized its processes, without ever disclosing to his readers that he had taken a role in the investigation. Yet he presented himself as a neutral journalist.[37]

Mollenhoff may have been the leading muckraker of his era to take on the judiciary, but he was by no means the only person instrumental in obtaining evidence against Douglas and other judges. Several citizens and one judge had a role in this as well. In 1962 Congressman Emanuel Celler, the long-serving chairman of the House Judiciary Committee, received a complaint against a federal judge from Harlan Grimes, a disbarred Oklahoma attorney. Up until the time of the letter Celler would not have had any reason to know of Grimes; nor had the federal judge Celler complained of, Stephen Chandler, yet come to the committee's attention. Grimes alleged that Chandler received kickbacks from wealthy litigants after issuing them favorable rulings. Celler assigned Congressman Jack Brooks, a Texas Democrat, to investigate Chandler. "I have not heard of any reports along the lines Mr. Grimes relates in his letter," Brooks responded, "and as a matter of fact, I don't believe I have ever heard of this particular charge before." In spite of Brooks's initial review, Grimes persisted over the ensuing four years in trying to prove Chandler was corrupt. In 1964 he claimed to Celler that Chandler had forced a landowner to sell property at $5,000 per acre when the property was valued at $15,000 per acre. The same year W. H. O'Bryan, another Oklahoma attorney, sued Chandler for making defamatory statements against him. Chandler had disbarred O'Bryan from the federal court, and the lawsuit was ultimately dismissed by the Court of Appeals for the Tenth Circuit.[38]

Grimes's accusations against Chandler were misdirected, but he helped publicize the fact that Chandler was unbalanced and irascible. The accusation also pushed Chandler to inform Senator Williams that other federal judges, including Douglas, were corrupt. Perhaps Chandler believed that if he helped Williams ferret out corruption in the judiciary, he would be viewed as an ethical judge. Yet Chandler had a checkered past. When Franklin Roosevelt nominated him to the district court, there was unusual opposition in the Senate, and it took three years to secure his confirmation after it was discovered that he had paid $3,000 to a stenographer who had accused him of assault. After becoming a judge, Chandler engaged in an open feud with Alfred E. Murrah, a pro–civil rights judge on the Court of Appeals for the Tenth Circuit. Chandler had several perceived enemies. He disliked oil billionaire Armand Hammer and excluded Hammer's corporate attorneys from meetings with opposing counsel. Known in the law as an ex parte meeting, a judge is not supposed to hold a conference with only one of the litigants' attorneys.

In 1964 the Tenth Circuit ordered Chandler to recuse himself from a trial involving Hammer's Occidental Petroleum Corporation. In response, Chandler motioned the appellate court to disqualify Murrah from serving on appeals that involved his court, on the basis that Murrah was hostile to him. There was, and is, no legal theory that would have entitled Chandler to make this argument. In an almost identical replay a year later, the Tenth Circuit ordered Chandler disqualified from a trial involving the Texaco Oil Corporation. There was a basis for the order. An attorney representing Chandler against O'Bryan's lawsuit represented the Oklahoma-based company opposing Texaco. Chandler responded by accusing the Tenth Circuit's judges of corruption.[39]

Shortly after Chandler was removed from the Texaco trial, he assigned himself to the trial of the two state supreme court justices accused of accepting bribes, but he had a personal knowledge of some of the litigants, which should have disqualified him from the court. In 1956 he oversaw a corporate bankruptcy in which the corporation's chief executive officer went to prison for fraud. The former corporate executive officer was a key witness against the two state justices. Although the state justices were convicted, Chandler was convinced that the US attorney as well as the local district attorney had done little to stem the state supreme court's corruption, and he gave several news interviews on the subject. In doing so, Chandler tried to build a reputation as a crime fighter. His accusations against Douglas and Parvin might have been given credence by legislators, but he undermined his own reputation.[40]

In early 1965 Chandler told the *Oklahoma Journal* that O'Bryan had masterminded the bribery scheme. In what can be characterized as a revenge prosecution, the local district attorney secured an indictment against Chandler for "appropriating public roads" for the development of a housing tract construction that Chandler had invested in. Although the state and federal courts quashed the indictment, this episode brought Chandler's ethics into question, and it proved to be the final straw for the appellate court. In response the appellate court convened a judicial council—an administrative board composed of judges—to prevent Chandler from hearing future cases. This highly controversial action, akin to an impeachment, resulted in congressional criticism and a 1970 Supreme Court decision that upheld the appellate court's ruling, but that ironically also resulted in a stinging dissent from Black and Douglas, who sided with Chandler. In spite of Douglas's support for Chandler, Chandler continued to give Williams "evidence" against Douglas. E. L. Albright, an aggrieved litigant, insisted to Chandler after he lost a patent appeal involving an ice-making machine that the reason for the Court not granting certiorari was because Douglas owned shares in the competing company. Chandler conveyed this false claim to Mollenhoff, who in turn passed it to Williams.[41]

As Nixon worked to revive his career, Mollenhoff and Williams began their campaign against Douglas, and Grimes and Chandler clumsily tried to uncover corruption in Oklahoma, a private citizen named Sherman Skolnick challenged the United States District Court for the District of Northern Illinois. Whether or not Skolnick intended it at the time, his actions gave momentum to Ford's eventual efforts against Douglas. On January 1, 1967, Judge William Joseph Campbell announced that he had resigned from the Parvin Foundation's board after Skolnick motioned Campbell to recuse himself from a specialized judicial panel composed of three federal judges. Campbell in fact had served as one of the founders of the Parvin Foundation, and his resignation drew suspicion. During the previous year, when Chief Justice Warren collected information from Douglas and Ashmore, Campbell protested against their statement that all of the board members knew of Douglas's $12,000-a-year payment. Skolnick's lawsuit had nothing to do with Parvin. He claimed that the voting districts in Cook County disadvantaged Chicago by underrepresenting the city's voters in the country's government. Chicago had fewer representatives per capita than the suburban and rural areas in the county. In essence, Skolnick had tried to apply *Baker v. Carr* to the county government's districting, and in response the county sought an expedited judicial review by a three-judge panel such as had been used in challenges to state laws governing apportionment. Decisions of such panels were appealable directly to the Supreme Court. Skolnick did not object to the specialized panel, but he opposed Campbell's service on it both because of his ties to the Parvin Foundation and because he owned property in Chicago.[42]

It would be easy to characterize Skolnick as a gadfly—the *Chicago Daily*

News called him this in 1969—but to do so understates his influence. In May 1969, Congressman John Ashbrook, an Ohio Republican, lauded Skolnick's efforts to uncover corruption in the federal district court in Chicago to Congress. Born in Chicago to immigrant Jewish Lithuanian working-class parents in 1930, and confined to a wheelchair for most of his life after falling victim to polio as a child, Skolnick set about to challenge Chicago's city government. He was not an attorney. Indeed, he was a self-taught detective who began his career by investigating his high school woodshop teacher, and in 1964 he formed an organization called the Citizens Committee to Clean Up the Courts. Sometimes his claims proved true. But he also went on to accuse corporations such as Coca-Cola and Chicago's newspapers, the *Sun Times* and *Tribune,* as well as the CIA, of controlling the federal courts, and he became staunchly anti-Catholic in echoing Henry Ford's claim that the Vatican planned to control the US government. However, in an analogous reprise of the Oklahoma supreme court scandal, Skolnick uncovered that two Illinois supreme court justices, Roy J. Solfisburg and Ray Klingbeil, had accepted stock from a litigant corporation before issuing a favorable decision for the corporation. Both state justices resigned in 1969 after an extensive investigation headed by future Supreme Court Justice John Paul Stevens. Beginning in 1965 newspapers reported on Skolnick's private investigations into politicians and judges, and in 1967 the *Chicago Tribune* informed its readers that Skolnick had accused Campbell of taking money from the Chicago's organized crime leaders. If Campbell were to be investigated for receiving payments in exchange for his rulings, it could cause an investigation into Douglas.[43]

Unlike Douglas, Campbell received no money from the Parvin Foundation, but Campbell believed that a relationship with Parvin at any level carried the risk of being accused of ties to organized crime, and for a judge who presided over organized crime trials in Chicago, such an accusation could have severe consequences. Before Roosevelt appointed him to a judgeship, Campbell served as a United States attorney and gained Attorney General Robert Jackson's praise for his prosecutions of Alphonse Capone and Moses Annenberg. Campbell also correctly believed that he was himself a potential Supreme Court nominee. When in 1968 Chief Justice Warren informed President Johnson of his intent to retire, Senator Everett Dirksen lobbied for Campbell to replace Warren. Johnson agreed that Campbell was a viable nominee, but then decided against him because Brennan already occupied the so-called Catholic seat. In reality Johnson had already determined to elevate Fortas to chief justice and select Homer Thornberry as Fortas's replacement. In an odd alignment with a president he considered corrupt, Skolnick would have embraced Johnson's decision not to nominate Campbell. Skolnick also won a victory of sorts against Campbell for another reason. In 1967, when he challenged Campbell's judicial service on the specialized panel, Campbell refused to recuse himself, but in late 1967 the Supreme Court determined that the specialized panel had been improperly constituted. The justices bypassed the issue of whether Campbell had to recuse himself—indeed, the decision ordering a new trial is a brief paragraph—but Campbell took no role in the new trial. The Court of Appeals for the Seventh Circuit determined that Skolnick's claims against the city's commissioners were meritless. In turn, Skolnick complained to Senator Williams that judges such as Campbell were beholden to organized crime. Skolnick also began to associate Douglas with Campbell, and Williams believed there was merit to Skolnick's claims.[44]

The Beleaguered Men in the Federal Judiciary

By the time Nixon was sworn in as president, the federal judiciary was under attack on several fronts. On June 13, 1968, Earl Warren informed Johnson that he would resign as soon as a successor was confirmed. This was an unusual mode of retirement, and it angered conservatives such as Senator Samuel Ervin, who rhetorically questioned, "Does the refusal of Chief Justice Warren to resign until an agreeable successor is appointed dilute the constitutional 'advise and consent' function of the Senate?" Warren's actions did not doom Fortas, but Johnson's appointment of a longtime friend, Homer Thornberry, to replace Fortas, assuming Fortas replaced Warren, gave rise to charges of cronyism. Johnson and Fortas had long been friends, and it was Fortas who represented Johnson during Johnson's contested Texas Senate primary victory over Coke Stevenson in 1948. Fortas moreover had been a protégé of Douglas's since he had been a law school student of Douglas's at Yale. When Douglas left Yale for the Securities and Exchange Commission (SEC), he took Fortas with him. In 1946 Douglas vouched for Fortas in a letter to the United States Maritime Commission director that he had "known Mr. Fortas for fifteen or sixteen years and was without a doubt a man of the highest moral character and integrity." What Douglas wrote in 1946 might have been true, but had the letter come out, it would have provided Ford with fodder to attack Douglas's judgment.[45]

When Johnson nominated Fortas to the Court in 1965, he was easily confirmed by a voice vote with little Southern opposition. But the three years between his confirmation as associate justice and his nomination to chief justice had altered the political landscape. Some of the same senators who were willing to have him on the Court in 1965 no longer felt beholden to Johnson and would rather have risked waiting to see if Nixon would be elected instead of Humphrey. There were significant impediments to Fortas's confirmation. Several senators voiced their opposition to the Court's overturning obscenity statutes, and Fortas had played a role in some of the disputed decisions. Another impediment arose from Fortas's continued political advice to Johnson. Johnson sought Fortas's assistance in matters ranging from the president's policies in Vietnam and the Dominican Republic to confronting increasing domestic dissent. Fortas would not be the first justice to advise a president. Chief Justice Frederick Vinson told President Truman that he believed it was lawful to seize steel mills during the Korean War in order to avert a stoppage in the production of war matériel. Justice Felix Frankfurter advised President Franklin Roosevelt on several matters involving national security and economic recovery. Justice Louis Brandeis had a direct role in drafting the nation's conscription laws in World War I before voting on the law's constitutionality. During Fortas's confirmation hearings to become chief justice, however, he disclaimed that he had advised Johnson, and this proved easy to debunk as a set of canards.[46]

Fortas may not have been ready to truthfully answer questions about his relationship to Johnson, and the Republican senator who served as an inquisitor on the subject, Robert Griffin, was relatively new to the Senate. Born in 1923 in Detroit, Griffin served in the infantry in World War II, then attended Central Michigan College followed by the University of Michigan's law school. He was elected to the House of Representatives in 1956, and in May 1966 Governor George Romney appointed him to the Senate to fill a vacancy. Like John J. Williams, Griffin was convinced that Johnson had engaged in cronyism of "the worst sort" and was loath to permit Johnson to nominate federal judges. Unlike Southern legislators and anticommunist organizations, he could appear to be reasonable in his efforts. He had criticized conservatives who called for Warren's impeachment, and he answered his constituents that if he spoke against Warren or any other judge, then he would have to recuse himself from any impeachment proceedings that might ensue. In this regard Griffin equated himself to an impartial juror on a criminal trial before the trial heard any evidence. He was, however, eager to defeat Fortas.[47]

As Griffin was considered a "minnow" by senior senators, his questioning of Fortas might not have proved devastating to Fortas's confirmation chances. Indeed, Dirksen not only came to Fortas's defense during Griffin's questioning but also belittled Griffin. But Fortas's lies to Griffin were obvious, and this resulted in doubts as to the integrity of his answers regarding his jurisprudence. Without Griffin, the Southern opposition to Fortas might have been viewed as an effort to return to Jim Crow segregation, and Northern conservatives in both parties might have distanced themselves from the anti-Fortas efforts. After Fortas testified, *Life Magazine* reported that he was paid $15,000 for teaching a seminar class at American University. This was an exorbitant sum, one far in excess of what a normal adjunct professor received. Indeed, it constituted slightly less than half of a justice's salary. More troubling was the source of the income. The seminar was wholly funded by corporate interests, and this drew considerable attention because some of it came from parties that were potentially due to appear in appeals before the Court. By the beginning of October 1968, Fortas's nomination was locked in a filibuster, and it was doubtful that it would come up for a vote. While Fortas only needed a majority vote on his confirmation, he needed a two-thirds vote to break a filibuster so that the Senate would actually vote. In late October he withdrew from consideration; he assumed that he would return to the Court to serve as associate justice until he decided otherwise.[48]

Shortly after Nixon became president, *Life Magazine* published another article detrimental to Fortas. Louis Wolfson, an investor who had been convicted of securities fraud in 1967, had created a charitable family foundation in 1965, and Fortas served as its advisor in exchange for $20,000 per year. The ostensible purpose of the foundation was to advocate for integrated housing. Fortas accepted one payment from the foundation but returned it eleven months later. Before becoming a justice Fortas had been a legal advisor and friend to Wolfson, and there was a strong implication in the article that Wolfson expected Fortas to lobby Johnson for a pardon. During the final days of Johnson's presidency, Attorney General Ramsey Clark notified Fortas that the Justice Department had learned of his relationship to Wolfson and that he had never reported the $20,000 to the Internal Revenue Service. Because Fortas had returned the money to the foundation, he countered that he did not need to report this money as income. Fortas's wife, Carol Agger, was a prominent tax lawyer and likely advised him that there was no requirement to report unclaimed income. But once Nixon became president, William Wilson, the Justice Department's new chief of the criminal division, decided to investigate Fortas further for practicing law on Wolfson's behalf and trying to influence the prosecution of Wolfson. Wolfson also supposedly told a *Wall Street Journal* reporter that Fortas had tried to intercede on his behalf with Johnson. In reality Wilson was the source of information for *Life* and the *Wall Street Journal* against Fortas, and while Hoover notified Mitchell that he knew of this fact, Mitchell cagily responded that the Justice Department would begin an investigation "to ascertain the scope of the leaks."[49]

In early May 1969, Griffin, Thurmond, and Goldwater publicly called for Fortas's impeachment. Williams wrote to Warren that "the acceptance of the $20,000 fee by Justice Fortas under the circumstances as outlined was a violation of the standard of conduct the American people have a right to expect of a man holding membership in the Supreme Court." Unless Fortas's judicial allies were willing to become a part of the political fracas, they could do little more than offer him sympathy, and several judges believed Fortas had undermined the judicial branch. During the summer of 1968 Brennan attended a seminar with New York's appellate judges and learned that a consensus opinion against Fortas had developed regarding Fortas's nonrecusal in Vietnam cases. Douglas, too, informed Brennan that he was surprised at the level of opposition Fortas faced. Only a few judges were willing to put their support of Fortas in writing. Harold Leventhal, a judge on the Court of Appeals for the District of Columbia, wrote to Fortas that he and his fellow judge, Carl McGowan, were "happy to see [Fortas] undaunted, and showing a courage not seen since the dark days of Senator Joe McCarthy." But by this time Fortas's chances of survival on the Court were dimming. On May 17 Minnesota senator Walter Mondale became the first Democrat to publicly voice a demand that Fortas resign from the Court.[50]

In mid-May, Attorney General Mitchell showed Earl Warren the Justice Department's "evidence" against Fortas. Warren in turn spoke with Fortas, and soon afterward Fortas announced that he intended to resign from the

Court. In the end Fortas was never prosecuted, in part because the evidence against him was not enough to prove that he had accepted money from Wolfson in exchange for seeking a pardon or that he had conducted legal work on behalf of Wolfson's foundation. Later Nixon would try to have Wolfson turn on Douglas, but this effort failed to gain any embarrassing information against Douglas. Echoing their efforts against Fortas, Mitchell and Wilson would promise Ford evidence that their allegations against Douglas were prosecutable. In the end they would fail to provide any evidence that Douglas had performed legal work or accepted money in exchange for judicial votes on appeals.[51]

Fortas's resignation had a deleterious effect on the federal judiciary not only because it brought to the public's attention the possibility that a justice serving in one of the nation's most important constitutional institutions had undermined that institution's efficacy, but also because judges and justices now had to examine their own conduct. Many judges had accepted payments for making speeches, had served on boards, and had written articles and books. Judges also held financial interests in corporations, and there was the possibility that they had failed to recuse themselves. Future justice Harry A. Blackmun wrote to a friend, "The serious aspect about it all, is that the entire federal judiciary, and not Mr. Justice Fortas or the Supreme Court alone, is under attack. For some reason I felt this very keenly when I ascended the bench in a court session the day after his resignation."[52]

Fortas was only one of the beleaguered men on the judiciary. Nixon's actions were to add two more judges to a growing list of publicly humiliated men. In place of Fortas, Nixon nominated Clement Haynsworth, a Southerner whom Eisenhower had appointed to the Court of Appeals for the Fourth Circuit in 1957. In terms of experience, Haynsworth was qualified to serve on the Court, and no less a personage than Hugo Black lauded his nomination. But Haynsworth was the embodiment of the Southern strategy, which placed states' rights and "freedom of choice" over civil rights, and he could be accurately accused of slow rolling the implementation of civil rights laws. He authored a decision that enabled a county to shutter all of its public schools to avoid integration because the denial of access to public education applied equally to whites and African Americans, and was therefore constitutional in light of *Brown*. He also upheld a freedom-of-choice plan that enabled the de facto continuation of segregated schools. In almost all of the cases in which

Haynsworth upheld school districting plans, the Court overturned his rulings.[53]

There were other markers for civil rights organizations to worry about. In *Griffin v. County School Board* a majority of the Fourth Circuit's judges agreed that contempt citations were appropriate against school board officials who held secret meetings to maintain segregated schools at the time of an appeal. Virginia's public schools remained segregated, particularly after the state's constitution was amended to permit tuition funding for children to attend private schools. The state legislature passed legislation permitting the defunding and closure of integrated schools, and extended state retirement benefits to private schoolteachers. After the state supreme court invalidated several of these provisions, the legislature enacted a "freedom-of-choice plan" and repealed a law requiring mandatory schooling. While most of the counties complied with the state supreme court's decision, the Prince Edward County government closed all of the county's high schools rather than integrate. Wealthier white students were able to gain a high school education, but African American and poor white students struggled. While a federal district court determined that the county's school closure violated the US Constitution's equal protection clause and ordered the county to reopen the public schools, the Fourth Circuit, with Haynsworth in agreement, reversed this decision. After the Supreme Court reversed the Fourth Circuit's decision, the district court reassumed control over the case. They ordered the school board to reopen the public schools and prohibited the county from paying tuition reimbursements for private schools. The county complied with this order, but in a secret meeting distributed $180,000 to white parents for future private school tuition payments. The appellate court determined that school board's conduct was contemptuous, but Haynsworth dissented on the basis that because no judge had expressly prohibited such a meeting, the officials could not be held in contempt.[54]

Perhaps Haynsworth's most offensive judicial acts were his role in *Eaton v. James Walker Memorial Hospital* and in *Simkins v. Moses Cone Memorial Hospital*. In *Eaton*, the Fourth Circuit determined that a private hospital that received no direct funds from the federal or state government could discriminate against licensed African American doctors because there was no "state action" involved in the discrimination. The decision was written by Morris Ames Soper, a judge thought of as having a sound record on civil rights, with

Simon Sobeloff and Haynsworth joining. In *Simkins*, six African American doctors and three dentists were denied staff privileges at the Moses Cone Memorial Hospital and the Wesley Long Community Hospital in Greensboro, North Carolina. Both hospitals were privately owned but were nonprofits in their charters and operated under the state's supervision. More importantly, both hospitals had earlier received federal funding under the Hill-Burton Hospital Construction Program. In 1946, Congress, in the Hill-Burton Act, authorized the use of federal monies to construct hospitals in medically underserved areas, and although the law expressly prohibited discrimination in terms of allocating monies, it also enabled the continuation of "separate but equal" in terms of hospital construction. The Fourth Circuit determined that because federal monies had been used to build the two hospitals, the hospitals could not discriminate against minority doctors. Haynsworth dissented. He argued that because the two hospitals had predated the Hill-Burton Act, and indeed the Moses Cone hospital was first established as a gift from the Cone family in 1911, the hospitals were free to discriminate.[55]

Eaton was decided in 1958 and *Simkins* in 1963. In 1964 the appellate court took up a challenge arising from the James Walker Memorial Hospital's discriminatory policies once more. This time, in *Eaton v. Grubbs*, the Fourth Circuit, in a decision authored by Sobeloff, determined that because the hospital received funds from the county government as well as the city of Wilmington, it could not discriminate against African Americans in either the admission of patients or the granting of privileges to African American medical professionals. Sobeloff recognized that between the issuance of the first *Eaton* decision in 1958 and the newer appeal, the Supreme Court had required a more thorough investigation as to whether a state or municipal government had participated in the governance or funding of an institution such as a hospital. This time Haynsworth concurred, but he did so with the caveat that he was bound to follow the Court's newer rulings, which had enlarged the federal government's power. Implicit in Haynsworth's concurrence was his opposition to the extension of civil rights beyond public education.[56]

Haynsworth had another significant problem, particularly in the aftermath of Fortas. In 1963 the Fourth Circuit heard argument in an appeal entitled *Darlington Mfg. Co. v. National Labor Relations Board*. The National Labor Relations Board (NLRB) determined that because Darlington's directors had shut down a mill in South Carolina in response to a union's organization efforts, the corporation had committed an unfair labor practice. The NLRB's decision, if permitted to stand, could have cost the parent corporation millions of dollars in back pay to the closed mill's former workers. Before becoming a judge, Haynsworth founded Vend-A-Matic, a vending machine company, and he was listed as its vice president well past his judicial appointment. He resigned from the company's board of directors only after a judicial council opinion advised him to do so, and he continued to own corporate stock valued at $450,000 at the time of the *Darlington Mfg.* appeal. Vend-A-Matic's contracts were exclusive in the sense that Darlington's employees could purchase foodstuffs and drinks only through Vend-A-Matic machines. If Darlington's parent company were to lose on its appeal, it stood to lose millions of dollars, which arguably could have resulted in the loss of its other mills. Thus, Vend-A-Matic would either preserve or improve its financial position if the NLRB's decision were reversed. The question then became whether Haynsworth had a duty to recuse himself from the decision.[57]

When the Fourth Circuit determined the appeal, it did so en banc—that is, with all of its judges—and Judge Albert Vickers Bryan authored the majority decision in which Haynsworth joined. The appellate court, with Sobeloff and J. Spencer Bell dissenting, concluded, by a vote of 3 to 2, that because Darlington was a single corporation—that is, it was not a chain of factories and therefore the owners had not used the closure as a threat against other unionization efforts—it could close for any reason. Haynsworth made no mention of a possible conflict of interest with his continued judicial role in the proceeding, thereby denying a litigant the opportunity to seek his recusal. At any rate, the Supreme Court overturned the Fourth Circuit's decision and determined that because Darlington was actually owned by a holding company that owned other mills, it had committed an unfair labor practice.[58]

Between the oral argument and the decision's issuance, Darlington's parent company awarded Vend-A-Matic another exclusive contact, which resulted in additional vending sales valued at $50,000 a year. In 1964 one of the union's attorneys asked Sobeloff to investigate Haynsworth. Although Sobeloff in his capacity as chief judge conducted an inquiry and concluded that Haynsworth had not violated any of the canons of judicial ethics, this did not stop news organizations from questioning Haynsworth's ethical fitness to serve on the Supreme Court. Nor did the fact that Robert Kennedy, while serving as attorney general, concurred with Sobeloff's judgment stem criticism against Haynsworth. In August 1969 the *Los Angeles Times* published an editorial claiming that Haynsworth had violated the judicial canons of ethics for over a decade. Perhaps because the *Los Angeles Times* had criticized Douglas and Fortas, its reporting on Haynsworth also had credibility.[59]

Nixon asserted a defense of Haynsworth that made Ford's claim that Douglas had accepted money from sources without recusing himself appear to be politically motivated. Shortly after Haynsworth's relationship to Vend-A-Matic became an issue, Attorney General Mitchell assigned Assistant Attorney General William Rehnquist to mount a defense of Haynsworth. In a memorandum to Nebraska senator Roman Hrsuka, the Republican leader of the Senate Judiciary Committee, Rehnquist tried to exonerate Haynsworth. The central thrust of Rehnquist's argument was that Haynsworth's financial interests in regard to the Darlington case were "too remote and insubstantial" to merit disqualification. Rehnquist acknowledged that Haynsworth assisted in Vend-A-Matic's financing before his judicial appointment and that, at least in regard to the corporate records, the judge continued to serve as a corporate vice president until 1963. However, Rehnquist insisted, neither factor evidenced any unethical judicial conduct. At the administration's behest, Senator Robert Dole, a Kansas Republican, insisted that the negative information about Haynsworth was nothing more than the product of "some segments of the media [attempting] to discredit [the judge] in the eyes of the public." Contemporaneously, Mollenhoff tried to convince New Mexico senator Joe Montoya that there were vast differences between Bobby Baker and Haynsworth, even though the two men attended vending trade conferences together.[60]

The level of Senate resistance to Haynsworth surprised Nixon. Republicans Charles Goodell, John Sherman Cooper, Clifford Case, Margaret Chase Smith, Mark Hatfield, Jacob Javits, Charles Matthias, and Richard Saxbe voted against Haynsworth. More importantly, two of the leading Republican senators who opposed Fortas turned on Haynsworth. On November 11, 1969, Griffin addressed the Senate against confirming Haynsworth. "Quite frankly, the hearings brought to light a number of matters of concern regarding the nominee's sensitivity to the high ethical standards expected of those who are to sit on the Supreme Court," Griffin began before insisting that at a minimum Haynsworth had created the appearance of having violated the canons of judicial ethics by not divulging his Vend-A-Matic shares to litigating parties. John J. Williams, the "conscience of the Senate," voted against Haynsworth as well. Thus, the senator who began the process of removing Douglas displayed his consistency in regard to Haynsworth.[61]

Nixon's second choice, G. Harold Carswell, proved more contentious than Haynsworth. In 1948 Carswell made a speech that could only be described as racist, and he had joined a country club that excluded minorities. He also drafted a restrictive housing covenant which excluded African Americans from residential communities. Carswell did not confront the same type of ethical challenges as Haynsworth, but his judicial record caused several Republican senators to wonder why Nixon had thought he was qualified to serve on the Court in the first place. On April 8, 1970, Senator Mathias, a Maryland Republican and friend of Vice President Agnew, explained his opposition to Carswell with the observation, "None of [Carswell's decisions] seem to belong in the great tradition of Anglo-American jurisprudence in which judges over the years have contributed to the growth and understanding of the law. Some of them are marked by basic errors." In the end the same alliance that opposed Haynsworth also defeated Carswell. This defeat would set into motion the attack on Douglas, but it would not be the only impetus for it.[62]

While Nixon's anger was well publicized—he publicly spoke of the impossibility of appointing a Southerner to the Court—several of his administration's actions were not well known. If Nixon's retaliation plans had become public and Ford went forward in demanding Douglas's removal, the House may not have investigated Douglas at all. On April 4, 1970, H. R. Haldeman instructed the White House deputy assistant for congressional relations, Franklin "Lyn" Nofziger, to compile a list of attorneys who had opposed Haynsworth and Carswell, and to ensure that none of them be permitted to enter the federal workforce. Republicans who opposed Haynsworth and Carswell were to be considered personae non gratae in the White House. Nixon also asked Murray Chotiner, his former campaign manager, to present the success of his third nominee as proof that Haynsworth and Carswell were denied confirmation on the basis of their Southern geographic origins, rather than celebrating the successful confirmation.[63]

On April 14, 1970, Nixon nominated Harry A. Blackmun, a Minnesotan and longtime friend of Burger, to replace Fortas. Although the Senate easily confirmed Blackmun, Deputy Attorney General Richard Kleindienst had to defend him against accusations that he had failed to recuse himself from three appeals involving a party in which he held a small stock interest. Perhaps if Nixon's first two nominees had not been defeated in a contentious manner Blackmun would have undergone greater scrutiny. Nonetheless, the fact that a deputy attorney general defended Blackmun in a public forum on which the major media outlets in the English-speaking world reported would later benefit Douglas against charges that he had failed to recuse himself from appeals in which he had received a small payment from a party.[64]

A further scandal arose out of the conduct of Frank Gray, a district court judge in Tennessee. Appointed by Kennedy in 1961, Gray had presided over the trial of three defendants accused of jury tampering during the criminal trial of Teamsters Union leader James Riddle "Jimmy" Hoffa in 1962. In the early 1960s John J. Hooker, a prominent lawyer and friend of both Kennedy and Douglas, opened a fried chicken franchise in Tennessee along with singer-comedian Minnie Pearl. In 1966 Hooker was narrowly defeated in the state's gubernatorial race, and he intended to run once again in 1970. However, the franchise declared bankruptcy and the value of its public stock plummeted. Before the public stock offering, Hooker invited a small number of friends to invest in the company at 50 cents per preferred stock share. Included on this list were two federal judges, William Miller and Gray. When the public stock sales reached peak value, the early private investors were able to sell shares at as high as $50 each, even though the financial value of the company was more speculative than real. Gray and Miller made small personal fortunes. By the time the franchise collapsed, thousands of Tennesseans had lost their investments. This episode of boom and bust in the fast food restaurant industry was not unique, but it was problematic that two judges profited from their personal relationships, and the *New York Times* reported this fact.[65]

On October 20, 1970, the *Wall Street Journal,* on its front page, reported that Gray had invested $2,000 in Hooker's venture in 1964 and earned a profit of close to $200,000 out of it. After Hooker's company declared bankruptcy, Gray oversaw its reorganization, including the restructuring of its debts. Fyke Farmer and Charles Morgan Jr., two liberal attorneys who normally supported Douglas, argued that Gray had a duty to recuse himself from overseeing the reorganization and that Congress needed to enact legislation preventing judges from serving on cases or appeals in which the judge held a financial interest. Although a number of judges and scholars came to Gray's defense, including Roger Traynor, the former chief justice of the California

Supreme Court, who headed an ABA effort to enact new judicial ethics canons, the publicity given to this issue, just like that of Fortas and Haynsworth, was not helpful to the image of the federal judiciary.[66]

Judicial and Legislative Efforts at Reform

To Earl Warren's credit, at the end of his judicial tenure he tried to create a new code of ethics that bound all of the judiciary. To do so, he convened the Judicial Conference, an administrative agency, to convince the justices to adopt a more stringent ethics code, mirroring the code governing the lower federal judiciary. The justices for the most part resisted his efforts. On June 10, 1969, the Judicial Conference issued guidelines to govern the conduct of lower court judges. The guidelines included the creation of a judicial board to monitor judges' income and assets, including the justices' accounts and investments. Several judges opposed this measure and petitioned Warren Burger to reevaluate its potential to undermine judicial independence. Black refused to acquiesce to Burger or the conference about filing an income statement. At the same time he also informed the *Los Angeles Times* that he would not provide his opinions on the guidelines. Douglas took the step of writing to the justices, informing them of his reasons for opposing the Judicial Conference's new rules. Any new requirements on judges, he urged, had to be enacted by Congress. "Judges have no authority to tell other judges what to do," he challenged before asking whether the Supreme Court would also be monitored and overseen by appellate and district court judges. Another rule that galled Douglas was that judges would have to first seek the conference's approval before publishing an article or traveling, or before accepting compensation for lecturing or writing. He claimed that he "deplored seeing judges withdraw into a cloistered life," and any rule requiring judges to submit their literary work or speeches for review was merely a form of judicial censorship.[67]

It was problematic that there was no uniformity of conduct among the justices. While Douglas and several other justices were willing to publicly associate with causes they deemed important, Thurgood Marshall took a more cautious approach. When a Christian antipoverty organization asked Marshall to attend a Sunday sermon, he responded that he "was prohibited from engaging in controversial matters." Douglas felt this cautious approach was unnecessary. Part of the problem with the judicial ethics rules in the late 1960s is that they had not been updated since the ABA issued the first canons of judicial ethics in 1923. The first judicial ethics canons were rudimentary, and their author, Chief Justice William Howard Taft, focused on financial improprieties of a direct nature. The 1923 canons did not prohibit federal judges from advising charitable foundations or universities, and judges could be paid income outside their judicial duties. In point of fact, Taft served on a foundation funded by industrialist Andrew Carnegie.[68]

There was no direct prohibition against either Fortas or Douglas serving on a foundation. Several other justices had done so, and so had the judges on the courts of appeals and district courts. In 1969 Charles Wyzanski, the chief judge of the United States district court for Massachusetts, informed Warren that from the time he became a judge in 1942 he had given dozens of lectures in Asia, Africa, and South America arranged by the Ford Foundation; he had also served on the boards of Princeton's Institute for Advanced Study, Smith College, and the Phillips Exeter Academy. In addition to receiving honoraria of $5,000, Wyzanski also earned $2,000 per term for teaching as a visiting lecturer at Harvard. Wyzanski was by no means alone among the district court judges, as most of them served on foundations, managed estates, and lectured on a large variety of subjects.[69]

Just as there was no uniform standard on teaching or serving on foundations and boards, there was no uniform standard on providing policy and political advice to a president. In 1934 James Beck, a former solicitor general who served under President Warren Harding and was one of Taft's confidants, wrote to the National Recovery Administration's director that during his legal career, which stretched over forty years, Supreme Court justices had often made public their opinions on various government programs, taught at universities, and advised presidents. The director, General Hugh Johnson, had sought Beck's opinion on Justice Brandeis's taking part in an appeal involving the agency. Brandeis had advised Roosevelt on creating the agency, and Johnson had publicly criticized Brandeis. Although Beck was a conservative who had earlier allied with Taft against Brandeis's nomination, he insisted that in terms of ethics, Brandeis "had an unblemished record on the bench."[70]

On June 29, 1969, six days after being confirmed as Chief Justice, Burger appointed seven federal judges, including some of Douglas's allies, such as

Elbert Tuttle on the Fifth Circuit and Harold Leventhal, to an advisory group on reforming judicial ethics. The purpose of this committee, the Interim Advisory Committee on Judicial Activities, somewhat mirrored Chief Justice Taft's efforts on judicial ethics standards in 1924. The federal judges appointed to the interim committee were not responsible to the ABA but rather were charged with creating ethics rules that were applicable to judges serving on the lower federal courts. Burger also designed the interim committee to focus its efforts on extrajudicial activities, whether or not such activities were compensated or free. Burger charged the interim committee to issue advisory opinions by using the ABA's canons "as a base." Within a week of the appointment of the judicial members, the interim committee issued five advisory opinions. These included approving a judge serving as a part-time or adjunct lecturer at a law school, provided that the compensation matched the normal compensation of part-time lecturers. The interim committee also advised that uncompensated service on the Salvation Army's board of directors and participation in an uncompensated college seminar panel, a church arbitration board, or as a testamentary trustee for a deceased family member would likewise not violate the canons of ethics.[71]

Douglas for his part took exception to the interim committee's use of the ABA's canons. In a letter to the Court, he argued that "those who purport to speak for the Association represent rich corporate clients." He claimed that he had once been an ABA member but had terminated his membership more than thirty years earlier because its conservative leaders, such as John Foster Dulles and John W. Davis, used it as a means "to defeat President Roosevelt's New Deal programs." Moreover, he reminded the justices that in 1916 ABA president Elihu Root aligned with Taft and others "representing the money trust and other manipulators of high finance" to try to discredit Brandeis during his confirmation hearings. Douglas, however, did not stop with his criticism of the use of the ABA canons of ethics. He encouraged the justices to renounce their affiliation with the association. In May 1969, the ABA's board of directors asked its ethics committee to consider whether Douglas should be investigated. While ultimately the ethics committee argued that it would damage the ABA to take a position on Douglas, newspapers reported on the board of directors' request.[72]

By the end of 1968 there was a general perception in Congress that the federal judiciary's ethics were far too malleable. On July 23, 1968, Senator Ervin introduced a bill to make it impossible for a president to nominate a justice unless the federal and state judiciaries had first recommended the candidate. The next year he referred a draft bill to the Senate Judiciary Committee that would have prohibited federal judges from "engaging or participating" in "the exercise of any power, or the discharge of any duty, which is conferred or imposed upon any officer or employee of the executive branch or the legislative branch of the government." In essence, Ervin sought to prevent judges from advising a president on the drafting of legislation, or advising on domestic, foreign, and military policies. Ervin explained that both of his proposed bills were in response to Fortas. "Concerning suggestions for improving the Supreme Court, I believe that many of their decisions could have been avoided if our government provided an adequate measure of insuring that only the most qualified men serve on the Court," Ervin argued.[73]

At the same time, Senator Joseph Tydings, a Maryland Democrat, introduced a bill to create a Commission on Judicial Disabilities and Tenure, which would have been composed of five judges and chaired by the Chief Justice. This commission would have the power to inquire into the conduct of all federal judges. If four of the judges agreed that a federal judge had violated judicial ethics standards, then the commission was empowered to recommend to the House Judiciary Committee that a judge be subject to impeachment. On November 6, 1969, Tydings addressed the Catholic University Law School on the need for judicial reform and claimed that Congress had to legislate a standard of "good behavior" for the judiciary because the judiciary had failed to follow its own standards. Tydings cited Fortas's resignation and Haynsworth's failed nomination, as well as "the Chandler case," as evidence of the need for judicial reform. He also reminded the audience that when on June 10, 1969, Chief Justice Warren had directed the Judicial Conference to prepare a code of ethics, his efforts had faltered because of the "Supreme Court's dimming judicial resolve." Tydings moreover argued that mandatory reporting of income and gifts as well as regulations on judicial activities were not a threat to the judiciary's independence but rather would serve to bolster public confidence in the judiciary. "The threat will pass only when the members of the federal judiciary realize that not every attempt to monitor their conduct constitutes hazing," he concluded.[74]

Tydings's efforts were defeated by several judges. Most notably, Black lobbied several judges to protest that Tydings's proposals for reform would undermine the judiciary's independence. Black and Tydings had a history of disagreement. In 1966 Black cautioned Tydings against creating multiple avenues to remove judges as it would undermine the Constitution's protections of an independent judiciary. Two years later Black took Tydings to task for recommending a law requiring judicial retirements at age seventy. "This is not because I happen to be over 70 but because I have known many district judges who have performed their best judicial services after they reached the age of 70," Black countered. Black was the most prominent opponent of Tydings's proposal, but he was not the only one. On October 17, 1969, Tydings wrote to Judge David Bazelon seeking his guidance on recusal policies. Bazelon turned to his peers on the Court of Appeals for the District of Columbia, and in turn the other judges agreed that the proper response to Tydings was that each judge should independently determine when recusal was necessary.[75]

In the House, Minnesota Republican Clark MacGregor offered three judicial reform bills. The first would require the IRS to remove tax-exempt status from any organization that offered payments to federal officials. This bill was aimed at the entire government, but he conceded that Fortas and Douglas were his reasons for introducing it. A second bill, HR 11369, would require all legislators, cabinet officers, and judges to report earnings and properties to the comptroller general. MacGregor wanted to make public the net worth of federal judges. The third, and most draconian bill, entitled HR 11370, made it a felony for any person in the federal government to receive a payment of over $500 for any activity, including speeches. MacGregor's efforts coincided with Fortas's withdrawal from consideration to be chief justice. On the day of Fortas's resignation MacGregor asked Celler to convene a subcommittee to investigate the outgoing justice and force Chief Justice Warren to publish Fortas's personal resignation letter to the Court.[76]

On May 8, 1969, Ohio Republican Robert Alphonso Taft Jr. introduced a bill entitled HR 1119 that would require federal judges to provide to the comptroller general their complete tax filings, including spousal incomes, as well as the names and addresses of professional corporations, businesses, foundations, or other enterprises in which the judge served as a compensated officer or consultant. The bill also required judges to disclose their real and personal property interests valued at over $10,000 and list all trusts valued at over $10,000. Finally, the bill required judges to list all financial liabilities such as home loans and lines of credit valued at over $5,000. Ostensibly this bill was introduced as a means to build public confidence in the impartiality of federal judges after Fortas's resignation. For reasons that are unknown or absent from the available record, Celler did not forward the bill for a committee review.[77]

On November 4, 1969, Taft, along with Ford, formally requested that Celler schedule a hearing on HR 11109, particularly because three days earlier the Judicial Conference had rejected Earl Warren's proposed prohibition against judges earning outside income. Celler remained noncommittal about the bill. Taft's inability to move the bill to a House Judiciary Committee hearing proved frustrating, and he complained to a University of Cincinnati law school professor that he "saw no reason why a thorough investigation of such conflicts of interest should not be carried out," adding that Ford was in the process of investigating "at least one member of the Court." Four days later, Ford publicly "hinted" that he was going to demand an investigation into Douglas. Three days after issuing his hint, Ford expanded on his statements, adding that he had been studying Douglas's financial relationships and that this would form the basis for his eventual demand to have Douglas investigated by the House. Later in the month Ford informed several congressmen that by the end of 1970 he would call for a special investigation into Douglas[78]

The death knell to Tydings's, Macgregor's, Taft's, and Ford's proposals was not only the result of judiciary's reticence; the actions of Senator Ervin also contributed to an impasse. In a surprising statement to the Senate Judiciary Committee, he argued that their proposed bills, "while well intentioned, would introduce new extra-judicial influences into the Federal court system" and would undermine the judicial branch's independence. Ervin attempted to work with the retired Warren on judicial ethics. In doing so he determined that the best means to ensure an ethical judiciary was in the appointment of judges rather than the regulatory process. To this end, he argued that judicial nominees should be required to permanently divest themselves of investments before taking their oaths of office. One week before Ford spoke against Douglas, Ervin issued an opening statement in a committee hearing criticizing the proposals.[79]

Douglas Entrenched

By the 1968 campaign cycle, the judicial liberals, with the exception of Douglas, understood that the Court was beleaguered. When Warren issued a draft of *Terry v. Ohio*, upholding the authority of police officers to "pat down" suspects if there was a "reasonable suspicion," Brennan cautioned that the Court would become a scapegoat for increasing crime if it had determined to reverse the conviction. But he also worried that the decision would stoke further resentment in the "poorer cities," because as written, the draft enabled a police officer to search a person if the officer subjectively suspected that the person was engaged in illegal activity. *Terry* stood as an exception to the Court's jurisprudence, and it had the possibility of disproving Nixon's claim that the Court sided with criminals over the police. Douglas dissented and remained true to his jurisprudence of distrusting law enforcement. The Court issued *Terry* on June 10, 1968, and the Republican convention began on August 5.[80]

Nixon's election emboldened Douglas to amplify his criticism of the federal government and continue his multifaceted writing. In addition to writing on conservation, he authored an article espousing folk music in a Ginzburg-owned nonpornographic magazine. The magazine paid Douglas $350 for the article. In a different magazine Ginzburg had published an article about Goldwater that a jury later determined constituted libel. Douglas had not recused himself from an appeal arising from the jury's libel verdict. When on May 29, 1969, Senator Paul Fannin, an Arizona conservative Republican and Goldwater ally, demanded Douglas's impeachment after the justice voted to overturn Ginzburg's obscenity conviction, Douglas responded by laughing. To conservatives, it was problematic that Douglas had a minor financial relationship with Ginzburg. In the end Fannin's demands against Douglas were unrealistic and had no basis in law, but Douglas was foolish not to take seriously the increasing attacks on him. One particular aspect of *Ginzburg* should have concerned Douglas. On September 25, 1969, Assistant Attorney General Rehnquist assured the House Judiciary Committee of the administration's support for two pending bills that would have criminalized the direct mailing of obscene material through the mail. He noted that Mitchell highlighted the *Ginzburg* decision as a basis for arguing the constitutionality of the proposed law.[81]

Shortly after Nixon became president, a Justice Department official lobbied Brennan to have the Court reconsider its *Alderman v. United States* decision. In that decision, the Court determined that the government was required to provide all defendants with transcripts of recorded conversations that had been taken through wiretaps. This meant that conversations recorded in other countries' embassies and consulates, even if damaging to national security or diplomatic relations, had to be given to defendants. The Justice Department officer implied that it was possible that a new congressional effort to curb the Court's jurisdiction as a result of the decision would occur. In spite of the Justice Department's efforts, the Court formally denied reconsideration to the government. Although this was not the first occasion that a government officer had approached a justice in a less than proper manner, it foreshadowed Nixon's efforts to reshape the Court.[82]

In March 1970 the Court debated an appeal arising from an Illinois state trial judge's determination to find a disruptive defendant in contempt of court. Because the contempt had occurred thirteen years earlier, it had nothing to do with dissent over the Vietnam conflict. Indeed, the person held in contempt was mentally ill and on trial for robbery. After threatening the trial judge, the defendant was removed from the court, and his counsel remained to present a defense. The Sixth Amendment articulates a defendant's right to be present in a criminal trial and assist in his or her defense, but this right is necessarily qualified on the basis of a defendant's behavior. In conference, Black argued that although the Bill of Rights cannot be abridged, in this instance the trial judge was confronted with the choice of either permitting Allen to remain in his own criminal trial but gagged and physically restrained, or to be removed from the trial until such time as he could behave. None of the other justices opposed Black's position, and Burger assigned Black to write the decision. Burger had a political motive in the timing of the decision's issuance, and he asked Black to accelerate writing the opinion. Judge John Murtagh, a New York state trial judge, had established a trial date for several members of the Black Panthers accused of plotting to bomb department stores. Not surprisingly, the trial was heavily covered in the media. During the pretrial hearings a number of spectators as well as the defendants were disruptive. After establishing a trial date, members of the Weather Underground, an antigovernment organization, bombed Murtagh's home.[83]

Burger feared that the Black Panther defendants would intentionally disrupt the courtroom as a means of delaying the actual trial, and he wanted to provide Murtagh with clear authority to remove the defendants. He also worried that Douglas would dissent in *Allen* on the basis that freedom of speech was sacrosanct to the point that the only judicial remedy available would be for the judge to order delays in the trial. However, Douglas had no intention of dissenting, and he wrote a terse letter to Burger on this point. Although Burger apologized to Douglas, this episode evidences that the conservative chief justice, mirroring the fears of many conservatives, distrusted Douglas. Moreover, Burger's determination to speed *Allen*'s issuance to benefit a state trial judge in a pending well-publicized trial shows that political motives were not confined to the Court's liberals. Finally, Douglas's concurrence in *Allen* would later be used by his supporters to prove that he was neither antigovernment nor a threat to national security.[84]

3

Douglas, Extrajudicial Activities,
and the Vietnam Conflict

On July 16, 1969, Dean Acheson testified to Congress on the need to enact new laws prohibiting federal judges from accepting money for making speeches, serving on boards, or teaching academic courses. Shortly afterward, former Supreme Court justices Arthur Goldberg and Tom Clark informed Congress that they agreed with Acheson. Acheson was a longtime civil servant who had been mentored in law school by Felix Frankfurter. He began his legal career as a clerk to Justice Oliver Wendell Holmes Jr., served as President Harry Truman's secretary of state, and advised President John F. Kennedy during the Cuban missile crisis. Acheson criticized both Abe Fortas and William O. Douglas with the admonition, "Where a lectureship has a stipend to it, it should be declined—or better not offered." Although Acheson's comments could have applied to other justices, and he singled out Frankfurter as an example of the dangers of judges giving political advice to the executive branch, his testimony would have established a basis for impeaching Fortas had Fortas remained on the Court. Acheson may not have known the extent to which Douglas had advised foreign governments, and given Douglas's rapid distancing from the Oval Office between 1964 and 1969, he may not have understood the full scope of Douglas's efforts to convince Johnson to deescalate the Vietnam conflict. Yet Acheson insisted that "a justice who accepted payments for writing on population control, the conflict of generations, and the iniquity of foreign undemocratic regimes invited trouble," and this comment was aimed directly at Douglas.[1]

Acheson's criticism of Douglas was noteworthy for several reasons. Both men had been New Dealers who were loyal to President Franklin Roosevelt. Both men believed that Nixon had unfairly targeted Alger Hiss; indeed, Acheson came to Hiss's defense in court. Like Douglas, Acheson deplored the conservatives' tactics of smearing opponents as procommunist. Although after he retired from the Court Douglas disparaged Acheson as a "status quo lawyer," the two men were like-minded in several respects on matters such as civil rights and the need to strengthen democracy by not resorting to repressive domestic measures such as government surveillance of citizens or outlawing political ideologies. Nonetheless, Acheson's public excoriation of Douglas contained valid criticisms. Douglas had long been involved not only in the nation's Vietnam policies but also in assisting in the creation of South Vietnam's government. Moreover, he frequently championed foreign policy causes that the Truman, Eisenhower, Kennedy, and Johnson administrations disfavored. More troubling to Acheson was the fact that Douglas was not popularly viewed as a foreign affairs novice. Because he had widely traveled and conferred with foreign leaders, including those of the Soviet Union and China, and because Roosevelt had approved his early foreign activities, he was often presented as being knowledgeable in world affairs. In 1957 Henry Usborne, a member of parliament in the United Kingdom and a senior Labour Party officer, sought Douglas's backing to lobby for a permanent United Nations peacekeeping force. One year earlier Sir Roger Makins, Britain's ambassador to the United States, informed Foreign Secretary Selwyn Lloyd that Douglas was the Court's foreign affairs expert.[2]

Douglas's extrajudicial activities in terms of military and foreign policy dated to his early Court tenure. On March 20, 1945, Roosevelt sent General William Donovan, the commander of the Office of Strategic Services, to seek Douglas's guidance on the asylum rights of political refugees in neutral countries. Roosevelt worried that Switzerland, Sweden, Ireland, Portugal, the Vatican, Turkey, and Argentina would offer Nazi war criminals asylum, which had enabled Kaiser Wilhelm II to escape prosecution after World War I. Douglas advised Donovan in a cryptic note that he did not consider neutral governments to possess the lawful authority to offer asylum to persons accused of war crimes. Three months later, Secretary of the Navy James Forrestal asked Douglas to lead a committee to propose postwar military requirements and examine "the relationship of civilian and military control, as well as relations between the United States and Soviet Union." Forrestal also asked Douglas to serve on a commission to review the navy's administration of local governments in the Pacific, and if Douglas were unable to take part, whether he "could recommend judges or prominent lawyers to take his place." Douglas obliged Forrestal with several recommendations, and he placed William Campbell at the top of his list. This was the same William Campbell whom Sherman Skolnick had accused of improper financial dealings in Chicago and who had served on the Parvin Foundation's board with Douglas.[3]

In 1959 Robert Hutchins, a former dean of Yale University's law school and onetime mentor to Douglas, founded the Center for the Study of Democratic Institutions (CSDI) in Santa Barbara, California. Pulitzer Prize–winning journalist Harry Ashmore joined Hutchins shortly after. The CSDI provided a forum for leading intellectuals to protect and strengthen democratic institutions across the world. On Hutchins's invitation, Douglas became an integral part of the CSDI. Its other participants included Democratic Party senators William Fulbright and Hubert Humphrey, Nobel laureate Linus Pauling, Swedish economist-sociologist Gunnar Myrdal, Republican senator John Sherman Cooper of Kentucky, and Republican governor George Romney. At its founding, the CSDI was not specifically focused on Vietnam, but by 1965 the Southeast Asian conflict consumed much of its members' attention. In 1963 Hutchins and Ashmore took notice of Pope John XXIII's *Pacem in Terris* encyclical and planned for a conference in New York two years later. (The pontiff had called for a meeting of the world's leaders to promote peace and an end to the Cold War.) The CSDI's Pacem in Terris conclave brought in Humphrey, Dwight Eisenhower, Earl Warren, Adlai Stevenson, justices on the International Court of Justice, and prominent foreign leaders to formulate a means to reduce tensions with communist governments.[4]

In 1967 the CSDI hosted a second Pacem in Terris conclave, this time in Geneva, Switzerland. With the State Department's approval, Hutchins invited North Vietnam's leaders to attend. Contemporaneously, Douglas lobbied Johnson to approve a private visit by Ashmore and Hutchins to North Vietnam where the two men would make informal inquiries as to the possibility of ending the conflict and meet with Ho Chi Minh. Ford's allies later insisted that Douglas had played a secretive role in the CSDI's connections to North Vietnam and then claimed that any communication with the North Vietnamese government violated a seldom-used law, the Logan Act. This law prohibits US citizens from conducting foreign policy in their private capacity without government sanction. Because Johnson had approved of the CSDI's activities after conferring with Douglas, accusations that its members were violating the Logan Act were meritless. Douglas moreover believed that he had established a foreign policy record that would appeal to the North Vietnamese, and Johnson wanted to find a peaceful solution before the 1968 election. Finally, neither Douglas nor Ashmore tried to make his attempted overtures to North Vietnam a secret, and indeed, in 1968 Ashmore published a book entitled *Mission to Hanoi: A Chronicle of Double Dealing in High Places* detailing their efforts.[5]

Douglas, Foreign Policy, and Extrajudicial Activities

Douglas followed a meteoric path to the Supreme Court. He was born in Minnesota in 1898, at the age of two moved to California, and after his father died four years later moved with his mother and sister to Washington. As a child he suffered a long-term illness that he later claimed to be polio. Like Nixon, Douglas grew up in an environment that could be charitably characterized as one step above poverty. He attended Whitman College in Walla Walla, served briefly in an army commissioning program in World War I, and then attended Columbia University's law school. He married the first of his four wives during law school, and after graduation in 1925 he took a job with one of the nation's most prestigious law firms. Within two years of Douglas's graduation, Hutchins hired him onto Yale University's law school faculty, where he taught commercial law. In 1934 Joseph Kennedy brought Douglas to the Securities and Exchange Commission (SEC) as its counsel, and when Kennedy departed two years later, Douglas became the commission's chairman. In this capacity he investigated stock market manipulations and enforced regulations to protect the national economy. Most importantly, he developed a keen, and personally helpful, friendship with Roosevelt, to the point that he became a regular member of the president's card games. When Roosevelt nominated him to the Court in 1939 to replace Louis Brandeis, only four senators voted against his nomination. By 1940 Douglas was thought to be a possible future president, and Roosevelt considered him as his vice presidential running mate in both 1940 and 1944.[6]

Once on the Court, Douglas became a prolific writer of books and articles. In addition to writing standard law books for law school students, he authored history treatises, travel journals, arguments for environmental protection, and quite a lot about his personal life. In this latter category Douglas gained a reputation for exaggeration, if not outright fiction. His public statements, whether while giving a speech or in writing, were often controversial; or at least they evidenced that he was willing to express opinions in a manner that went beyond the traditional bounds of judicial propriety. At times he savaged the historic justifications that segregationists and political conservatives insisted proved the rightness of their beliefs. By the time Douglas published *America Challenged* in 1960—a book that would become central to Ford's demand for his impeachment—he had already argued that the United States' approach to domestic and foreign communism was flawed and that the government had abandoned a basic principle that the protection and expansion of individual rights was the best guarantor of defeating oppressive political ideologies such as communism and fascism. No president since Roosevelt, Douglas insisted, had understood this principle.[7]

Several authors have posited that it was only his unrivaled intellect that made Douglas suited for the Supreme Court. In several other ways he would have been better suited for service in different governmental capacities. Part of this had to do with his penchant for political activity and questionable associations. By the 1960s he viewed himself as a protector of the environment; he participated in public protests against mining activities, sewage dumping, and dam building. Like Frankfurter, he advised Roosevelt and other New Deal political leaders. There was a difference between Douglas and Frankfurter. While Frankfurter departed from judicial ethics norms by advising Roosevelt's cabinet on wartime issues, including a joint defense agreement between Canada and the United States, as well as the military trials of captured German saboteurs, he did not seek political office, whereas Douglas did. By the time Douglas ascended to the Court, his circle of friends included prominent New Deal men, leading academics, and of course Roosevelt. Some of the New Dealers he became associated with included Secretary of the Interior Harold Ickes, James Landis, Abe Fortas, Tommy Corcoran, Clark Clifford, Frankfurter, and Hugo Black. He also befriended rising politicians such as Nelson Rockefeller, Johnson, and Truman. Douglas's friendships, however, were hardly permanent. Early in his Court tenure he and Frankfurter became antagonists, and Justice Robert Jackson also became a bitter opponent. Although Truman was personally fond of Douglas, he became exasperated with the Justice's behavior. [8]

During World War II, Douglas protected the nation's wartime policies by joining with the majority of the Court in upholding the detention of US citizens of Japanese descent, administrative control over commodity pricing, and the extension of military jurisdiction—and commensurate denial of jurisdiction of the federal judiciary—regarding captured enemy combatants in US military trials. However, after Roosevelt's death, Douglas transitioned from siding with the president; he sought limits on federal power in regard to national security. His judicial efforts included ending military trials of citizens, reducing the military's jurisdiction over its own service members, and giving the federal courts unprecedented jurisdiction over the military. Before Douglas's judicial tenure, military and national security programs were largely immune from the reach of the courts, and one of Douglas's legacies included opening the federal courts to aggrieved persons challenging governmental decisions on mandatory retirement, inequities in military pay and promotions, challenges to courts-martial convictions, and security clearance denials for civilians working in the government.

Douglas opposed several programs created to limit communists from holding public employment or in the professions of law and medicine. He refused to limit free speech or freedom of assembly rights for persons who adopted disfavored political positions. When the federal government created mandatory registration lists for "subversives," he stood in opposition. He also infuriated conservative anticommunists by adhering to a jurisprudence that did not distinguish communism from other political beliefs. Douglas was a key participant in the Warren Court's extension of the Bill of Rights into state criminal trials, including the right to defense counsel for indigent defendants, a mandate for state juries to come from a cross section of society and not exclude African Americans or women, the right of defendants to have full access to the government's evidence (even when there were national security concerns), and the requirement for police to inform suspects of their constitutional right against self-incrimination. [9]

By 1949 Douglas made it clear that state laws designed to limit the equality of African Americans were inherently unconstitutional. He sided with employees over management in pay disputes and working conditions, and he opposed race discrimination in employment or education. He played a

prominent role in the reapportionment of voting districts and the overturning of Jim Crow laws that had excluded minorities from voting. Some of the
reapportionment decisions angered Northerners as well as Southerners because the rulings resulted in the political power of rural voters being eroded.
Douglas was hardly alone in the altering of criminal law and voting rights,
but he was far more vocal in justifying the Court's decisions than the other
justices.[10]

In 1947, in a speech recognizing the one-hundredth anniversary of the
birth of former Illinois governor John Altgeld, Douglas posited that judicial
injunctions had been a historic tool of "the industrial class" against union
labor. The actions of federal judges, Douglas argued, enabled the owners of
industry and banks to subjugate workers into poverty and a never-ending
state of powerlessness. "Too many times and for too long," Douglas argued,
those in power had used the law to prevent the majority of a population
from taking part in government or increasing their wealth. Douglas carried
this view of history not only into his domestic jurisprudence but also into his
foreign policy philosophy. In 1952 he wrote to a group of legal scholars that
the best means by which to effectuate change in Southeast Asia was to "work
through the peasant groups" and to remove them "from the feudal classes."
He cautioned that unless the United States removed its support from the
"ruling classes," communist revolution was inevitable. On May 30, 1964, in
a speech in Charleston, West Virginia, Douglas argued that the United States
had wasted its global credibility on "vain military adventures." His claim was
hardly new. For the previous fifteen years he had traveled much of the world
and written magazine articles on the people he met and how they perceived
the United States.[11]

During the summer of 1951 Douglas journeyed to Asia, and when he
passed through San Francisco on his return flight he stated to a local bar
association that the US government should formally recognize the People's
Republic of China. Not only were Douglas's comments reported, but also
Truman rebuked him for his stance on China. Normally Truman and Douglas were allies, and Truman had previously offered Douglas a cabinet post
as secretary of the Interior as well as the role of running mate in 1948. But
Douglas resented Truman. In 1944 Douglas and Truman were advanced as
potential vice presidential candidates for Roosevelt's fourth-term candidacy.
To Douglas's dismay, the Democratic convention chose Truman. Douglas be-

lieved that he was superior to Truman in intellectual capacity, knowledge of the world, and leadership skills. When Truman offered Douglas a cabinet position as well as the vice presidential slot, he understood Douglas's reluctance to leave the Court, but he may not have known that Douglas still harbored anger about being left off the vice presidential ticket in 1944.[12]

Although Douglas was not alone in advocating China's formal recognition—and indeed Nixon later began the process of accepting the legitimacy of the communist government—at the time he was in the minority, and the United States was in a war with China on the Korean peninsula. Moreover, the majority of American political leaders still subscribed to the belief that communism was a monolithically led movement from Moscow. This was, after all, a time in which conservative congressmen and pundits were able to convince millions of Americans that communist sympathizers in the US government had contributed to Mao Zedong's communist victory over the nationalists, and in a few cases, government employees, such as Owen Lattimore, were prosecuted for perjury after being questioned by congressional committees about their role in China. It did not help Douglas when it became known that he and Lattimore were friends.[13]

Douglas created a political firestorm for Truman. Senator Everett Dirksen, an Illinois Republican, claimed that Douglas's comments proved the administration was soft on communism, and Senator Herman Welker, an Idaho Republican, accused Truman of using Douglas to articulate the administration's position on China, even though Truman had clearly tried to isolate the communists in China. Even Truman's Democratic allies, who normally would have defended Douglas, did not do so in this instance. Senator Tom Connally, a Texas Democrat and confidant of Lyndon Johnson, openly criticized Douglas for privately undertaking a foreign policy role to the detriment of the nation. Truman fumed, but rather than publicly denigrate Douglas, he wrote a private letter to the justice. "I was somewhat embarrassed by your statement on Communist China," Truman began. "As long as I am President, that cut-throat organization will never be recognized by us as the government of China and I am sorry that a Justice of the Supreme Court has been willing to champion the interest of a bunch of murderers by a public statement." Although Truman professed his personal fondness for Douglas, he ended the letter with an admonishment to give "his best effort to the Court and let the President of the United States run the political end of foreign and domestic affairs."[14]

Truman's rebuke did not end Douglas's activities in trying to influence foreign policy. Although the letter upset Douglas and led him to apologize— a process that took several drafts, including questionable protestations that he had never sought the vice presidency in 1944—he encouraged Truman to consider that by prying China from the Soviet Union, Southeast Asia would move away from the Kremlin's influence, and in the long term this would enable the "free world" to avoid becoming mired in endless conflicts. Moreover, Douglas assured Truman that his hatred of communism had only been increased by his travels to various communist countries. He further challenged Truman that it was impossible to defeat communism militarily because a majority of the world's population had already fallen under some type of communist control.[15]

Douglas's foreign policy commentary did not generate any immediate calls for his impeachment, but it would later be brought up after he tried to prevent the government from executing Ethel and Julius Rosenberg in 1953. After Douglas's granting of a stay of execution, Georgia Democrat Don Wheeler introduced a resolution to the House accusing Douglas of "high crimes and misdemeanors" and called him "a modern day Sanhedrin Court in the spurious conviction of Jesus Christ." Wheeler had little congressional support, and Douglas, after all, had not acted alone. Frankfurter and Black also opposed the executions, although on a different basis. Louis Graham, a Pennsylvania Republican who had been appointed as chairman of the investigation, and Emanuel Celler, who was the ranking Democrat on the investigation, concluded that Wheeler did not understand the role of the judiciary and agreed to table the resolution. In the end nothing came of Wheeler's efforts to impeach Douglas, and because the House overwhelmingly disapproved of an impeachment, Douglas barely took notice of it, other than to later inform a news reporter that he had survived previous impeachment attempts.[16]

Douglas did not end his foreign policy advocacy simply because Truman had excoriated him or because he had been accused of treason. In all likelihood both of these events emboldened him to advocate for foreign causes. In 1949 he traveled to Iran and began a friendship with Mohammad Mossadegh, a liberal prime minister who was seeking to secularize the government. Because of Iran's proximity to the Soviet Union, Mossadegh was tolerant of communism. Yet he had no intention of Iran's becoming communist or a part of the Soviet sphere of influence. Instead, he tried to remove British postcolonial control of Iran's economy. The British had established control over Iran's petroleum reserves as a result of administering Iran after World War I. After William Donovan sought his advice on relations with the Iranian government, Douglas responded that Truman's policies "played to Russian hands—unwittingly and unnecessarily."[17]

Douglas also recruited for the CIA in Iran and the Mediterranean. In 1951 he introduced Kurish Shabazz to the CIA after describing him as a friend and "a Christian with very high moral standards and character." Shabazz was fluent in Farsi as well as several other languages, and when the CIA informed Douglas that they could not hire him, Douglas then asked the State Department to offer Shabazz a position. Douglas believed that if he could place reliable Iranians into the CIA, American policy would become pro-Mossadegh. When in 1970 the CIA's leadership informed the House Judiciary Committee investigation that the agency possessed no information related to Ford's claims, they omitted the fact that Douglas had recruited for them.[18]

In addition to recruiting for the CIA, Douglas's trip to Iran had a military aspect to it. The US Army supplied his hiking stove, clothes, and boots for his climbs on Mount Ararat and in the Zagros mountains. He reported to the army's Quartermaster's Corps that most of their equipment had withstood the various environmental challenges, but the army would be ill prepared to deal with sunburn, and the "general-issue sleeping bags" were too warm for summer temperatures. Douglas did not suspect that the United States would send the military into Iran for aggressive reasons; he hoped that the Department of Defense would send military aid to protect the Iranian government.[19]

In 1951 Douglas hosted Mossadegh at the Supreme Court and feted him as a champion of freedom who could overcome communism without resorting to oppression. In a televised interview on CBS, Douglas lauded Mossadegh's resistance against British efforts to commandeer Iran's oil and insisted that the United States needed to help build Iran's economy. As Douglas developed a deeper understanding of Iran, he also discovered that Winston Churchill, at the behest of British oil interests, backed a coup to topple the Iranian monarchy, and once this coup succeeded, it resulted in Mossadegh's murder. Douglas may not have known the extent to which the Eisenhower administration supported the coup against Mossadegh, but conservatives later used Douglas's advocacy for Mossadegh as proof of his intent to undermine foreign policy.[20]

In 1955 Douglas journeyed with Robert Kennedy to Iran and the Soviet Union. Joseph Kennedy had asked Douglas to take Robert with him on one of his journeys in order to provide an educational experience, and Douglas felt he owed a debt to his former mentor. When Douglas first tried to visit the Soviet Union in 1951, Joseph Stalin's intelligence service had branded him a spy and refused him entry into the country. In 1955, however, Nikita Khrushchev reversed the ban and permitted the two men, in addition to an interpreter, leave to travel. Douglas debated several Soviet professors and government officials during his journey, and he was able to see the effect of Stalin's brutal governance on the people in the southern Soviet republics. He presented his impressions of Soviet communism in a book entitled *Russian Journey*, and nothing in the book could be interpreted as an endorsement of communism.[21]

New governments arising from Europe's colonial retreat approached Douglas for guidance. In 1963, as the small African nation of Nyasaland gained its independence from Britain and its government changed the country's name to Malawi, its foreign minister sought Douglas's advice on strengthening its judiciary to protect democracy. William Campbell had earlier formed a relationship with Malawi's minister of local government and enabled a meeting between the minister and Douglas. When Douglas advised the minister, he did so in the company of Representatives Charles C. Diggs, Adam Clayton Powell, and Edith Green, and of Senator Frank Church. Each of these legislators defended Douglas after Ford's attack in 1970. Douglas's advice was consistent in that he argued that the best two means of preventing communism were to prevent the accumulation of power in a chief of state and to remove all censorship of competing ideas. Douglas was not heeded. Shortly after the meeting Malawi lapsed into a one-party government that militarily repressed opposition.[22]

Douglas's overseas experiences led him to embark on writing projects in books and magazines, many of which criticized US policy. In 1952 he published an article in *Look* magazine entitled "We Have Become Victims of the Military Mind." In it he argued that the federal government had become overly militarized and was therefore less likely to use diplomacy to confront communism. The government's emphasis on the military, he warned, would lead to a diminishment of freedom in the United States and abroad. In other *Look* magazine articles published between 1952 and 1956, he criticized government policies in Korea, Malaya, and several former European colonies in Asia. Douglas's warnings were threefold. First, because presidents since Roosevelt had decided to defeat, if not contain, communism by military means, this resulted in alliances with dictators rather than with prodemocracy leaders, who merely allowed leftist politicians into their governments. In the long term, this policy would undermine the appearance of the United States as an advocate of worldwide democracy. Second, the overemphasis on military security led to intrusive federal policing in the name of national security, and this in turn led to a loss of individual freedom domestically. Finally, the specter of communism enabled reactionary political and economic leaders to defeat civil and individual rights movements in the United States. Douglas's fears proved prescient, but he did not always exercise sound judgment in his advocacy of foreign leaders, particularly in regard to Vietnam.[23]

In 1953 Douglas openly supported Ngo Dinh Diem, South Vietnam's leader, writing to him that "millions in the free world" had "great and abiding faith in him." Diem, of course, was an ally of the United States and an anticommunist; it would therefore have been difficult for Douglas's conservative detractors to find fault with his choice of ally. But Diem was a Catholic in a Buddhist country, and notwithstanding his family's dictatorial conduct, his faith undermined his credibility with South Vietnam's population. In 1955, when an Austrian émigré named Joseph Buttinger founded a lobby group to influence American support for Diem's government, Douglas enthusiastically joined this group, which was called American Friends of Vietnam. Buttinger convinced liberals such as Emanuel Celler, John F. Kennedy, Edmund Muskie, Arthur Schlessinger Jr., and Adam Clayton Powell to take part in its activities. Douglas later took credit for introducing Diem to the organization, and for a brief time its members were enamored with South Vietnam's leader.[24]

Diem was more than an acquaintance to Douglas. In 1952 Douglas sent him a copy of his book draft of *North from Malaya* to make sure that he did not misrepresent conditions in Vietnam. In an interview conducted at the John F. Kennedy Library in 1967, Douglas recalled that Diem was "the one man who had survived the French and preserved his integrity." In order to strengthen Diem's position against the French government before Vietnam's independence, Douglas introduced him to Kennedy and Senator Mike Mansfield in the hopes of presenting the French with congressional solidarity for Diem. In late 1953, while Diem was negotiating with the French government in Paris for Vietnam's independence, he apprised Douglas of his difficulties with the French. In response, Douglas advised him on how to proceed with a peaceful separation. These meetings occurred before the French military disaster at Dien Bien Phu in May 1954. In June of that year, Diem called Douglas "a great friend of Vietnam." With the independence of Vietnam and its division into the communist north and the noncommunist south, Douglas continued to advise Diem. "The position of the Mendes-France government which wishes to be done with this before July 2, does not leave us the time necessary to bring about a political and military realignment, when we can count on many chances, in particular the warm reception which the masses have kept for me, to triumph over communist Vietnam," Diem wrote to Douglas. In 1957 Douglas insisted to Tran Van Chuong, South Vietnam's ambassador to the United States, that he be permitted to entertain Diem in the United States. Although the Eisenhower administration did not disapprove of Douglas's actions toward Diem, Douglas should have understood that he had taken a role in shaping the government's Vietnam policies that went far beyond his judicial duties.[25]

Diem's assassination in 1963 altered Douglas's views on US policies on Vietnam, but he did not initially denounce increased American military involvement. Instead, he was silent on Vietnam until 1965, a year after Johnson secured the gulf of Tonkin resolution from Congress. That year Douglas asked for his name to be removed from the American Friends of Vietnam's letterhead because it "entered the broader political field." The organization had in fact called for an increased military response to combat communism, and Douglas made it clear that he opposed any military buildup in Vietnam. During a lecture at Hobart College in New York, Douglas openly doubted that a military victory in Vietnam was achievable.[26]

Well before the publication of the Pentagon Papers in 1971, Douglas suspected that Johnson had been less than transparent in explaining the purpose of the nation's military involvement in South Vietnam. He was not alone in his suspicions. By the end of 1964 there was a growing public demand for Johnson to explain why the government was in the process of committing more young men to the conflict. Douglas also believed that the war in Vietnam was distracting Johnson from fulfilling his Great Society pledges. In November 1965, 30,000 people demonstrated against the war in Washington, DC. That same year large-scale urban riots broke out in Los Angeles, and two years later Detroit experienced a similar upheaval. In both instances, governors used the state national guard to bring order to the cities, and in Detroit Johnson ordered the army to assist the national guard. While the riots did not begin as a protest against the Vietnam conflict, the inequities inherent in conscription mirrored those in society, and as a result the upheaval highlighted the war, police conduct, and the failures of Johnson's administration, which had campaigned on the Great Society but which was believed to have abandoned the president's promises of equality, urban renewal, and increased employment opportunities made during the campaign.[27]

One inequity that the social unrest highlighted was the means by which young men were brought into the military. Known as Selective Service, the national conscription program enabled deferments for college, graduate school, certain professions, religious beliefs, and religious ministers. Disproportionate numbers of African Americans were ordered into the military, and it was clear by 1967 that the exemptions favored wealthier young men. African Americans constituted almost 35 percent of South Carolina's population, but only one African American was appointed to the state's Selective Service boards. In Georgia less than one-fifth of 1 percent of 509 of the Selective Service board members were African American even though more than 25 percent of the state's population was African American. In 1967 the National Advisory Commission on the Selective Service Act found that twenty states' boards did not have a single African American serving in a capacity to vote on conscientious objector appeals. In 1968 the chairman of the Atlanta, Georgia, Selective Service board publicly called civil rights leader Julian Bond a "nigger."[28]

For Douglas, the racism in compelled military service was an appalling part of the war, though he professed that it had been predictable. In 1962 Secretary of Defense McNamara appointed Gerhard Gesell, a Douglas protégé, to chair a national investigation into the military's treatment of African American soldiers, and two aspects of it were appallingly apparent to Douglas. First, African American servicemen stationed in the Southern United

States remained subject to intense discrimination. Thus, the failure of Southern governors to appoint African American citizens to the state Selective Service boards was not surprising. Second, at the time of Gesell's report, African American men made up 6 percent of the military; by 1967 this figure was more than 12 percent. Although the Selective Service boards did not actually bring men into the military, they decided conscientious objection and family hardship appeals. Douglas justifiably believed that the boards were far more lenient on white men than African Americans, and this led to an increased number of African American men serving in Vietnam.[29]

In 1967, in nationwide campus protests known as the Vietnam Summer, speeches denouncing the war from Martin Luther King Jr. and other civil rights leaders, as well as an antidraft movement as powerful as the Civil War anticonscription movements, stymied the government's national defense and military policies. Even high schools experienced student walkouts to protest the war. The modes of conscription and a deferment scheme that favored wealthy white men became a powerful symbol for a growing antimilitary feeling. The Vietnam conflict brought the military's internal governance into a public forum unequaled in history, and fears of an erosion of the military's subservience to the elected civil government were also articulated in a manner not seen since the Civil War.[30]

The 1968 Tet offensive was an important demarcation point in both the conflict and the judiciary's reaction to hundreds of lawsuits from conscientious objectors, free speech and civil rights advocates, reservists, and draftees who argued that the war was illegal and therefore they could not be lawfully sent to Vietnam. On January 31, 1968, the Viet Cong launched a massive attack during Tet—one of the more important celebrations in Vietnam. The communist offensive was defeated, and the combined US and South Vietnamese forces secured a military victory, almost destroying the Viet Cong's ability to fight. However, because McNamara, General William Westmoreland, and others in the military establishment had previously claimed that the Viet Cong were close to defeat, the size of the attacks was seen as proof that the United States was engaged in an unwinnable war. After the Tet offensive, antiwar demonstrations and refusals to submit to induction increased, as did appeals to the courts.[31]

In 1968 Douglas made three decisions that would indirectly enable Ford's charges that he had undermined national security. He rescinded his membership in the American Friends of Vietnam organization after alleging that not only had the CIA infiltrated the group but also it had convinced Butt-inger to use the group to front CIA interests. While Buttinger denied that he was working with the CIA, he shared Douglas's letter with the organization's prominent members. Although Douglas had been critical of the CIA in the past, the tenor of his letter to Buttinger could be interpreted in such a way that Douglas viewed the CIA as a threat to democracy. This letter, conservatives argued, made Douglas's votes on the decisions regarding the United States' intelligence activities suspect.[32]

After leaving the American Friends of Vietnam, Douglas turned to the CSDI to convince Johnson that peace with North Vietnam was possible. In March 1966 Douglas secured Johnson's permission to discuss a settlement with Ho Chi Minh while the two men attended the Pacem in Terris II conference in Switzerland. Perhaps because Truman's earlier rebuke had resulted in criticism from both political parties, Douglas took an uncharacteristic step and independently obtained Attorney General Nicholas Katzenbach's support. Johnson placed limits on the CSDI's discussions with Ho, namely that no discussions regarding military operations would be undertaken. In the end Douglas did not personally meet with North Vietnam's leader. Instead, Hutchins and Ho met, and little was accomplished. Nonetheless, Ho might have believed that Douglas was the best person to secure a peace agreement. Through the end of Johnson's administration, Douglas received messages from North Vietnam favoring peace, which he provided to Johnson's administration.[33]

Douglas also tried to secure for Johnson an intermediary to negotiate with Ho by asking Pernendu Kumar Banerjee, India's ambassador to Costa Rica, to serve informally as a go-between for Johnson and Ho. Douglas and Banerjee had formed an intellectual friendship in the early 1950s, and in 1968 Banerjee lauded Douglas as "an unsurpassed man with intellectual tolerance, understanding, and perspective." However, Secretary of State Dean Rusk advised Johnson to avoid using Banerjee. Rusk's actions infuriated Douglas, who vented to Banerjee that Rusk had lied to Johnson. Failing to convince Johnson on Banerjee, Douglas returned to his speech making and the CSDI. By early 1968 Douglas's opposition to US involvement in Vietnam was so well known that a government official in Hanoi sent him a communiqué through a neutral country inquiring whether Clark Clifford, who had replaced McNamara as secretary of Defense, was sincere in his willingness to scale back the conflict. Douglas forwarded Clifford the communiqué without his personal analysis but noted, "It has not apparently been presented as yet to the Department of State."[34]

On May 30, 1967, Douglas was the keynote speaker at the Pacem in Terris II conference in Geneva. He stressed that he supported the International Criminal Court and explained his efforts to have the United States submit to its jurisdiction. "I have spoken in almost every one of our 50 states urging the revocation of our Connelly Amendment which so qualified our acceptance of the jurisdiction of the International Court as to make it virtually impossible for that Court to deal with a controversy involving the United States without the consent of the United States," he claimed. This was not all. Douglas also assured the audience that he believed "the west has no monopoly on concepts of justice," and that its jurists, including those in the United States, should be more open to incorporating foreign legal concepts. Undoubtedly the most disturbing part of Douglas's comments to conservatives was his laudatory observations of how Ho Chi Minh had instituted literacy and health programs in North Vietnam.[35]

Sitting alongside Douglas as he spoke were Muhammed Khan, the former foreign minister of Pakistan; Phillip Jessup, a US citizen serving as a judge on the International Court of Justice; and Louis Padilla Nervo, a Mexican jurist also serving on that court. Former justice Arthur Goldberg and Senator William Fulbright were also in attendance. While Douglas was no doubt sincere in his beliefs that international law and an end to the Cold War would benefit the cause of human rights and force the United States to leave Vietnam, the fact that he explained his political lobbying efforts and criticized the United States to a distinguished group of international leaders gave conservatives even more fodder for his removal.[36]

Douglas, the Legality of the War, and the Response of Conservatives

It was one matter for Douglas to lobby Johnson to extricate the US military from Vietnam or make public statements against the war, but it was quite another to insert his opposition to the war into the decisions of the Court. This, however, is precisely what Douglas did. To be sure, Douglas wanted the

Court to rule on the constitutionality of sending conscripted servicemen into a faraway conflict without a formal declaration of war or a United Nations Security Council resolution; the latter had occurred in the Korean War. There was nothing untoward in Douglas pushing the Court to at least determine an appeal on this subject, and on more than one occasion Justice Potter Stewart joined Douglas to do so. In 1967 the Court denied certiorari to Private Dennis Mora, a soldier who tried to prevent his shipment to Vietnam by having a court declare the war "illegal." On the one hand, when Douglas and Stewart dissented from the Court's refusal to consider the issue, they received dozens of commendatory letters from university professors and lawyers. On the other hand, Douglas's detractors noted that Mora was on a "watch list" of potential subversives. Having failed to convince the Court to make a ruling on the war, there were four areas in which Douglas made his opinions on the war a part of his jurisprudence: appeals arising from challenges to draft boards, reservists challenging their call-up to active duty, sundry free speech cases, and appeals arising from courts-martial prosecutions.[37]

On February 1, 1969, Paul V. Winters, a Marine Corps reservist, appealed to the District Court for the Southern District of New York to prevent his activation to active duty. Winters had enlisted in 1965, and although his enlistment contract stated that he could not be involuntarily called to active duty under normal circumstances, statutorily, in a national emergency, marine reservists could be involuntarily ordered to active duty for a twenty-four-month period. Additionally, reservists who failed to take part in at least 90 percent of their drill weekends could also be ordered onto active duty. One year after Winters enlisted, Congress legislated to the president the authority to call marine reservists to active duty who had not previously served on such duty. In 1967 the Department of the Navy increased marine reserve drill requirements to 100 percent attendance. Winters failed to make the 100 percent requirement, though he had fulfilled the terms of his original contract by making 90 percent of his reserve drills. Thus, while Winters's order to active duty was statutorily permissible, a question remained as to whether Congress had the authority to alter the enlistment contracts of reservists because that is what it essentially had done. Problematic to Winters's defense was that it appeared that he altered a hospital record to have his command characterize a missed drill as "excused." When Winters lost in the district court and court of appeals, Douglas saw an opportunity to make it clear that he believed that, absent a constitutionally declared war, the government could not send reservists into a foreign conflict without their consent. If Douglas prevailed, a significant military resource would be blocked from serving in Vietnam unless its members consented to going.[38]

At the same time Winters tried to prevent his call-up in New York, so too did a unit of 113 army reservists in a case entitled *Morse v. Boswell.* The army reservists were stationed in Virginia and appealed first to the district court, then the Court of the Appeals for the Fourth Circuit. Like Winters, the army reservists pointed out that when they enlisted, they had done so on a contractual basis, and that if Congress declared a national emergency, then the reservists could be called into active duty for the duration of the emergency, with an additional six months of service. Absent these conditions, only in instances of substandard performance could the reservists be ordered to active duty. Although not in the language of the enlistment contract, after the Korean War, Congress authorized the president to call up army reserve forces if the president declared a national emergency. After the 113 reservists had enlisted, Congress, in response to the Tet Offensive, enacted another law that enabled the president to order army reserve forces into active duty for a twenty-four-month period. This made the army reservists' challenge to their call-up to active duty more difficult to fight than Winters's case. Undermining the reservists' contention of an unlawful call-up to active duty was that the army had in place an application process for exemption from call-up, and only nineteen reservists had made use of this process. Yet because the reservists alleged an unconstitutional act by the executive branch, they urged the Court that the application procedure was not applicable to their appeal. They argued that most of the applications for exemption were rejected by the army. Ultimately, however, the appellate court denied the reservists relief after ruling that the courts did not possess jurisdiction to determine the appeal. In another case, entitled *McArthur v. Clifford,* the appellate court denied the reservists relief.[39]

The Court denied certiorari to McArthur, Morse, and Winters, and Douglas vehemently dissented from the denials. In regards to the reservists in *Morse,* Douglas issued a stay against the secretary of the army from shipping the 113 reservists to Vietnam. In response, the *Washington Post* accused him of conducting "a judicial shop-around." Even Judge Simon Sobeloff, who was normally Douglas's judicial ally, accused him of being "sui generis" (an independent legal classification, without precedent). Clement Haynsworth, who was soon to be nominated by Nixon to the Court, noted that Douglas had acted "extraordinarily because Warren who is also the circuit justice" had already denied the reservist's stay application. Haynsworth was charitable in this description of Douglas's conduct. After all, Douglas, without any other justice's support, had basically tried to trump the Chief Justice's decision.[40]

In his dissent from the denial of certiorari, in *Morse,* Douglas argued that the Court had to enforce the plain language of an enlistment contract. But he also believed he had to concede that Congress possessed the authority to change laws, regardless of the effect on the nation's citizenry. Douglas issued his *Morse* dissent on October 7, 1968. Two weeks later he issued his dissent in *Winters.* In it he accused the military of "secretly cloaking their decisions" and insisted that the Court had a duty to protect people from military discipline. "Civil Liberty and Military Control are irreconcilably antagonistic," he concluded. Finally, on December 16, 1968, Douglas dissented from the Court's denial of certiorari to McArthur, arguing that a unique question was raised regarding presidential power to use military forces without a declaration of war.[41]

Douglas's vehemence provided an outlet for aggrieved service members and their families. By 1968 he had received hundreds of letters from service members and reservists imploring him for help against their shipment to Vietnam. The *Morse* file alone contains more than a hundred such letters. Mr. A. R. Morse, the petitioner's father, thanked Douglas for his "courageous decision." He also expressed his worries over the army's treatment of his son and was convinced that his son's duty assignments were in retaliation for being the named petitioner on the decision, expressing, "Morse is a Lehigh Graduate with an M.E. Degree, and two MOS [military occupational specialties], one as a computer programmer and another as a radio mechanic, yet the War Machine has assigned him to wash uniforms in Vietnam for 2 years!" While a tour of duty in Vietnam was limited to a year and the younger Morse did not receive a two-year deployment order, the lack of trust antiwar citizens had toward the government was symbolized in this letter.[42]

Douglas realized he could not prevail, even among his liberal allies on the Court, in his quest to terminate the war through the reservists' appeals. On December 5, 1968, he angrily issued a denial of a stay against sending 368 Washington state national guardsmen to Vietnam. In it he lamented that the

Court had already made it impossible for reservists to seek a lawful means to challenge their orders in the courts. Failing to gain a majority of the justices to terminate the war through the reservists' cases, he turned to attacking the military justice system.[43]

In June 1967 the army court-martialed Captain Howard Levy, a dermatologist stationed in South Carolina. Levy's court-martial was not particularly unique for its time, except that by the time his appeals reached the Court in 1973 Douglas had thrice attempted to intervene in the trial and prevent Levy's imprisonment. Levy openly encouraged soldiers to refuse to go to Vietnam despite being given ample warning from his command against doing so. In 1969 Douglas issued a stay against Levy's imprisonment (meaning the army would be temporarily prevented from imprisoning Levy) until bail was considered. But neither the Uniform Code of Military Justice (the code governing the military) nor any other federal law permitted bail to convicted servicemen. Levy had previously applied for bail, been refused, and tried to appeal to the Court, which denied him certiorari. After the Court's denial Levy should have been sent to prison, but Douglas issued an order releasing Levy.[44]

In response to Douglas's order for Levy's release, Congressman Felix Edward Hebert, the chairman of the House of Representatives Armed Services Committee, tried to remove Douglas from deciding appeals against the military. First elected to Congress in 1940, Hebert was a conservative Southern Democrat who opposed integration, signed the Southern Manifesto, and served on the Armed Services Committee from 1958 until his retirement in 1977. In 1975 he tried to prevent a congresswoman as well as an African American congressman from serving on the committee after claiming that minorities and women were not qualified to legislate military affairs. On August 8, 1969, Hebert, along with South Carolina Democrat Mendel Rivers, complained to Chief Justice Burger that Douglas's act of ordering the secretary of the army to release Levy threatened the army's readiness and discipline.[45]

Hebert, apparently in ignorance of the principle of judicial independence, believed that Burger could order Douglas to be disqualified from "passing judgment on any cases involving Vietnam, the draft, or the military in general." This was not Hebert's first complaint against Douglas. In 1968 he penned two letters to Warren asking the Chief Justice to prohibit Douglas from deciding appeals arising from the Vietnam War. In all three letters Hebert claimed that Douglas's issuance of stays against the Department of Defense from sending called-up reservists to Vietnam empowered domestic antiwar movements as well as the communist forces in Vietnam. Not surprisingly, in April 1970 Hebert joined with Ford to impeach Douglas.[46]

By this time Hebert was not alone in claiming that Douglas had weakened national security. In 1967 Congressman Ben Blackburn, a Georgia Democrat, complained to the State Department that Douglas had evaded prosecution even though the justice had violated the Logan Act. In 1969 Blackburn allied with Hebert in seeking Douglas's removal from all national security decisions. And in June 1970 Senator Herman Talmadge, a Georgia Democrat who had supported Haynsworth and Carswell, informed his constituents that in several Selective Service exemption cases, Douglas endangered national security. Talmadge wanted Georgia's voters to demand that Douglas be removed from the Court, or at least censured in the Senate.[47]

The Levy case was hardly an aberration for Douglas, but for conservatives it did color Douglas as being hypocritical in his jurisprudence. In 1950 Congress enacted the Uniform Code of Military Justice to bring several important due process rights into military trials and to partially align the military justice system with federal criminal trials. In 1969 in *O'Callahan v. Parker*, Douglas led a majority of the Court to curtail the military's court-martial jurisdiction over its service members. Between 1950 and 1969 the military's jurisdiction expanded over almost all crimes. That is, a service member anywhere in the world accused of a crime could be court-martialed. This included off-base crimes in which a civilian was the victim. In several appeals in the 1950s Douglas tacitly approved of the expanded jurisdiction, but in *O'Callahan* he led a bare majority of the Court to determine that because military trials were historically suspect, the military's jurisdiction had to be significantly narrowed.[48]

Sergeant James O'Callahan was not a war protester. In 1956, while stationed in Hawaii, he broke into a hotel room and sexually assaulted a young woman. He confessed to committing rape to the Honolulu police, and a court-martial convicted him. O'Callahan spent the next decade trying to have his conviction and jail sentenced overturned, and there was no particular legal reason for the Court to take an interest in his appeal. Eight years after his conviction, and after he had exhausted the military's appellate processes, he unsuccessfully tried to appeal to federal courts. None of the five federal courts that O'Callahan appealed to found that his court-martial was unfair, or that he had been denied due process in any manner. But while serving his sentence in a federal prison, O'Callahan had the luck of being assigned as a cellmate to James Riddle Hoffa, the imprisoned former president of the International Brotherhood of Teamsters. This coincidental cellmate assignment led to Victor Rabinowitz's (Hoffa's attorney) representing O'Callahan. Rabinowitz, an admitted onetime communist, had not only defended citizens accused of communism such as Alger Hiss but had also defended Julian Bond and had taken part in several high-profile cases.[49]

Although O'Callahan argued that his trial was bereft of due process, the Court, in a decision Douglas authored, determined that because the nation had long had a "distrust of standing armies," this distrust equated to only permitting the most limited military jurisdiction. As a result of the decision, the military could court-martial its service members overseas for a variety of crimes but could court-martial its service members who were stationed in the United States only for purely military offenses, such as desertion and refusal to follow orders. This decision, which was overturned less than two decades after its issuance, was controversial for a number of reasons. At one time Douglas had lauded the military justice system, and now he turned on it. Moreover, the decision was devoid of historical analysis, and once more he was accused of trying to weaken the military. And, of course, the fact that Rabinowitz prevailed added to the conservatives' claims that Douglas sought to undermine national security.[50]

Less than two weeks after O'Callahan, the Court issued, Noyd v. Bond, a decision that further defined the ability of service members to appeal court-martial convictions to the federal courts. Air Force captain Dale E. Noyd refused to train junior officers; he was court-martialed and sentenced to a year in prison and dismissal from the military for his refusal to obey lawful orders. Noyd wanted to create a defense of his actions by arguing that the United States was involved in an "illegal war" in Vietnam, and therefore his actions were lawful. With three days remaining on his sentence, he petitioned Justice Byron White to order the military to release him from his imprisonment. White refused, but one day after his refusal, Douglas issued an order freeing Noyd from prison. The *New York Times* and several radio and television stations covered Noyd's trial and appeals, and it became well known that Douglas had infuriated White.[51]

Conservatives did not know the extent to which Douglas wanted to protect *O'Callahan*. In February 1970 a convicted service member appealed his court-martial conviction for rape and kidnapping to the Court on the basis that the military did not have jurisdiction over him in the first place. Although the appeal was a means to clarify, if not strengthen, *O'Callahan*, Douglas convinced Black to vote against certiorari out of a fear that if the Senate confirmed Carswell, there would be enough votes to overturn *O'Callahan*. Ultimately neither Marshall not Brennan joined with Douglas and Black, and the Court took up the appeal. In the appeal, entitled *Relford v. Commandant*, the Court simply clarified when the military could exercise court-martial jurisdiction over its personnel. Nonetheless, Douglas's actions evidenced a fear that conservatives would undo his efforts to limit the government's authority over its drafted citizens.[52]

To war hawks and conservatives Douglas's jurisprudence was bad enough. But in February 1970 Douglas published his most controversial argument regarding the federal government, the Vietnam conflict, and the "intrusion" of the military into the daily lives of Americans. In a small book entitled *Points of Rebellion*, he appeared to argue that because the government had utilized the military and CIA to surveil US citizens and undermine academic freedom on college campuses, citizens could assume a right to overthrow the government, just as the colonists had removed George III's authority over them. *Points of Rebellion* contained passages that were sure to offend not only hawkish officials but also moderate Americans who still possessed faith in governmental institutions.[53]

Douglas used the campus terminology of the day, such as "big brother" and "the establishment," in describing the federal government. He wrote that the Pentagon had "a fantastic budget that enables the dream of putting down much-needed revolutions which will arise in Peru and in the Philippine Islands, and with other be-knighted countries," then asked, "Where is the force that will restrain the Pentagon?" Douglas also observed, consistent with the views of many liberals, that military spending had grossly overtaken the government's ability to aid the nation's poor or support public education. Unlike federal funding for social programs, Douglas considered military spending to be a means to suppress democracy; he thought that the nation was on a precipice as to whether it would fall into a dictatorship or its citizens would regain the essential freedoms guaranteed by the Bill of Rights and the prior three decades of the Court's jurisprudence.

To conservative congressmen and former New Deal centrists alike, one of Douglas's sins was in his historical interpretation of why universities had become co-opted by the Pentagon and intelligence agencies, why the government compiled "growing dossiers on people," and how intelligent and creative citizens were kept from government service. Conservatives, he argued, had used the threat of communism to undermine basic liberties. Douglas, true to his allegiance to Roosevelt, did not criticize any of Roosevelt's actions in World War II; instead he began his criticism with Truman, characterizing him as a weak president who had failed to confront McCarthyism. But he directed his sharpest criticism against Johnson and accused him of circumventing the Constitution with "lies, half-truths, and phony excuses" in order to wage war in Vietnam. He also accused Johnson of using conscription to penalize antiwar dissenters.[54]

More than a thousand ordinary citizens wrote to Douglas praising *Points of Rebellion.* Some of the writers urged Douglas to remain on the Court, and others assured him that they would lobby their representatives and Nixon against using the book as a basis for impeachment. These citizens ranged from lawyers and professors to blue-collar workers and parents who had children serving in Vietnam. Douglas's fans included Republican senator Robert Packwood of Oregon, who asked Douglas for an autographed copy. Senator Philip Hart, a Michigan Democrat, lauded Douglas's attempt to bring to the public's attention "the need to solve those problems in our society which have caused so much alienation and frustration among many groups." However, the book was not without its literary detractors. Congresswoman Florence Dwyer, a New Jersey Republican, informed her constituents, "Undoubtedly Justice Douglas will make a great deal of money out of the sale of his book because of the fact that it is so controversial and that perhaps is the real reason for writing the book."[55]

Dozens of readers, including Douglas's supporters, pointed out that in *Points of Rebellion* he wrongly attributed a quote to Adolf Hitler. Initially there was no public criticism of Douglas's use of the quote, but when in early March 1970 Senator Edmund Muskie of Maine also used the quote, several researchers discovered that there was no record of Hitler's making the statement that Muskie and Douglas attributed to him. Hitler's alleged quote, if he said it, could have served as a focal point for comparison to the law and order arguments of conservatives. On page 58, the quote read: "The streets of country are in turmoil. The universities are filled with students rebelling and rioting. Communists are seeking to destroy our country. Russia is threatening her with her might and the republic is in danger from within and without. We need law and order." When confronted with this error, Douglas's secretary, Fay Aull, merely responded that the Library of Congress was unable to authenticate the quote, and it would be redacted from future editions of the book. To Douglas's critics the misquote was proof that he would fictionalize history in his "anti-American" efforts to paint the Nixon administration of taking Gestapo-like measures against his dissenting allies who undermined the war.[56]

After publication of *Points of Rebellion,* several critics called for Douglas's removal from the Court. On March 17, 1970, Congressman William Scott insisted that the book was "grounds for Douglas's impeachment." A month later Scott spoke to a mostly empty Congress, claiming that Douglas "encourages violence and resentment against the activities of numerous branches of our government." He earlier responded to a constituent that Douglas was a "drooling and doddering old nursing home case whose presence on the Court represents a clear and present danger to our social order." Senator Robert C. Byrd accused Douglas of "declaring his support of efforts to radically alter the social, economic, and political structure of this nation while turning a blind eye to communist aggression." Byrd echoed the opinions of several legislators by claiming that Douglas had led the Court to permit communists to freely work in defense industries and children to be exposed to pornography, and had overburdened the nation's budget by siding with "freeloaders" over hardworking Americans. To Byrd, *Points of Rebellion* was part of a deliberate effort to topple the government and turn the United States into a socialist domain.[57]

Even conservative legislators who did not favor impeachment expressed their anger at Douglas over *Points of Rebellion.* Congresswoman Catherine Dean May of Washington shared her disgust with Douglas to Scott. Although ultimately May would not side with Ford, she forwarded to Scott a disparaging book review from Albert Yencopal, a Washington state municipal judge. Yencopal accused Douglas of acting as a modern-day George III rather than the government. "Among the first judges [Roosevelt appointed] who would judiciously develop a strong central government was Douglas," Yencopal asserted. "Because of this, the citizen's voice has grown weaker and weaker until now it is barely a whisper." May likewise found Douglas's criticism of the federal government hypocritical because he had taken a prominent role in the growth of it.[58]

Once more, conservative organizations took on Douglas. The United States Anti-Communist Congress published an open letter asking Douglas to resign. Unlike the John Birch Society, the Anti-Communist Society had "excused" Earl Warren's actions on the Court because Warren had claimed that he merely interpreted the Constitution in arriving at his decisions. However, the organization distinguished Douglas from Warren with the claim that because Douglas had encouraged the government's overthrow, he had disregarded the Constitution rather than interpreted it. Failing Douglas's retirement from the Court, the organization lobbied Burger to force Douglas's removal from all appeals in which the government was a litigant. Newspapers joined in the criticism of Douglas. The *Chicago Tribune* accused him of "disgracing the Court." So too did the *New York Times* and *Los Angeles Times.* The *Orlando Sentinel's* editorial staff headlined its opinion page "Douglas Has Forfeited His Right to Sit on the Court" and insisted that Douglas encouraged revolution before claiming "he has little respect for the average American's ability to decide things for himself." The editors of the *Daily News* of Greensboro, North Carolina, observed "the spectacle of a judge endorsing resistance to arrest—as if this were a legal or reputable way to assert a constitutional right—is an astonishing commentary on the erosion of political rationality that has reached such proportions in American life today."[59]

Douglas had some defenders in Congress, who tried to explain that the conservatives' interpretation of *Points of Rebellion* was flawed. Senator Frank Church, an Idaho Democrat, urged one constituent that Douglas had merely warned of the possibility of rebellion if the government continued to spy on dissenters and force young men into unpopular conflicts. Former senator Wayne Morse, an Oregon Republican turned Democrat, defended Douglas and insisted that the conservatives had long been trying to find reasons to have Douglas removed from the Court. Ironically, *Points of Rebellion* was hardly a noteworthy read. Had it been written by an ordinary citizen, it likely would have been ignored. But because it was written by a Supreme Court justice, the reaction was far different than had it been written by a professor or student. *Points of Rebellion* was evidence of Douglas's frustrations with a government that had taken the nation into an unnecessary war and ignored basic democratic principles. Yet Douglas had not consorted with campus radicals. He never appeared in demonstrations or associated with people who sought to overthrow the government. However, he did have a questionable relationship with Albert Parvin.[60]

Douglas, Parvin, and the Internal Revenue Service

In spite of Douglas's extrajudicial activities at the government's behest, early in his judicial tenure he was cautious about his associations. For instance, in 1947 the United States chapter of the World Federal Movement asked him to serve on their board. The World Federalists espoused the same type of global political beliefs as Douglas. That is, they advocated for international law and diplomacy, as well as for a recognition that global poverty would lead to fascism or communism. The organization's membership included Albert Einstein, Mahatma Mohandas Gandhi, and later Martin Luther King Jr. Although Douglas was delighted to have been asked to serve as a presiding officer, he responded that it would be incompatible with his judicial position to do so.[61]

From the time that Ford alleged Parvin was connected to organized crime, several authors have used Ford's language in making the same suggestion. For instance, James F. Simon, in *The Center Holds: The Power Struggle Inside the Rehnquist Court*, wrote: "Parvin reputedly had ties to organized crime." In a study on the influence of Italian Americans on the development of Las Vegas, Professor Albert Balboni linked "men with backgrounds in organized crime" to Parvin's corporation. Although Parvin hired men like Edward Levinson and Edward Torres, who were suspected of ties to organized crime, to manage his corporation's casinos, it was the Nevada Gaming Commission that approved their employment. It is true that Parvin retained Sidney Korshak, an attorney noted for representing Chicago's Mafia leaders, but Korshak was also retained by other casino owners such as Kirk Kerkorian, Hollywood moguls, movie stars, and the Los Angeles Dodgers. Finally, in 1961 and again in 1966 the FBI received information from anonymous sources that Parvin, and by implication the foundation, had ties to organized crime. Thus, while

Parvin associated with reputed organized crime figures, there is innuendo but no firm evidence that he committed any crimes with them.[62]

Despite Ford's characterization of Parvin as "a mysterious person" with connections to organized crime, he was not a semimythical Mafia criminal. Parvin was born to middle-class parents in Chicago in 1900 and died in 1992 in Beverly Hills, California. After World War II he donated several million dollars to UCLA's medical school and established the foundation that later became the focus of the House's inquiry. Parvin started an interior design company in Los Angeles in the early 1930s after leaving Chicago. In 1944 noted real estate developer Del Webb introduced Parvin to Benjamin "Bugsy" Siegel, and Siegel contracted with Parvin to furnish the Flamingo Hotel and Casino. If to Ford this relationship constituted evidence of a Mafia tie, then Del Webb would also have to become suspect. Yet Webb played golf and associated with Barry Goldwater and Bing Crosby, and in 1945 became part owner of the New York Yankees. In 1947 Siegel was murdered in Los Angeles, in all likelihood because he failed to make his Flamingo Casino venture profitable, and he had become irrational in the opinion of his Mafia benefactors, Meyer Lansky, Charles Luciano, and Frank Costello. By 1955 Parvin's corporation secured a major interest in the Flamingo.[63]

In 1960 Parvin read *America Challenged*. The book was a compilation of lectures that Douglas had given at Princeton University as part of the school's Walter Edge lecture series. In it Douglas attacked loyalty oaths as well as the government's propensity to seek military solutions for solving ideological differences across the world. He reminded his readers that Benjamin Franklin had once labeled loyalty oaths as "the last resort of liars," and that Abraham Lincoln believed such oaths were antithetical to democracy as well as "unchristian." Douglas also turned to the theme he developed in "We Have Become Victims of the Military Mind," arguing that the decline of dissent in the nation's political life was a result of "the mighty military cabal whose reach into our affairs becomes greater with each national budget." On July 25, 1960, Parvin wrote to Douglas that *America Challenged* had "moved and impressed" him and that he was determined to try to promote understanding between peoples in both the developed and developing world: "It is regrettable that with the billions spent for ways to destroy civilization, so little is available to promote better understanding." After meeting Parvin in Santa Barbara, California, in late July, Douglas responded that he "would be happy to serve as a trustee and officer." The contents of this letter hardly seem like the words of a Mafia figure.[64]

Until 1960 Parvin had been a reclusive businessman. When during that year Albert entered Douglas's life, Douglas was in need of money; his judicial salary did not cover his personal debts. His divorce to his first wife had proved costly, and he was soon to have a second divorce that resulted in a further loss of income. For a time Douglas took to sleeping in his office. Before 1960 it is doubtful that Douglas knew Parvin's name. Like several wealthy Americans, Parvin wanted to create a foundation that would provide scholarships to students and would be aligned with a political or social cause. Because *America Challenged* partly focused on Central and South America, Parvin believed that a foundation affiliated with Princeton University could be created with Douglas's help, as well as that of Robert Maynard Hutchins and Robert Goheen, Princeton University's former president. As one of the world's leading universities, Princeton would add gravitas to Parvin's foundation.[65]

From the beginning of their relationship, Parvin idolized Douglas, and Douglas thought highly of Parvin, to the point of inviting the businessman to attend President Kennedy's inauguration. When in January 1961 Douglas sent Parvin a rough draft of a press release explaining why he joined the foundation and asked Parvin to contribute to the final copy, the businessman responded, "That's like asking Mickey Spillane to read and correct Shakespeare." Douglas did not overtly seek a compensation scheme from Parvin. Parvin's attorney, Victor Mindlin, advanced the idea of a specific $12,000 annual payment in a January 1961 meeting that Douglas did not attend. There is nothing in either the House's investigation records or Douglas's voluminous correspondence to indicate that he was initially aware of a discussion about his annual payment. Nonetheless, when he was offered this money, he willingly accepted it.[66]

Douglas planned to focus the foundation's efforts on South and Central America, but he made it clear to Parvin that it was critical the foundation do nothing to upset Kennedy's foreign policy. Douglas recruited John Cooper Wiley, a retired foreign service officer who had served in Austria as the United States chargé d'affaires when that country's voters decided to welcome a Nazi takeover in 1938, to develop a "school of democracy" for Cuban refugees arriving in the United States and other countries. Wiley was also Truman's ambassador to Iran. He recruited Cuban professors to operate a college focusing on training a future free Cuban government. Douglas also recruited Don K. Price, the dean of Harvard University's graduate school of public administration, to advise the foundation on its expenditures, though Price cautioned that the expenses would be high. Finally, Douglas urged Parvin to meet with Judge William Campbell in Chicago, and on October 17, 1960, Campbell assured Mindlin that he had reviewed the foundation's articles of incorporation and would enthusiastically serve on its board. Campbell also declared to Douglas, "It is always a pleasure to be engaged in worthwhile work but when this can be done and at the same time have the pleasure of association with such dear friends as yourself, it becomes a joy indeed."[67]

When in January 1961 Douglas explained his enthusiasm for serving on the Parvin Foundation as its chairman, he did so in a press release with Parvin's input. Douglas noted that the foundation was the first organization "dedicated solely and exclusively to the promotion of improved relations between nations and to the dissemination among the peoples of underdeveloped nations of democratic ideas of freedom and justice." Douglas moreover proffered that he embraced the foundation's goal of educating future "prime ministers, political leaders, judges, and legislators imbued with democratic ideals and trained in the democratic tradition." He echoed his argument from "We Have Become Victims of the Military Mind," maintaining that "military solutions against communism could not end poverty misery, hunger, or illiteracy which were the very ills that communism grew from." He was particularly proud that Princeton had become the foundation's sponsoring university. At the end of the press release he engaged in some hyperbole by predicting that because Parvin was a believer in expanding freedom "in the traditions of Jefferson, Madison, and Lincoln, the name Parvin, like those three names, will become a symbol of justice and equality for all men."[68]

The worst that could be said about Parvin is that he was involved a single act of youthful indiscretion. In 1928 he pled no contest in a Chicago court to receiving stolen property and was sentenced to probation. The 1928 crime appears to have occurred as a result of his business accepting stolen property for resale when he should have known that the goods, in this case, furniture, had been stolen. The sealed court record was still contained in the state courthouse in downtown Chicago, and it would have remained there, unknown to the public, had not Bryce Harlow, a former aide to Eisenhower and Nixon speechwriter, obtained it through a third party. Harlow conveyed Parvin's minor criminal record to Mollenhoff, who shared it with Senator John J. Williams on November 27, 1968, more than a month before Nixon's inauguration. The importance of this date cannot be overstated. Two years earlier the *Los Angeles Times* had favorably reported on Douglas and Parvin. In late 1968 the *Times* reversed course and challenged Douglas's fitness. Williams does not appear to have been aware of Parvin's background until Harlow and Mollenhoff shared it with him and the *Times*. This is the first evidence that the Nixon administration had planned to force Douglas from the Court, even before Nixon had been sworn in as president.[69]

Parvin remains a difficult study. By the 1940s he had moved to Los Angeles, and his business of furnishing hotels and restaurants had made him a wealthy man. He was more of a large-scale interior decorator than an ally to the Mafia, but because his business had expanded into Las Vegas and furnished several casinos, he became connected to some of the nation's leading underworld figures, including Meyer Lansky. In 1958 he purchased the Dohrmann Company, which led to his company's becoming the largest hotel supplier in the Western United States. (The Dohrmann Company was the oldest hotel supply business in the United States.) That year, the Parvin-Dohrmann Corporation acquired the controlling interest in the Flamingo Hotel and Casino, and by 1960 the company held substantial shares in the Stardust, Aladdin, and Fremont casinos. Parvin sold the Flamingo in 1960, and part of the sale's proceeds enabled his foundation to begin. Additionally, Parvin donated 1,000 of the Flamingo's shares to the foundation so that it would be able to begin its operations with a positive cash flow. Yet there was a dark side to Parvin's casinos. Bobby Baker had visited them and discussed opening the Dominican Republic to the casino industry with Edward Levinson. Douglas and Parvin did not take part in these plans, and Parvin was retiring from his business. However, given Parvin's interest in supporting democratic movements in Latin America, Baker's presence in his casino appeared suspicious.[70]

In the end all that can be determined about Parvin was that he tried to avoid publicity and was a successful businessman. The fact that he owned a casino and even paid half a million dollars to Lansky as a "finder's fee" might appear suspicious, but the reclusive Howard Hughes had similarly paid for his casino. In late 1968 Parvin announced his intention to retire from the corporation, and several of the investors purchased more than 300,000 shares of Parvin-Dohrmann stock, putting the investors in charge of the company. Delbert Coleman, another casino owner, became the corporation's new president. In March 1969 Parvin-Dohrmann shares sold at an inflated rate, resulting in the American Stock Exchange suspending all sales. One month later the Denny's Restaurant Holding Group publicly offered to buy Parvin-Dohrmann for $200 million, but within thirty days Denny's had reduced its offer by $69 million. In late 1969 Parvin sold most of his shares in the Parvin-Dohrmann Company. Shortly after the sale the SEC opened an investigation against the company for stock manipulation. SEC investigators discovered that one of Parvin's former managers had schemed with the Speaker of the House of Representatives's chief of staff in an attempt to stymie their investigation. The IRS also investigated Parvin for tax underpayments, but this was not unusual because casinos were a likely place where underpayments of taxes occurred.[71]

On May 27, 1969, the *Los Angeles Times*, the *New York Times*, and several other newspapers published articles detailing a letter that Douglas had written to Parvin in which he called the IRS's investigation into the Parvin Foundation a "witch hunt." The letter was impolitic, and it earned Douglas a public rebuke from Congressman Emanuel Celler, the chairman of the House Judiciary Committee, who later led the investigation into Douglas. After all, the IRS determination was a legal matter that could reach the Court on appeal. For a justice to have declared a governmental operation to be a witch hunt when a district court judge would likely be called on to make a ruling put the district court judge in an unpleasant position of not only having to ignore Douglas's comments but also assuring the public that the decision was independent from external influences. While Douglas had never intended for the letter to become public, and neither the public nor Celler learned of the source of Douglas's anger underlying the letter, it put Douglas in a poor light.[72]

Nixon understood that an IRS audit was a powerful weapon against political opponents, and even when the opponent's actions were legally defensible, a public relations nightmare remained possible. Nixon aide Patrick Buchanan tried to convince IRS commissioner Randolph Thrower to remove tax-exempt status from the Southern Christian Leadership Conference after its newsletter criticized Nixon. Thrower resisted Buchanan's lobbying, but in another matter he met with the secretary of the Treasury, David Kennedy, and assured him that the IRS would take steps to ensure that publicity surrounding an audit of Republican governor James Rhodes of Ohio would remain out of the public's attention. The IRS had previously concluded that Rhodes had converted his campaign funds for personal use and then failed to pay federal income taxes on these funds. At the time of the audit, Rhodes, who had served four nonconsecutive terms as governor, was planning to run for the Senate in 1970, and Nixon nominally favored him over Republican congressman Robert Taft III as the party's candidate. Additionally, at the same time as the IRS audit, there was speculation that Rhodes owed a favor to organized crime after he commuted the prison sentence of Thomas Licavoli, an elderly bootlegger who had been sentenced to life in prison in 1933. By the time Rhodes granted parole in 1969 Licavoli was in ill health, and there were sound reasons for granting parole; Licavoli was sixty-five years old and had served more than thirty years in jail. However, the parole enabled Rhodes's opponents to accuse him of accepting Mafia bribes. Although Rhodes was spared from public opprobrium over the tax audit, under pressure from Nixon, he ultimately did not run for the Senate and remained governor.[73]

Given Nixon's plans to weaken nonprofit organizations that opposed his policies, Douglas's witch-hunt claims would have been given credence had the public known of Nixon's intentions. Although it was true that the IRS had the previous year investigated the foundation's investments, on the basis of Carol Agger's advice Parvin assigned an outside investment company to manage future purchases and sales of stocks. Douglas held Agger in high esteem, but she was married to Abe Fortas, which could give an appearance of linking Douglas to Fortas in a manner unhelpful to Douglas. "The best chances for administrative resolution of the matter will lie not only in showing that the charges are spurious, but also in showing that Mr. Parvin has no Mephistophelean designs on the Foundation's property," Agger informed Douglas. "This can be accomplished by showing that the Foundation has taken steps to totally divorce Mr. Parvin from any control over the financial activities of the Foundation." Moreover, several of the IRS's reasons for revocation were based on untrue assertions made by Douglas's opponents. IRS auditors claimed that Parvin had financed the publication of *America Challenged,* that Parvin paid a $24,000 premium on a retirement annuity for Douglas, and that Douglas had been given stock in the Parvin-Dohrmann Corporation. One day after the IRS's issuance of its revocation notice to

Parvin, Douglas fired off an angry letter to Parvin via Agger, denouncing the investigation. This was the letter shown to the public.[74]

Douglas and the Dominican Republic

In 1970 Ford alleged that Douglas had promoted organized crime and communism in the Dominican Republic. Douglas had a decade-long goal of bringing democracy to the Dominican Republic, but prominent foreign policy experts in the United States viewed his ally in that country, Juan Bosch, as an anti-American leftist. The reason Douglas believed that Bosch was the leader most likely to succeed in navigating the Dominican Republic between communism and totalitarianism had to do with US policy in the Caribbean. After Fidel Castro's takeover in Cuba in 1959, the US government aggressively tried to stem the further spread of communism throughout Latin America, and in particular the Caribbean. Rafael Trujillo's dictatorial rule over the Dominican Republican led to a heightened danger of communism taking root in that country. Although Trujillo was anticommunist, during his presidency he oversaw the massacre of well over 10,000 of the Dominican Republic's Haitian minority and the murder of nuns; he supported an attempted overthrow of the Venezuelan government with arms and finance; and he was also brutal in suppressing socialists and communists, and wanted to assist in the removal of Fidel Castro from Cuba. In 1959 Dominican forces loyal to Trujillo were able to defeat insurgents who had trained in Cuba alongside Castro's forces. Although Trujillo was anathema to both Eisenhower and Kennedy, he was also a potential ally in the containment of communism, and as one scholar has pointed out, Nixon, while serving as vice president, praised Trujillo's quest to defeat communism in Latin America.[75]

On May 31, 1961, Trujillo was assassinated, and the Dominican Republic's military took over the government. An election in December 1962 resulted in Bosch's becoming the Dominican Republic's president. After Bosch assumed the presidency, Kennedy sent Johnson to the Dominican Republic to represent the US government at Bosch's inauguration. The Kennedy administration quickly suspected Bosch of being procommunist, particularly after Bosch complimented Castro. Moreover, the US ambassador to the Dominican Republic informed Kennedy that Bosch was "a deep cover communist." In September 1963 the Dominican Republic's military leaders deposed him, and he fled to Puerto Rico. Bosch, however, never intended his country to become communist. He believed that if more Dominican Republicans were landowners, there would be a commensurate growth of a middle class, and in turn the emergence of a liberal democracy.[76]

One of Ford's allegations against Douglas was that he had attended Bosch's inauguration without Kennedy's approval and therefore violated the Logan Act. However, not only did Douglas not travel to the inauguration for independent political reasons, but the State Department also approved his travel. On January 23, 1963, Bosch personally contacted Douglas through the Dominican Republic's embassy in Washington, DC, and the invitation was forwarded from the embassy through the State Department to Douglas. "The installation of the of the first freely elected government, which will rule our country after thirty-two years of ruthless dictatorship, will provide an occasion of profound rejoicing for the Dominican people," Bosch noted in his invitation to Douglas. "Knowing your keen interest in the furtherance of democratic freedom and social progress within our continent, the Dominican Government and the Dominican people fervently hope that you and Mrs. Douglas will honor this event with your presence." Douglas attended the inauguration with Parvin, who in turn invited his lawyer, corporate executive Harvey Silbert. One month after Bosch was removed from the presidency, Douglas informed the CSDI that they would be unable to host him at a seminar because it would appear to sanction Bosch's government over that of his successor.[77]

After Bosch's ouster, Kennedy supported Donald Reid Cabral, a pro-Western dictator. Two years later the Dominican military deposed Cabral, leading to a civil war in which Bosch attempted to return to power. In response Johnson ordered US military forces into the Dominican Republic. Johnson wanted to thwart Bosch's return to power and at the same time prevent a Trujillo-like dictatorship. In sending military forces to the Dominican Republic, Johnson did not have the express approval of either Congress or the Organization of American States, and there was public outcry against his actions. Johnson had bipartisan backing from senior congressional leaders, including Senate Minority Leader Dirksen and Speaker of the House John McCormack.[78]

Douglas's activities in the Dominican Republic later became central to Ford's attacks on him. When Parvin, Douglas, and Silbert went to the Dominican Republic in 1963, at the invitation of Bosch, they intended to utilize the foundation's resources to help the Dominican Republic build its democratic institutions by creating new educational centers. But there were problems with their choice of employees. In the early stages of the Parvin Foundation's foray into the Dominican Republic, the foundation utilized Sacha Volman, a European émigré. Volman was born in Romania, fought against the Nazis in World War II, and later fought against the Romanian communist regime before fleeing to South America in the late 1940s. In 1959 he set up an educational initiative called the Institute of Political Education in Costa Rica to train anticommunist, prodemocracy forces. This institute trained several Dominican Republic students.[79]

Volman communicated with Douglas on obtaining World Bank support for the Dominican Republic while Bosch was president, but nowhere in their correspondence is there evidence that Douglas actually assisted in this effort. What may not have been known to Douglas, Parvin, or for that matter their accusers, was that although Volman appeared to be a "shadowy figure" who conversed with anti-American elements throughout Latin America, he was in reality a CIA operative. For other reasons, Douglas had significant doubts about Volman and went so far as to write the US ambassador a confidential letter seeking his opinion on whether Volman was trustworthy.[80]

Douglas not only advised Bosch on strengthening his government but also offered the assistance of others to help build educational institutions and improve the Dominican Republic's infrastructure. One of Douglas's recommendations would have enabled Ford to further his allegations that Douglas sought to undermine national security and promote socialism. On February 1, 1963, Douglas introduced Edward Lamb to Bosch. Douglas characterized Lamb as "a friend, an agricultural expert and owner of Lamb Industries," and "a liberal forward thinking progressive man." There was more to Lamb than Douglas described. In the late 1920s Lamb served as the city attorney of Toledo, Ohio, before becoming a member of National Lawyer's Guild and the Congress of International Organizations. He later became a millionaire who purchased industries and television stations, and he was a contributor to the Democratic Party as well as the CSDI. In the 1940s and 1950s conservatives insisted Lamb was a communist.[81]

Allegations of Lamb's supposed communism originated in the Depression. After representing an Ohio auto workers' union during a strike in 1938,

an Ohio judge attempted to disbar him. The judge accused Lamb of disrespect to the court and then appointed a committee to investigate him. The
committee concluded that Lamb supported communism and sought to disrupt Ohio's legal system. Unsurprisingly, the judge adopted the committee's
recommendation to disbar Lamb. Robert Jackson, while serving as solicitor
general, undertook a highly unusual act, albeit with Roosevelt's approval: he
filed an amicus brief with the Ohio supreme court in support of Lamb. The
Chicago Tribune reported on public criticism against Jackson for filing an
amicus brief as a solicitor general, as this had never before occurred in a state
court, and it represented a federal intrusion into the state's legal system. The
Tribune also published Jackson's response that he had an obligation to ensure
the judiciary's fairness to all litigants and attorneys. In answering a critic,
Jackson responded, "We can have no worthy judicial system unless we protect
the right of advocates to champion the cause of any person who becomes
involved in the machinery of the law." In reality Lamb was not a communist. Like Parvin, he believed that liberal and socialist-leaning governments
in Latin America were more likely to enable democracy's long-term growth
than were dictatorships. Nonetheless, had Ford discovered Lamb's involvement in the CSDI as well as Douglas's advocacy for his role in the Dominican
Republic, it could have resulted in another matter for the latter to defend
himself against.[82]

Renewed Conservative Interest in Douglas

Nixon articulated his disgust with Douglas as early as 1956. In a speech to
the American Legion the vice president decried "well-intentioned but misguided people" who believed the government had taken too hard a stance
against communism. "There are some who tell us from a practical business
standpoint we are foolish in our refusal to recognize Red China and admit
its representatives into the United Nations," Nixon claimed, before reminding his audience that "the executive and legislative branches of government
have flatly rejected cowardly expediency in this matter." In this part of his
speech it would be difficult not to conclude that Nixon had rebuked the very
foreign policy position Douglas had subscribed to, if not Douglas himself.
But Nixon did not end with this comment. He called "those who parrot the
cliché that if we could give every Asian another bowl of rice there would be

no communism in that part of the world" superficial and a danger to national security. This was a direct criticism of the very arguments that Douglas had made earlier in the decade.[83]

Shortly after the *Los Angeles Times* reported on Douglas's accusation that the IRS had harassed Parvin as part of a Nixon administration vendetta, Senator Strom Thurmond accused Douglas of weakening national security by issuing stays against the call-up of reservists for shipment to Vietnam. "Twice within the past few weeks a Supreme Court Justice has arrogated to himself the privilege of countermanding military orders," Thurmond argued to the Senate, before erroneously adding that the reservists did not yet "have a case pending before the Supreme Court." Thurmond did not stop with pointing out Douglas's activism, and indeed insisted that the justice had "lessen[ed] respect for authority" and increased "contempt for lawful commands." In addition to weakening military discipline, Thurmond claimed that Douglas had engaged in an "outrageous attack on law and order . . . [that] will have far-reaching effects both on the structure of our military and the whole framework of constitutional government."[84]

On June 12, 1969, Thurmond gleefully proclaimed to a New Jersey audience that Fortas's resignation was "an important advance in the reform of the Court," then turned to Douglas and the Parvin Foundation. He accused Douglas of helping the foundation "falsify its tax returns" and of supporting procommunists like J. Robert Oppenheimer. In addition to these accusations, Thurmond insisted that because the CSDI had "propagandized" its studies, Douglas's service on its board was incompatible with the judicial duty of impartiality. But Thurmond also hurt his own cause by centering on "the specter of black rebellions" and how Douglas had enabled these to occur. If African Americans demonstrated against the government, Thurmond alleged, white Americans should place the blame on Douglas. Three days earlier Thurmond had given a truncated version of this speech on the Senate floor, adding that Douglas had not only espoused a theory of fighting communism by aligning with "leftwing governments" but had also, by working in the CSDI as well as allying the Parvin Foundation with the Inter-American Center for Economic and Social Studies, co-opted the CIA. At the end of June, Thurmond traveled to Arizona and championed Barry Goldwater while once more accusing Douglas of unethical conduct by writing for *Avant Garde,* then not recusing himself from appeals involving the magazine's owner.[85]

On March 2, 1970, Clark Mollenhoff spoke with Benton Becker about the revocation of the Parvin Foundation's tax-exempt status. "This sets the stage for unwinding the tangled tale involving Bobby Baker and William O. Douglas," Becker concluded to Mollenhoff before characterizing Douglas's as "shadowy." Becker also claimed to Mollenhoff that Douglas had tried to gain a visa extension for an Iraqi Kurdish professor who was at risk of being sent back to Iraq, where he would face a possible political trial. Implicit in this information was the fact that Douglas had tried to circumvent the normal immigration proceedings at the professor's behest. By this time Nixon knew he had Ford's support when and if an attack on Douglas was believed to be needed. There was, however, a question as to whether there was enough support in Congress to order an investigation.[86]

It takes more than a single legislator to trigger an impeachment. It takes 218 representatives if the entire House is present to vote. Moreover, an impeachment against a justice cannot occur without an impassioned core of legislators. In addition to Ford and many conservative Republicans, Nixon relied on Southern legislators. In the Senate, Strom Thurmond, Barry Goldwater, Robert Griffin, and John J. Williams were likely to lead an impeachment trial, but this had to wait until the House acted. On June 8, 1969, Mollenhoff announced in the *Des Moines Register* that Thurmond had aligned with Republican senators Carl Curtis of Nebraska and Paul Fannin of Arizona to have Douglas impeached. Mollenhoff's article did not focus on claims that Douglas had imperiled national security, though he mentioned Douglas's connection to Juan Bosch. Rather, the article mainly concentrated on the Parvin-Dohrmann Corporation's stock manipulation as well as a reputed relationship between Bobby Baker, suspected mafiosi, Fortas, and Douglas.[87]

Douglas's Prescience

After the 1968 election Douglas sensed that Nixon would press for his impeachment. In February 1970 he told his former clerk, Charles Ares, that he was likely to retire at the end of the Court's term. "I'm the lightning rod now that Warren has retired," Douglas penned to his friend Charles Horowitz. Douglas could have added that he had long been a "lightning rod" because of his public statements on foreign policy, the Vietnam War, and a federal government that monitored its own citizens to the point of endangering their freedom. For years conservatives were appalled with Douglas about his jurisprudence and criticisms of the government. But they opened a new front against him with allegations of financial improprieties and ties to criminal figures. Thus, the anti-Douglas forces characterized their target as a protector of organized crime and pornography, an enabler of pornography and social decay, and a stoker of rebellion who bolstered communism and socialism to weaken the United States.[88]

In 1969 he wrote to Burger that from the time he had joined the Securities and Exchange Commission in 1934, he had not owned any corporate stocks or bonds, and that his only interest-bearing investments were in US bonds. He informed Harry Ashmore that he had "reliable information" from "newspaper friends" that Congressman Clark MacGregor, a Minnesota Republican, and Congressman Charles Rarick, a Louisiana Democrat, were going to introduce an impeachment bill against him. On November 25, Rarick alleged to his constituents that Douglas had "furthered the communist conspiracy," and MacGregor claimed that Douglas "had intimate associations with known criminals and subversives." In May 1969 Douglas discovered that Wilbur Mills, the chairman of the House Ways and Means Committee, had directed a review of the Parvin Foundation's finances. Elected to Congress in 1938, Mills was an Arkansas Democrat who had signed the Southern Manifesto and voted against major civil rights laws. Mills intended to topple Douglas, but his efforts rapidly imploded when the rest of his committee appeared uninterested in following suit.[89]

When in October 1969 the *Washington Star* reported that Parvin had funded his foundation with proceeds from his casino profits, Douglas complained to Clifford that the casino funding had occurred before his meeting with Parvin, and that all Parvin had done was to transfer the "fractional interest" from his casino to "kick start" the foundation. The *Star* also noted that Thurmond had called for Douglas's removal. More concerning to Douglas was that the National Broadcasting Corporation, in its Huntley-Brinkley news hour, negatively reported on his relationship to Parvin. In November Douglas learned that Mollenhoff had tried to "plant a story with the press" that he lobbied Bosch to enable the Mafia to establish casinos in the Dominican Republic in exchange for assuring his continuance as that country's president. On December 31, 1969, Douglas asked Clifford to quietly gather former judge Simon Rifkind, as well as Sidney Davis, a former law clerk to

Hugo Black, and Joseph Ball, the Warren Commission's counsel and a gifted trial attorney, to map out a defense strategy in case Nixon's administration convinced congressional conservatives to demand his impeachment. In addition to Rifkind, Ball, and Davis, Douglas also asked William Gossett, a Detroit-area attorney and the son-in-law of former chief justice Charles Evans Hughes, to represent him. Gossett, however, would never be able to join in Douglas's defense because there were four attorneys at his Detroit firm who had already advised Ford on the best means to impeach Douglas.[90]

Although Douglas joked about calls for his impeachment, he was in fact becoming increasingly desperate for others to represent him. On April 7, 1970, one week before Ford's speech, he leaned on Clifford to secure former attorney general Ramsey Clark as well as former Oregon senator Wayne Morse for his defense team. Douglas also insisted that former ambassador John Bartow Martin could defend against any claims that Douglas had tried to connect Bosch to American gambling interests. It does not appear that Douglas knew that Ford would become Nixon's instrument to initiate an impeachment, but it is clear that from the time of Nixon's inauguration that a significant impeachment attempt was likely.[91]

One week before Ford called for Douglas's impeachment, Attorney General Mitchell contacted Douglas. When charges had first been contemplated against Fortas a year earlier, Mitchell had informed Earl Warren that an indictment against Fortas was likely. Mitchell's threat, though overstated, was enough to drive Fortas off the Court. Douglas had earlier told his friend, Charles Horowitz, that he would remain on the Court to fight any charges against him. Now, he responded to Mitchell, "Well Mr. Attorney General, saddle your horses." After hanging up the phone with Douglas, Mitchell instructed William Wilson to provide Ford with the Justice Department's files on Douglas. Thus, with the Nixon administration's assistance, if not prodding, a belief that the political and social environment was favorable for conservatives, and that there were enough legislators in agreement for impeachment, Ford launched his campaign against Douglas. He did so with full knowledge that although the country and most of Congress were ignorant of a key Nixon decision on Vietnam, an invasion of Cambodia was imminent.[92]

4

Ford's Attack on Douglas Begins

On Monday, April 13, 1970, the *Las Vegas Sun* reported that an impeachment resolution was likely to be introduced against Douglas by the end of the week. That evening, Vice President Spiro Agnew, in a *CBS News* interview, insisted that Douglas had undermined national security. When asked how the administration would react in the event Ford moved for an impeachment against Douglas, Agnew answered, "It would be pretty hard to prospectively comment on that." Despite his noncommittal response, Agnew went on to express that he doubted Douglas's fitness to serve on the nation's highest court. "I think that if we are talking about qualifications of Supreme Court justices, it may be appropriate to look at some of his beliefs, among which, as I recall, is a statement that rebellion is justified in cases where the establishment has acted in the way it is acting at the present time," Agnew claimed. "It seems rather unusual for a man on the bench to advocate rebellion and revolution."[1]

On the basis of the timing of Agnew's statements, it would be difficult for a dispassionate observer on April 15 not to conclude that Nixon advised Ford that the time had arrived to publicly demand Douglas's removal. Had Ford not acted, Agnew would have looked foolish, as Agnew had made it clear that was speaking on behalf of the administration in the interview. In the same interview, Agnew also criticized university administrators who failed to curb student demonstrations. Given that conservatives had accused Douglas of stoking student unrest, Agnew's claim is additional evidence of the administration's encouraging Ford to act. What the nation did not know is that in the same week that Ford called for Douglas's impeachment, Agnew pushed Nixon to order the invasion into Cambodia over the objections of other cabinet officers. Agnew, moreover, knew that, after the publication of *Points of Rebellion,* large numbers of Southern voters had implored their congressmen to remove Douglas, and several Southern legislators had spent the early part of the year demanding that Douglas retire or face impeachment. Thus, Agnew's comments to CBS also signaled to Southern Democrat legislators that the administration would support Douglas's impeachment.[2]

Agnew's signal to Southern Democrats was an important moment in the impeachment campaign against Douglas. Southern legislators almost universally believed they were not in a position to lead a campaign against Douglas. Florida Democrat James A. Haley informed his constituents that although many of his congressional peers sought Douglas's impeachment, they would be unsuccessful if it were led "with a Southerner taking the initiative." To one constituent, Haley complained, "The honest truth is that action against Justice Douglas initiated by a Southerner would be ineffective for the obvious reason." Although Haley's Southern victimization theory was fallacious, he and his peers did not need to worry about Nixon's commitment to the Southern strategy. In addition to Ford and Nixon, they also had an ally in Louis Wyman, a conservative Republican from New Hampshire who was prepared to introduce a resolution calling for an ad hoc investigation of Douglas through the House Rules Committee. In late 1969 Wyman accused Douglas of soliciting donations for Alaska senator Ernest Gruening's unsuccessful reelection campaign. When in 1970 Wyman introduced a resolution to investigate Douglas, he included this allegation among several other charges.[3]

Although Wyman came to the House only in 1962, he was an old-guard conservative who had been in politics since the end of World War II. In 1946 he became counsel to the Senate Investigations Committee, and one year later Senator Styles Bridges hired Wyman as his secretary. In 1956, after the Court's decision striking down Pennsylvania's espionage statute, Bridges and Wyman—by then a state legislator—joined Senator Joseph McCarthy in condemning the Court for aiding communism. As a state attorney general, Wyman testified to Congress on the dangers of communism and again condemned the Court for having issued several decisions that recognized basic constitutional rights for persons suspected of communism. He also aligned with Herbert Philbrick, one of the leading anticommunists in the 1950s and 1960s, in attacking the Court. An alliance of Wyman and Ford with Southern Democrats such as Haley reflected Nixon's Southern strategy goal to establish a legislative power base. Even so, the alliance would have to be strong enough to bypass congressional leadership and circumvent the traditional investigative machinery of the House Judiciary Committee.[4]

Ford's Speech and Initial Reaction: April 15–May 1

When on April 15, 1970, Ford detailed his allegations to the House of Representatives, he claimed that he had received hundreds of letters criticizing Douglas and that this had led him to "quietly [undertake] a study of both the law of impeachment and the facts about the behavior of Mr. Justice Douglas." Ford articulated several complaints before specifying his charges against Douglas: that HR 11109—Congressman Robert Taft's reform efforts—had remained "dormant" in the Judiciary Committee; that the Warren Burger–led Judicial Conference's newly promulgated ethics rules did not apply to the Supreme Court; and that the thirty-six-year-old canons of judicial ethics were merely advisory for the federal judiciary. Ford also tried to reassure the House that he had not moved against Douglas on the basis of the Justice's jurisprudential philosophy or because he held a personal animus against Douglas.[5]

Ford began his attack by reminding the House that federal judges did not constitutionally serve in their offices for life but rather remained on the bench only during periods of "good behavior," and he conceded that the term "good behavior," found in Article III of the Constitution, was no different than the language accompanying the terms of office for federal legislators found in Article I. But he insisted that because voters had the ability to remove a legislator, president, or vice president through the electoral process, federal judges had to be held to a higher standard of decorum than elected officials. While the Constitution does not differentiate between judicial impeachment and impeachments of elected officials, Ford's statement was somewhat understandable because of the life tenure of judges. Yet he weakened his own position by failing to articulate a clear standard for what constituted an impeachable offense. Instead of a finite standard, he claimed that "an impeachable offense is whatever a majority of the House of Representatives considers it to be at a moment in history; conviction results from whatever offense or offenses two-thirds of the other body considers to be sufficiently serious to require removal of the accused from office." In essence Ford insisted that impeachment was a political rather than a constitutional process, and this enabled Douglas's defenders to claim that Ford had disregarded a solemn constitutional process. In making his claim Ford also departed from a fundamental conservative tenet of strict constructionism. For decades conservatives who opposed the New Deal and civil rights insisted that the government had to adhere to the Constitution's "original intent" by not adding interpretations beyond its plain text. Now, Ford failed to adhere to conservative dogma.

After giving his opinions on the nature of judicial tenure, Ford went on to provide his reasons why Douglas should face an impeachment hearing. He began with the claim that Douglas had consorted with pornographers, particularly Ralph Ginzburg, "an editor and publisher of a number of magazines not commonly found on the family coffee table." Ford then asserted that Douglas's relationship to Ginzburg created a twofold conflict. Ginzburg's magazines had thrice published Douglas's articles. In 1963 a United States District Court found Ginzburg guilty of violating a federal obscenity statute by mailing a magazine entitled *Eros* to hundreds of subscribers. The Court upheld the conviction, but Douglas, along with justices Hugo Black, Potter Stewart, and John Harlan, dissented. Douglas's dissent was not a defense of pornography. Rather, he was challenging the government's regulation of speech and worried that dissent would be more easily suppressed. Although Douglas's free speech jurisprudence was consistent—and indeed aligned—with Black's, Ford obviously hoped that the general public would not make a distinction between Douglas's broad defense of free speech and the protection of a pornographer who dabbled in politics.[6]

To this end, Ford reminded Congress that in 1964 another Ginzburg magazine article had attacked Senator Barry Goldwater, the Republican Party's presidential candidate, and Goldwater had successfully sued Ginzburg. Douglas dissented from the Court's decision not to grant certiorari to Ginzburg's appeals in that case. Ford believed that because Douglas had written an article in *Avant Garde,* another of Ginzburg's magazines, during the period, and because the libel suit and conviction were under judicial review, he had violated a basic tenet of judicial ethics by entering into a financial arrangement with a party in an appeal before the Court. Douglas's article was not on the law but in praise of folk music, and he was paid $350 for it. Nonetheless,

Ford insisted that a federal law required a judge to recuse himself in "any case in which he has a substantial interest, has been counsel, is or has been a material witness, or is so related to or connected with any party or his attorney as to render it improper, in his opinion, for him to sit on the trial, appeal, or other proceeding therein." In this instance, Ford overreached because Douglas did not have a financial stake in the outcome of Ginzburg's appeals. Indeed, Douglas's financial relationship to Ginzburg was far less in value than Clement Haynsworth's was to his vending company. But linking Douglas to a purveyor of material that conservatives considered to be obscene added to their argument that Douglas was contributing to destabilizing society. Additionally, Ford urged that because excerpts from *Points of Rebellion* appeared in *Evergreen* (another Ginzburg-owned magazine) that contained a "hybrid of hippie-yippie" diatribes against the government, Douglas condoned every *Evergreen* magazine article, including those that encouraged violence.[7]

At this point in his speech it became evident to Ford's opponents that he had blundered. Before his speech he had handed reporters a text of what he intended to say, but shortly after he began his speech, Congressman William Fraser interrupted with a request for a "point of order." This type of interruption is permissible when a legislator seeks a clarification from the representative speaking to the House, but the speaking representative does not have to yield, except under limited circumstances. When Ford refused to yield, House Majority Leader Carl Albert ordered a roll call—an attendance record—of the members. (Albert was in charge of the House in the absence of Speaker of the House John McCormack.) Albert then enabled Fraser, a Minnesota Democrat, to point out that Ford's speech differed from his press handout. In the press handout, Ford insisted that Ginzburg paid Douglas at a time when Ginzburg had an appeal pending before the Court. Because there was no evidence this was true, Ford omitted this charge from his speech.[8]

Ford next turned to the first of several allegations that Douglas had undermined national security. *Points of Rebellion* was the obvious "evidence" that Douglas's detractors could point to in making this claim. After all, conservatives argued, the book was open to the interpretation that Douglas had insisted that the nation's freedom was at risk because of an overarching and intrusive military-industrial complex. Douglas had also warned that because of governmental surveillance on individuals protesting the Vietnam conflict as well as other social inequities, the right of people to dissent was in peril, and that before this right was lost, the people should warn their government to cease its surveillance. Ford focused on a section in *Points of Rebellion* to allege that Douglas encouraged social strife. He asserted that Douglas had championed the idea that just as there had been a right to rebel against the British crown during the War of Independence, this right continued in the event the federal government did not curtail the expansion of the military's influence into the lives of Americans. In this regard Ford linked Douglas with organizations such as the Black Panthers and the Weathermen.[9]

While Ford found *Points of Rebellion* appalling and argued that it had the potential to further stoke national unrest, he also disparaged it. "The kindest thing I can say about this 97-page tome is that it is quick reading," he began, before claiming it otherwise would have been of no more value to the nation than had a college sophomore written it. Nonetheless, Ford could not ignore the facts that publishing giant Random House had produced the book and that it had significant distribution potential. "It is a fuzzy harangue evidently intended to give historic legitimacy to the militant hippie-yippie movement and to bear testimony that a 71-year-old Justice of the Supreme Court is one in spirit with them," he concluded before turning to Douglas's association with Albert Parvin.

In addition to claiming Parvin "and a mysterious entity known as the Parvin Foundation" were antithetical to the interests of the United States, Ford insisted that Douglas had conducted legal work for Parvin, including drafting the Parvin Foundation's articles of incorporation. To prove that Parvin was linked to organized crime, Ford used the furniture magnate's city of birth and casino ownership as evidence. "Albert Parvin was born in Chicago around the turn of the century, but little is known of his life until he turns up as president and 30-percent owner of Hotel Flamingo, Inc.," Ford asserted, before claiming that Parvin had close ties with mafiosi such as Bugsy Siegel, William "Ice Pick" Alderman, Sanford Adler, and Gus Greenbaum. Beyond these associations, Ford's chief "evidence" for a Mafia connection was that Parvin had paid Meyer Lansky a $200,000 finder's fee for the sale of the Flamingo, a Las Vegas casino.

The difficulty with Ford's accusation against Parvin was that billionaire Howard Hughes had also paid "fees" to Mafia men such as Moe Dalitz for the purchase of his Las Vegas casinos. In the late 1960s alleged mafiosi who controlled Nevada's casinos had been looking for a means to divest from large-scale legal gambling out of a fear that the Justice Department had learned of their tax-skimming schemes. In retrospect, in considering Nixon's and Attorney General John Mitchell's "tough on crime" policies, their 1968 political campaign against the Court, and Clark Mollenhoff's claims that the Department of Justice had protected racketeers during Lyndon Johnson's presidency, it is understandable why Ford attempted to "give life" to the fiction that Douglas's votes on appeals were influenced by his underworld associations. In reality, however, Ford's attempt to directly tie Douglas to the so-called underworld through Parvin were too tenuous to succeed, and they partially contributed to the ultimate failure to move the investigation through the subcommittee to the full committee.[10]

This is not to ignore the fact that Parvin, as a youth, had been convicted of a petty crime, or that the Securities and Exchange Commission had targeted the Parvin-Dohrmann Corporation for fraudulent stock manipulations, which ultimately brought the office of the Speaker of the House of Representatives into disrepute. Yet Parvin had sold his major interest in the corporation by the time this scandal occurred. And even though the business associations between corporations and casino owners in Nevada would at the time necessarily create a link between corporate owners and shareholders on the one side, and suspected underworld figures on the other, the Nevada Gaming Commission concluded that Parvin had not committed any felonious crimes and therefore was entitled to own casinos. Guilt by association, then, was the evidence Ford relied on in making his allegations regarding organized crime and Douglas.[11]

In this vein Ford tried to tie Douglas with Robert "Bobby" Baker and Edward Levinson. Baker, as noted earlier, was a protégé of Lyndon Johnson who was enmeshed in a fraud scandal involving vending machines in defense industries. Ford reminded Congress that Fortas had represented Baker's vending machine company before his Supreme Court appointment and that Carol Agger also gave legal advice to both Baker and Parvin. Levinson had connections to organized crime figures through his ownership of the Sands Casino and directorship of the Flamingo Casino. As a tie between Douglas and organized crime, Ford reminded Congress that Parvin had business dealings with both Levinson and Baker. As final proof of Douglas's unlawful conduct, Ford claimed that Douglas and Baker had met clandestinely in a Parvin-owned casino to support gambling interests in the Dominican Republic. Had Douglas and Baker consorted in Las Vegas, it might have brought clarity to Ford's next charge that a former socialist president of the Dominican Republic was receptive to overtures from organized crime, with Douglas acting as an intermediary.[12]

Ford alleged that after Baker's and Douglas's hotel rendezvous, Baker met with Juan Bosch to convey Douglas's continued support to Bosch. This accusation carried an implication that Baker's purpose of meeting Bosch was to obtain a license to open a casino in the Dominican Republic, and that Douglas had helped him do so. It is true that in the 1950s organized crime leaders had dominated the casino industry in Cuba, and that after the communist takeover of that nation they had explored the possibility of other Caribbean locations. But any attempt to link organized crime to Bosch was problematic because like Fidel Castro, Bosch intended to nationalize much of the Dominican Republic's economy, including its hotels and casinos. Ford either was unaware of or ignored this aspect of Bosch's plans. If Douglas had met with Baker and Bosch, Ford posited, he had also likely interfered with the foreign policy of the United States, particularly because neither the Kennedy nor the Johnson administration had fully backed Bosch's presidency in 1962 or his attempt to return to power in 1965. However, there was no evidence at all that Baker and Douglas were in Las Vegas for a shared purpose, and the investigation later uncovered that the two men were not even in the city at the same time. Moreover, there was no evidence of any correspondence between the two men regarding the Dominican Republic.[13]

Having tried to tie Douglas to organized crime, Ford next turned to the Parvin Foundation's reason for existing. "The ostensible purpose of the Parvin Foundation was declared to be educating the development of leadership in Latin America," Ford claimed before hinting that the real purpose behind the foundation was to protect Mafia assets in Cuba during the communist revolution. Again, Ford focused on Latin America. He claimed that when in February 1963 Bosch had returned from exile to become the Dominican Republic's president, Baker, Parvin, and Douglas were present to welcome him. But Ford had to concede that Senator Hubert Humphrey and the first lady, Lady Bird Johnson, had also attended in a formal capacity. Ford then emphasized that Douglas's resignation from the Parvin Foundation after Fortas's departure from the Court constituted direct evidence that Douglas knew his association with the foundation violated judicial ethics.[14]

In terms of the CSDI, Ford claimed that through its Pacem in Terris II sponsorship, its leaders, including Douglas, encouraged left-wing rebellions in Latin America and Asia. In this latter category, Ford's allies would later hint at a relationship between Ho Chi Minh and Douglas. Once more these allegations were meritless. The CSDI had partnered with the Parvin Foundation on several projects, but it had not been involved in any matters contrary to the United States' foreign policy. Indeed, as the investigation uncovered, many of the CSDI's acts had President Lyndon Johnson's support.[15]

Toward the end of his speech Ford reiterated that Douglas had aligned with a combination of organized crime, left-wing campus radicals, and other "subversive persons" whose interests ran contrary to those of the United States. Finally, Ford attempted to create an aura of guilt by association regarding Fortas because Fortas had been one of Douglas's prized pupils at Yale University. In comparing the two justices, Ford concluded by claiming that Douglas had violated judicial ethics rules far beyond what Fortas had done. "There is no evidence that Louis Wolfson had notorious underworld associations in his financial enterprises," Ford propounded in making his comparison. "Whatever he may have done privately, Mr. Justice Fortas did not consistently take public positions that damaged and endangered the fabric of law and government."[16]

As Ford finished, Phillip Burton spoke in defense of Douglas. A liberal California Democrat, Burton personified the country's political and social divisions when juxtaposed against Ford and his allies. "Few members in the history of the Supreme Court can match the consistently outstanding record of Justice William O. Douglas in his defense, preservation, and strengthening of the constitutional rights of the American people," Burton challenged. "As for me I want to be the first to decry this attack on one of the most outstanding justices in American judicial history."[17]

Democratic congressman Joseph D. Waggonner, a conservative prosegregationist Louisianan, took the podium after Ford. He reminded the House that in 1966 he had introduced a resolution to remove Douglas. First elected to Congress in 1960, Waggonner had opposed civil rights, and he supported the US involvement in Vietnam. He also urged the United States to ally with Rhodesia's apartheid government, despite the fact that only the Portuguese and South African governments had done so. Waggonner was hardly loyal to his party. In 1968 he campaigned for Nixon over Humphrey, and in 1974 he fought against Nixon's impeachment. After Nixon resigned, Waggonner continued to profess the former president's innocence. In his short statement, Waggonner seconded Ford's allegations, and he emphasized an alleged linkage between Douglas and the "pornographic" publications of Ginzburg, as well as between Douglas, Lansky, and the "radical Hutchins." Waggonner's speech was brief—and hardly helpful to Ford, as he articulated a meritless interpretation of the judicial system. "Douglas's least whim," Waggonner argued, "his most causal aberration can suddenly and for all intents become the law of the land." This claim lacked any efficacy for the most obvious of reasons: Douglas was only one of nine justices, and the idea that the Court's most liberal and iconoclastic justice could sway Burger, Harlan, Stewart, White, or the newly confirmed Blackmun stretched credulity.[18]

While Waggonner's statements may not have undermined Ford, a misjudgment on the part of Wyman, one of Ford's staunchest Republican allies, shifted whatever momentum existed for creating a special ad hoc investigation to a traditional investigation headed by the Judiciary Committee. Wyman was a states' rights congressman, and it would be difficult to find a more outspoken and often careless anticommunist in the House. In 1957 he excoriated President Eisenhower for sending federalized military forces into Little Rock, Arkansas. While serving as state attorney general he convinced New Hampshire's legislature to pass a statute banning subversive persons from holding state government positions; this same legislation empowered his office to investigate persons suspected of ties to the Communist Party of the United States. He accused well over one hundred of New Hampshire's citizens of supporting communism. But the Supreme Court could, and did, keep him from carrying out some of his more egregious plans. In 1957 the Court reversed a professor's criminal conviction that Wyman had set in motion. The professor, whose sin had been to exercise his First Amendment free speech rights, also exercised his Fifth Amendment right against incrimination and refused to answer Wyman's interrogation, and a state judge imprisoned the professor for criminal contempt.[19]

Although Wyman did not always lose before the Court—two years later the Court upheld a civil contempt against Willard Uphaus after he refused to provide Wyman with the names of people who attended an alleged communist summer camp—he remained angry with the justices who opposed him. In 1957 Wyman addressed the Georgia state legislature and derided *Brown* and other civil rights decisions. He also claimed that Douglas had shown an allegiance to subversive organizations. In 1966 Douglas led the Court to destroy many of Wyman's efforts to sanitize New Hampshire of alleged subversives. In *DeGregory v. Attorney General*, the Court determined that the reasons Wyman had used to investigate New Hampshire's citizens were stale and violated the First Amendment. Douglas took pride in criticizing Wyman's earlier treatment of Uphaus, to the point that Brennan and Fortas worried about the tenor of the decision. Had Ford intended to make the investigation a constitutional rather than a political process, he would have had to stop Wyman, if for no other reason than Wyman was the antithesis of an impartial representative in either fact or appearance. Given that Ford's earliest vocal allies were outspoken racists, the effort to oust Douglas had a remarkably unpromising start. This was not the only reason the effort floundered.[20]

Almost immediately after Majority Leader Albert recognized Wyman to deliver his statement, Congressman Andrew Jacobs, an Indiana Democrat, asked Wyman to yield for "a three-second statement." Wyman assumed that Jacobs only sought a minor point of order to obtain a clarification from Ford, and he yielded the podium to Jacobs. Instead of seeking a minor point of order, however, Jacobs introduce a formal resolution that called for an investigation by the Judiciary Committee. The fundamental difference between Jacobs's proposal—listed as HR 920—and Wyman's—listed as HR 922—was that Wyman, at Ford's behest, sought to place the investigation in the Rules Committee. As long as the investigation remained in the Judiciary Committee's control, it would consist of a proportion of congressmen based on the House's composition. That is, three Democrats and two Republicans would investigate Douglas. And this investigation would be overseen by Congressman Emmanuel Celler, a long-serving liberal New York Democrat.[21]

Wyman acted churlishly after he spoke. Not only did he submit HR 922, but he also went on to submit four additional resolutions, listed as HR 923, HR 924, HR 925, and HR 926, all essentially duplicating HR 922. Even if all of the signatories were added up, it would fall far short of the number who had affixed their names to HR 920. All of Wyman's resolutions placed the Rules Committee in charge of the investigation. Two other congressmen introduced separate resolutions against Douglas. Florida Democrat Charles Bennett introduced his own resolution, HR 927, which called for a select committee to investigate Douglas. A prosegregationist, Bennett—who had lobbied Eisenhower to permanently place the motto "in God we trust" on currency—believed the Court was decidedly anti-Christian, and this was enough of a basis to have Douglas removed. New York Republican Frank Jefferson Horton, with Connecticut Republican Lowell Weicker and New York Republican Hamilton Fish Jr., introduced the last resolution, HR 928. All three of these representatives were moderates within their own party; indeed, they had chastised segregationists for undermining the Constitution. While their resolution called for a special committee to investigate Douglas, they sought to limit the scope of the investigation to "Douglas's official conduct." In other words, Horton, Weicker, and Fish wanted to limit the grounds for impeachment to the commission of an actual crime.[22]

The few historians who have written on Douglas's impeachment do not seem to have discovered how and why Jacobs acted to keep the investigation in the House Judiciary Committee. Jacobs was a liberal from Indianapolis who supported the 1964 Civil Rights Act and who campaigned for Robert Kennedy in the 1968 Indiana primary. He did not leave behind a collection of historical documents when he died in 2013. However, Congresswoman Edith Green, an Oregon Democrat, left in her collection a memorandum detailing that Jacobs and a small number of other Democrats met "in executive session led by Speaker McCormack" before Ford's speech and determined to preempt Ford's demand for a special investigation by calling for a vote to permit an investigation through the normal means of the Judiciary Committee. In essence Jacobs acted to protect Douglas against an investigation that would have permitted a Southern conservative legislative bloc that was already desirous of removing Douglas to lead it. On April 24, 1970, Page Belcher, an Oklahoma Republican, accused Jacobs of "being an extreme liberal who introduced an impeachment resolution for the very purpose of having the Judiciary Committee turn it down." Belcher's accusation against Jacobs was incorrect. Under Celler, the Judiciary Committee would be able to refashion Ford's charges and then determine whether there was any evidence to substantiate the charges. The investigation would have, at a minimum, three members who supported civil rights. In the end the investigation would have four pro–civil rights congressmen serving on it.[23]

Ford's First Defeat: The News Characterizes His Efforts, April 1–May 5, 1970

News editors and media owners have the power to effect public perceptions of significant events not only in the reporting of the events but also in the decision regarding where to place the reporting. Professor Laurel Leff points out in her study of the *New York Times* and the Holocaust that in 1939 the New York Times was managed by Arthur Sulzberger, a Jewish publisher who was concerned that the paper could be perceived as a "Jewish newspaper." For a variety of reasons beyond Sulzberger's concerns on the perceptions readers might have for the nation's largest circulating newspaper, the *New York Times* often buried stories of anti-Semitism and the Holocaust deep within the paper. Neither Ford nor Nixon—nor for that matter Douglas—could control reporting on the impeachment effort; it became apparent that the major news media uniformly abandoned the impeachment effort as a front-page story within days of Ford's speech. In part this abandonment was unsurprising because the Vietnam War had dominated the news, but also because other events would rapidly overtake Ford's demand for the removal of a long-serving justice.[24]

On the morning of April 15 the *Wall Street Journal*'s editorial staff chastised Nixon and Ford for preparing to attack Douglas. The *Journal*'s editors had endorsed Nixon in 1960 and 1968, and they were highly critical of Douglas. But the editors believed that Ford's motives were political and that he had little understanding of the long-term harm he could cause to the judiciary. Indeed, they labeled Ford's allies "foolish." In an editorial entitled "Political Reprisal," the *Journal*'s editors conceded that Haynsworth had been rejected "on the flimsiest of charges," but then argued, "What the House Republicans propose to try, with little hope of success, could only continue the deterioration of the Court's prestige, something the nation can ill afford." Given that this editorial appeared in a proadministration newspaper before Ford spoke, he would have been prudent to curtail his speech. But he did not do so.[25]

There was a fundamental aspect of the United States' democracy that undermined Nixon's and Ford's campaign against Douglas. The two men could not control the content of the nation's newspapers or the television media, and the spring and summer of 1970 were globally chaotic. The ongoing conflict in Vietnam as well as violence in Cambodia and protests against the war dominated the news. For instance, on the eve of Ford's speech, the *New York Times* informed the nation's readers that hundreds of ethnic Vietnamese had been murdered in Cambodia. Other prominent news stories reported that Nixon had entered into nuclear arms reduction discussions with the Soviet government and had also announced personnel cuts in the army. In addition to these news items, during the week of Ford's speech, three US astronauts engaged in the Apollo 13 mission struggled to return to earth after a destructive explosion occurred in the third stage of their Saturn V rocket. The grand jury proceedings investigating the drowning death of Mary Jo Kopechne and Senator Ted Kennedy's involvement was reported on. After a Palestinian attack on the US embassy in Amman, Jordan, which occurred on the same day as Ford's speech, King Hussein demanded that Harrison Symmes, the American ambassador, be recalled to the United States. Labor riots in Poland resulted in a Soviet crackdown on union activity in that country. In Quebec a separatist movement undertook kidnappings and other violent acts before being suppressed by the Canadian military. For the first time since World War II, the Canadian government instituted martial law. Finally, the breakup of the Beatles was garnering significant attention from fans of rock music.[26]

Generally, in April 1970 the nation's newspapers did not side with Ford, and the reporting ranged from neutral to skeptical of his intentions. The *Boston Globe* gave little space to Ford's attack on Douglas; they placed the story on the twelfth page of its April 15 evening edition. The *Globe* informed its readers that "Douglas's dealings with Parvin began in 1960 when he aided in setting up the Albert Parvin Foundation and became a director and later its president at $12,000 a year," but then reminded them that he had resigned from the foundation eleven months earlier. Two days later the *Globe* headlined with the fact that more than one hundred congressmen had aligned with Ford. At the same time the newspaper informed its readers that Celler established a subcommittee investigation, but by this time the grand jury investigation of Kopechne's death, the Apollo 13 rescue, and the attack on the US embassy in Amman were of more interest than the investigation into Douglas.[27]

On April 16 Mollenhoff's former newspaper, the *Des Moines Register,* headlined that Ford had called for Douglas's impeachment, and in an effort to provide Nixon protection against the allegation that he had spurred Ford to act, it also quoted Nixon's press secretary, Ronald Ziegler, insisting that the president had not "discussed the matter with Ford." Of the nation's major newspapers, only the *Register* appears to have reported Ziegler's canard, and it did so in a neutral manner. But the next day the *Register*'s editors made it clear that they did not support Ford. After reminding its readers that the *Register* had once criticized Douglas for his relationship to Parvin, they now alleged that Ford acted incautiously. "An impeachment drive heavily tinged with politics can only do further damage to the Court," the editors wrote. "Architects of the 'Impeach William Douglas' move will be performing a major disservice if they persist in the effort."[28]

The *Cincinnati Enquirer*'s editors suggested that neither Ford nor Nixon intended for an impeachment to succeed, but rather accused the two men of trying to embarrass senators who had voted against Haynsworth and Carswell. James Reston, in his syndicated column, sarcastically questioned whether Douglas's book could be considered a misdemeanor, if not a high crime, because of the decline of literature. The *Atlanta Journal-Constitution* merely headlined that Ford had sought a bill for Douglas's impeachment. The *Detroit Free Press* informed its readers that Ford's allegations against Douglas were "based on all of the innuendo of recent years." The editors of the paper wrote that they "could take Ford's attack on Douglas seriously if they had greater faith in [Ford's] objectivity." There were exceptions to the general tenor of the news. The *Arizona Republic*'s editorial staff argued to its readers that Douglas was unfit to remain on the Court before concluding, "The impeachment of William Douglas might well be unprecedented. But this is an instance in which a break with precedent would be a statesmanlike move."[29]

The *Philadelphia Inquirer* serves as one media example, among many, that contextualizes Ford's early inability to use his allegations against Douglas as a means for capturing the nation's support. On April 12, 1970, its banner headline read, "Apollo 13 Heads toward Moon." On the bottom of the first page ran the headline, "Agnew Attacks Douglas, Asks Examination." Under this headline the *Inquirer* informed its readers, "Douglas often involved in controversy drew publicity this week after publication of his 20th book, *Points of Rebellion.*" However, the newspaper also reported that Senator Richard S. Schweicker, a Pennsylvania Republican, claimed that Nixon had pressured him to vote for Carswell's confirmation. Two days later, the *Inquirer* reported under its lead headline that the Apollo 13 mission had had to abort its lunar goal as a result of a power failure. Underneath this article, the newspaper reported that a Soviet nuclear submarine had sunk off the coast of Spain, the Israeli air force had attacked targets near Cairo, and four "Viet Cong" rockets missed the US embassy in Saigon. Interestingly, and perhaps related to Ford's effort to shore up Nixon's popularity, the *Inquirer* reported that the president's popularity had fallen as a result of the administration's military policy regarding Laos. On page three, the newspaper not only informed its readers that Ford had indicated he would move the House to investigate Douglas but also that he denied any linkage between the failed Haynsworth and Carswell nominations, and his pending effort against Douglas.[30]

On April 15 the *Inquirer* once more headlined the troubled Apollo 13 mission; underneath this story it reported that Nixon had nominated Blackmun to the Court as well as Admiral Thomas Hinman Moorer as chairman of the Joint Chiefs of Staff. On the second page the newspaper reported that Pennsylvania's state legislature was considering a bill to prevent the use of its national guard forces in Vietnam until such time as Congress formally declared war. On its third page, the newspaper informed its readers that Blackmun was "a moderate" in his civil rights jurisprudence, and that the US envoy to Sweden had been heckled by a large crowd. There were no reports on Douglas even though Ford had indicated he would speak on the subject.[31]

When the newspaper reported Ford's speech in Congress on April 16, it placed the story on its fifth page. The two dominant news items on the front page were that Apollo 13 had been set on a course to return to earth and that twenty-five American soldiers had been killed in Vietnam. On its second page, the newspaper reported that a House of Representatives investigation had questioned Captain Harold Medina over the My Lai massacre, and on page three, it reported the attack on the embassy in Jordan (Medina was part of the chain of command involved in the massacre). On its fourth page the *Inquirer* informed its readers of Blackmun's net worth as well as his past rulings.[32]

Although the hearings into Douglas continued, by the beginning of May, reporting on it seldom appeared in the *Inquirer*. On May 2 the newspaper reported that the US military invaded Cambodia, which resulted in college campus demonstrations throughout the country. On Sunday, May 3, the *Inquirer* reported on its front page the continuation of the attack in Cambodia as well as Senate opposition to the expansion of Vietnam conflict into Cambodia. Further in the newspaper were reports that the Soviet Union had denounced the United States' actions in Cambodia; that the Egyptian and Israeli militaries had clashed; and that an army reserve officer training corps building at Princeton University had been firebombed. The next day the newspaper printed a report on its second page detailing a clash between students at Kent State University as well as a report on its sixth page informing its readers that more than 65 percent of California's men who had been ordered into military service had evaded the draft. On Tuesday, May 5, the *Inquirer* headlined that Ohio national guard soldiers had killed four students, with the underline that "violent dissent is an invitation to tragedy." On the newspaper's third page ran a story that senators from both parties claimed Nixon had usurped powers beyond the war powers conferred on a president. It was not until May 6 that the newspaper reported on any matters involving the Court; that article appeared on its eighth page, where it reported that the Senate Judiciary Committee approved of forwarding Blackmun's nomination by a unanimous vote of seventeen members.[33]

Unsurprisingly, Southern newspapers were not only more likely to side with Ford than their Northern counterparts but they also referred to Ford's efforts as "bipartisan." The Rolla, Missouri, *Daily News* called Douglas "a suspected cancer in our body of states" and likened Ford to a medical intern. Alabama's *Birmingham News* reported that Ford was heckled with "demands for time-consuming quorum calls" throughout his speech. In an editorial the *Birmingham News* noted that the Rules Committee as favored by the conservatives could produce articles of impeachment within two weeks. The Charleston, South Carolina, *News and Courier* informed its readers on April 15 that Ford had planned to speak against Douglas, but the next day the front-page coverage contained reports on the grand jury investigating Kopechne's death, a pending Teamsters Union walkout, and the attack on the embassy in Jordan. That day's news editorial gave milquetoast approval to Blackmun's nomination before accusing the Warren Court of making "Americans unhappy" by "twisting the old Constitution out of shape." On April 17 the *News and Courier's* editorial staff responded to an allegation that Ford's actions were destined to weaken the Court, writing, "Since the liberals have enjoyed control of it for many years, they will employ political humbug to confuse the public rather than yield this source of power at a time when the pendulum of opinion is swinging another way."[34]

The *Richmond Times-Dispatch* assailed the Senate for rejecting Haynsworth and Carswell, and leveled criticisms against Virginia senator William Spong, who had voted against Carswell. When on April 8 Spong defended himself by pointing out that he had voted to confirm Burger and Haynsworth, and that Carswell was not the "best possible choice," the *Times-Dispatch*'s editors responded by linking Spong to Indiana's liberal senator, Birch Bayh, who had led the liberals' efforts to reject both Haynsworth and Carswell. The newspaper also insisted that Vermont senator Winston Prouty, a Republican, had backtracked on his promise to vote for Haynsworth and Carswell because of liberal pressure in his state. On April 16 its editors argued that the nation was entitled to know the full story about Justice Douglas's behavior and associations, including his "inflammatory calls for revolution" and the "Albert Parvin Foundation which was deeply involved with notorious underworld figures." The only way to discover the depth of Douglas's conduct, the editors argued, was a formal investigation.[35]

Although there was a tendency for the Southern newspapers to side with Ford, some took a more neutral position. The Mississippi-based *Clarion-Ledger* simply headlined "Douglas Removal Motion Introduced" on April 16, and the following day it reported that there was a growing movement to remove the justice. The *Ledger* also headlined the Palestinian attack on the US embassy in Jordan, but in terms of providing any anti-Douglas materials, only a few of Wyman's statements were reported. The *New Orleans Times-Picayune*'s editorial staff predicted that the debate over Douglas would become a political issue in the November midterm elections in which incumbent senators who opposed Haynsworth would have to explain their support of Douglas to their constituents.[36]

Finally, international newspapers characterized Ford's attack on Douglas as a political reprisal rather than a legitimate constitutional action, and presented Douglas as an innocent target. The *Times of India* reported that Ford had embroiled the Court in further controversy. The *New Zealand Herald* linked the Senate's rejections of Haynsworth and Carswell to Ford's efforts to oust Douglas with the comment, "It is now being said in private conversation that it is time to nominate a man who fits added the requirements of the Court rather than fitting the desires of Strom Thurmond." While the opinions of government officials or the general public in India or New Zealand were unlikely to affect Nixon and Ford, it is noteworthy that both countries possessed legal systems stemming from Great Britain's and therefore possessed similarities to the United States.[37]

If the opinions of the press in India or New Zealand were unlikely to influence Nixon or Ford, then the major newspapers of the United States' three most important allies should have given both men pause. On April 17, 1970, *The Times,* Britain's largest-circulation newspaper, informed its readers that Ford had engaged in "a conservative–liberal vendetta and there is some suspicion that he has the tacit support of the White House." The British newspaper added that Blackmun had taken part in three cases involving corporations that he held stock in while serving on the Court of Appeals for the Eighth Circuit. In another article, *The Times* reported that a new wave of campus violence had broken out on college campuses in the United States. Scotland's largest-circulation newspaper, the *Glasgow Herald,* observed on April 15— before Ford had even delivered his speech—that although conservatives disliked Douglas and "generated a lot of sound and fury," the impeachment was likely to fail."[38]

In Canada the *Toronto Globe and Mail* reported that Ford had accused Douglas of consorting with organized criminal leaders and with Juan Bosch, but then failed to provide evidence for his accusations. The next day the *Sydney Morning Herald* reported that Ford's "virulent attack launched efforts by a group of conservative Republicans and Democrats to have the Judge, noted for his liberal views, removed from the Bench." That the major newspapers of the United States' three closest allies doubted the veracity of Ford is an important aspect of the impeachment effort. Given the *Times*'s, the *Globe*'s, and the *Herald*'s reporting, their readers could have easily concluded that Ford's allegations were made for nefarious reasons, in turn casting greater doubts on the integrity of Nixon's presidency. In Australia, which had its military forces fighting alongside American forces in Vietnam, Ford's campaign against Douglas could have had significant foreign policy repercussions by creating public doubts as to Nixon's commitment to the rule of law, treaties, and economic agreements.[39]

Overseas news sources are only one means to assess foreign opinions on Ford's actions. On April 28, 1970, J. Robert Schaetzel, the State Department's special representative to the Federal Republic of Germany, wrote to Dean Acheson that although West German leaders believed Nixon had made an unfortunate choice in selecting G. Harold Carswell, the attack on Douglas was irresponsible. Perhaps Schaetzel was expressing his own views, but before April 1 he told Acheson that Nixon had deftly balanced domestic and international crisis and enjoyed confidence from Europe's leaders. In the same letter Schaetzel also called Douglas "foolish." Most importantly, he observed to Acheson that the attack on Douglas could also undermine trust in Nixon overseas.[40]

Ford's Second Defeat: The Administration's Response and the Cambodia Invasion

From the time of Cambodia's independence from France in 1953, its neutrality proved difficult to maintain because of its geographic position. The governments of North and South Vietnam, as well as China and Thailand, made territorial claims against Cambodia and tried to manipulate its government. Over the course of the Vietnam conflict, US intelligence agencies conducted operations in Cambodia. Likewise, North Vietnamese forces and the Viet Cong used Cambodian territory as a means of transit as well as a place to hide troops and matériel. Led by Prince Norodom Sihanouk, Cambodia had nominally aligned with the communists. Beginning in March 1969 Nixon ordered an aerial campaign, Operation Menu, to bombard communist strongholds in Cambodia, and on March 18, 1970, while Sihanouk was traveling abroad, the Cambodian legislature voted to depose him. After Sihanouk's ouster the government was led by Lon Nol, an official more amenable to the United States than Sihanouk had been. On March 21 Lon Nol ordered all North Vietnamese forces to leave Cambodia, and two days later Sihanouk broadcast his opposition to Lon Nol from China. Thus, not only were foreign military forces operating in Cambodia but there was also a real possibility of a Cambodian civil war.[41]

Throughout March the North Vietnamese military increased its presence in Cambodia, with the intent of toppling Lon Nol and creating a communist government. In response, some of the rural population loyal to Lon Nol began to slaughter Cambodia's ethnic Vietnamese minority. This expanded the purpose of North Vietnamese forces in Cambodia to protecting the ethnic Vietnamese minority. In early April, Nixon and Kissinger, along with the chairman of the Joint Chiefs of Staff, began to plan for a ground offensive operation in Cambodia. Even before his inauguration Nixon intended to pursue a different policy than Johnson in regard to Cambodia and Laos. Johnson feared that a widening of the war into Cambodia and Laos could result in a broader conflict with China. Nixon intended to maximize the application of American military force as a means for strengthening his Vietnamization policies. But Nixon had several political hurdles beyond straightforward political opposition to "widening the war." Both Secretary of Defense Laird and Secretary of State Rogers opposed committing US forces in Cambodia. In 1969 they had opposed Operation Menu, and after the *New York Times* reported on the "secret bombing campaign," Kissinger convinced Nixon that neither Laird nor Rogers could be trusted to participate in planning military operations in Cambodia and Laos. Indeed, on April 26, 1970, Kissinger informed Nixon in a confidential memorandum, "Care should be exercised at today's meeting not to surface the fact that General Wheeler has been conducting intensified planning to implement the attacks on Base Area 352/353 without full knowledge of the Secretary of Defense."[42]

As important as Laird's opposition was the fact that bipartisan group of senior senators opposed the use of any force in Cambodia. Senate Majority Leader Michael Mansfield and ranking Senate Republican Hugh Scott lobbied Nixon not to send ground forces into Cambodia. This was not all. Senators John Sherman Cooper and Frank Church drafted a bill to refuse funding for operations in Cambodia and Laos, in effect informing the president that the use of forces in either country would not have congressional approval. Although Nixon realized that Rogers's fears of international opposition to a large-scale bombing operation and Laird's fears of domestic upheaval were rational, this did not dissuade him. Instead, he limited sharing the plans for an invasion to a select small number of legislators, including Ford.[43]

On April 30, 1970, Nixon announced that American and South Vietnamese military forces had invaded Cambodia in an effort to destroy Viet Cong and North Vietnamese military units. Roughly 12,000 US soldiers, along with a larger number of South Vietnamese military forces, crossed thirty miles into Cambodia. The campaign met with resistance, and both sides suffered losses. While the attack may have initially been a military success in the sense that it disrupted North Vietnam's transport of weapons, the strategic implications of the invasion were devastating for other reasons. First, whatever the perceived necessity of the invasion may have been, it was at odds with Nixon's promise not to expand the conflict, and it was difficult for millions of Americans to reconcile Vietnamization with this action. Congressman Sam Gibbons, a Florida Democrat who had earlier supported Nixon's Vietnamization policies, went so far as to accuse Nixon of being the cause of the nation's unrest. In 1969 he told his constituents that Haynsworth's nomination would have a positive effect on limiting dissent. In regard to Vietnamization, Gibbons claimed, "Under the circumstances, the President has taken the right course in handling the Vietnam situation," before concluding that Nixon's "opponents had [made the job] exceedingly difficult, particularly in foreign policy matters, if [they] are continually criticizing his policies." But on May 15 Gibbons excoriated Nixon over the Cambodian invasion.[44]

The term "difficult" in relation to the domestic reaction may be charitable. Massive demonstrations against the war were occurring across the nation, and congressmen who had been left in the dark over the Cambodian operation responded by trying to curb Nixon's authority as commander in chief. On May 5 Ohio national guard soldiers killed four students demonstrating against the Cambodian invasion. A day earlier Ohio's governor, James Rhodes, called the demonstrators the "worst type of people in America." By the end of the week more than 100,000 protesters had gathered in Washington, DC, thirty ROTC offices had been bombed, and sixteen state governors had mobilized their national guards. In New York construction workers supportive of the administration attacked demonstrators, and Nixon was spirited away from the capital to Camp David for two days while army leadership determined how great the danger to the government was. For the first time Nixon gave serious consideration to using the Huston plan for using the military to arrest opposition. If he had done so, it is unlikely that Congress would have remained silent.[45]

Nixon should have anticipated congressional resistance. On April 28 the *New York Times* headlined that the Senate Foreign Relations Committee had opposed sending military aid to Lon Nol's Cambodian government. The next day twenty-four congressmen sent a petition to Nixon opposing military operations in Cambodia. The signatories to this petition included Douglas's supporters, such as Abner Mikva, Patsy Mink, Don Edwards, Jerome Waldie, and Edward Koch. "The decision of your administration to expand the war bodes ill for both the cause of world peace and the well-being of the American people," the petitioners argued. On May 1 fifty-nine congressmen added their names to the petition. In addition to the petition, Michael J. Harrington, a Massachusetts Democrat, urged Congress to prevent the funding of military operations in Cambodia. Senator William Fulbright demanded that the administration constitutionally justify its actions. At the same time New York Democrat Benjamin Rosenthal and Rhode Island Democrat Robert O. Tiernan introduced two resolutions asking Congress to consider the unconstitutionality of Nixon's actions. On May 7 Koch introduced a resolution, backed by thirty-two other signatories, for a national day of mourning. The military invasion quickly overshadowed Ford's impeachment efforts. Moreover, the fact that the majority of Douglas's detractors in Congress backed Nixon placed their efforts against Douglas in a broader context of supporting an unpopular war that Douglas opposed. By the beginning of May more than half of the senators publicly expressed their opposition to the invasion, including Republican Senate Minority Leader Hugh Scott.[46]

Thus, two weeks after Ford alleged that Douglas had violated judicial ethics, broken the law, and constituted a threat to national security by stoking dissent, and three days after Celler had formed the House Judiciary Committee investigation, large swaths of the nation appeared to be in the midst of a rebellion against the government. Nationwide protest on a never-before-experienced scale was precisely what Douglas had warned of in *Points of Rebellion,* as well as in his earlier writings and speeches—to his misguided critics precisely what he had intended all along. Congress for its part would spend much of the late spring and summer debating a means to curtail Nixon's authority to use the military outside Vietnam without its express legal sanction instead of debating Douglas's fate. In the midst of a historic debate over a president's authority to send forces into a foreign conflict, Celler's committee would use the resources accorded to it to investigate Douglas.

Ford's Third Defeat: The House Judiciary Committee Remains in Charge

There were several reasons that Ford's efforts to create a special investigation headed by the Rules Committee would have provided a more likely means to have articles of impeachment drafted and then passed on to the whole House for a full vote. The Rules Committee would have adopted the ad hoc investigation's findings on Douglas and then voted on any articles of impeachment without further debate. However, this course of action would have constituted a significant departure from more than a century of precedent in which the Judiciary Committee investigated judges. Another reason was that William Colmer, a conservative anti–civil rights Southern Democrat from Mississippi, chaired the Rules Committee. Although Ford had once claimed his intent to distance conservative Republicans from Southern Democrats, his attempt to forge an alliance with Colmer to upend the House investigative machinery evidenced a significant act contrary to his claims. In addition to Colmer's being a Southern Democrat, Ford had another hope that his efforts to get the Rules Committee to oversee the investigation would succeed. The second-ranking Democrat, New York's James Delany, appeared ambivalent and did not openly oppose impeaching Douglas.[47]

Colmer, a World War I veteran and supporter of US involvement in Vietnam, had been in Congress since 1933. He had signed the Southern Manifesto, disparaged the Warren Court after *Brown,* and claimed that the Southern states constituted "the real America." Colmer also equated antiwar demonstrators with communism. In 1961 Speaker of the House Sam Rayburn, a longtime Texas Democrat, tried to purge Colmer from the Rules Committee after accusing him of disloyalty to President Kennedy by "bottling up bills in the committee." In fact Colmer had not only aligned with anti–civil rights legislators to challenge the Voting Rights Act but had also openly backed Nixon in the 1960 election against Kennedy. In 1966, with both Rayburn and Kennedy dead, and with Speaker of the House McCormack desperately trying to keep the vestiges of the New Deal coalition in authority, Colmer ascended to the Rules Committee chairmanship.[48]

In 1969 Colmer headed a "study group" to examine, among a myriad of possible alterations to the relationships between committees and the House leadership, whether the Rules Committee should be empowered to conduct congressional investigations against persons in the other two branches of government. Colmer's purpose in seeking more power for the Rules Committee had to do with maintaining the influence of Southern Democrats in the House. That is, the Rules Committee had a large number of Southern legislators. On June 17, 1969, Colmer introduced a draft bill to the House that would have given the Rules Committee the power that he sought. For over a year a McCormack-led coalition of Northern and Western Democrats and liberal Republicans blocked Colmer's efforts to expand his committee's authority. However, on October 26, Congress passed the Legislative Reorganization Act, which, among its other aspects, maintained the Judiciary Committee's primacy in investigations of federal officials. While Colmer's purpose had little directly to do with the impeachment effort against Douglas, the timing of his effort and possible impact on the investigation cannot be ignored. If the Rules Committee were to investigate Douglas, its members would first have to agree on a set of rules to follow, and such rules would be proposed by Colmer. Given the makeup of the Rules Committee, there were enough Southern Democrats and Republicans to create a set of rules favorable for an impeachment to occur. More distressingly, Colmer would select the three Democrats for the investigation.[49]

Although McCormack and Albert sought to keep the Rules Committee from investigating Douglas, it was a midtenure congressman from Boston who became instrumental in swaying Colmer not to do so. Elected to replace John F. Kennedy in the House in 1953, Thomas "Tip" O'Neill was tasked by McCormack to lobby Colmer not to insert the Rules Committee into the investigation of Douglas. In 1955, at McCormack's behest, Rayburn assigned O'Neill to the Rules Committee; there he developed a friendly relationship with both Colmer and Colmer's predecessor, Howard K. Smith, another Southern Democrat and anti–civil rights congressman. Initially Colmer informed the *Times-Picayune* that he was not opposed to a separate Rules Committee investigation. However, on April 24, 1970, he issued a press statement briefly describing his reasons for not pursuing an investigation against Douglas. He posited that the best that his committee could accomplish with Wyman's resolution would be to "study the charges made against Mr. Justice Douglas." In other words, Colmer disingenuously claimed that his committee could not be used as a means to draft impeachment articles. Yet Colmer would also have likely voted to impeach Douglas. O'Neill informed his constituents that because "Celler, an extremely fair man who is greatly concerned with civil liberties, has created a Special Committee to consider all charges against Justice Douglas," a Rules Committee investigation was unnecessary. Moreover, he insisted that the Rules Committee investigation would have been inherently biased against Douglas.[50]

On April 21, 1970, having gained Colmer's promise to block Ford's efforts to use the Rules Committee, Celler selected Jack Brooks, a Texas Democrat, and Byron Rogers, a Colorado Democrat, to join the investigation. Celler promised the public that the investigation would not be a "whitewash of Douglas," but at the same time it would also not be a "witch hunt." Brooks was a liberal who had supported Johnson's domestic policies and civil rights, but also the escalation of force in Vietnam. However, by 1970 he had joined with congressmen who called for an end to the war. He was also a longtime antagonist of Nixon; during the 1960 presidential campaign, Brooks had accused Nixon of various acts of wrongdoing, including manipulating federal agencies to financially benefit his family and friends during Eisenhower's presidency. Byron Rogers had served in the army in World War I, and after the war he began a career in state politics, including a period as Colorado's attorney general. In 1950 Denver's voters elected him to Congress, where he served ten consecutive terms. Rogers, like Celler and Brooks, supported civil rights. In 1967, in response to a firebomb attack on the NAACP headquarters in Mississippi, he pushed for legislation to federalize law enforcement in that state, in effect authorizing the FBI to hire and fire local police officers. While Rogers had never been a public supporter of Johnson's escalation of forces in Vietnam, he also had not opposed it.[51]

William M. McCulloch, the ranking Republican on the committee, selected himself and Edward Hutchinson, a Michigan Republican, to serve on the investigation. Although Ford lobbied McCulloch to appoint Hutchinson to the committee, there is nothing in either Ford's or McCulloch's papers that indicates Ford's lobbying was the reason for the appointment. Ford may have believed that McCulloch would push for the House to draft articles of impeachment because he had proven himself to be a stalwart conservative and national security hawk. But McCulloch could also be wholly independent of his party. He had been close friends with Celler for more than a decade, and the two men had allied over civil rights legislation. McCullough had not only voted for the 1964 Civil Rights Act and the 1965 Voting Rights Act but had also given impassioned speeches in the House encouraging Republicans to not to temporize the importance of equality by analogizing basic constitutional rights with their commitment to shrink the federal government's power over the states and municipalities. In 1967 he cosponsored Rogers's bill to federalize law enforcement in Mississippi in spite of the fact that most Republicans opposed the expansion of federal authority. When in December 1969 Nixon expressed a desire to not extend the Voting Rights Act for another five years, McCulloch dissented and pushed congressional Republicans to oppose the president. According to Majority Leader Carl Albert, McCulloch was the Republican that Democrats in the House most respected, even though he was an anti–New Deal conservative. On learning of McCulloch's appointment, Washington Democrat Thomas Foley lauded McCulloch as "a man of universal respectability and integrity." If Nixon and Ford were able to secure McCulloch's vote in favor of impeachment, this would send a powerful signal to the nation that Douglas's support for civil rights had not been a basis for impeachment. If McCulloch opposed impeachment, then Douglas's allies would have a further means to argue that Ford was motivated by politics rather than a respect for the law.[52]

Like many congressmen, constituents lobbied McCulloch to impeach Douglas. In 1969 as Ohio constituent wrote to McCulloch, "Since the Senate has such high standards for Supreme Court nominations, I would like to see you participate in an effort of impeach Douglas." McCulloch noncommittedly responded, "An investigation would be a most difficult and technical undertaking." On April 9, 1970, a petition of more than one hundred Ohioans insisted that McCulloch join with Wyman to impeach Douglas. The petitioners again received the same response on the difficulty of investigating a justice. McCulloch received dozens of constituent letters expressing the view that Douglas had invited socialism and communism, as well as crime, into the United States. Yet McCulloch delivered a calm and reasoned response to the writers. On April 21 he issued a press release expressing his confidence in Celler and promising his "objective consideration of evidence" before making a recommendation. "In view of the political whirlwind that surrounds this controversy, there arises the need for completely honest and impartial judgment," he concluded. After reading the press release, the Ohio supreme court's chief justice lauded McCulloch's "statesman-like" restraint.[53]

McCulloch supported Celler in several fundamentally important matters regarding Ford's allegations. For instance, he insisted that the twenty-one charges against Douglas in HR 922 were incorporated into HR 920, albeit in a different format. HR 920, however, did not adopt Ford's standards for impeachment, and implicit in this was Celler and McCulloch's agreement that traditional constitutional standards had to apply. Most of the charges in HR 920 accused Douglas of abandoning his duty of impartiality and accepting monies contrary to established law. However, one charge accused Douglas of undermining confidence in the federal government by publishing *Points of Rebellion*. A further charge involved an article that Douglas had authored in *Evergreen* magazine entitled "Redress and Revolution," which likewise was designed to erode confidence in the government. Another charge claimed that because Douglas served as the chairman of the executive committee of the CSDI, and that organization had sought relations with the Soviet Union and stoked campus unrest, he was responsible for the student unrest.

A separate charge involving Douglas and the CSDI claimed that during Pacem in Terris II, he tried to communicate with Ho Chi Minh without presidential sanction. The specific language of this charge was "the *Pacem in Terris,* to which Ho Chi Minh was publicly invited and all the while the United States was in midst of war in which the communists directed by the same Ho Chi Minh were killing American boys fighting to save South Vietnam the independence and freedom we had promised that Nation." In other words, the charge alleged that Douglas had tried to undermine the US government's promise to the people of South Vietnam. Douglas was also accused of undermining national security by publicly advocating that the government "recognize Red China" and by criticizing the government to Brazilian college students during a lecture in Rio de Janeiro. In regard to Douglas's position in the Parvin Foundation, HR 922 contained claims that Douglas had consorted with "gangsters" and had tried to reestablish the "leftist" Juan Bosch as president of the Dominican Republic. HR 920 did not include these two allegations in the same language as in HR 922, but the allegations were nonetheless incorporated into the investigation with slightly different wording.[54]

In addition to the charges contained in HR 922, Celler permitted other congressmen to add allegations against Douglas. On May 5 William Lloyd Scott forwarded several news stories critical of Douglas and suggested to Celler that the investigation call the reporters to testify. On May 11 Mississippi Democrat Jamie L. Whitten informed Celler that "there is a real connection between present considerations facing the country and actions of Justice Douglas and other judges." Virginia Democrat Watkins Moorman Abbitt insisted that Douglas was culpable in the decay of "social order" and that he "had convinced foreigners that the United States had been morally oppressive in its various policies." In addition to these new allegations, and perhaps providing circumstantial evidence of why Ford had lobbied for Hutchinson's appointment, Hutchinson alleged that on at least three occasions Douglas had violated the Logan Act. The Logan Act is designed not only to give the president a virtual monopoly over foreign policy but also to ensure that the United States does not become obligated to a foreign government or cause without the express command of the executive branch, tying the act to national security. Yet not once in the Logan Act's two centuries of existence has there ever been a successful prosecution of a violation. Mollenhoff promised Hutchinson information that Douglas had illicitly tried to gain a visa extension for an Iraqi Kurdish professor and that this constituted a Logan Act violation. Hutchinson in turn insisted on adding this "charge" to the investigation. It proved to be a foolish move.[55]

In one sense Celler satisfied Ford's, Wyman's, and Waggonner's demands. After all, the committee had determined to investigate each of the charges contained in HR 922 as well as open the investigation to other charges. What HR 920 did not permit was a bypassing of the Judiciary Committee to better Ford's chances of having articles of impeachment drafted for the full house to consider. Ford and his allies, however, professed their dissatisfaction with HR 920 and claimed that it did not contain all of their allegations against Douglas. Ford's chief complaint against HR 920 was that it did not incorporate his flexible standard for defining what constituted an impeachable offense. As late as July 29, 1970, he protested that HR 920 failed to mention the legal standard that the federal judiciary had to be held to higher standards than elected officials. However, by this time HR 920 and its commensurate investigation were well underway.[56]

Ford's Fourth Defeat: The Investigation Begins and Douglas Mounts a Defense

Moments after Ford, Waggonner, and Wyman left Congress, Douglas wrote to his former clerk, Charles Ares, that instead of retiring, he would fight Ford. By this time Ares had become the dean of the University of Arizona school of law. Many of Douglas's former clerks rallied to his defense. Jerome Falk wrote to Douglas, calling Ford and his allies "cretins," and promised that he would "be on the next plane." Falk, along with Warren Christopher, gathered nine other former clerks to strategize Douglas's defense. The former clerks were now law firm partners and professors. UCLA law professor Bernard Jacob, who had clerked for Douglas in 1960, expressed to Celler, "While there is room enough in this country, as Mr. Justice Douglas has always taught, for even the incoherent ideas which these gentlemen spread upon the Congressional record on April 15, 1970, Congress had to recognize Douglas's wit, insight, and courage that protected this country's proud tradition of freedom." Contemporaneously, University of Oregon professor Hans Linde, who had clerked for Douglas in 1950, drafted a letter to Celler expressing similar sentiments.[57]

By April 20 Douglas received hundreds of letters of support from across the country and as far away as Vietnam and Sweden. The letters came from university professors such as Wallace Caldwell from the State University of New York at Oswego, who praised Douglas's three-decades-long defense of the Bill of Rights. A student begged Douglas to "stand firm and not give into the forces of fascism now in our midst." A "housewife" professed her admiration for Douglas and accused Ford of being part of "a malicious group of petty men." The president of the Democratic Youth for Action told Douglas to "be proud of his friendship with Juan Bosch and stand up to Nixon, Ford, Southern strategists, and ultrarightists who would return to the past at the expense of your career." One person sent Justice Byron White a telegram insisting that he step down from the Court to defend Douglas. Douglas also received hundreds of telegrams. These messages empowered Douglas to fight. The writers not only had to take the time to compose their thoughts but also had to pay postage costs or Western Union telegram fees, which in 2018 dollars equated to $29 per telegram. Although the letters and telegrams came from working men and women, young men in fear of the draft, and parents who had lost a child in Vietnam or who had had children drafted into the military, one letter gave Douglas reason to believe that Congress would not side with Ford. Just as Oregon senator Robert Packwood had asked for an autographed copy of *Points of Rebellion,* his chief of staff conveyed to Douglas the senator's message: "Stick to your guns. The Stone Age guys in the past tried to impeach Socrates, Archimedes, and FDR—they weren't right then and they aren't right now!"[58]

Ford did not foresee that his attack would result in prominent members of the legal academy coming to Douglas's defense. Had he merely questioned Douglas's judicial ethics regarding financial relationships, the legal academy's response might have been tepid or even split. It was not only because Ford had aligned with Southern conservatives but also because a number of fringe organizations had rallied to him and he had refused to renounce them that the attacks from the legal academy resulted. On the morning of Ford's speech, Fred Rodell, Ford's former Yale Law School professor, in a *New York Times* editorial, argued that if Ford's "absurd" standard for impeachment was applicable to all federal judges, then both Haynsworth and Carswell should have been impeached after their failed nominations. Ford was apparently taken aback by Rodell's use of the word "absurd" and complained to his former professor. When Rodell challenged Ford to disavow extremist religious figures such as James Hargis in Arkansas, who claimed that Ford's campaign against Douglas was directed by God, Ford refused to distance himself from Hargis. While the impact of Christian evangelical leaders in Ford's efforts was minimal, the fact that leading evangelical ministers—such as the Los Angeles–based W. S. Birnie, who claimed that Douglas was "a communist bent on destroying Christianity" and that civil rights constituted "a sin," and James Hargis, who publicly professed similar allegations against Douglas— supported Ford enabled Douglas's supporters to paint Ford as allying with a fringe that did not adhere to constitutional principles such as racial equality. When Ford tried to defend his silence in regard to the two ministers as being an unfair criticism of the reasons underlying his effort against Douglas, Rodell characterized Ford's defense as "a new and rather whining letter from Gerry Ford." Douglas chuckled to his attorneys that Ford's allies would turn out to be his worst enemies. More importantly, Rodell's colloquy with Ford was a foreshadowing of how Douglas would be defended.[59]

On April 20, 1970, Emanuel Celler appointed Kenneth Harkins as the investigation's counsel. Harkins normally served as the chief counsel for the Antitrust Subcommittee, and he would later be appointed as a judge on the Federal Court of Claims. An army veteran who had fought at the Battle of the Bulge, Harkins had worked with Celler since 1955. Harkins was instrumental in the investigation's final conclusion that Douglas had not violated any laws or canons of ethics. In spite of this, in 1971 Nixon appointed Harkins to the federal bench. Three other attorneys served the investigation: Thomas Hutton, Franklin G. Polk, and Howard F. Fogt. Celler appointed Hutton and Polk, and McCulloch selected Fogt. Celler did not personally conduct the subcommittee's interviews, but he supervised the investigation.

Shortly after the investigation team was assembled, Fogt outlined to McCulloch a suggested legal framework for conducting the investigation. On the one hand, he noted to McCulloch that the House's role was not the equivalent of a trial, and therefore Douglas was not entitled to the Sixth Amendment's right of confrontation or the right to present a defense such as would have existed in a criminal trial. On the other hand, he cautioned, the House had a duty to ensure that it remained impartial and to provide to Douglas all evidence it obtained in the course of its investigation. Thus, the Republican counsel agreed that the House had to consider whatever evidence Douglas provided to the investigation. Fogt's advice to McCulloch was sound, but it would later result in Ford's accusing the investigation of giving Douglas undue influence in the outcome. It is ironic that Ford's accusations against the subcommittee giving Douglas too much influence in the investigation's outcome originated in a bipartisan agreement between the subcommittee and the investigators to permit this to occur.[60]

One week after Ford's speech Douglas informed Celler that he had retained Simon Rifkind, a longtime friend, as his counsel. Rifkind was born in Russia in 1901 and immigrated with his parents to New York nine years later. After graduating from the City College of New York, he attended Columbia University's law school and entered the bar in 1925. Rifkind was a consummate New Dealer who assisted in drafting the National Industrial Recovery Act. In 1941 Roosevelt appointed him as a judge on the United States District Court for the District of New York. But by 1950 Rifkind had become bored with being a judge and left his judicial position to form a law firm. In 1980 Douglas publicly lauded Rifkind as the greatest litigator of their generation. Interestingly, Rifkind had testified in the same Senate investigation as Acheson and opposed any new laws designed to limit a judge's extrajudicial activities. Douglas asked Rifkind to see if his former clerks Vern Countryman, a Harvard law professor, and William Cohen, a Stanford law professor, would join his defense team, as well as former senator Wayne Morse. In a sense Rifkind's defense of Douglas would be partly based on arguing that Douglas had comported his behavior to the requirements of a status quo.[61]

Although Cohen, Countryman, and Morse were unavailable to serve as defense counsel, after Douglas retained Rifkind he added Warren Christopher, Clark Clifford, Gerald Stern, and William Ramsey Clark to his defense. These five men formed a formidable team with powerful political connections. Clifford had intermittently served in Democratic administrations, beginning with his tenure as a White House attorney under Truman and continuing as a member of the Presidential Intelligence Advisory Board under Kennedy and as secretary of defense in Johnson's last year. Clark, the son of a former Supreme Court justice, had served as attorney general in the last two years of the Johnson administration. Christopher was Douglas's clerk in 1949 and served as deputy attorney general under Johnson. In 1962 Douglas lobbied California governor Edmund G. Brown to appoint Christopher to the state supreme court: "He is unusually able, young, and industrious and a person of the highest character," Douglas penned. "But equally important, he has a liberal progressive outlook on law and is not wedded to the clichés of bygone days." In 1977 President James Earl "Jimmy" Carter appointed Christopher as deputy secretary of state, and in 1993 Christopher became secretary of state under President William Jefferson "Bill" Clinton. Stern worked in Fortas's former law firm and was a gifted litigator who had fought polluters in the federal courts. In 1994 Stern was appointed as a special counsel to prosecute the leaders of a prominent Middle Eastern bank. In essence Douglas was represented by a formidable team of Washington insiders. These men quickly debunked some of Ford's more egregious claims. For instance, Ford had insisted that Douglas's article praising folk music in *Avant Garde* constituted a personal relationship between the justice and Ginzburg. But Clark was able to point out that Douglas had sent the article to several magazines and had intended it as a dedication to musicians Pete Seeger and Joan Baez.[62]

Douglas spent the first month of the investigation scouring his files and contacting former clerks and office personnel who could assist in compiling evidence for his defense. His former clerks included prominent Washington, DC, lawyers, professors of law, and politicians such as LeRoy Collins, who had served as Florida's governor from 1955 through 1960. Collins offered to lobby Florida's democrats to side with Douglas. He also noted to his daughter that he had to be cautious in answering "an avalanche of mail," even though most of it was supportive. The one bright spot for Douglas was that Ford's attack had resulted in increased sales for *Points of Rebellion*.[63]

The investigation's first action was to contact Albert Parvin and request that he provide all correspondence, memoranda, and records of telephone conversations between Douglas and the ranking members of the foundation held in Parvin's possession. The investigation also sought a full list of the foundation's activities as well the foundation's relationship to the CSDI. Finally, the investigation wanted access to the foundation's finances as well as the sources of Douglas's income. Four days after receiving the investigation's request, Joseph A. Ball, an attorney retained by Parvin, responded that all of the material the investigation sought was in Rifkind's possession and that he would provide these materials to Harkins. Celler was unhappy with permitting Rifkind to become the source of material because he represented Douglas; at a minimum this would create an appearance that Douglas controlled the investigation. Ball acquiesced to Celler's concerns and arranged for the investigators to travel to Los Angeles to review the foundation's legal and tax records.[64]

On May 18 the investigation interviewed Robert Baker, who conceded that he had been in the Dominican Republic with Edward Levinson for Juan Bosch's inauguration in 1962. However, Baker insisted that he had not seen or interacted with Douglas on that trip. The investigation would later be able to conclude that Ford's allegations against Douglas in regard to influencing Bosch at the behest of gambling interests were meritless, and in fact Douglas had traveled to the Dominican Republic in a semiofficial capacity at a different time. In essence, Douglas was no more guilty of consorting with Baker than would be two random American travelers to London who happened to arrive and depart from that city within the same week. Ford's source for this allegation was William Wilson; problematically, Wilson had based the allegation on nothing more than the State Department's passport records.[65]

On May 20, 1970, Sherman Skolnick wrote to Celler that he had evidence that Douglas had failed to recuse himself from appeals involving Parvin. Skolnick believed that E. J. Albright, one of Senator Williams's informants, could tie Douglas to appeals arising from real estate cases in Chicago in which Parvin had interests. In the end this allegation came to nothing. Skolnick also alleged that because Parvin's hotels had purchased ice-making machines from an Albright competitor, Douglas had a duty to recuse himself from any appeals brought by Albright or the rival company. When on June 5 the investigation traveled to Chicago to interview Skolnick, it became clear that although Skolnick might have information regarding Judge Campbell, he had little to offer the investigation on Douglas. More tellingly, Skolnick used the investigation's presence as a means to draw media attention to his own efforts. The committee report later commented that when the investigators arrived at Skolnick's residence, they were greeted by "news reporters and TV photographers" who were there by Skolnick's invitation. Once inside Skolnick's residence, the investigators concluded he was "disorganized and confusing." At the conclusion of the interview, the investigators asked Skolnick to provide a narrative statement, but as of December 3, 1970—the day the subcommittee voted on closing the investigation—he had resisted doing so.

In the end, whatever evidence Skolnick may have possessed regarding Douglas did not affect the investigation.[66]

The same day the investigation discovered that there was no existence of a tie between Baker and Levinson on the one side, and Bosch and Douglas on the other, they received the first of several competing memoranda between Rifkind and two Detroit-based attorneys that Ford had retained. Rifkind's key argument was that although a federal judge could be impeached if he had committed acts of judicial misconduct while serving in a judicial capacity, in order to impeach a judge for extrajudicial conduct—that is, conduct that occurred in the judge's personal life—the House would have to find that the judge had actually committed a crime. Rifkind cited several examples in making this argument. The most prominent incident had to do with the impeachment of Judge Robert Archbald in 1912. Archbald had purchased coal-laden properties at discounted prices from railroad litigants appearing in his court in exchange for issuing favorable rulings to the railroads. Senator Elihu Root presided over Archbald's impeachment trial; he insisted that in pressuring the railroad litigants to sell him discounted property, Archbald had committed a crime. Specifically, Archbald committed the federal offense of extortion.[67]

Rifkind promised to cooperate with the investigation and attached over six hundred documents to his memorandum, including correspondence between Douglas and Parvin, minutes from Parvin Foundation and CSDI meetings, and information critical to defeating the allegation that Douglas had conducted legal work for either group. Rifkind added at the beginning of his letter that his "exhaustive inquiry vindicated [his] faith in the character and integrity of the man who in the 1920's helped revitalize legal education in the United States, who in the 1930's helped reform the nation's securities and bankruptcy laws and their administration, and who in the past thirty years has participated in the effort to give genuine meaning to a Bill of Rights which too often in the past was honored more in the breach than in the observance." Implicit in Rifkind's memoranda was a future political defense strategy of portraying Douglas as a target of Nixon's assault on individual rights.[68]

Rifkind next defended Douglas's writings, accusing Ford and his supporters of taking passages from *Points of Rebellion* in order to decontextualize the book's overall theme for nefarious reasons. Ford's accusation that Douglas had attempted to foment an antigovernment revolution made Rifkind's counterargument easy. The passages Ford selected as examples of Douglas's unfitness for continued service were isolated from their full meaning. For instance, Ford alleged that Douglas had insisted the federal government was controlled by "special interests" that "perpetuated tyranny and oppression." But Rifkind reminded the investigation that the paragraph preceding that passage stated that this was merely a belief of "the coming generation." Rifkind went on to point out that in 1962 President Kennedy had warned South American governments that when a government suppresses dissent, violence is often the result, and that in 1920 Felix Frankfurter had espoused the same caution. Moreover, he reminded the investigation that Wallace Hickel, Nixon's secretary of the Interior, had publicly recognized that the country's youth believed they were deprived of their political voice. Finally, Rifkin insisted that Douglas's concurrence in *Illinois v. Allen* proved that *Points of Rebellion* consisted of warnings rather than a call to arms. Although as earlier noted Burger and the other conservative justices worried that Douglas would dissent from the decision, instead Douglas concurred with the admonition that "the social compact calls for tolerance, patience, and restraint, but not for sabotage and violence."[69]

Rifkind next turned to the question of whether Douglas would have to recuse himself from decisions arising from challenges to national security. If, Rifkind reasoned, many distinguished judges in the twentieth century had made public speeches on matters such as equality under the law, segregation in schools, or the parameters of free speech, then recusal would be the required norm. Yet when Justice Louis Brandeis criticized the effect of big business on democracy, or when Judge Learned Hand had written a treatise that became the definitive statement on the right of free speech, neither of them recused himself from appeals involving these issues. Rifkind juxtaposed Brandeis and Hand against the instances—more than a dozen of them—when Douglas had recused himself from the Court because he had a relationship to a party or had spoken publicly on a specific issue pending before the Court.

In terms of Douglas's relations to Ginzburg, Rifkind pointed out that while it was true that Douglas had written an article praising folk music in *Avant Garde*, there was no evidence that Douglas knew that Ginzburg owned this magazine. The $100 Douglas received for writing this article was too de minimis, Rifkind argued, to require that Douglas recuse himself from Ginzburg's appeals from either the libel case or the criminal conviction. And the fact that *Evergreen* had printed an excerpt from *Points of Rebellion* was not a product of Douglas's doing. Rather, Random House had permitted *Evergreen* to do so. Moreover, Douglas had not dissented alone. In both appeals he joined with Black and Stewart in his dissents. These dissents were merely reflective of Douglas consistently placing greater protection on free speech than many of his contemporaries. Finally, Rifkind pointed out that no comprehensive set of rules existed governing recusal, except where a judge had a direct financial interest in the outcome or had participated in the trial in some capacity. Because Deputy Attorney Kleindeinst had defended Harry Blackmun against the allegation that he had sat on three appeals involving parties in which he had a minor stock interest, and because Rehnquist had argued that Clement Haynsworth's ties to a vending machine company were too tangential to require recusal, Rifkind argued it was clear that Douglas's onetime payment of $100 passed ethical muster. Besides, Douglas did not own any stocks of corporate holdings.[70]

Rifkind was next able to debunk Ford's two most serious allegations: that Douglas had engaged in legal work for the Parvin Foundation by drafting its articles of incorporation and then by providing tax advice to its members. In 1961 Parvin's attorney, Victor Mindlin, drafted the foundation's incorporation articles and oversaw its tax compliance. Judge Campbell signed the articles in Mindlin's presence alongside Douglas. From that point forward, Rifkind insisted, the evidence clearly showed that Douglas and Campbell had stayed away from any legal oversight of the foundation. When in 1969 the IRS threatened to revoke the foundation's tax-exempt status, Parvin retained Agger as the foundation's counsel. Douglas's opponents used the fact that Agger—Fortas's wife—had at one time defended Robert Baker to prove a link between Douglas and Baker. Once more, Rifkind noted that Kleindienst had recently defended Blackmun's status as a board member of the Mayo Clinic as well as the fact that Blackmun had received more than $8,500 in executor's fees for managing the wills and trusts of his friends. Moreover, Rifkind reminded the subcommittee, Burger also served on the Mayo Clinic's board, and historically other justices had likewise engaged in extrajudicial activities, such as Chief Justice Harlan Stone's serving on the board of a New York foundation and Justice Owen Roberts's chairing an investigation into the Japanese attack on Pearl Harbor.

Rifkind easily attacked Ford's other allegations, such as the allegedly criminal source of the Parvin Foundation's funding. Rifkind contextualized Parvin's casino ownership by pointing out that several insurance companies and pension funds also held shares in casinos. So too did millionaires Howard Hughes and Kirk Kerkorian. In terms of Douglas's relationship to the Dominican Republic, Rifkind showed that Douglas had traveled to the island nation with Parvin, but for the purposes of overseeing a literacy project, and at no time was Baker with them. This project had the full support not only of the Dominican Republic's government under Bosch but also of the US ambassador as well as President Kennedy. While it was true that Douglas received $12,000 per year for his work with the foundation, Rifkind pointed out that because Douglas had never claimed any travel expenses or reimbursements for hiring assistants, the $12,000 was truly a stipend, and Douglas did not materially benefit from it. As for Douglas's role in the CSDI, Rifkind noted that two former presidents had taken part in its activities. Finally, Rifkind debunked the charge that Douglas had consorted with "underworld" figures. While it was true that Parvin's company owned several casinos, not once had the government pursued criminal charges against Parvin. Rifkind ended his memoranda with an admonition that legislators who made false allegations against other government officers should be held to a standard akin to disbarment. That is, if the allegations were proved false, then the legislators should be prohibited from drafting legislation.

Rifkind's memorandum infuriated Ford, Waggonner, Wyman, and several other legislators, each of whom protested what they believed to be a threat of their removal from Congress. In reality Rifkind had simply outclassed them. His memorandum was not only a thorough refutation of Ford's allegations but also contained a constitutional and legal analysis that was difficult to counter, particularly in regard to the legal standard required for the House to vote for impeachment. Equally importantly, Rifkind produced a volume of documentary material that undermined several of Ford's remaining allegations regarding Douglas's role in the formation of the foundation as well as the management of the foundation's finances.[71]

Although the investigation had been planned to end on August 24, the investigation's staff realized that far more time was required, and on June 20 Celler requested an additional sixty days to investigate the charges against Douglas. The Judiciary Committee voted to grant this request four days later.

In response, Waggonner insisted once more that the investigation be handed over to Colmer and the Rules Committee, but without explaining why the Rules Committee would proceed more rapidly. Celler, however, was able to explain to the House that the main reason for seeking the extension was a lack of cooperation from the executive branch itself. He had contacted to Nixon and on June 2 had gained Nixon's promise of full cooperation from the Internal Revenue Service, the CIA, the State Department, the FBI, and the attorney general. If Douglas had broken any laws or undermined national security, then ostensibly these agencies would have some information. Yet as of July 1 none of these agencies had provided the investigation with any material on Douglas.[72]

Douglas actively participated in constructing counterattacks against Ford's allegations. For instance, Ramsey Clark was in charge of developing defenses against the charge that Douglas had profited from his relationship with Ginzburg, and on April 30 Douglas informed Clark that he had withdrawn from cases in which he knew a litigant and the litigant had inadvertently informed him of the pending appeal. On May 5 he provided examples to Clark of his ethical conduct as a justice. He claimed that when he initially joined the Court, he had sought out Justice Louis Brandeis's advice on when it was necessary to recuse from a pending case. Douglas adopted Brandeis's position that the financial amount in an interest was irrelevant to judicial disqualification because "a $1000 interest in one litigant may be as important to one judge as a $500,000 interest would be to another." He then claimed that Brandeis instructed him that the justices did not consider an interest in an insurance policy to be automatically disqualifying, but this was an exception to the general rule. Douglas informed Clark that in 1958 he had withdrawn from taking part in *Columbia Broadcasting System v. Loews* because a news reporter had approached him about the appeal. The issue in that appeal had to do with CBS's satirizing a Loews movie and with whether a copyright protected against parody. Douglas also noted that in 1968 he had withdrawn from *United States v. Southwestern Cable Corporation* because his son had an investment in a small cable television company in Los Angeles. Although his son's company was not a party to the litigation, the potential effect of the Court's decision on the burgeoning cable television industry could indirectly benefit his son. As it turned out, the Court, in a closely divided decision, ruled adversely to the cable television industry, indirectly to the detriment of his son.[73]

Douglas next approached the issue of Ford's charge that he was partisan by noting that justices had historically been accused of this conduct. For instance, Douglas pointed out, justices Stephen A. Field and Pierce Butler had served as attorneys for major railroads and then tended to side with railroad litigants over their adversaries. Yet Field and Butler sat on dozens of appeals where a railroad was a party. Douglas accused justices James Byrnes and Frederick Vinson with having "racist leanings," and he rightly claimed that justices Warren and Marshall had been noted for being pro–civil rights. All four of these justices decided civil rights cases. The simple facts that Justice Charles Evans Hughes had run for president and that justices Black and Sutherland had served in the Senate and "were identified with the burning issues of the day" did not mean that they were unqualified to serve on the Court. Moreover, in several matters neither Sutherland nor Black had recused themselves from appeals that arose from challenges to laws that they had earlier voted on in their legislative capacities.[74]

Douglas contrasted himself to his peers by noting that, with the exception of Frankfurter in one administrative law decision, he had recused himself from appeals in which he held strong political views. In *National City Bank v. Republic of China,* the newly created Taiwanese government under Chiang Kai-shek asserted a claim against an American bank to recover monies deposited by the prerevolutionary Chinese government. The bank countersued against a million-dollar default by the Chinese government with the argument that if the Republic of China in Taiwan could assert a claim against the bank for its predecessor government's monies, then it should also be held responsible for the predecessor's loan default. Douglas claimed his recusal from the appeal was based on his "deep-seated animosity to the Formosa regime on account of its corruption and its cruel oppression of civil rights."[75]

On May 7 Douglas drafted a legal brief for Clark's consideration. He began by dissecting the intent underlying 28 USC 455, a law that prohibited judges from serving on cases in which they held "a substantial interest in" or were "connected with" one of the parties. The statute did not define either "substantial interest" or the degree to which a judge might be "connected" to one of the parties. However, he pointed out that his interests and connections with Ginzburg were far less than Haynsworth's interests and connections in the *Darlington* decision. Douglas tried to prove that he had acted cautiously in regard to conflicts of interest and used his two-decade-long relationship with *Look Magazine* and its publisher, Cowles Brothers, as an example. "My relationship with the Cowles Company and with *Look* has been so close that I recused myself from all Cowles cases," Douglas insisted. In contrast, he reminded Clark, he had occasionally written articles for the *New York Times* "at the going rate" of "between $150 and $300—somewhere in that zone," but he "had not hesitated to sit in a *New York Times* case." To Douglas, the $300 payment from Ginzburg for his *Avant Garde* article fell squarely in line with his work for the *New York Times*. In other words, Cowles, which had paid for three of Douglas's trips to Asia and published several articles and books, could be interpreted as having an ongoing financial relationship with Douglas. In contrast, neither the *New York Times* nor Ginzburg fell into this category because Douglas had only written occasional articles and had received individual small sums of money. Douglas also argued that he had no role in Random House's permission for Ginzburg to publish an excerpt from *Points of Rebellion* in *Evergreen* magazine, and explained that his decision to publish articles in *Playboy* was not to strengthen the pornography industry but rather "to reach young people, particularly on conservation."[76]

Two weeks after giving Clark his appraisals of Ford's allegation that he had violated 28 USC 455, Douglas provided Clark a list of protest activities that he and his fourth wife had involved themselves in. He admitted to attending a public protest against sewage dumping in Boston in 1964, a "protest hike" in against the Kennecott Copper Company's attempts to open in the North Cascade Mountains in 1967, and eleven other public protests against actions likely to degrade the environment. He also called Congressman Wyman's claim that he had raised funds for Senator Ernest Gruening's failed reelection campaign a lie.[77]

Two months after assisting Clark to build a defense against Ford's claims that he had been politically motivated, or had failed to recuse himself from appeals in violation of law or the canons of ethics, he responded to Skolnick's assertion that he had failed to disqualify himself from serving on three appeals to the Court. Douglas recognized that he and Campbell were "old, old friends" and had served on the foundation's board together, but he stated that they "never had any business relationships of any kind." Moreover, no party had challenged Douglas from serving on the appeal arising from Skolnick's demand that Campbell recuse himself from the three-judge panel deciding whether Cook County's voting districts favored the wealthy suburbs and disadvantaged Chicago's voters. The first time Douglas heard of Skolnick's allegation was when the subcommittee investigation determined that it was of interest to them.[78]

The Volatile World of Nixon

In several ways beyond the Cambodian invasion, Nixon contributed to Ford's early defeat. On April 16, 1970, according to John Ehrlichman, Nixon informed his staff that Ford's efforts were likely to fail because Speaker of the House McCormack would block any investigation against Douglas. Perhaps for this reason Nixon did not overtly support Ford, and his behind-the-scenes efforts only emboldened the judiciary and media to come to Douglas's defense. On the day of Carswell's defeat in the Senate, H. R. Haldeman instructed White House Staff assistant Jeb Stuart Magruder to "keep the heat on the [*Washington*] *Post, Time,* and *Life* regarding both Carswell and their decision to come out against Mitchell." In addition, Magruder was directed to compare Douglas with Carswell and Haynsworth, with the admonition that if either of Nixon's nominees was unfit to serve on the Court, then Douglas failed judicial standards. None of the magazine editors followed Magruder's lead.[79]

On April 16 the president of WETA, a Washington, DC, television station, terminated a journalist's employment after Attorney General John Mitchell's office hired the journalist's wife as an assistant. One week later, Congressman Dan Kuykendall, a Tennessee Republican and strong supporter of the administration, objected to the firing during a congressional speech. This story, in light of all of the other news, was nothing more than a *Washington Post* paragraph, but Haldeman believed that it could be used to put California senator Alan Cranston on the defensive. The wife of Cranston's chief of staff worked at WETA, and the administration tried to tar Cranston with the brush of being the beneficiary of a liberal double standard. To this end, Haldeman assigned both Deputy Assistant to the President for Congressional Relations Lyn Nofziger and Mollenhoff to damage Cranston through a public relations campaign to prevent either WETA or Cranston from coming to Douglas's defense or criticizing the Cambodian invasion. The public relations campaign failed to curb either the station or Cranston.[80]

The administration's most appalling conduct was its effort to threaten Earl Warren against protecting Douglas. Nixon worried that Warren would try to publicly defend Douglas or admonish the government that the Cambodian invasion was unlawful. To this end Nixon turned to Rehnquist to draft a statement that any public pronouncement from Earl Warren on either Douglas or Cambodia would violate judicial ethics. Rehnquist drafted a brief synopsis on how the judicial ethics canons continued to apply to retired justices; he argued that because Warren could serve on future trials and appeals, there was an absolute prohibition against the former chief justice from engaging in "political activity." The memorandum had no effect on Warren. Indeed, the former chief justice would later assist a California Republican to counter Ford's allegations and assist Celler.[81]

The morning after Nixon announced that military forces had entered Cambodia, Attorney General John Mitchell spoke at a Law Day luncheon in Washington, DC, and warned that "irresponsible and malicious criticism of the Court" endangered constitutional liberty by undermining the people's confidence in the federal judiciary. Mitchell appeared to support some of the Court's decisions limiting the scope of police conduct and concluded that "responsible citizens supported the principles behind the Court's rulings on desegregation, obscenity, reapportionment and separation of church and state." The New York Times headlined Mitchell's speech on its front page between two reports on the Cambodian invasion. Mitchell did not mention Douglas by name, but people who listened to his speech or who later read about it might have believed that the speech was an effort to defuse the impeachment investigation.[82]

On May 6 the Grand Rapids Free Press, Ford's hometown newspaper, thanked Mitchell and surmised that he had aimed this comment directly at Ford. Although the Free Press generally backed Ford, it opposed the impeachment efforts and noted that the Court was "determined that the least of us are protected through a series of decisions pertaining to the individual's rights while in the custody of the police or in court." Mitchell, of course, did not intend to oppose Ford. Instead he lauded Ford's efforts against Douglas. After Ford read the editorial and queried Mitchell on why he had made the speech, Mitchell wrote to the editors that his speech was "not intended to make any judgment as to whether Representative Ford's activities are anything but the responsible type of activities he has engaged in in the past." Thus, although Mitchell made it clear to Ford that the administration had not retreated from its desire to remove Douglas, the nation did not know this.[83]

Nixon's actions toward Republicans who disagreed with him undermined both the Cambodia invasion and Ford's efforts against Douglas. On April 29 New York City's Republican mayor, John Lindsay, warned Nixon against sending forces into Cambodia and accused the administration of weakening "faith in the judicial system." Lindsay's comments demonstrated a lack of Republican unity on either the Cambodia invasion or the attempted impeachment against Douglas; Nixon's response highlighted a willingness to have the Republican Party shed any pretense of moderation. By the end of the first week of the Cambodian invasion, Nofziger urged Haldeman to begin a public campaign "inviting Lindsay to leave the party." Nofziger concluded, "I think Middle America would be well-pleased and well-served," by removing liberal Republicans from the party."[84]

5

The House of Representatives
Responds to Ford and the
Cambodian Invasion

One day after Ford's speech, North Carolina Democrat Roy Taylor accused Douglas of "pouring oil on the fires of civil unrest by publishing a book advocating rebellion and revolution." Contemporaneously, Georgia Democrat Maston Emmett O'Neal Jr. introduced HR 924, requiring the Speaker of the House to appoint a special subcommittee comprising six congressmen with both parties evenly represented. Elected to the House in 1965, O'Neal was openly honest in his reasons for seeking a Rules Committee takeover. He admitted to prejudging the result of any investigation before all of the evidence could be analyzed; he explained that he wanted Celler removed from the investigation to reduce the possibility of Northern liberals absolving Douglas. He also noted that Douglas was a threat to the national security. "In my opinion, Justice Douglas is an evil man and one of the most dangerous in America," he argued. "His behavior has been far from 'good' as required by the Constitution, and I think he should go to trial for it." The same day O'Neal filed HR 924, he also cosponsored HR 925 with William Nichols, an Alabama Democrat. By joining with Joseph Waggonner, L. Mendel Rivers, and F. Edward Hebert in contending that Douglas was a threat to national security, O'Neal, Nichols, and Taylor became an integral part of Ford's Deep South alliance against Douglas.[1]

Notwithstanding Ford's failure to have the Rules Committee take control of the investigation, in order to have a hope of success, the anti-Douglas forces would have to ensure that the alliance of conservative Republicans and Southern legislators operated in lockstep;

Ford would also have to add other Democrats. On April 15, 1970, there were 192 Republicans and 243 Democrats in the House. Of this number there were eighty-nine Southern Democrats, including those elected from the Southern periphery states of Texas, Arkansas, West Virginia, Missouri, Kentucky, Maryland, and Florida. However, some of the Democratic congressmen in these periphery states embraced the Great Society, and a group of the older representatives had come into office in support of the New Deal. They would not uniformly support the impeachment campaign. In addition to the difficulty of getting more than the half of the House to support him, Ford had another problem. The demographic alignments in his efforts were visible from the start. Not one of the House's nine African American congressmen backed Ford; nor did any of the House's four Hispanic congressmen, including Republican Manuel Lujan from New Mexico. All of the seven congresswomen, including the three Republicans, Massachusetts's Margret Heckler, New Jersey's Florence Price Dwyer, and Washington's Catherine Dean May, refused to sign a resolution and informed their constituents that Ford was in the wrong. Ford's allies consisted of white men who were politically conservative, anti–civil rights reactionaries, or both.[2]

Ford needed Northern and Midwestern Democrats to join in his efforts for another reason. The House minority leader's alliance with congressmen who had signed the Southern Manifesto threatened to tar the impeachment attempt as a constitutionally ignorant assault on civil rights. The Southern signatories to HR 922 and the other resolutions often evidenced an outright hatred for African Americans. In addition to prosegregationist William Lloyd Scott of Virginia, who had been elected on an anti–civil rights platform and who infamously attributed the need for zip codes to alleged African American illiteracy, other Southern signatories to the various resolutions included opponents of the 1964 Civil Rights Act, such as Florida's Robert Sikes, Louisiana's Speedy Long, Georgia's George Eliot Hagan, Alabama's Walter Flowers, North Carolina's Roy Taylor, Mississippi's Gillespie Montgomery, and Virginia's Wilbur "Dan" Daniel. Anti–civil rights men who supported Ford were not relegated to the South. Oklahoman John Jarman and Ohioan John Ashbrook opposed federal laws to ensure equality and sought Douglas's impeachment.[3]

Ford would have difficulties in the House beyond allying with Southern segregationists. Among liberal Democrats there was a consensus that civil and individual rights were under increased threat, and Douglas was the Court's leading guardian of these rights. On May 9, 1969, Democratic congresswoman Patsy Mink of Hawaii informed her constituents that she "would continue to do all in [her] power to protect our individual freedoms." This promise meant protecting Douglas against Ford and Nixon. In addition to the general belief that Ford's campaign against Douglas was a small part of a greater Nixon administration attack on individual freedom, liberals and moderates doubted the trustworthiness of Nixon's administration. In late April, Secretary of State William Rogers testified to the House Appropriations Committee that no decisions had been made in regard to sending the US military into Cambodia and Laos, and he assured the committee that the administration would consult with Congress before commencing any military actions in either country. Because neither the congressmen on the Appropriations Committee nor Rogers knew of Nixon's plans, when on April 30 Nixon announced that military forces had entered Cambodia, it was unsurprising that Republican Paul McCloskey from California and Democrat Clarence Dickinson Long from Maryland excoriated Rogers for lying to them.[4]

Gerald Ford v. Carl Albert

By the time Ford demanded Douglas's impeachment, Speaker of the House John J. McCormack's long congressional tenure was at an end. Elected to the House in 1928, he had steadily risen in leadership positions until he became majority leader in 1940. For twenty-two years after becoming majority leader, McCormack labored as a loyal understudy to Speaker Sam Rayburn until Rayburn's death in 1962. Although McCormack had been a loyal New Dealer and civil rights advocate, because of his support for Johnson's Vietnam policies, a younger generation of Democratic Party representatives determined to remove him from the speakership and nominated Arizonan Morris K. Udall as a challenger. McCormack handily defeated Udall in late 1969, but his campaign to retain power was difficult, and he announced his plans to retire after the 1970 election. He also handed House Majority Leader Carl Albert the power to schedule House debates and voting. McCormack's congressional tenure was at an end not only because of his age but also because his chief of staff and a longtime friend had used his office letterhead to try to convince the Securities

and Exchange Commission not to investigate the Parvin-Dohrmann Corporation. After Parvin had sold his company, its public stock price soared above
its real value, and a number of investors, including the actress Jill St. John, lost
fortunes. On November 29, 1969, the *New York Times* accused McCormack of
being "derelict in his duties" for permitting his office to be used in this manner, and on January 18, 1970, McCormack announced his retirement. Neither
the *Times* nor Ford argued that a connection between McCormack and Parvin
proved that the foundation or Douglas were corrupt.[5]

Although McCormack had initially been effective in keeping Colmer's
committee from taking over the investigation by having Andrew Jacobs introduce HR 920 before any of the other resolutions were filed, it was Albert
who was instrumental in protecting Douglas from Ford by keeping the Judiciary Committee in charge of the investigation throughout the spring and
summer of 1970. Known as "the little giant," Albert was diminutive in size
but was well respected as a tough majority leader who brought Democratic
Party liberals and conservatives together on budgetary issues. Albert voted
in favor of the 1964 Civil Rights Act and the 1965 Voting Rights Act. Like
McCormack, he supported Johnson's Vietnam policies, and he did not oppose Vietnamization. His only opposition to the Court's civil rights decisions had to with busing students as a desegregation measure, which he called
"social rather than judicial judgments." Albert was also the only member of
Oklahoma's congressional delegation not to sign a resolution for Douglas's
impeachment. And although he and Ford were friends, he both trusted and
admired Celler.[6]

When in late March 1970 McCormack announced his intention to retire,
all three of the Democrats investigating Douglas pledged their support for
Albert to advance to the speakership. A coalition of "hard hat"—construction and heavy manufacturing industry constituencies—Northern and Midwestern Democrats also supported Albert. His two main rivals were Wilbur
Mills, an anti–civil rights Democrat from Arkansas who chaired the House
Ways and Means Committee, and Udall. Waggonner and Abernethy promised Mills their votes, but by the middle of April, Mills disclaimed interest in
leaving his committee to become Speaker. Udall's support was limited to a
small number of newer Democrats, and he lacked committee leadership experience. Albert's control over the House was such that he determined when
a resolution would be open to debate or a vote. At no time did he permit a

challenge to HR 920 to be debated; instead he held firm that Celler's committee was to remain the sole overseer of investigation into Douglas. In spite of Albert's unyielding refusal to permit Ford and the Southern Democrats to commandeer the investigation away from Celler, several Southerners, such as Tom Bevill of Alabama, backed his ascension to become Speaker well before the investigation concluded. To Southerners the Douglas impeachment was important, but there were other considerations, and Albert's defense of Douglas did not detract from his effectiveness in obtaining government expenditures for regional projects or his ability to command from the political center. To party conservatives he was a better choice than the liberal Udall, and backing Albert also prevented the Republican minority from elevating a Speaker that the a majority of the Democrats opposed.[7]

Albert proved his toughness in another way. Although the majority of his constituents favored impeaching Douglas, disliked the Court's civil rights decisions, and believed the Court was soft on communism and crime, this did not alter his position of keeping Celler in charge of the investigation. "I hope you will do everything in your power to help impeach Justice William O. Douglas," wrote one constituent. "I feel he is one of the most extreme persons in the US and is one of the reasons we have so much disrespect for our way of life." Another constituent accused Douglas of being "an old sex maniac and a communist" before imploring Albert to "rid the Court of the Justice." Not all of the writers sided with Ford. One writer from California implored Albert to "please use your power to help tell the country how rotten Ford's political ploy is, and to counter it." Albert drafted a singular response to both Douglas's detractors and supporters. While he insisted that the Judiciary Committee's investigation was consistent with the House's rules, he stressed his trust in both Celler and McCulloch before promising that he would withhold his vote until reviewing the evidence the investigation produced. Until the final report's publication, Albert did not call a House vote any vote or debate on the other resolutions.[8]

The Cambodian Invasion, Days of Rage, and Ford's Failed Hard Hat Foray

By 1970 a majority of Americans wanted the United States to exit Vietnam, but this did not mean they supported antiwar demonstrations or the counterculture movement. A recent study on the foreign relations of the United States notes that one of the lessons of Lieutenant William Calley's court-martial for his role in the My Lai massacre is that opponents of the war did not constitute a clear-cut majority. Calley had commanded soldiers in one of the most heinous war crimes ever committed by US military forces. His soldiers murdered more than three hundred innocent villagers, including children, and the ensuing coverup by senior army officers added to a growing belief that the nation was involved in a lawless war. The army court-martialed Calley and sentenced him to life in prison, but letters demanding Calley's exoneration poured in from all parts of the country. This contributed to Nixon's insistence that not only were critics of the war more vocal than the "silent majority," but they also constituted a danger to the United States' continuing status as a superpower. While the antiwar movements may have been a vocal minority, Nixon misjudged their ability to affect the government. By May 1 it became apparent that the vocal minority had the capability to deliver a socially and politically powerful response to the Cambodian invasion, and that in terms of news reporting, the invasion would eclipse the investigation into Douglas.[9]

On May 1, 1970, the *New York Times* lead headline blazed, "Nixon Sends Combat Troops to Cambodia to Drive Communists from Staging Zone." Beneath this headline were reports of a clash at Ohio State University between antiwar students and national guardsmen, as well as a pending Black Panther demonstration in New Haven for which the Connecticut governor had asked Attorney General John Mitchell for army protection. In addition to news reporting on the grand jury investigating Mary Jo Kopechne's death and a court-ordered injunction against a potential New York City police "work stoppage," the *Times*'s front page also informed its readers that Nixon had briefed "key congressmen" before the invasion. The *Times* did not list all of the congressmen Nixon had briefed, but it did report that New York Republican Ogden Reid had introduced an amendment to cut off all funding for the Cambodian operation. Although Reid was a newer legislator, having been elected to the House in 1962, his family owned several newspapers, and he had served as President Eisenhower's ambassador to Israel. In turn, Ford asked the House to delay voting on Reid's amendment until after Nixon explained his reasons for the invasion. Reid's action highlighted that Ford's own party was not uniformly aligned with him in either his attack on Douglas or the Cambodian operation. It also evidenced that the Republican minority leader was unable to focus the House's attentions on Douglas's alleged wrongdoings.[10]

On May 4, 1970, Ohio national guardsmen killed four Kent State University students and injured nine others while the students were demonstrating against the Cambodian invasion. Across the nation more than four million students walked out of their university classes, and several occupied campus administrative offices. High schools also experienced student strikes. Fringe antigovernment groups bombed ROTC buildings and police stations. On May 8, 100,000 demonstrators coalesced in Washington, DC, and Nixon's security team concluded that the president's life was in danger. In response, the army increased its presence in the capital. Seven days later, police in Mississippi opened fire at protesting students at Jackson State University. This time two students were killed and twelve injured.[11]

There was, however, opposition to the antiwar movement. The same day as the massive demonstrations in Washington, DC, and other cities, a group of construction workers belonging to the Building and Trades Council Union in New York assaulted antiwar demonstrators in downtown Manhattan. This incident—which became known as the Hard Hat Riot—was triggered by construction workers becoming enraged after Mayor John Lindsay ordered the city government's flags to be flown at half mast in response to the Kent State shootings. Union leaders accused the mayor of siding with communists. The unions had resisted racial integration, and a sizable minority of New York City's protesters were African Americans who challenged the nation's political leaders that a military induction system that forced them to fight in Vietnam in greater proportions than it did whites was inherently undemocratic. While no antiwar demonstrators were killed in New York, violence being perpetrated by people on both the right and left fringes appeared uncontainable. Douglas had warned that violence would increase because people who were certain of their inherited status were fearful that people who had finally achieved equal rights posed a threat. "The release of the Blacks from the residual institutions of slavery has filled many white communities with fear, and the backlash has had profound political consequences," he observed.[12]

Although from the outset the smaller-than-hoped-for numbers of signatories to HR 920, HR 922, and HR 924 appeared to diminish the chance of impeachment, Douglas remained at risk; this was partly because of an unusual political dynamic in the industrial North and Midwest. Douglas personified the social upheaval that the hard hats detested. Congressmen backed by organized labor tended to support Nixon's Vietnamization policies and were aghast at the antiwar movement and counterculture. Yet they also realized that Douglas was the Court's longest-serving reliable ally of labor unions. Despite Douglas's repeated votes in favor of union actions, congressmen from districts weighted with industrial union votes had to balance laborers' support for the continued involvement in the Vietnam conflict, and their anger at both the social upheaval occurring on college campuses and the effect of civil rights in the workplace.

Daniel Rostenkowski serves as a case in point. Born in Chicago in 1928, he fought in the Korean War before being elected to Illinois legislature in 1952. Six years later he began a thirty-six-year tenure in the House of Representatives, representing a majority-white working-class constituency. In the early 1960s McCormack and Albert viewed him as a rising star. Rostenkowski supported Johnson's Vietnam escalation as well as Vietnamization. However, during the 1968 Chicago convention, he angered Albert and McCormack, and they stripped him of his committee assignments. When in 1969 Rostenkowski received letters from constituents asking him to work for Douglas's removal because "the justice was promoting anarchy and revolution," he thanked the writers for expressing their views rather than disagreeing with them.[13]

Rostenkowski was the type of Democratic congressman whom Nixon believed he could rely on for his "tough on crime" platform as well as for support for the Cambodian invasion. Rostenkowski informed his constituents that the Cambodian invasion could not "rightfully be characterized as an escalation of the war in Vietnam." Instead, he claimed, it was "a means whereby Vietnamization can be hastened and carried out with a minimum loss of American lives." Perhaps of greater value to Ford and Nixon regarding Douglas was that Rostenkowski had spoken in support of Clement Haynsworth, and had gone so far as to inform a local organization that "many of Haynsworth's accomplishments were very worthwhile, and I think had he been confirmed to the Supreme Court, he would have done an outstanding job." Rostenkowski responded to another constituent who hoped that he would side with Ford "so as to rid the Court of this patriot of anarchy";

the constituent could "be assured that I will keep your views in mind as the House debates this issue and that I will act in a manner compatible with the principles on which our democracy was founded." In spite of hopes that Rostenkowski and others like him would support Ford, this did not occur. At no time did Rostenkowski sign an anti-Douglas resolution or publicly speak against the justice.[14]

Like Rostenkowski, John J. Rooney represented a white working-class district, albeit in Queens, New York. His constituents included thousands of union construction workers who had attacked demonstrating college students during the Hard Hat Riot. Led by Peter J. Brennan, the Building and Construction Trades Council of Greater New York repeatedly endorsed Rooney since his first congressional election in 1944. Brenan also supported Nixon and later became his secretary of labor. Rooney, like Brennan, was an outspoken proponent of the United States' involvement in the Vietnam conflict. He was also a confidant of J. Edgar Hoover, and he only tepidly endorsed the 1964 Civil Rights Act and 1965 Voting Rights Act. Rooney was an outspoken anti-internationalist and tried to curb the State Department's budget. He claimed that programs such as Voice of America were useless in fighting communism and that only a large military was effective in safeguarding democracy. Other than a prounion record, Douglas had little in common with Rooney. Douglas's belief that diplomacy and the reduction of global poverty were the best weapons against communism were antithetical to Rooney. Yet Rooney was reluctant to join in the impeachment efforts and voiced his confidence in Celler. Other Democratic congressmen from hard hat constituencies such as Pittsburgh's William Moorhead and the Bronx's Mario Biaggi were likewise reluctant to join with Ford.[15]

In Detroit, Democrat Martha Wright Griffiths represented auto assembly workers. She received anti-Douglas mail throughout the investigation. She responded that the investigation would make its recommendations to the House and that she would have to wait to decide how to vote. In terms of Cambodia, after receiving hundreds of letters and petitions denouncing the invasion, she informed her constituents that it was imperative for Congress to bar the use of force in Cambodia and Vietnam because in addition to widening the war, Nixon had acted unconstitutionally. Pennsylvania Democrat Fred Rooney was also a hard hat. He represented a district populated by steel workers, and like Rostenkowski, he refused to join Ford. There was a critical aspect of Fred Rooney's conduct that did not catch Ford's attention. In the midst of the investigation, Rooney asked Douglas to preside over his daughter's wedding. Douglas responded that although he admired Rooney, beginning with Justice Holmes, the justices had concluded that they lacked the lawful authority to conduct marriage ceremonies. He also added that if he did perform the ceremony, "it might come back to haunt a lovely couple later on." Had Douglas presided over the wedding, it would have signaled that a prominent Northern hard hat Democrat had complete faith in the justice.[16]

Hard hat Democrats were not isolated to the industrial Northeast and Midwest. In California Jeffrey Cohelan represented Berkeley, but he was out of step with his district's university students. Elected to Congress in 1958, Cohelan supported Johnson's escalation of force in Vietnam and was a labor union ally. Before his congressional tenure he drove a milk truck and was an International Brotherhood of Teamsters officer. When in 1966 Berkeley students staged a sit-in at his office, he denounced their political activity. Thus, even though he represented a student population known for its opposition to most conservative causes, he was far more of a hard hat Democrat than a university liberal. Yet when Ford sought Douglas's impeachment, Cohelan criticized Ford. To one constituent, Cohelan wrote that he had contempt for Ford and admired Douglas's refusal to retire. He agreed with another constituent who accused Ford of "diminishing respect for the judiciary and cheapening his congressional office." Cohelan was more adamant in his opposition to the Cambodian operation than Rostenkowski and New York's Rooney; indeed, he suspected that Ford may have timed his speech against Douglas to deflect attention away from the expansion of the war.[17]

Republican Revolt in the House

As a signal weakness to his efforts, Ford was confronted with a small-scale but critical revolt within his own party. California's Paul McCloskey might have appeared to be an unlikely defender of Douglas. A decorated Marine Corps officer and Korean War veteran, on the surface McCloskey personified Nixon's Republican Party. He was appalled at the growing social disorder, and he believed that the government had become too permissive toward drugs and pornography. He was also a graduate of Stanford University's law school and had a command of constitutional law that was at least on par with Ford's.

Before 1970 he and John Ehrlichman had been close friends. Having won a special election in 1967, McCloskey was a part of the Republican sweep that owed much to Nixon. He defeated popular former actress Shirley Temple Black in the Republican primary and handily beat his Democratic challenger. But although Nixon expected McCloskey's loyalty because he endorsed him in the election, any expectation that the congressman would ally with Ford over Douglas or support the Cambodian invasion turned out to be illusory.[18]

McCloskey spoke to the House on April 24, one week after HR 920 was put into effect, and in doing so he became the first Republican to openly oppose Ford. His speech was more of an excoriation than a gentle disagreement, and it attracted a small number of Republicans to ally with him, including Michigan's Don Riegle and Maryland's Gilbert Gude. "I think that the hue and cry over the proposed impeachment of Justice Douglas may represent the gravest constitutional issue of the 91st Congress," McCloskey wrote to Gude. "As you may have noted, I have respectfully disagreed with Gerry [Ford]'s interpretation that an impeachable offense is whatever a majority of the House of Representatives considers it to be at a given moment in history." McCloskey went on to argue that opposition to Ford would not equate to party disloyalty; he further noted that although he could not personally defend Douglas's behavior, the justice's conduct had not risen to the constitutional standard for impeachment.[19]

In his speech McCloskey made it clear that Douglas's personal life and affiliation with the Parvin Foundation were distasteful, but he noted that the constitutional principle of judicial independence was at stake. All Ford had proven, McCloskey insisted, was a willingness to use impeachment as a political weapon. In the midst of his speech, Harold Royce Gross challenged him over the amount of evidence Ford possessed, insisting that Ford's argument requiring judges to be held to a higher standard than elected officials was constitutionally sound. "What the gentleman here is saying is if he wants to be a Lothario, that is alright as long as it does not involve what he is doing on the bench," Gross claimed. In response, McCloskey conceded that if Douglas had actually committed a crime, then his extrajudicial behavior could be grounds for impeachment. But, he reminded the House, most of the criticism against Douglas was that he had overtly expressed his political views and had been married four times. This formed no constitutional basis for removal. To impeach on this basis, he argued, would "have a ring of ex post facto to it."[20]

While Gross accused McCloskey of serving as Douglas's de facto defender in the House, others came to McCloskey's defense. Charles Whalen, an Ohio Democrat, disagreed with Ford's judicial impeachment standard. Whalen reminded his listeners that Congress possessed the ability to effect "life of death," and he turned to the Vietnam conflict as an example. "It would seem to me that the members of Congress, in approving the last number of years, military appropriations which were used and expanded in Vietnam are certainly responsible for the 40,000 deaths there," he claimed before drawing a connection between those in Congress who backed Ford and those who had earlier supported the 1969 covert aerial attacks on Cambodia. Ironically, because Whalen spoke a mere five days before the Cambodian invasion, he unwittingly uncovered a connection between Ford's attempt to impeach Douglas and a secret war plan. Nonetheless, to Whalen, Ford's move against Douglas was proof that Nixon intended to wage a war without limits. Shortly after Whalen came to McCloskey's defense, Illinois Democrat Richard William Yates joined in supporting McCloskey. "I want to congratulate the gentleman on what I consider the most important thrust of his argument, and that is the members of the House should not go off half-cocked or emotionally on this very grave charge which may lead to impeachment," Yates urged. After Yates concluded, Tom Foley commended McCloskey for safeguarding the principle of judicial independence. On April 28 Cohelan lauded McCloskey's "most brilliant attack on the Ford resolution."[21]

McCloskey's speech should have worried Ford. On June 24, 1970, McCloskey approached Earl Warren for help in finding a way to end the investigation. Warren in turn informed Douglas that McCloskey was seeking assistance in formulating his arguments, and he would help in the effort. Douglas responded that he was relieved that it "show[ed] a serious approach, not a witch hunt." Shortly afterward McCloskey conveyed to Celler a legal argument that Douglas had not committed any offense, even though his off-duty conduct had brought him personally into disrepute. On April 14 Illinois Republican John Anderson expressed his support to Ford by stating that the pending impeachment should at a minimum serve as a warning to Douglas. But by the end of the month he had determined that Ford's actions were purely political and not worthy of his support. Thus, early in the investigation, four Republicans made their opposition to Ford public. Although McCloskey, Riegel, and Gude were relative newcomers to the House, Anderson was not. Moreover, at the beginning of May, McCloskey gained another ally against Ford.[22]

New York Republican Ogden Rogers Reid had had enough of Nixon's administration. He vehemently opposed the extension of the war into Cambodia, and he believed Ford's quest against Douglas was a danger to the Constitution. Within an hour of Nixon's April 30 address to the nation about the Cambodia invasion, Reid informed Congress that he would introduce a bill to cut off all funding for the war. This concerned Nixon to the point of ordering Haldeman to "deflect the Reid Amendment." By this time the attempted impeachment of a Supreme Court justice did not sufficiently deflect from the invasion. When in early May McCloskey wrote to Reid that "the proposed impeachment of William O. Douglas may present one of the gravest constitutional issues of the 91st Congress," Reid concurred and agreed to help McCloskey prepare a constitutional argument against Ford. By the end of May, Reid compiled the House's record on judicial impeachments and provided McCloskey with an analysis of Ford's mistaken standards for judicial impeachment. From this point forward, McCloskey's legal arguments had Warren's and Reid's assistance.[23]

Ford's Deep South Democratic Allies
Go to War against Douglas

From the time of Douglas's attempts to stop the Rosenbergs' executions, no grouping of elected federal legislators evidenced an antipathy to Douglas more than the congressmen of the Deep South. As enthusiastic participants in Nixon's Southern strategy, Southern Democrats echoed Nixon and fanned a popular yet historically flawed sentiment that there was a prohibition against a Southern appointment to the Supreme Court. Georgia's John W. Davis claimed to an Atlanta television news station after learning that Haynsworth had been denied confirmation, "Southerners have long been excluded from being possible Supreme Court Justices." This of course was untrue in light of the fact that Hugo Black remained on the Court. However, Black was hardly the type of justice that Southern Democrats desired.[24]

Ford had a fundamental problem with his Southern congressional allies in that they made little effort to shield their racism, and they fought against human rights across the world. One month before Ford's speech, the State

Department had considered discontinuing an embargo against Rhodesia, and Southern Democrats supported this move. In 1965 the white-dominated Rhodesian government declared its independence from Great Britain after the British government insisted that the majority African population had to attain legal equality and the right to vote. Led by Ian Smith, the white Rhodesian government began a brutal suppression campaign against its majority African citizens seeking equal rights and self-governance. In response the United Nations voted to embargo all Rhodesian exports. The Johnson administration joined in the embargo, but several Southern congressmen, along with Senator Goldwater, insisted that Smith's government was in the right and that Rhodesia was an important bulwark against communism. The Southern Democrats' insistence on recognizing an apartheid regime abroad evidenced that they had not accepted civil rights anywhere in the world.[25]

To Southern legislators, Douglas's persistent pro–civil rights jurisprudence had instrumentally contributed to upending a way of life that hierarchically placed whites above African Americans, and they saw Ford's efforts as an opportunity to exact revenge. Six of North Carolina's seven Democratic representatives signed HR 920. In South Carolina, Mendel Rivers, William Jennings Bryan Dorn, Thomas Gettys, and Albert Watson voted to impeach Douglas. The two South Carolina representatives who absented themselves from the initial vote, John McMillian and James Mann, would likely have voted to impeach as well. Both of these men had signed the Southern Manifesto but were away from Congress on April 15.[26]

Louisiana's nine-member congressional delegation were all Democrats, and eight of them joined with Ford. Waggonner and Hebert had already expressed their opposition to Douglas. Otto Passman, John Rarick, Patrick Caffrey, Edwin Edwards, and Speedy Long followed suit. Only Hale Boggs did not sign any of the resolutions to remove Douglas. If a House vote were to be taken on an impeachment article, it is unclear how he would have voted. Boggs, a senior legislator, served as majority whip, but he supported several Great Society programs. After serving with Ford on the Warren Commission, he dissented with the report's conclusion that Lee Harvey Oswald had acted alone in assassinating Kennedy. Boggs had signed the Southern Manifesto and had voted against the Civil Rights Act in 1964. Yet unlike the rest of Louisiana's delegation he supported the Voting Rights Act the following year, as well as laws to prevent discrimination in housing. He was also closely aligned with Carl Albert and supported his ascension to the speakership.[27]

Four of Mississippi's five Democratic Party congressmen openly endorsed Ford. Jamie Whitten and Charles Griffin assured their constituents that they would vote to impeach Douglas. Both men insisted that Douglas intended to weaken the nation and make it impossible to secure a military victory overseas. Gillespie Montgomery voted with Ford but did not leave to posterity his reasons for doing so, and his personal correspondence remains sealed from the public. Colmer would likely have voted to impeach Douglas, but as the Rules Committee chairman, he determined to remain apart from the other Southerners in case he took over the investigation at a later time.[28]

It would be harder to find a representative who epitomized the core tenets of segregation more than Mississippi's Thomas Abernethy. Elected to the House in 1943 at the age of forty, he would serve in Congress until 1973. Like Colmer, he signed the Southern Manifesto and advanced bills to limit the Court's jurisdiction from challenges to voting laws as well as equality in education. In 1956 he wrote to a constituent that he expected justices Frankfurter, Harold Burton, and Sherman Minton to retire, but he worried that Eisenhower would appoint "political pinheads such as [Attorney General Herbert] Brownell and his ilk." Abernethy's disgust with Brownell was based on the Eisenhower administration's support for civil rights in *Brown*. He also intensely opposed Franklin Roosevelt, and he criticized the Court for upholding New Deal programs. "The Court has been going down since the Roosevelt era," he claimed to another constituent. "[Its] wild and ridiculous decisions have certainly encouraged communist activity." In 1965 he introduced a resolution to the House that would have prohibited a president from appointing a justice who had previously been a president, governor, legislator, or cabinet officer. "One who studies law but spends his life in the field of politics can hardly qualify as being supreme in the knowledge of the law," Abernethy claimed. In 1968 Abernethy alleged that a "Jewish lobby" was campaigning to keep Fortas on the Court.[29]

On May 5, 1970, at the same time as Abernethy was demanding that the United States side with Ian Smith's white-only Rhodesian government, he reminded his constituents that he had joined with other Southern congressmen to remove Douglas. He also insisted that Nixon's policies in Vietnam and Cambodia were necessary to win the war. Although HR 922 also listed non-Southerners, Aberncthy assured his constituents that Douglas's impeachment would be a Southern victory. They key to regaining Southern prominence, Abernethy believed, was in removing Celler's committee from the investigative process and giving Colmer the opportunity to command an investigation. To this end, he expressed confidence that Colmer would eventually supplant Celler.[30]

Nine out of ten of Georgia's representatives voted to investigate Douglas, including the state's two Republicans, Benjamin Bentley Blackburn and Standish Fletcher Thompson. The one Democrat absent from the vote, Robert Grier Stephens, intended to join with the others, which would have made Georgia one of three state congressional delegations to uniformly seek Douglas's removal. John William Davis had championed segregation and decried the 1964 Civil Rights Act. In a press release to the *Atlanta Journal-Constitution*, he now urged that the proof of Ford's rightness was in the "bipartisan support" for removing Douglas. Davis went on to argue that if the House failed to appoint an investigation composed of three Republicans and three Democrats as envisioned by Ford, Wyman, and Waggonner, then "an immediate vote for impeachment [would be] in order." In another press release Davis announced his anger at the Senate's failure to confirm Haynsworth and Carswell as being the reason for his action against Douglas.[31]

Georgia Democrat Maston Emmett O'Neal had sought Douglas's removal since he first came to the House in 1965. A prosegregationist and World War II veteran, on July 25, 1966, O'Neal introduced HR 928 calling for Congress to investigate Douglas on the basis of the justice's marital infidelities. The first paragraph of O'Neal's 1966 resolution attacked the "moral character of Justice William O. Douglas, in view of the fact that he has been divorced by three wives on grounds of alleged cruelty, including in the case of one wife, alleged personal indignities." Douglas hardly cared about O'Neal's resolution, and Celler never forwarded it to the Judiciary Committee for a vote. Nonetheless, it was unsurprising that O'Neal would join with his fellow Georgians and Ford in attacking Douglas. Indeed, even before *Points of Rebellion* was in print, O'Neal claimed that Douglas had undermined national security in issuing *Gutknecht v. United States,* a Selective Service decision in which the Court found that a draft board could not make use a person's failure to comply with an induction order as a basis to later draft him. In other words, a person's refusal to answer a draft order into the military could be prosecuted as a crime, but it could not become a means to actually draft the person in a later order. O'Neal believed that *Gutknecht* was proof of Douglas's treason, even though other five justices had voted in that opinion. But Douglas could have countered that Georgia, with O'Neal's acceptance, had ordered African American men into the military without giving them fair representation in their appeals against the draft.[32]

After joining with Ford, O'Neal displayed his certitude that Douglas was a threat to the United States. "I get the idea from reading your letter of April 19 that you don't think too highly of Justice Douglas," he responded to one constituent. "There is no doubt in my mind that he is a dangerous man, and I hope our efforts to impeach him are successful." It should have been of little surprise that not only would O'Neal join with Wyman and Waggoner, but he also introduced his own resolution to the House with the express purpose of taking the investigation away from Celler's supervision and placing it squarely under Colmer in the Rules Committee.[33]

In Alabama, William Nichols responded to a constituent who accused Douglas of "encouraging students, militants, and fanatics who are out to destroy our country" that he "wholeheartedly supported Ford." In addition to Nichols, Alabama's remaining four congressional Democrats voted to investigate Douglas. Only one of Alabama's representatives, Robert Emmett Jones, had served in Congress at the time of the Southern Manifesto, and in a predictable pattern, he had signed it. The others—George William Andrews, Thomas Bevill, and Walter Flowers—opposed civil rights. Like Georgia, Alabama had transitioned to electing Republicans to federal office. Alabama's three Republicans, William Jackson Edwards, John Hall Buchanan, and William Dickinson, maintained the states' rights demands of segregationists and sided with Ford.[34]

The Deep South, consisting of Louisiana, Mississippi, Alabama, Georgia, South Carolina, and North Carolina, was the only region to be wholly unified against Douglas. In contrast, Democratic congressional delegations on the Southern periphery, such as Tennessee, where none of the five Democratic congressmen signed a resolution against Douglas, posed a problem for Ford. To be sure, three of Tennessee's four Republicans signed HR 920, but the absence of Democratic votes showed where the Deep South ended and the broader South began. In Virginia three of the state's five Democrats signed

HR 920, and only two of the five Republicans joined them. Absent from this list was Richard Poff, who served on the Judiciary Committee and would later be advanced as a possible Supreme Court justice after Black left the Court. Poff had signed the Southern Manifesto early in his congressional tenure, but he intentionally stayed away from the impeachment effort against Douglas.[35]

Maryland's congressional delegation consisted of four Democrats and four Republicans, and only one of these eight congressmen signed a resolution to have Douglas investigated. But this vote was hardly beneficial to Ford. Clarence Dickinson Long's reason for adding his name to HR 920 was to ensure that Celler maintained control over the investigation. He also added his name to HR 926—essentially Wyman's reiteration of HR 922—in order to gather information for Douglas's defenders. Long had been a civil rights advocate; he supported McCormack and Albert, and he implored student advocates to taper their antigovernment rhetoric so as not to empower conservatives in the government to suppress free speech. On April 30 Long excoriated Nixon over the Cambodia invasion. "For six years we have tried to win a war in one nation with as many as a half-million men," Long challenged Nixon. "The administration has broken its promise and its constitutional obligation to consult with Congress before committing American troops, American treasure, and American prestige to the defense of one more nation that lacks the will to defend itself." At the same time as Long signed HR 920, he also supported Edward Koch's petition accusing Ford of having ulterior reasons in demanding Douglas's impeachment.[36]

Of Missouri's ten representatives, only three signed HR 920. Democrats William Raleigh Hull and Richard Ichord, along with Republican Durward Gorham Hall, decided to join Ford. In response to *Points of Rebellion,* Hall questioned Douglas's mental fitness to remain on the Court, going so far as to sarcastically suggest that the justice had been attacked by a flock of birds. William Hull likewise determined that Douglas's book constituted a threat to national security. Ichord was most vocal of the three legislators against Douglas. At the same time he joined with Ford, Ichord fought to keep Congress from dissolving the House Un-American Activities Committee and was waging a personal war against United States district court judge Gerhard Gesell, who had been one of Douglas's lawyers at the Securities and Exchange Commission thirty years earlier. Gesell had issued a ruling preventing Ichord's committee from harassing individuals who had spoken against the United States' conduct in Vietnam or supported civil rights. A staunch anticommunist, Ichord believed that communism had motivated civil rights leaders, antiwar movements, and liberal judges such as Gesell and Douglas. In Ichord's battle to prevent his committee's dissolution he fought with John McCormack, Emanuel Celler, and Abner Mikva. Just as Celler fought to keep the investigation of Douglas in the Judiciary Committee, he also challenged Ichord that "defining espionage is the sole province of the Judiciary Committee" and, since Ichord did not serve on the Judiciary Committee, he had "no business" advocating new criminal laws.[37]

Florida's congressional delegation was split against Douglas. On April 16 the *St. Petersburg Times* headlined Ford's speech and then reported "with Republican William C. Cramer sounding the battle cry and Rep Robert L. F. Sykes piloting strategy, most of Florida's House delegation swung behind Ford's effort to investigate Douglas." This was not a wholly accurate news report because there were both dissenters and abstentions in Florida's delegation. Six of the state's twelve congressmen signed HR 920, and Charles Edward Bennett introduced a separate impeachment resolution based on Douglas's alleged anti-Christian conduct. Democrats Robert Sikes, Don Fuqua, James Haley, William V. Chappell, and Paul G. Rogers had voted against both the 1964 Civil Rights Act and the 1965 Voting Rights Act. Haley, Sikes, and Rogers had also signed the Southern Manifesto in 1956. Republican J. Herbert Burke also joined with Ford, though he did not sign HR 920. After the release of *Points of Rebellion,* Haley renewed his earlier efforts to have Douglas removed from the Court. This time, however, Haley did not focus on Douglas's personal life; he instead insisted that Douglas was a threat to the nation. "He has certainly made a heavy contribution to the unrest and dissension we have in the country today," Haley claimed before arguing that the nation's founders would have demanded a special congressional committee to investigate Douglas. To Haley, *Points of Rebellion* was merely a reflection of Douglas's alleged long-term goal to weaken the United States. He believed the proof of Douglas's intent could be found in the justice's tax and investment records. Although Haley doubted that Southern Democrats would be enough to sway the rest of Congress to begin impeachment proceedings, he had greater doubts that the justices would police each other and remove Douglas. "I had hoped that the Court itself would take some action," he lamented to a constituent before concluding that the decisions in which Douglas was in the majority also contributed to a decay in the social order.[38]

Like Haley, Louis Frey was a prosegregationist legislator who sought Douglas's removal, but unlike Haley, Frey was a Republican. In this sense Frey could align with Ford without Ford's having to explain why he backtracked on his promise that Republican conservatives would "go it alone." On April 8, 1970, he argued to the House that Carswell's defeat had occurred "because of the liberals' revulsion to strict construction and an anti-south bias." As a representative of Florida's Fifth District, Frey's constituency included Cocoa Beach and Orlando. In 1968 he promised the residents of both cities that he would fight against the Court's busing decisions. After Ford called for Douglas's removal, Frey told his constituents that he intended to vote for impeachment. "Douglas's interpretation of the US Constitution is far from what our founding fathers intended," he claimed, before contending that Carswell was far more qualified than Douglas to serve in the judiciary. Nowhere in Frey's argument was there an assurance that Douglas's jurisprudence would not be the basis for a removal vote. Instead he openly insisted that impeachment was a means to rid the Court of a liberal justice.[39]

Although half of Florida's Democrats sided with Ford and signed resolutions calling for the Rules Committee to take over the investigation, there were others, such as Samuel Gibbons, who had criticized the Court and who lamented the Senate's denial of confirmation to Haynsworth and Carswell, but who did not join with their delegation against Douglas. Elected to the House in 1963, Gibbons opposed the Court's decisions on busing and criticized the 1968 *United States v. Robel* decision in which the Court struck down the government's rules excluding persons who were suspected to be communists from working on military bases. When one constituent complained that the Court had damaged the government, he responded that he agreed the justices had "usurped" Congress and the president. "Certainly, there are many who are disturbed over many of the decisions reached by the Court, and I surely share your views that there should be a separation of powers between the legislative and judicial branches of government as provided for in the Constitution," he concluded. Although Gibbons was not a vocal segregationist, in certain matters he evidenced a reluctance to embrace civil rights, or even permit advocacy that challenged discrimination on the public's airwaves. He threatened to have Congress withhold funds for Voice of America if H. Rapp Brown or Stokely Carmichael were permitted to become a part of that program. He also opposed the United States' adoption of the United Nation's trade ban with Rhodesia. Yet Ford's actions worried Gibbons because he suspected that the impeachment effort had been undertaken for purely political reasons and that it would set a dangerous precedent. Although he was initially unwilling to denounce Ford, he articulated to constituents who wanted him to join with Ford a simple statement that he trusted Celler to conduct the investigation. Gibbons's quiet approach soon changed.[40]

In early May, Gibbons denounced the invasion of Cambodia as a widening of the war. He then took the surprising step of backing Udall to replace McCormack as Speaker of the House. Udall had been a pro–civil rights legislator who opposed recognizing Rhodesia and was an outspoken critic of Nixon's war policies. By the end of June, Gibbons concluded that Douglas's criticisms of the government surveillance of its citizens were true, and he excoriated the executive branch for overclassifying information that he believed the public had a right to know. "So much information is now classified as "secret which has nothing to do whatever with national security. . . . Too often the information jeopardizes nobody except some agency or official," Gibbons claimed before insisting on a congressional investigation into federal intelligence activities. In August, Gibbons chastised the CIA for its conduct in Guatemala and Vietnam. By this time Gibbons made it clear that he believed Ford's allegations against Douglas were "a dangerous farce," and that although Douglas had not comported himself with the expectations inherent in being a federal judge, the justice's public warnings about the government were meritorious.[41]

There was one vocal Florida Democrat who refused to join in a Southern chorus to impeach Douglas. Elected to the Senate in as a pro–New Deal Democrat in 1936, only to be defeated by a primary challenger in 1950, Claude Pepper embraced Douglas's civil rights jurisprudence and his opposition to the Vietnam conflict. In 1962 Florida's Third Congressional District voters elected Pepper to the House of Representatives, where he would remain until 1989. Pepper served in the army in World War I, encouraged Roosevelt to side with Britain before Pearl Harbor, denounced the Southern Manifesto, and opposed Nixon. Shortly after Ford called for Douglas's removal, Pepper argued to Celler that Ford's attacks were irresponsible. Pepper also accused

Wyman of trying to have the Rules Committee take over the investigation as a prelude to dismantling civil rights.[42]

In Texas, four Democrats and no Republicans signed HR 920—or for that matter any other resolution calling for Douglas's impeachment. Ovie Park Fisher insisted that *Points of Rebellion* required Douglas's impeachment. Having served in Congress since 1941, Fisher had signed the Southern Manifesto and opposed significant parts of the New Deal and the Great Society. Likewise, John Vernard Dowdy, who also signed the manifesto, joined Fisher in demanding Douglas's removal. A third signer of the manifesto, Wright Patman, allied with Dowdy and Fisher to support Ford. Olin Teague joined with Fisher, Dowdy, and Patman in seeking Douglas's removal as well. In Teague's case, he had already acted against Douglas. In May 1969 he introduced an impeachment bill, but no congressmen signed it. Teague agreed with a constituent that Parvin's interests in casinos necessarily meant that Mafia money had been funneled to Douglas. Less than a year later, and a month before Ford's speech, Teague promised his constituents that in light of *Points of Rebellion,* he "would be glad to impeach the anti-American Douglas." Two days after Ford's speech Teague announced his alignment with Ford, but he insisted that the nation's newspapers—he called them the "fourth estate"—would back Douglas. Teague's politics were different from the other three Texans. He had supported the Equal Rights Amendment and generally aligned with Sam Rayburn, the New Deal, and Johnson. Nonetheless, he noted to one constituent that his "voice against Douglas was added a long time ago." However, shortly after Teague signed HR 920, Carl Albert rebuked him for permitting his name to be used in an advertisement for a luxury resort owned by H. L. Hunt, one of the wealthiest men in the United States. Albert's admonishment appears to have diminished Teague's ardor against Douglas. In his responses to constituents, he defended Celler's remaining in control of the investigation.[43]

In spite of the four anti-Douglas congressmen, Texas's Democrats proved to be less than a united front for Ford. After Wyman finished his April 15 speech against Douglas, he faced a challenge from Robert C. Eckhardt. In 1975 Eckhardt would call Douglas the twentieth century's most influential protector of individual rights. By the time he was elected to Congress in 1966 Eckhardt had already developed a pro–civil rights and otherwise liberal voting record in the state government. Wyman had not specifically addressed his intention to impeach Douglas when he introduced HR 922, but Eckhardt painted him into a corner by forcing him to concede that he considered impeachment to be a foregone conclusion. Eckhardt did so to set the stage for Tom Foley, who followed with the argument that because both Ford and Wyman were predisposed to impeach Douglas, they had to recuse themselves from appointing congressmen to the investigation because any of their appointees could hardly be considered impartial. Eligio de la Garza and Henry B. Gonzales were staunch Great Society supporters. Both men opposed the invasion of Cambodia and insisted that Ford had acted out of malice against Douglas. So too did Jim Wright, who eventually became the Speaker of the House, only to resign in a scandal. Wright initially supported Vietnamization, but he opposed the Cambodian invasion. James Jarrell Pickle, another Texas Democrat, supported the Great Society and civil rights, and opposed the Cambodian invasion. Not surprisingly, he also denounced Ford. Finally, Jack Brooks served alongside Celler on the investigation, and he was not well disposed toward the Nixon administration.[44]

Douglas's Defenders: Richard Bolling, Brock Adams, Edith Green, and Patsy Mink

On April 14 Brock Adams, a Democrat from Seattle, took on the *Seattle Times*, which in its previous day's editorial had concluded that if Douglas had been a nominee, he would have been disqualified on the basis of temperament alone, and therefore impeachment was necessary. In response, Adams countered in a press release that because Ford had threated to impeach Douglas after Haynsworth's rejection by the Senate, and because he had made a similar threat regarding Carswell, the public should conclude that Ford's conduct was both "partisan and unfortunate." Adams responded to a constituent who agreed with him, "There are no grounds at present that would justify the impeachment of Justice Douglas under the terms of the United States Constitution, as expressed in Article II, Section 4 and Article III, Section 1."[45]

Like many of his peers, Adams was not immune from constituent lobbying to impeach Douglas; in fact he received more than a hundred letters and telegrams asking him to support Ford. One writer encouraged him to "terminate Douglas's sordid tenure on the US Supreme Court," while another accused Douglas and his supporters of being part of a "liberal pro-communist–

Zionist clique" before asking, "Well who's side are you on?" A more rational constituent, who nonetheless supported Ford, complained that under
Douglas the Court had "taken the power away from our police force whereby
law-abiding citizens are not safe in parks or in the streets." Another writer
expressed that Douglas would find a way to prevent Nixon from pursuing
the antiballistic missile system and that it was therefore necessary to "remove
the communist from the Court." Although Adams disagreed with these constituents, he did not detail his constitutional argument for opposing Ford.
"At present, I know of no reason which would justify the impeachment of
Justice Douglas and I support efforts to block the proceeding," he countered
in a form letter.[46]

Douglas had a staunch ally in Oregon's Edith Starrett Green. A liberal
Democrat who fought for the inclusion of women into the professions of
law, medicine, and engineering, Green was elected to the House in 1954 and
was at one time considered the most powerful woman in the House of Representatives. Both Adlai Stevenson and John F. Kennedy asked her to open
their respective presidential conventions. Green is chiefly remembered for
the passage of Title IX, a law which mandated equal opportunity for women
in higher education, and the Equal Pay Act, which required that women receive the same pay as men. (She was also instrumental in securing funding
for several NASA projects.) Before her congressional tenure she worked as
a teacher and was elected to Oregon's legislature. Despite a volume of constituents imploring her to support Ford, she became one of Douglas's most
reliable allies. Unlike McCloskey or Brock, Green did not leave room for the
possibility that Douglas had actually committed any offenses. "The fact that
Justice Douglas, intentionally or unintentionally, has succeeded in attract-
ing more personal notoriety than his fellow jurists in a profession traditionally notable for its circumspect and decorous conduct is, in my view, hardly
grounds for impeachment proceedings," she insisted.[47]

Green noted to several of her constituents that most of the mail she received from Oregon's voters was anti-Douglas. But some of Douglas's supporters insisted that Ford's efforts were simply an extension of the John Birch
Society's earlier campaign to have Earl Warren impeached. One constituent
compared Ford's actions against Douglas to a fulfillment of George Orwell's
novel, 1984. Another wrote a letter to both Ford and Green in which he challenged Ford "to leave his smear tactics out of Congress and impeach Nixon."

Green responded to both anti-Douglas and pro-Douglas constituents with a form letter that supported the Judiciary Committee's investigation. "I have never supported House Minority Leader Ford's proposal," she answered. "Chairman Celler's committee is the appropriate body to do this." Like Cohelan, Green also linked Nixon's Vietnam policies and the Cambodian incursion to Ford's attack on Douglas. "In my opinion the Congress has let slip too far away its prerogatives in its power to make or not make war, and it would be equally regrettable if it defaulted in its constitutional obligations to ensure the integrity of the Supreme Court," she urged.[48]

Within a week of Ford's speech, Democratic congresswoman Patsy Mink of Hawaii had voiced her opposition to impeachment and had insisted that the Judiciary Committee maintain control over the investigation. Mink's position was consistent with her past approach to the judiciary. In 1966 she responded to a correspondent who wanted Douglas removed on the basis of the justice's fourth marriage, arguing that unless there was proof that Douglas had committed a crime of "moral turpitude," she would not join an impeachment resolution. She had also opposed Carswell's nomination to the point of publicly shaming Senator Hiram Fong into backtracking on his promise to vote for confirmation. Mink called Carswell "an affront to the women of America," and she gained the support of professional women's organizations. But she was the recipient of a large volume of hate mail from across the nation. An Alabaman questioned her whether she was "both a nigger and a white hater," and several men and women questioned her femininity. None of this mail deterred her commitment to civil and individual rights, or her opposition to Ford. "By way of background, it is my belief that the matter is basically a political attack on the beliefs represented by Justice Douglas," she informed a sailor stationed in Vietnam. "You may be sure I will do my best to prevent further action which stems from the Senate rejection of two conservative nominees." Mink promised another constituent that she "would do everything possible" to resist any attempts at impugning the integrity of the Supreme Court for political purposes. Within a short time, Hawaii's other representative, Democrat Spark Matsunaga, informed his constituents that he agreed with Mink.[49]

Richard Bolling represented a Missouri district encompassing part of Kansas City and its suburbs. Missouri narrowly voted for Nixon over Humphrey by a margin of 44.8 percent to 43.7 percent, but it is noteworthy that Wallace received more than 11 percent of the statewide vote. Nixon also barely carried Bolling's congressional district; had Wallace not run as an independent, presumably Nixon would have captured most of these votes. Aside from a risk of alienating his constituents, there were other factors that made Bolling's pronounced support for Douglas somewhat surprising. Although Missouri was a part of the "upper south," Bolling grew up in Alabama. He was educated in Tennessee and earned a master's degree at Vanderbilt. His service in the army in World War II culminated in his appointment as assistant chief of staff to General Douglas MacArthur. After the Japanese surrender, Bolling settled in Kansas City, where he became the chairman of the American Veterans Committee, a more liberal organization than the Veterans of Foreign Wars but one still dedicated to national security causes. In 1948 Bolling decided to run for Congress, and although local party leaders did not support him, Speaker of the House Sam Rayburn did, and this was enough for a victory. Bolling politically aligned with Rayburn until the Speaker's death, and he was generally supportive of Kennedy and Johnson.[50]

The day after Ford's speech, Bolling promised that he would fight Douglas's removal "every step of the way," and he accused Ford of threatening the judiciary's independence. At the end of the first week, Bolling formally spoke to the House and inserted a statement from the editor of the *International Student Press* into the *Congressional Record* that the attack on Douglas was calculated to create an election issue for the 1970 midterm elections. There was a political risk to Bolling—not only because he stood in the minority in the South but also because, like Albert, many of his constituents wanted Douglas's removal. Moreover, Bolling's defense of Douglas was widely reported across his state. On April 26 the *Kansas City Star* headlined that Bolling supported Douglas while Hall, Hull, and Ichord intended to have Douglas removed from the Court.[51]

Like many Southern congressmen, Bolling encountered constituent pressure to side with Ford. Two weeks before Ford's speech, the owner of a Kansas City grain corporation urged Bolling to join the "movement in the House of Representatives, to remove the unethical and un-American" Douglas from the Court. Another constituent implored him to "get Douglas out of the Supreme Court," adding, "He is no doubt a communist." Echoing this sentiment, a Kentuckian accused Bolling and Douglas of "acting on behalf of communism instead of being loyal Americans." A fourth writer asked Bolling to "join the great silent majority and support [their] *'points of rebellion'* by voting to impeach Douglas." As in the case of several politicians, dozens of anti-Douglas letters urged impeachment. Several writers accused Bolling of hypocrisy in opposing Haynsworth and Carswell. Other writers claimed that Douglas was allied with organized labor at the expense of the country. Bolling resisted constituent pressures and responded that his fight was not about support for Douglas or the justice's positions of law; rather, it was for the protection of the Supreme Court itself. In response to constituents who advocated that public pressure should require Bolling to vote with Ford, Wyman, and Waggoner, he countered with a quote from Edmund Burke, eighteenth-century member of parliament and political philosopher, who noted that an elected representative owes his constituents his best judgment, not adherence to a dangerous popular opinion.[52]

Ford's Republican Minority: Opponents, Half Efforts, and Flawed Men

Three Republican women served in the House: Florence Dwyer of New Jersey, Catherine Dean May of Washington, and Margaret Heckler of Massachusetts. All three had a well-deserved reputation for toughness. Florence Dwyer won her congressional seat in 1956 and focused her energies on consumer protections as well as attacking government overspending. Before her congressional tenure, she served in New Jersey's legislature, raised a son, and attended Rutgers University Law School at the same time. She became an advocate for women's equality and is remembered for describing the path of success for women in Congress as follows: "A Congresswoman must look like a girl, act like a lady, think like a man, speak on any given subject with authority, and most of all work like a dog." Although Dwyer was disgusted with *Points of Rebellion,* she issued a single form letter to respond to constituents regardless of whether they backed Ford or Douglas. "I disapproved of Representative Ford's action in relation to Justice Douglas and am sure it does not reflect the thinking of the majority of Republicans," the letter stated. At no time did Ford challenge Dwyer over her stance.[53]

Just as Dwyer was hardened against Ford's actions, so too were Catherine Dean May and Margaret Heckler. May was elected to Congress in 1958 and served until 1971. Although she was an advocate for women's rights, she also had a national security background, having served on the Joint Committee on Atomic Energy. In this capacity she fought to protect the nation's nuclear weapons arsenal, and she supported Vietnamization. But she criticized Ford and refused to back the impeachment effort. May drafted form letters to her constituents noting her trust in Celler and urging patience with the investigation. Shortly after the investigation against Douglas began, when a constituent asked May to "disassociate herself from Ford," she responded that she had never been associated with the impeachment effort. In July, May practically belittled Ford's charges as "having everything, including the kitchen sink, thrown into it."[54]

Elected to the Congress in 1966, Heckler unseated Joseph Martin, the prior Speaker of the House, in a primary contest even through the state party sided with Martin. Heckler was the only woman in her law school class at Boston College. Not only was she the editor in chief of the law review, she also founded the school's student Republican Party. A party centrist, she opposed Johnson's Vietnam buildup and supported Vietnamization insofar as Nixon remained committed to reducing the United States presence in South Vietnam. She criticized the Cambodian invasion and refused to side with Ford on Douglas. Ford never confronted Dwyer, May, or Heckler over their stance, and indeed he appeared to shrink from them.[55]

When Frank Jefferson Horton, Lowell Weicker, and Hamilton Fish IV introduced HR 928, they weakened Ford's efforts by essentially siding with McCloskey. HR 928 would have given the Rules Committee jurisdiction over the investigation, but then limited the investigation to Douglas's "official conduct." The three congressmen did not seek articles of impeachment to be the result of the investigation, but rather only whether Congress should codify new prohibitions against judges teaching courses, being paid for public speaking, or serving on nonprofit boards. Horton was a moderate Republican who voted to appropriate funds for the Great Society and supported the Civil Rights and Voting Rights acts. He also supported federal environmental protections and endorsed the Equal Rights Amendment. Both Weicker and Fish were also moderates, and none of the three men wanted to be associated with anti–civil rights legislators. In 1984 Weicker was arrested for staging an antiapartheid protest outside the South African embassy. Republican congressman William Ayers, whose constituency included industrial areas along the shore of Lake Erie, indicated he would sign HR 928, but for undiscovered reasons he opted not to.[56]

To be sure, Ford had a core of loyal Republican supporters in the House, but many of his Republican anti-Douglas allies had opposed anti–civil rights legislation and supported Nixon's Vietnam policies. Ohio Republican John Ashbrook had long criticized the Court for siding with criminals and communists. A graduate of Harvard and the Ohio State University law school, he was one of the early leaders of the John Birch Society's college organization, Young Americans for Freedom. From the time he was elected to Congress in 1960, he accused Martin Luther King Jr. of fomenting "lawlessness" and insisted that King intended urban riots as part of a "master plan." Unsurprisingly, Ashbrook voted against the 1964 Civil Rights Act, and equally unsurprisingly, he signed HR 923. Oklahoma's two Republicans, Page Belcher and John "Happy" Camp, provide another example of Ford's allies. First elected to Congress in 1950, Belcher voted against the Civil Rights and Voting Rights acts. He insisted that HR 920 had been designed by liberals to defeat Ford, and he had agreed with a constituent that the Supreme Court had become "a dictatorship that permitted the Negro minority [to dictate] its terms to the Court." He thanked another constituent who called Douglas's appointment "Roosevelt's worst mistake." Camp did not enter the House until 1966 and therefore was not able to vote on the 1964 and 1965 acts, but he signed HR 922 and HR 923, and he argued that the Cambodian invasion was legal and necessary.[57]

The few Southern Republicans in Congress joined in the effort against Douglas as well. These men tended to have similar racist politics as their Democratic counterparts, and they tried to criminalize free speech. In late 1969 Republicans William Lloyd Scott of Virginia, William Cramer of Florida, James T. Broyhill of North Carolina, Wilmer Mizell of North Carolina, and Marion Snyder of Kentucky sponsored a bill to create a crime to deny a person "the benefits of any educational program or activity where such program or activity is receiving federal financial assistance." The proposed law was aimed at antiwar and civil rights protesters on college campuses. If enacted, it would have permitted any university student to complain to a US attorney, who could then seek an indictment against the student demonstrators. The maximum penalty for the offense was a $1,000 fine and a year in prison. Cramer unabashedly advocated for the bill as a means to "rid colleges of radicals." Each of these congressmen signed one or more of the resolutions seeking Douglas's removal, and undoubtedly they viewed *Points of Rebellion* as proof that Douglas stoked dissent.[58]

Arizona Republican John Jacob Rhodes was a natural ally of both Ford and Southern Democrats. In spring 1970 he expended considerable effort to defeat school busing; he promised Arizonans that he "would do his utmost to preserve neighborhood schools." Born in Kansas in 1916, he attended Harvard law school and served in the army in World War II. In 1952 he was elected to Congress with the enthusiastic support of his mentor, Barry Goldwater. In 1964 he vigorously campaigned for Goldwater, and four years later he did the same for Nixon. Although the House had no constitutional role in the nomination of justices, like Patsy Mink, Rhodes actively campaigned against judicial nominees, although he directed his efforts against Thurgood Marshall and Abe Fortas. In September 1968 he insisted to his constituents that Congress's pending omnibus crime bill was "a critical means for overruling many of the Court's decisions." In the first month of Nixon's presidency, Rhodes promised his constituents that he would consider bills to curb the Court's jurisdiction, but he cautioned that he would also oppose measures "which interfered with the balance of our governmental powers as established by the Constitution."[59]

By 1969 Goldwater was lobbying Rhodes to pursue impeachment against Douglas. In turn Rhodes told his constituents that Douglas had conducted himself in a manner similar to Fortas, and Congress was likely to investigate the justice. "It is hard to tell what action will be taken at this time, either by Congress or the Judicial Branch itself," he wrote to a Phoenix attorney. "However, it is apparent that some action will be taken, particularly in light of further disclosures about Justice Douglas." After the publication of *Points of Rebellion,* Rhodes began his efforts to have Douglas removed from the Court. On February 17, 1970, he informed another Arizonan that he had joined with Iowa Republican William Scherle to insist on an investigation of Douglas's disloyalty to the United States. Shortly after Rhodes indicated his support for Ford; Sam Steiger, Arizona's other Republican representative, likewise announced support.[60]

Although Steiger endorsed HR 926, Rhodes was not in full agreement with Ford on the means to investigate Douglas. That is, unlike Ford and the anti-

Douglas Southern Democrats, he did not disparage the Judiciary Committee or insist on a Rules Committee takeover. When Charles Ares, dean of the University of Arizona's law school, challenged Rhodes that Ford's standard for impeachment was not only "in constitutional error, but so novel as to be an abandonment of strict constructionism," Rhodes responded by promising Ares that his only intent in seeking an investigation was to discover whether Douglas had violated the law by doing legal work on behalf of the Parvin Foundation. Rhodes assured Ares that Ford's other allegations were not enough of a basis to seek impeachment. Moreover, Rhodes and Steiger had allied with Southern Democrats in regard to the Court's civil rights jurisprudence. When Ares warned Rhodes that Ford had sought Douglas's impeachment for political purposes and that "grave damage [would] be done to the Supreme Court if the present proceedings [were] pushed to their ultimate conclusion," Rhodes responded that "the denigration of the Court has progressed over long period of time, and its collective and individual actions have been at least partially responsible." Rhodes added, "Insofar as public esteem is concerned, many of these decisions constituted radical departures from a previous norm of American life." Given Rhodes's antibusing efforts and his opinion that the Court's civil rights jurisprudence had "angered the laity" by allegedly upending constitutional rights, he would have likely voted to impeach. Yet with his acceptance of Celler's control over the investigation, it can hardly be said that he gave Ford his full backing.[61]

Although Southerners formed the largest bloc of anti–civil rights legislators, they were by no means alone, and a similar correlation between anti–civil rights politics and an effort to remove Douglas could be found elsewhere. In Southern California, Orange County's politics mirrored Mississippi more than California's. Sandwiched between Los Angeles County to the north and San Diego County to the south, Orange County was a Republican stronghold. It was also Nixon's birthplace. In 1970 Republican James Utt represented the northern part of the county. A decade before Ford called for Douglas's impeachment, he introduced a resolution to amend the Constitution to require federal judges to publicly disclose their income and investments. He voted against the 1964 Civil Rights Act and the 1965 Voting Rights Act. He insisted that Ian Smith's apartheid government in Rhodesia was in the right, and that the concepts of majority rule and equal rights for Africans were an impossibility. Utt vociferously denounced Douglas after the release of *Points of Rebellion,* but in March 1970 he died suddenly. His replacement, John G. Schmitz, promised to continue his policies. A John Birch Society member who opposed federal and state civil rights laws, Schmitz unsurprisingly voted to investigate Douglas. Like Utt, he supported Ian Smith and campaigned for Goldwater in 1964.[62]

Seventeen California Republicans served in Congress, but of this number only Delwin Morgan Clawson, Charles Samuel Gubser, Craig Hosmer, and H. Allen Smith signed HR 920. Clawson and Gubser were also the only Californians to sign to HR 922, and Hosmer signed HR 924. Even in adding Schmitz and Barry Goldwater Jr.—the son of the Arizona senator—to this number who would have voted to impeach Douglas, and taking into account that when all of California's Republican representatives voted for Ford over Charles Halleck, it is remarkable that fewer than a third of the state's Republican representatives supported Ford. This lower number reflected a dynamic that saw some of the state's Republicans supporting causes similar to those espoused by Douglas. For instance, in 1968 Northern Californian Don Clausen won reelection with more than 70 percent of the votes cast, and he campaigned on strengthening antipollution laws and other environmental protection measures. He informed his constituents that although the House did not have a direct role in judicial confirmations, he opposed Fortas's nomination to become chief justice. While he endorsed Nixon's plan to create an environmental protection agency, he sided with McCloskey on Vietnam and Cambodia. In order to gain Clausen's vote to impeach Douglas, the investigation would have to prove that Douglas had actually committed a crime. Some of California's Republican legislators simply believed that Ford's actions were unwise. Similarly, Burt Talcott informed his constituents on California's central coast that he opposed Ford because impeachment would turn Douglas and his cause into martyrs.[63]

Ford garnered no support from either John Dellenback or Wendell Wyatt, Oregon's two Republican congressmen. Not only had had Dellenback aligned with Nelson Rockefeller and focused much of his congressional tenure on conservation, but he also made it clear that Ford's standard of impeachment was more of a danger to the rule of law than was Douglas's conduct. "To interpret the Constitution so loosely on a vital question such as this would surely set a dangerous precedent," Dellenback wrote to a constituent. "A temporary majority of Congress would be empowered to remove from any position in government anyone who did not agree with them." Like Clausen, Dellenback would have to be certain that Douglas had committed a crime before voting for impeachment. Before his election to congress in 1964, Wyatt had been an FBI agent, and he was generally supportive of Nixon's Vietnam policies. But in early May he "expressed reservations" about the Cambodian invasion, and he did not provide to the press any comments on Douglas. However, he informed a constituent that while he believed all of the justices should retire on reaching the age of seventy, Ford's campaign "had all the earmarks of vindictiveness."[64]

Like Oregon, neither of Washington's two Republican legislators sided with Ford. Serving in the House alongside Catherine Dean May, Washington's other Republican, Thomas M. Pelly, was elected to the House in 1952 and spent much of his career trying to protect his state's economy by advocating for enforcement of commercial fishing limits by foreign corporations. Pelly opposed antiballistic missiles, but he supported the United States' involvement in Vietnam. On April 12 he received the first anti-Douglas letter from a constituent asking him join with Ford. He agreed that claims against Douglas were "a serious matter," but he was noncommittal about how he would vote because Ford had yet to speak to Congress on the matter. On April 20 Pelly sent out a form letter assuring his constituents that he "would study all developments in this case very closely," but again he resisted calling for impeachment. One day later, Pelly created a new form letter in which he assured his constituents that Ford's allegations were serious. He added that the Judiciary Committee had begun a "closed-door investigation," and he would have to wait until the investigation concluded before committing to any course of action. In a letter to another constituent who called Douglas "a dirty old man unfit for public office," Pelly insisted that because of the large number of congressmen who sought Douglas's removal, "the House Judiciary Committee had no choice but to name a special investigative committee."[65]

Whether a constituent accused Douglas of seeking the government's overthrow or attacked Ford for launching "a vindictive political agenda," Pelly answered all writers by expressing his faith in the "Celler-led Judiciary Committee." On April 24 Pelly gave a radio interview in which he defended Celler and expressed his belief that the Judiciary Committee would not "whitewash" Ford's allegations or "witch hunt" Douglas. Whether a constituent accused

Douglas of seeking the government's overthrow or attacked Ford for launching "a vindictive political agenda," Pelly answered all writers by expressing his faith in the Judiciary Committee. Pelly's cautious and thoughtful answer was hardly the type of response Ford sought from a Republican congressman. Yet it typified the response of the majority of West Coast Republicans.[66]

On the opposite side of the country, Ford confronted a Republican opponent in Maryland. Elected to Congress in 1966 with Nixon's support, Gilbert Gude represented Maryland's newly created Eighth District, which stretched from the north-central part of the state into Washington, DC's wealthier northern suburbs. The Eighth District's voters were economically diverse, ranging from farmers to wealthy suburban lobbyists. In 1968 he won reelection with 59 percent of the vote. Despite Nixon's support, Gude's political positions were more aligned with those of Nelson Rockefeller. In 1967 he feuded with Ichord and informed his constituents that the House Un-American Activities Committee had outlived its usefulness. One year later he promised to repeal the 1950 McCarran Act, which had enabled the attorney general to detain citizens suspected of subversive activities without a trial. In 1970 Gude assured his constituents that he supported civil rights for minorities and opposed legislators in his own party who tried to foil school desegregation. He also publicly championed enforcement of the Voting Rights Act, and in 1970 he introduced to the House a draft bill that would ultimately become known as the Equal Rights Amendment. Although the amendment failed to become a part of the Constitution, Gude established himself as politician who rose above party ideology and fought for equal rights.[67]

Although Gude had broken with his party's more conservative ideologues, this alone did not mean that he would oppose Douglas's impeachment. In 1969 he indicated to the chief of oncology at Georgetown's medical school that he supported Fortas's removal from the bench. Moreover, Gude also endorsed not only Nixon's Vietnamization policies but also the 1969 Cambodian aerial bombing campaign. Although he was deluged with thousands of letters demanding that Congress cease funding the Vietnam conflict, he sided with the administration, assuring both the American Veterans of Foreign Wars and the American Legion that he supported Nixon.[68]

Shortly after Ford issued his demand to the House of Representatives, Gude created a draft letter to his constituents in which he noted "only if the evidence now being gathered shows that Justice Douglas is probably guilty of such serious misconduct will I support a resolution of impeachment." By May he began to inform his constituents that he believed "the integrity of the Supreme Court and all its members is a keystone of respect for law in this country" and promised that he would not allow political ideology to direct his actions. In June, he openly expressed doubts in Ford's actions. "The matter of impeachment must be taken with utmost seriousness and I regret that the effort in the House, even if well-intentioned, has the appearance of political overtones that do not reflect well on this body," he wrote. "The issue has quieted down in the wake of the Cambodian invasion and I am hopeful that it will be handled more coolly and responsibly when it comes to the House floor." Notably absent from his responses was the fact that by the time Gude had authored his June letter, he had also joined with Douglas on a project to preserve the historic Chesapeake and Ohio Canal.[69]

The Interim Report

On July 20 the investigation published its interim report to the House. After reviewing Parvin's finances, the investigation concluded that there was no evidence of tax fraud or money laundering by either Douglas or Parvin. To be sure, the IRS had yet to provide information to the subcommittee, and the interim report did not state that Douglas had been cleared of financial impropriety charges. Likewise, the SEC determined that Parvin's successors who had purchased the Parvin-Dohrmann Corporation had inflated the company's stock value and that Parvin had benefited financially. Yet this had no direct bearing on Douglas. The interim report described the charges Ford made against Douglas as well as the investigation's jurisdiction to investigate Douglas. Because Ford jumbled his accusations, Celler categorized the various claims made against Douglas. One category focused on Douglas's relationship to Ginzburg and any improper judicial conduct that might have occurred as a result of it. To this end, the investigators looked at 28 USC section 455, a law that prohibited judges from serving on cases in which they had a financial interest in the outcome. The investigation next turned to *Points of Rebellion*. The interim report informed Congress that the central questions to arise from this publication were whether Doulas intended to encourage rebellion against the government, as well as whether he had to recuse himself from appeals involving national security. The investigation also examined the

April 1970 edition of *Evergreen* magazine with *Points of Rebellion*. Because the magazine had taken a chapter from Douglas's book, the key issue to the investigation was whether Douglas had the authority to prevent the magazine from printing the article. Here the investigation determined that Douglas was unaware of the magazine's publication of part of his book, and therefore the justice was partly absolved of the charge that he and Ginzburg had entered into a continuous publishing arrangement.[70]

After the interim report was published, Ford had his assistant, Robert Hartman, supply the investigation with the names of seven former Parvin-Dohrmann employees who could ostensibly give information on the connections between Douglas and organized crime, and between Douglas and socialists and communists. Ford also provided Celler with his staff's investigative notes from the previous year. The fact that Ford waited a year to do this cast suspicion on his motives. Further, Ford was "helpful" in other ways. When in late May Celler ran into difficulties with Attorney General Mitchell's not opening the Justice Department files on Douglas, Ford arranged a meeting between the investigators and the Justice Department. Yet while Ford's contributions were driven by his desire to have impeachment articles brought before the House for a predetermined vote, he clumsily tried to present himself as a neutral assistant to the investigation. Time and again, his actions belied his professed neutrality. When in early August Celler had the interim report published, Ford complained that the investigation had failed to give him any credit for his efforts, then accused the subcommittee of personally attacking him.[71]

The interim report offended Ford for another reason. He complained that HR 920 misrepresented his arguments and accused the investigation of giving Douglas "all of the rights contained in an adversarial proceeding." He went so far as to argue that Douglas did not have a right to defend himself in the investigation, and he expressed his dismay that his arguments on the judiciary's being held to a "separate, additional, and more exacting standard" was not a part of HR 920. Ford moreover accused the investigation of giving Douglas's attorneys more leeway in presenting a defense and claimed that this proved a pro-Douglas bias. Oddly, he also complained to Celler that Rifkind had been given communications between the congressmen who had aligned against Douglas and Celler, and that this had violated the privacy of those congressmen.[72]

Ford conceded that had Douglas faced a formal trial, as was contemplated in the Senate, he would have been entitled to obtain a greater degree of evidence, but he equated the House investigation to a grand jury in which there were no rights to the prosecution's evidence. The problem with Ford's assessment in this matter was that he ignored the fact that customarily a judge or member of another government branch, when investigated by the House, was provided evidence based on the charges, and nowhere in the Constitution is there an absolute correlation between a House investigation and a grand jury. In other words, House members must decide whether an investigation into a government officer is a judicial act, akin to the truth-seeking function of a trial, or simply a political act. Ford's complaints to Celler were thus yet another unintended admission that he meant the impeachment to be a political rather than a constitutional activity.[73]

On August 1 Waggonner accused the investigation of "running roughshod over members of Congress who wanted nothing more than a fair inquiry into the conduct and behavior of Associate Justice Douglas." He complained that little had been done to investigate Parvin and instead that the subcommittee had produced a report "larded with a correspondence log, containing a crude threat of disbarment." Additionally, he took exception to Rifkind's analysis of the Parvin Foundation's finances. The Louisianan insisted that alleged mafiosi figures such as Sidney Korshak, Meyer Lansky, Edward Levinson, and Edward Torres be placed under oath and questioned. Three Republicans from Iowa's congressional delegation, Harold Gross, John Kyl, and Wylie Morse, joined Waggonner in accusing Celler of whitewashing the investigation.[74]

Waggonner unintentionally provided Celler with a potential bombshell that could have undermined Ford from that point forward. He announced that he had retained Benton Becker as a special counsel to assist in the investigation of Douglas. For unknown reasons, Celler did not use Becker's association with Waggonner against Ford. Moreover, by this time Ford and Waggonner, if they had consulted with Becker, must have known that the Nixon administration would not provide any damning evidence against Douglas because Becker knew that none existed. Indeed, shortly after Ford's speech, Becker had advised him that Wilson's allegations could not be substantiated, then tried to help extricate Ford from his more outlandish claims against Douglas.[75]

Although Waggonner and Wyman called the interim report a whitewash and accused Celler of stalling, the investigation had vigorously continued. Moreover, while the House and Senate were focused on bills limiting the president's authority in Cambodia and expanding his authority to protect the economy, Waggonner's new shadow investigation into Douglas overstepped a basic maxim of legal ethics. Yet just as Rifkind did not take advantage of Benton Becker's association with Ford and Waggonner in leading the shadow investigation, neither Rifkind nor Celler revealed an action by Becker in regard to Louis Wolfson. Ford and Nixon believed that Wolfson had information to tarnish Douglas, and perhaps at first this was a reasonable belief. But Wolfson disavowed knowing Parvin or having any information on the Parvin-Dohrmann Corporation. Moreover, Wolfson made it clear that he had met Douglas only on two social occasions. Even after Becker learned of these facts, he persisted in pressuring Wolfson to testify by virtually promising a pardon. Unless Nixon's administration had authorized Becker to make this promise—and there is no evidence available that any authorization had been given—Becker offered Wolfson an impossibility in exchange for false information against Douglas. The canons of legal ethics prohibit prosecutors and other attorneys from promising benefits that cannot be given. At any rate, Wolfson continued to insist that he had no information against Douglas and in fact admired him, and Becker, Waggonner, and Ford escaped from a political disaster.[76]

Waggonner was irritated with Celler to the point that, in addition to creating a shadow investigation into Douglas, he contacted the clerk of the Supreme Court and demanded copies of Douglas's reports of extrajudicial income. Although Douglas could have blocked Waggonner's access, he and Rifkind determined to provide the material to the congressman. Douglas's actions in this instance enabled his congressional allies to argue his innocence by using his cooperation. This time, instead of Wyman's hindering the impeachment campaign, it was Waggonner who did so. Indeed, Waggonner's misjudgment led to the *New York Times* reporting on Douglas's openness. On August 5 the *Times* reported that the disclosure showed that while Douglas "continued to carry on an active off-bench life," he owned no stocks, and the disclosure "appeared to contain little ammunition for his critics."[77]

Two weeks after Waggonner complained to Celler, Wyman once more tried to have Colmer and the Rules Committee take control of the investigation. Like Waggonner, Wyman provided a list of names he was certain would implicate Douglas with organized crime. Colmer informed Celler that his committee had been inundated with more than one hundred resolutions against Douglas, but he also implied that it would take until the end of summer before the Rules Committee would consider any of these resolutions. In an effort to strengthen Ford's argument that a judge's behavior outside his judicial duties could arise to impeachable offense, Wyman also forwarded a letter from Roger Traynor, a prominent legal scholar and California supreme court chief justice. Traynor had been a judicial liberal who was instrumental in overturning California's antimiscegenation laws and expanding civil rights, and he had worked on drafting a new code of judicial ethics for the ABA. But he had intentionally remained quiet over a possible impeachment of Douglas, and his correspondence with Wyman did not touch on any aspect of the investigation. Rather, Traynor had written to Wyman his opinions on Judge Frank Gray in Tennessee. At a minimum Wyman's use of Traynor's letter evidenced that he was willing to conceal important evidence from Celler.[78]

The Investigation Continues and the Battle of the Lawyers: Phase II

Although the interim report was published on July 29, and although Ford and his most ardent supporters denounced it, the fact that it was designed to inform the House that the investigation needed further time did not mean that it had finished. One of the main difficulties that the investigation encountered was that the executive branch had failed to cooperate. Nixon had promised Celler that the FBI, IRS, CIA, Justice Department, and State Department would fully cooperate with the investigators, but the president's promise remained unfulfilled by the time of the interim report's publication.[79]

On June 9 Celler and McCulloch met with Attorney General Mitchell and gained Mitchell's assurance that extensive documentation on Douglas would be forthcoming. However, by the time of the interim report, the Justice Department had transmitted only three documents to the investigation, and these contained nothing of evidentiary value. Mitchell later noted that the Justice Department received documents from both the Internal Revenue Service and the Securities and Exchange Commission, but then determined that investigation already had these materials. Mitchell tipped his hand as to his personal feelings about Douglas by adding that the justice had been "the subject of various allegations and complaints about his personal life" and that "his purported friendships and associations had been the subject of thirty years of suspicion." A similar lack of information occurred in the case of Will Wilson, who permitted the investigation to review unsourced material. That is, Wilson's information was anonymous, and this deprived the investigation of any means to assess the authenticity of what Wilson had to offer. On August 17 Mitchell forwarded a spurious allegation that Douglas had taken a $5,000 payoff to overturn a California trial judge's denial of bail to a defendant, Dr. Jerome Rehman, charged with "endangering the public health." This accusation came from Rehman's landlord, and there was no information to this effect from Rehman, his attorney, or the prosecution. Moreover, Douglas once more permitted the investigation to search through his files. The subcommittee investigated the allegations involving Rehman and concluded that they were meritless.[80]

Given Douglas's extensive travels throughout Asia, the Near East, and South America, it would have been surprising if the CIA did not have files related to his activities. Because Douglas had worked with General William Donovan at the Office of Strategic Services, the CIA possessed Douglas's written correspondence to Donovan. When in 1955 Douglas and Robert Kennedy returned from their trip to the Soviet Union, Douglas informed the CIA that a large number of Chinese workers were being trained in the Soviet Union, and that Soviet military forces were being employed in agricultural development and railroad construction. In 1957 the CIA brought Douglas to its headquarters to lecture on Iran and the Soviet Union.[81]

On June 22, 1970, Celler specifically asked CIA director Richard Helms for copies of "evidence in relation to any of the charges within the scope of the various resolutions." Celler's new request to Helms is important for its expansive language. He did not simply focus the investigation on HR 920. Instead, he enabled the CIA to consider all of the other resolutions and allegations in the hopes of full cooperation. In turn, Helms directed CIA general counsel Lawrence Houston to search through the agency's files to see whether there was any evidence that Douglas had undermined national security. One month later, Helms responded to Celler that after an initial review of the CIA's files, the only material relevant to the House's investigation was that Douglas had worked with Sacha Volman.[82]

The same day that Helms responded to Celler, the investigators visited the CIA to review its information on various matters that Douglas had been connected with. These were housed in sixty-four boxes of material. After doing so, the investigators accepted the CIA's conclusion that it had no evidence against Douglas. However, one classified memorandum noted that Volman had given the CIA information obtained through his CSDI work. Helms wanted assurance that this information would remain protected from public disclosure, but Harkins was unable to promise that this would be the case. The inability of the investigation's counsel to promise Helms that all evidence would remain classified led to Houston's counseling to congressmen Richard Poff and Mendel Rivers for assistance. Both men advised Helms to meet with Celler and Ford directly to tell them of the agency's concerns that Volman's identity remain confidential. Thus, by the middle of July, the CIA had not only debunked one of Ford's more outlandish charges against Douglas, but several congressmen, including Ford, knew that the charge Douglas had undermined national security through his foreign activities was frivolous. Moreover, Helms and Houston concluded that the impeachment attempt had been a political move from the start.[83]

Although Celler did not know of Helms's and Houston's conclusion that Ford had made a politically motivated set of allegations against Douglas, he was convinced that the CIA had not been as forthcoming as it should have been. While Celler recognized the importance of not divulging information that could be harmful to national security, he wanted a more specific answer from the agency that either Douglas had consorted with enemies of the United States or he had not. Helms and Houston continued to insist that the agency had no information helpful to the investigation. In essence, the CIA would not explicitly exonerate Douglas, even though it had implicitly done so. In the end the CIA proved more unhelpful to Ford than Douglas, but Helms had clearly exasperated Celler by withholding information that exonerated Douglas.[84]

The investigation also carried out several side inquiries including those demanded by Waggonner and Ford. On July 24 the investigators interviewed Edward Levinson, followed by several of Parvin's former employees. For the most part the investigators found the employees cooperative, and with the exception of one witness, there was little to cause to doubt their truthfulness. The most revealing evidence to the investigation was that the Nevada Gaming Commission, a state agency charged with ensuring that criminals did not own or manage casinos, had never concluded that Parvin had a criminal past that merited concern. Like the CIA, the IRS and State Department had no evidence that Douglas had committed any crime.[85]

After failing to convince Celler to alter the investigation in a manner that favored impeachment, Ford published his complaints against the interim report to the House and then submitted a legal brief to Celler outlining his arguments on the constitutional standards of judicial impeachment. This was partly to counter the arguments of Rifkind, Clifford, and Clark, and partly to gain a consensus that his arguments about the legal standard for judicial impeachment were both reasonable and grounded in the nation's legal history. Bethel Kelley and Daniel G Wylie, two attorneys employed at Dykema, Gossett, Spencer, Goodnow, and Trigg, authored the brief. Kelley and Wylie were not newcomers to Ford's efforts against Douglas, and Ford later noted that they had assisted him in researching Douglas before his April 15 speech. Known as the Kelley Memorandum, their legal argument for impeachment centered on the historic use of it against judges. However, Kelley and Bethel went further than simply advancing an argument: They accused Rifkind of basing his May 18 analysis on "historical inaccuracies."[86]

While the Kelley Memorandum was lengthy and filled with historical examples of impeachments, none of its analysis supported Ford's argument that "good behavior" was simply definable by a majority of the House. The Kelley Memorandum's opponents included more than Douglas's defense team. McCloskey remained convinced that the House had to adopt a standard definition such as would be found in a criminal trial. He argued that the Kelley Memorandum provided no definitive proof that Ford's proposed standard for judicial impeachment was constitutionally grounded. Ford's standard, he urged, would enable Congress to depart from the due process principle of defining conduct before criminalizing it. In 1808 the Supreme Court determined that common-law crimes, such as those that existed in Great Britain, were unconstitutional. That is, in order to make an otherwise lawful behavior unlawful, Congress would have to codify the prohibited conduct and then affix a sentence to it. McCloskey insisted that a judge's misbehavior while serving on the bench, such as the misuse of judicial power, could constitute an impeachable offense. In contrast, a judge's off-bench conduct would have to specifically violate the law. To McCloskey, a judge could engage in lecherous or boorish behavior, but as long as the conduct did not constitute a crime, the behavior was not a basis for impeachment.[87]

Rifkind responded to the memorandum by arguing that the historic record on judicial impeachments made it clear that McCloskey's position was correct. For instance, the 1805 impeachment trial of Justice Samuel Chase resulted in his judicial survival because there was no proof that he had violated any law. Rifkind also urged that in the impeachment trial of Judge Robert Archbald, there was a finding of guilt for a criminal violation, but Archbald had been acquitted the charges related to his personal behavior.

On August 12, Kelley and Wylie transmitted a second memorandum criticizing Rifkind's response to their arguments. They accused Rifkind of mischaracterizing the historic record and insisted that the Chase impeachment had only established a precedent that impeachments should not occur as a political weapon. (Ironically, this is precisely what Ford's detractors accused him of doing.) The second memorandum highlighted that in the impeachment trial of Halstead Ritter, the Senate found Ritter guilty of a general charge of bringing the judiciary "into disrepute." This argument was technically correct, though they also argued that impeachment trial acquittals were of little precedential value. In theory, according to Kelley and Wylie, the Senate established a precedent for permitting a judge's general behavior to become the subject of an impeachment. But the article itself did not distinguish between criminal and noncriminal activity.[88]

The central thrust of the new memorandum was to argue that a judge's noncriminal extrajudicial activities could form the basis for an impeachment if those activities brought the judge into disrepute. Rifkind in his earlier memorandum cited Senator Elihu Root's review of the 1912 impeachment of Archbald as proof that a judge could be impeached only if his extrajudicial conduct constituted an actual crime. Ford's attorneys countered that because Root had cited a law review article espousing that noncriminal conduct could form the basis for an impeachment, Root intended for judicial impeachment to be based on a judge's overall conduct.[89]

Before Rifkind could respond to the second Kelley Memorandum, McCloskey provided the investigation with his opinion of the legal battle being waged between Rifkind and Ford's attorneys. To McCloskey, Kelley had neglected to analyze the intent of the Constitution's framers and instead merely interpreted past impeachment practices. McCloskey insisted that because an impeachment proceeding was akin to a grand jury trial in the House, the House must first determine that Douglas had committed crimes in regard to his personal conduct, or that his judicial conduct had brought the Court into disrepute by violating a specific ethics canon. McCloskey also reminded the investigation that Justice Blackmun had not recused himself from appeals in which he held a minor financial interest in one of the parties, and he argued that this was comparable to Douglas's relationship to Ginzburg.[90]

On August 18 Rifkind responded to the second Kelley Memorandum by calling Ford's impeachment standard "utterly destructive of the principles of an independent judiciary" as well as "historically and legally as untenable as it is mischievous." He reminded Celler that during the first Congress, when Congressman Samuel Livermore had insisted that the impeachment of a federal judge for nonjudicial conduct could occur only as the result of a crime, none of the Constitution's drafters had disagreed. Moreover, in every impeachment conducted by Congress before Ford's demand, at least one of the underlying articles that a judge was found guilty of was also a statutory criminal offense.[91]

Rifkind also pointed out that nowhere in either of the two Kelley memoranda was there a citation of the Federalist Papers or the Constitutional Convention records. Given that impeachments are a serious matter, the lack of evidence as to the intent of the Constitution's authors was a glaring omission. Moreover, Rifkind discovered, the two Kelley memoranda had relied on a law review article that was written by one of the prosecutors of Judge Archbald and not by a dispassionate scholar. But even so, he pointed out, the author of that article conceded that no judge had ever been removed from the federal bench without having been found guilty of an actual crime. Indeed, the article noted that Senator Root, in explaining to the Senate why Archbald should be removed from the judiciary through impeachment, had explicitly argued that each of the articles constituted a crime. While there was little new in Rifkind's response to the Kelley memoranda, he had effectively countered Ford's attorneys. And while the battle of the attorneys may not have made a difference in the investigation's conclusion, Douglas's legal team was the clear winner.[92]

At any rate, after Waggonner, Ford, and Wyman protested the interim report and accused Celler of overseeing a slipshod investigation, the House quieted over Douglas. By August 5 the House was confronted with a Senate bill designed to limit Nixon's abilities to conduct future military operations in Cambodia and Laos. There were few news reports on the investigation. Indeed, the major news stories from August to December included continuing demonstrations against the war, Edward Heath's becoming the United Kingdom's prime minister, the women's rights movement holding an enormous rally in New York, a civil war in Jordan erupting between the government and the Palestinian majority, and the Soviet Union landing a probe on Venus. Chile and Bolivia experienced assassinations and kidnappings. In Canada a Francophone separatist group in Quebec seized hostages, resulting in the Canadian government's only instance of declaring martial law in peacetime and using its military forces to police the population in its history.[93]

6

A Long Summer of Discord
The Senate Awaits the House

On June 5, 1970, Justice Hugo Black wrote to Fred Rodell that he did not believe the Senate would act against Douglas. "There is nothing he has done to justify impeachment and I do not believe the Senate can be bamboozled into believing he has," Black concluded. Rodell had grown concerned that the Senate would launch an independent investigation into Douglas, but he doubted that Ford—whom he called "that damned fool ex-student of mine"—would succeed in the House. One month earlier Black had told Rodell that he would help Douglas "weather the storm," and added, "The present hub-hub about him will get exactly nowhere." Black's correspondence is salient for more than one reason. It represented the fact that although many judges outwardly met the impeachment attempt with silence, on the whole the judiciary did not side with Ford and Nixon and instead had faith in the Senate. In reality, by June the upper house was focused more on Vietnam and Cambodia than on Douglas. The Senate's attentions also included the creation of a federal agency solely dedicated to workplace safety, funding the nation's first national passenger rail company, and passing a comprehensive law to combat organized crime. The Senate had a keen interest in foreign policy because Vietnam was not the only foreign policy focus as Richard Nixon sought to strengthen the North Atlantic alliance, the Soviet Union enacted new oppressive measures in Eastern Europe, and the Chinese and Soviet alliance was becoming increasingly frayed. And, of course, the Senate, like the House, debated Rhodesia as Nixon signaled a willingness to open limited trade with that country despite the United Nations embargo.[1]

The Senate has been called the country's most deliberative body, and this title is applicable to the impeachment process. Constitutionally, after the House votes by a simple majority to forward articles of impeachment against a federal official, the Senate then conducts a trial in which two-thirds of the senators must vote in favor of a finding of guilty. A finding of guilt on a single article automatically results in the removal of the official. Perhaps because senators hold their seats for six-year terms, and perhaps because incumbents often prevail against challengers, senators are more likely to build alliances across party lines than their counterparts in the House. The Constitution's creators envisioned that the Senate would not only be a constraint against an authoritarian president but also a check against popular dissent that was likely to be manifest in the House. It is the Senate, after all, and not the House, that ultimately determines whether to have the United States bound by a treaty. In addition to approving treaties, senators are responsible for all of the major functions that are found in the House, but they also exclusively vote to confirm presidential nominees to cabinet positions, ambassadors, military officer promotions, and federal judges.

In 1804 the House investigated Justice Samuel Chase and forwarded eight impeachment articles to the Senate. Chase was an irascible judge who, because of the structure of the judicial branch at the time, conducted trials within his assigned circuit. In his capacity as a trial judge he offended counsel and issued rulings that many legislators found indefensible. Moreover, Chase was a Federalist, and by the time of his impeachment the majority of congressmen in both chambers were Democratic-Republicans. None of the eight impeachment articles applied to Chase's performance as a Supreme Court justice; rather, the articles related to his conduct as a trial judge. Perhaps because in the early part of the nation's history the principle of judicial independence weighed heavily on the conscience of several senators, they acquitted Chase of all charges. From the beginning of the twentieth century until Ford's call for Douglas's impeachment, a total of twenty-one federal judges were investigated in the House, but of these, only three went to the Senate for an actual trial, and two were convicted. The two convicted judges, Robert Archbald and Halstead Ritter, had violated specific statutes, though

Archbald had also been charged with "bringing the judiciary into disrepute." The Senate acquitted Judge Harold Lauderback of all charges, but that trial should be viewed as suspect because a majority of the House did not vote to forward impeachment articles and the Senate began its trial based on a minority report.[2]

The mechanics of the impeachment process provided only a narrow possibility for a Senate trial to convict Douglas. For one reason, senators would have to decide whether Douglas's noncriminal conduct formed enough of a basis to find him guilty of bringing the Court into disrepute, or whether actual evidence of a crime was necessary to do so. The Senate could move directly into a trial, or it could have the Judiciary Committee further investigate Douglas. Mississippi's anti–civil rights senator, James O. Eastland, remained the upper house's Judiciary Committee chairman, and he would be able to control a Senate investigation into Douglas in a manner that enabled a sordid public airing of Douglas's personal life along with unsubstantiated allegations of ties to the criminal underworld and Douglas's supposed empowering of communism. Eastland was in many respects more incautious than his House counterpart, Emanuel Celler. Yet a separate investigation into Douglas was unlikely because historically, when the House forwarded impeachment articles to the Senate, the Senate moved directly to a trial.[3]

In order to obtain two thirds of the votes, an anti-Douglas alliance would be difficult to achieve. In the Ninety-First Congress, the Senate consisted of fifty-seven Democrats and forty-three Republicans. Neither the Republican wave of 1966 nor the 1968 presidential election had dislodged a Democratic Party majority, which had held the upper house since 1957. Although in the preceding Congress the Democrats had held sixty-four seats and the loss of seven seats was significant, it largely related to dissatisfactions with the Vietnam War, the Great Society, and a perceived increase in crime. This did not mean that the newer senators would align against Douglas.

With the exception of John Tower from Texas, Howard Baker from Tennessee, Edward Gurney from Florida, and South Carolinian Strom Thurmond, who switched his allegiance to the Republican Party in 1964 after years of protesting against civil rights and racial equality, the Democratic Party remained in the majority as a result of its one-party strength throughout the South. But in contrast to the House, Southern Democratic senators were not in lockstep regarding Douglas. Arkansas's William Fulbright, Texas's Ralph

Yarborough, and Tennessee's Albert Gore Sr. were unlikely to align with their Southern brethren on the basis of fanciful claims that Douglas was a threat to national security. Although Fulbright had signed the Southern Manifesto, by 1970 he had become more accepting of civil rights and opposed the continuation of military activity in Vietnam. Gore and Yarbrough were Great Society liberals who supported civil rights, and they generally aligned with Douglas's jurisprudence.[4]

If the House were to forward articles of impeachment, an anti-Douglas alliance would need all remaining Southern Democrats to side with an overwhelming majority of Republicans. Numerically this was a possibility, though two factors made it unlikely. Moderate Republicans such as Massachusetts's Edward Brooke, New Jersey's Clifford Case, Kentucky's Marlow Cook, and Oregon's Mark Hatfield and Robert Packwood believed that they had a responsibility to protect the judiciary against political efforts to undermine it. In order for moderates from both parties to vote for impeachment, there would have to be clear evidence of Douglas's committing a crime. The other factor was the continuation of the war in Vietnam. The Cambodian invasion brought Republicans such as John Sherman Cooper of Kentucky into an alignment with Democrats who opposed the war. Reaction to the Cambodian invasion would be a predictor in assessing a senator's commitment to remove Douglas, just as a senator's earlier support for Clement Haynsworth and G. Harrold Carswell was a factor.[5]

Senate Leadership, Cooper–Church, and the Predisposed Vote

As dissent against the Cambodian operation roiled the nation, it also consumed the attentions of Congress members. Although there were senators who wanted to vote on Douglas's fate, they were denied the opportunity to force the Senate into a trial as a result of the efforts of a bipartisan opposition to Nixon's Cambodia strategy. New York Republican Charles Goodell called Nixon's reasons for the invasion "ghastly." In the late hours of April 30 Senator Charles McCurdy Mathias, a Maryland Republican, introduced a resolution for Congress to convene a committee to determine whether the Cambodian invasion was legal. In doing so, he implied that he believed Nixon had exceeded his constitutional authority. By May 1 Hatfield and South Dakota

Democrat George McGovern informed the Senate that they would introduce a bill to prohibit funding for military operations outside Vietnam. Although their efforts failed, Cooper and Democrat Frank Church of Idaho introduced a resolution to prevent the funding of ground forces in Cambodia and Laos after July 1. The resolution, which became known as an amendment, was in actuality part of a defense appropriations bill. Given Nixon's promise to remove army forces from Cambodia by the end of June, the Cooper–Church Amendment did not force Nixon to do anything that he had not already promised the nation. After a seven-week debate, on June 30 the Senate voted in favor of this bill by a vote of 58–37 (with five not voting).[6]

Although the House would eventually vote against the Cooper–Church Amendment as an unconstitutional limitation on presidential power, the Senate made it clear that a majority of its members thought that Nixon's actions imperiled the constitution. And because the debate lasted seven weeks, it garnered significant news attention. The list of twenty-three Republicans who voted for the amendment was emblematic of the administration's lack of party support for a significant national security measure. It included Delaware's James Boggs and John J. Williams, Hawaii's Hiram Fong, New Jersey's Clifford Case and Harrison Williams, Oregon's Robert Packwood and Mark Hatfield, Pennsylvania's Richard Schweiker, Ohio's William Saxbe, and Vermont's George Aiken and Winston Prouty. With the exception of John J. Williams, none of the Republican senators who supported limiting Nixon's power to order military operations in Cambodia and Laos was likely to vote against Douglas without compelling evidence of a crime. As a result of Cambodia, many senators distrusted Nixon's Vietnam policies. Moreover, because the Senate's leaders fell into the category of distrusting Nixon, an impeachment trial and guilty finding would be all the more unlikely.

After Lyndon Johnson became vice president in January 1961, Michael Mansfield succeeded him as Senate majority leader. Born in New York City's overcrowded Hell's Kitchen immigrant neighborhood in 1903, Mansfield moved to Montana seven years later. In 1918 he joined the navy at the age of fourteen, and then two years later joined the Marine Corps. His military duties took him to the Far East, where he gained an understanding of Japan, China, and ultimately Vietnam. After returning to Montana he attended college and played football before turning his talents to teaching history at the state university. In 1942 he was elected to the House of Representatives over Jeanette Rankin, the sole representative to vote against the declaration of war against Japan. A decade later Montana's voters placed him in the Senate. Although Mansfield was known as a foreign policy expert—and indeed Johnson appointed him to the Foreign Affairs Committee—he was also a staunch civil rights proponent. Mansfield had a relationship with Douglas that stretched to 1951. The future majority leader resisted joining in the attack against the justice after his public statements on recognizing the People's Republic of China. In 1953 Douglas introduced Mansfield to Ngo Dinh Diem. At no point did Mansfield intimate that he was unhappy with Douglas, and he had voted against Haynsworth and Carswell. He also vocally opposed the Cambodian invasion. The only guarantee that Nixon had in Mansfield was that he would fight for Douglas.[7]

In contrast to the Democratic Party, there was a significant change in the Senate's Republican leadership. On September 7, 1969, the Republican minority leader, Everett Dirksen, died, and the Illinois governor appointed Republican Ralph Tyler Smith in his place. But Smith's tenure was to be short lived. He lost to Democrat Adlai Stevenson III in a special election on November 3, 1970. Whether Dirksen would have ultimately sided with Ford or Douglas is purely speculative, but his death did not help the anti-Douglas faction. Dirksen had a powerful role in shaping the judiciary, and an examination of his last two years in the Senate evidences no inclination to become involved in undermining the Court. Dirksen was a conservative. Yet he supported civil rights, voted for Thurgood Marshall and Abe Fortas, and was a close friend of Lyndon Johnson. Early in his congressional career he spearheaded an unsuccessful effort to have Judge Samuel Alschuler impeached from the Court of Appeals for the Seventh Circuit. When it appeared that Fortas was likely to face impeachment, Dirksen developed a bland form letter indicating that the House would first have to act and that he was obligated to refrain from commenting. Throughout his career Dirksen refrained from attacking the judiciary for being soft on communism, and he occasionally defended the Court against political attacks. He had also been a proponent of Judge William Campbell, even after Sherman Skolnick had made public his accusations that Campbell had investments tied to Albert Parvin. However, Dirksen criticized the Court for protecting criminals at the expense of victims. This much can be said about Dirksen's death. Because he was silent on Douglas and had supported both Campbell and Fortas, his death did not provide a rallying point for the proimpeachment forces. Given the timing of the House Committee's report, the matter would have fallen to Stevenson to decide how to vote, and he too showed no inclination to support impeachment.[8]

In one fundamental respect Dirksen's death proved to be destructive to Ford's efforts. Hugh Scott, the new Republican minority leader, had little patience for Nixon's approach to the judiciary. Scott deplored the president's attempts to ally the Republican Party with Southern segregationists. Like Dirksen, he was committed to the advancement of civil rights, and although he believed the federal government had encroached into too many areas of American life, he also felt that aligning his party with segregationist legislators would be an immoral abandonment of his reasons for being a Republican in the first place. Moreover, while he had campaigned for Nixon in 1968 and supported Vietnamization, he also opposed the use of military force in Cambodia and Laos. And he voted against Haynsworth and Carswell.[9]

To Scott, Haynsworth's civil rights record was too poor to secure his vote. To his constituents who questioned his lack of support to Nixon's first failed nominee, he answered that he had "voted his conscience." Carswell fared worse in Scott's estimation. In addition to a poor legal intellect, Carswell had been openly hostile to civil rights, and Scott promised his constituents that he shared their concerns over "the advancement of human rights." He also undertook efforts to assure civil rights leaders that the Republican Party had not abandoned its origins. "Judge Carswell's racist speech which was of an exceptionally extreme nature and his racist action in helping incorporate an anti-Negro golf course have outraged all Americans who believe in equality and human dignity," he wrote to Roy Wilkins.[10]

Although Scott was hardly an ally to Nixon and Ford in regard to the judiciary, he backed Nixon's economic policies, an end to the draft, and measures to strengthen law enforcement. Scott's Senate leadership was not as powerful as Ford's in the House. When Scott became minority leader, he preferred a moderate senator such as Margaret Chase Smith of Maine to succeed him as whip. But Robert Griffin, the so-called minnow, ascended to the position, and he was determined to see Douglas impeached. The first test of Griffin's leadership in the impeachment campaign occurred after Senator Ted Kennedy criticized Ford's attack on Douglas on April 16. Griffin accused Kennedy of injecting politics into the impeachment process before the House investigation had had an opportunity to finish and before the Senate a chance to conduct its own investigation. To Griffin, Kennedy's conduct "was a serious breach of a senator's responsibility and obligations." Kennedy, however, did not permit himself to be goaded into a debate on Douglas.[11]

While Kennedy may have been predisposed to acquit Douglas, and certainly there were deep family ties between Kennedy and Douglas, there were senators who were equally predisposed to vote Douglas guilty. Clearly, Barry Goldwater, Strom Thurmond, John J. Williams, and Griffin were in this category, albeit for different reasons. Williams had no issue with Douglas's civil rights jurisprudence, and although he did not approve of the Warren Court's liberality, he was consistent in his view of judicial ethics. After all, Williams had voted against both Haynsworth and Carswell because he doubted their integrity. Because Griffin had also voted against Haynsworth and Carswell, there was a sense of purity to his and Williams's actions against Douglas. This could not be said to be the case of Goldwater and Thurmond, as they parroted Ford's allegations that Douglas had intentionally imperiled national security, and their hostility to civil rights had been the basis of their past attacks on the Court.

The Senate had time and space to reflect on Ford's impeachment campaign against Douglas. By the time of the interim report's publication in July, Congress's and the nation's attentions were no longer fixed on Douglas. There were other matters of national and international importance. At the time the Senate forwarded the Cooper–Church Amendment to the House, the House voted in favor of a bill giving Nixon immense control over the economy in a manner not seen since the New Deal. Known as the Economic Stabilization Act, the law empowered Nixon to freeze wages and consumer prices, as well as control the interest rate. In what became known as the Nixon Shock, the United States abandoned the post–World War II gold standard in an effort to maintain the nation's prosperity. The Senate would now have to determine the viability of this bill.

Another reason for the Senate's having time and space to consider a trial against Douglas was that the press barely noticed the interim report's publication, and although the Vietnam conflict still supplied the majority of news articles, there were other news items, such as dog owners giving their pets the hallucinogenic drug LSD. This story was given front-page coverage in the *San Francisco Chronicle* the day after the interim report's publication, evidencing that the public had other interests than only Ford's efforts against Douglas. The *Chronicle* reported Waggonner's complaints against Celler on its sixth page, the same day it reported the canine drug use issue. The *New York Times* waited until August 4 to report criticism against the report, and then it only did so on its twenty-first page. The same day, the *Washington Post* headlined that Nixon had insinuated that Charles Manson was guilty, but White House press secretary Ronald Zeigler denied that the president had given a definitive statement on Manson's guilt. It took until the sixth page for the *Post* to report criticism against the interim report. Much of the nation's news reporting was focused on Manson's murder trial. But there was also reporting on a new attempt at peace in the Middle East, inflation, and even ineffective mouthwashes. The *Post* gave greater precedence to these than the interim report. The nation's other major newspapers, including the *Los Angeles Times* and the *Boston Globe,* likewise barely noted the interim report. Overseas, the *Times* (London), *Sydney Tribune,* and *Toronto Globe and Mail* did not carry any stories regarding it.[12]

On June 20 the *Baltimore Sun* placed a story on its front page that Chief Justice Warren Burger intended to testify to Congress that more appeals were coming to the Court than any time since William Howard Taft was chief justice. (In 1922 Taft convinced Congress to give the Court greater control over the selection of cases to grant appeal, and this cut the number of appeals.) The *Sun* quoted a "Court official" as stating that "several clerks have collapsed physically from overwork." The article did not mention Douglas, though more than one reader may have wondered whether the justice's attentions were now equally divided between his judicial duties and his legal defense. The next day the *Sun's* front page was dominated by foreign policy and economic news ranging from trade quotas to Palestinian pressure on Arab governments to reject Israeli peace proposals. At no time in July did the *Sun* report on the investigation. On August 5 the *Sun* placed its report that five of the justices—but not Douglas—had released information on their income sources on its sixth page. One page earlier the *Sun* had a small article entitled "Douglas Foes Say Panel Is Dragging Its Feet."[13]

On July 21 the *Chicago Tribune* reported on its sixteenth page that the interim report was merely an outline of "the immensity of the task faced by the investigators." The *Tribune's* major headline was a story that a kidnapped girl's body had been found near Lansing, Michigan. Additionally, the paper reported that a milk industry strike had been settled, a Florida "bandit" had killed two women, and Nixon promised that despite economic growth there would be no tax hikes. The *Des Moines Register* did not report on the interim report until August 4, but then it headlined on its front page "Charge Whitewash on Justice Douglas." In a separate article published the same day, the *Register* reported that five Supreme Court justices, but not Douglas, had divulged the sources of their income. Two days later the *Register* reported that Douglas had independently listed his outside income. One day after the interim report was published, the *Detroit Free Press* headlined that the Federal Trade Commission determined that the McDonald's Corporation had engaged in deceptive marketing practices. Its editors also argued that FBI director J. Edgar Hoover had become "a menace to everyone's freedom." The *Press* did not publish any news on the interim report in June or early August, but it did report that Nixon had determined Charles Manson guilty of murder even before the trial began. Nixon, however, backtracked on his comments, but not before the newspaper's editors excoriated him. "If the present jury cannot be insulated from the President's prejudgment, then it may not be possible to get an untainted jury anywhere," the *Press* concluded.[14]

Southern newspapers varied in their reporting. The *Richmond Times-Dispatch* did not mention the interim report in July. On August 4 the *Times-Dispatch* carried an article on its fourth page that Waggonner and several other congressmen had called the investigation a "whitewash," but also that Celler had defended the investigation's progress. One day later the *Times-Dispatch* reported that Doulas had listed his off-bench earnings separately from the other justices. On August 4, Louisiana's *Shreveport Times* reported that Waggonner had called the investigation "a travesty," but this story appeared on the paper's eighth page. The *Clarion-Ledger* of Jackson, Mississippi, was the one notable exception to Southern newspapers. Before the interim report's publication, the *Ledger*'s editors accused the investigation of stalling and whitewashing evidence against Douglas. "There are grave charges of improper action and conduct on the part of this radical jurist," the editors cautioned, before casting aspersions on "New York's ultra-liberal Rep. Emanuel Celler, an admirer if not warm personal friend of Douglas." On August 5 the *Ledger* reported that five of the justices had filed income reports, and highlighted that Douglas had not done so.[15]

In August 1970 Edwin Palmer Hoyt, a military historian and *Denver Post* editor, wrote to Douglas, "I guess your enemies, I hope, have run out of gas. They don't seem to be heckling anymore. I trust they will cease and desist." Hoyt assumed that because the news media had lost interest in headlining Ford's allegations, so too had Congress given up on removing Douglas. Although the rancor against Douglas appeared to diminish, there were still legislators waiting to take him on. Two of them were in Arizona, getting ready to renew legislative efforts into a Senate trial.[16]

Two Arizonans Prepare to Lead a Senate Prosecution

If the Senate were to place Douglas on trial, there was little doubt Goldwater would lead the prosecution, even though technically a select group from the House served in a quasiprosecutor role. Six days before Ford called for Douglas's removal, Goldwater informed several constituents, "Douglas's impeachment was long overdue." Throughout the late spring and summer of 1970 Goldwater lauded Ford and continued a barrage of accusations against Douglas. Goldwater's conduct, however, was hardly novel. In fact the senator had spoken against Douglas since 1965 and against the Court since Warren had become chief justice. Goldwater opposed *Brown* and other civil rights decisions, and he lauded Burger, Haynsworth, and Carswell. While he was a Nixon ally, he privately expressed his disappointment that Nixon had not done enough to promote conservatism, and ridding the Court of Douglas would be a means to kick-start the administration into keeping its promises. The depth of Goldwater's animus to Douglas was also evident in his belief that a "deep state government," populated by older New Deal government employees, intentionally sought to undermine Nixon. In January 1970 he met with Agnew to encourage a Senate uprising against Hugh Scott, whom he deemed to be too liberal. And he expressed his dismay to Agnew at Nixon's reluctance to become involved in Senate matters. In March 1970, when it appeared that the Senate would defeat Carswell, Goldwater privately put the blame on Nixon for not forcefully advocating conservative policies to the Senate.[17]

On August 6 Goldwater met with Nixon and Mitchell. Other Republican senators present included Florida's Edward Gurney, South Carolina's Strom Thurmond, Texas's John Tower, and Kansas's Robert Dole. Three House Republicans attended as well. Goldwater recorded in his diary that the Southern legislators were frustrated with the Court's busing decisions. Goldwater agreed with the Southern position that busing was unconstitutional, but he turned the conversation to the nature of the federal government. He warned Nixon that just as Eisenhower had inherited 13,000 Truman appointees who undermined Republican policies, federal employees hired during Kennedy's and Johnson's administrations, as well as the New Deal holdovers, would stymie Republican efforts "unless something drastic is done." To Goldwater, Nixon's cabinet had done too little to curb "government by administrative regulation," and the worst offenders included Secretary of Defense Melvin Laird.[18]

Nixon's answer, as Goldwater recorded in his diary, is instructive as to the administration's response to the House's investigation of Douglas and the Senate Republicans' overall tepidness in joining with Ford: "When Nixon reminded me of the difficulties in getting rid of these people, and I told him there was no difficulty in getting rid of anybody if he worked hard enough, he asked me why I hadn't visited him since August 28, 1969." In the midst of national protests against the administration and the administration's defeat on the Cooper–Church Amendment, the White House remained silent on Douglas. The silence even included Vice President Spiro Agnew. Goldwater warned Nixon that if he did not work decisively to remove federal officers who opposed him, the midterm and 1972 presidential elections would be difficult. Goldwater's prediction proved true for the midterm elections, but not Nixon's reelection. All the Southern legislators at the meeting agreed with Goldwater—not only on the need to remove Douglas but also in the belief that Nixon had not done enough to fight communism. Goldwater later placed his advice in writing and received Nixon's thanks. Yet after their meeting Nixon did little in regard to Douglas.[19]

Goldwater's disgust with Douglas was not simply based on the senator's anger with judicial activism. He believed in an ongoing war with communism and that the Court had enabled domestic communists to undermine democracy at home and abroad. In the two decades after World War II, many foreign policy experts and politicians argued that if a single Asian nation fell to communism, others would follow suit. In 1970 Goldwater still clung to this belief; he justified the Cambodian invasion for this reason. Although Nixon did not inform Goldwater of the invasion before it occurred, Goldwater did not waver in his support for it. "The President's decision to send American troops together with South Vietnamese forces into Cambodia came as a surprise to the general American public, but only to those of us who have followed this war closely, it was the only decision he could make," he penned in a general mailer to Arizona's voters. Goldwater voted against the Cooper–Church Amendment.[20]

On racial matters Goldwater's record was reactionary and gave rise to reasonable charges that he accepted racism and inequality as an intrinsic part of American life. Three months before Ford demanded Douglas's removal, Goldwater fought to keep the federal government from recognizing a holiday for Martin Luther King Jr. "Although Martin Luther King did many good things for his race, I don't believe he was of the stature that deserves this type of memorial," he told one constituent. He also wanted the government to reestablish relations with Rhodesia's white-only government, and he accused Rhodesia's majority population of being procommunist. At the time Goldwater believed that Africans were incapable of self-government, and the costs of the repression of a majority population were far more acceptable than the possibility that Rhodesia would turn communist. He did not seem to consider that, notwithstanding the virtue of equality, supporting an apartheid regime might drive more of the majority into communism.[21]

On March 24, 1970, Goldwater agreed with a constituent that Douglas was "a clear and present danger to the United States." This was only one of hundreds of letters he received from across the country, perhaps because he was one of the best-known senators to seek Douglas's removal. When an Illinois resident called Douglas "a treasonous disgrace to our country," Goldwater responded, "Hopefully the pressure of public opinion will cause the Congress to take action on this matter." On April 16 Goldwater virtually promised Arizonans that he would vote Douglas guilty. He agreed with a constituent who wrote that she "would like to know why in hell our government doesn't do its work as well and start to clean out this scum and vermin" before concluding, "It appears to me that the Supreme Court should be overhauled." Douglas was symbolic of a government Goldwater detested. When the Court determined that various security acts intruded into the rights of citizens, Goldwater blamed the "butchering of the law" on Douglas's alleged penchant for communism. After Goldwater advocated imprisoning antiwar demonstrators in May 1970, Senator Ervin chastised him. "Imprisonment without trial is a dangerous concept to introduce into our law. We cannot dismiss from our minds the frightening possibilities inherent in a policy of imprisonment without trial for 'criminal' or 'socially dangerous' tendencies."[22]

Not all of Goldwater's correspondents supported Douglas's removal from the Court. When a naval officer's wife accused Ford of seeking to remove Douglas for political gain and asked Goldwater not to consider Douglas's personal life, he responded that although Douglas's personal life and liberal jurisprudence were "controversial," he did not regard these issues as "grounds for impeachment." "But," Goldwater continued, "the Justice's rulings are clouded by his personal bias and that there are several instances of conflict of interest which will be exposed during the proceedings." He challenged another constituent who alleged that Ford had acted out a revenge motive because of the Haynsworth and Carswell nominations, responding, "This would be a logical response to the hypocrisy of those who are judging the President's nominees to the Court, while overlooking the background and performance of Justice Douglas." Instead, Goldwater insisted, "impeachment of Douglas is overdue."[23]

Arizona's other senator, Republican Paul Fannin, was in lockstep with Goldwater. A Stanford University graduate and owner of a gas supply firm, Fannin was elected Arizona's governor in 1958. He campaigned for a Goldwater presidency in 1964 at the same time as he successfully ran for Arizona's other Senate seat. Once in office he backed anti–organized labor laws. Like Goldwater he wanted the government to recognize Rhodesia as a bulwark in the fight against communism. He was a leading spokesman against the United States' signing the Genocide Convention, and he accused the United Nations of having "become a voting bloc of Afro-Asians, dominated by communists and socialists."[24]

Fannin joined with Goldwater and Southern legislators in arguing that the Warren Court had eroded traditional values and made the country weaker. He disparaged the Court over *Miranda* and its civil rights and criminal law jurisprudence. In 1966 he told his constituents that he was repeatedly "appalled at the decisions emanating from this body that seems unreasonably obsessed with a concern for criminals in our country while it hypocritically overlooks the victim of crime." Fannin was not unusual in his expressing his disgust with *Miranda,* though he accused the Court of having "made a fetish out of protecting criminals."[25]

Fannin's choice word of "fetish" amply described how he viewed Douglas.

Throughout 1966 and 1967 he accused Douglas of empowering the pornography industry and despaired that the justice's four marriages enabled the erosion of families across the nation. In 1969 he joined with Thurmond and Goldwater to demand that Congress remove Douglas along with Fortas. Like Goldwater, Fannin attracted support from conservatives across the nation. As 1969 came to a close, the Republican mayor of Winthrop, Illinois, thanked Fannin for calling Douglas a threat to the nation—and this was before *Points of Rebellion* had been printed and before Nixon had ordered an invasion into Cambodia. If the United States failed in Vietnam, Fannin claimed, it would fail elsewhere, and Douglas would have contributed to the failure.[26]

Unsurprisingly, as a staunch conservative, Fannin had demanded the United States send military forces into Vietnam to defeat communism, and endorsed Vietnamization. He backed the Cambodian invasion and fought against the Cooper–Church Amendment. Fannin was also intolerant of dissent against the war. "With reference to the violence in this country, my feeling is that when legitimate dissent turns to violence and endangers lives and property, there is absolutely no excuse for the latter," Fannin wrote to a constituent. "The alternative to law and order is anarchy and the latter will not be tolerated in this country." While in a vacuum Fannin's statement appears reasonable, he equated campus demonstrators who temporarily blocked access to classrooms to a form of violence.[27]

Just as Goldwater's presidential campaign suffered a tremendous defeat, so too would his and Fannin's efforts to build a Senate coalition large enough to have the upper house separately investigate Douglas or put pressure on the House to find misconduct and then drive forward impeachment. The two Arizonans teamed with Thurmond and gave anti-Douglas speeches in Atlantic City, New Jersey, and Charleston, South Carolina. They also lobbied conservatives in both parties, and moderates in their own. They did not succeed in moving the Senate to independently investigate Douglas. Part of their failure rested in the Senate's deliberative nature, and partly it resulted from the Senate's preoccupation with Cambodia in the summer's first half. But it also had to do with the commitment of moderate senators to the Constitution and a growing distrust of Nixon.

The Disunified Broader South and the Mid-Atlantic

In 1970 the so-called Broader South ranged from Maryland to Florida and from Georgia to Texas. Inside this region, the Solid South included the core of the former Confederate states. There was a great deal of political diversity between the Broader South and the Solid South, which had voted for the Dixiecrats in 1948. For instance, Louisiana's Russell Long and Allen Ellender signed the Southern Manifesto, voted against the Civil Rights and Voting Rights acts, and voted to confirm Haynsworth and Carswell. But Ellender opposed the United States' involvement in the Vietnam conflict, and Long backed Johnson's and Nixon's Vietnam policies. In spite of Ellender's disagreement with the United States' involvement in Vietnam, it was likely that he and Long would have voted Douglas guilty of a noncriminal impeachment article. Both of Missouri's senators were Democrats, but they differed on Vietnam. Stuart Symington, a longtime defense advocate, believed that if the United States left Vietnam, communism would spread throughout Asia. Elected in 1968, Democrat Thomas Eagleton differed from Symington on the war. Both men had opposed Carswell, and Symington voted in favor of the Civil Rights and Voting Rights acts. Before his Senate tenure, Eagleton defended the Warren Court in a series of public speeches. Neither of Missouri's senators publicly indicated that they would vote to remove Douglas, but given their commitment to civil rights, it was unlikely they would vote Douglas guilty unless there was clear evidence of a crime.[28]

Texas senator Ralph Yarborough insisted that despite Douglas's political activities, the judiciary's independence required a much higher standard for impeachment than Ford or popular Southern opinion recognized. Texas's other senator, Republican John Tower, was an ardent conservative who had voted against the Civil Rights and Voting Rights acts, but he left no record of any desire to impeach Douglas. Tennessee's Gore and Arkansas's Fulbright were of like mind in desiring to protect Douglas. In Kentucky, neither Marlow Cook nor Cooper joined with Ford and Nixon. But other Southern senators such as Eastland wanted Douglas removed. Eastland had long sought to turn the federal judiciary back to a time when it found segregation constitutional. He also turned his efforts to having the United States formally recognize Rhodesia's white-only government under Ian Smith.[29]

By the time of Ford's call to impeach Douglas, Eastland—born in 1904 and elected to the Senate in 1942—had served in the Judiciary Committee for twenty-two years and as chairman for thirteen. In 1954 he ran his re-election campaign by promising to fight the Court, the NAACP, and labor unions. After the Court issued *Brown* in 1954, Eastland centered his efforts on preventing the appointment of nominees who would further advance civil rights, and he frequently claimed that communism and civil rights consti-tuted a united front against the national interest. Although Eastland had oc-casionally allied with Douglas's Northern supporters such as Philip Hart and Birch Bayh on other matters, and even advocated for Bayh's integrity against Nixon's attacks after Bayh voted against Haynsworth and Carswell, he was clearly going to vote for Douglas's impeachment.[30]

Mississippi's other senator, John Cornelius Stennis, had also signed the Southern Manifesto. A 1928 University of Virginia law graduate, Stennis had been a county prosecutor and circuit judge in De Kalb, Mississippi, be-fore being appointed to the Senate to replace the deceased Theodore Bilbo. Mississippi's voters returned Stennis to the Senate by large margins in the ensuing six elections before his retirement in 1988. In his pre-1970 voting record, Stennis seldom departed from Eastland. Although Stennis remained a Democrat, he was often an ally of Eisenhower, Nixon, and Ronald Reagan on national security matters. In 1965, during Senate hearings into the army's readiness, he claimed that the defense budget was woefully inadequate to operate in Vietnam. And he supported both Haynsworth's and Carswell's nominations.[31]

Stennis professed to his constituents that although he was disgusted with Douglas, he had to avoid making comments about the possibility of an im-peachment. To be sure, Stennis let some of his writers know that *Points of Rebellion* "shocked" him into believing that Douglas wanted to undermine the government. "The attitudes and activities of Justice William O. Douglas are and have been for many years of grave concern to me," Stennis wrote to several constituents. "I do not approve of his philosophy of government and would not have supported his confirmation had I been in the Senate at the time." When two military officers insisted to Stennis that Douglas had un-dermined national security, he agreed rather than caution them that because they were subject to the orders of the president, and because the military had to be subordinate to all three branches of government, they should be reluc-tant to openly support the impeachment process. Stennis earlier opined to a constituent that the Warren Court's "ultra-liberal philosophy was a danger to the United States."[32]

Georgia's senators, like its representatives, were in lockstep with Ford over Douglas. The aged Richard Russell had long advocated segregation, though unlike many of his peers who openly advocated public resistance to *Brown,* he did so quietly. He also supported Nixon's military policies, including the Cambodia invasion as well as antiballistic missiles. It is clear that Nixon trusted Russell to the point of secretly informing him of the details of the pending Cambodian invasion. First elected to the Senate in 1932, Russell served continuously until his death in 1971. He was upset with his former protégé, Lyndon Johnson, over the 1964 Civil Rights Act as well as Johnson's judicial appointments of Fortas and Marshall. In Nixon, Russell saw a means to stop desegregation. Indeed, Russell endorsed both Haynsworth and Carswell. When a Georgia state judge asked Russell to forward Carswell's name to Nixon in 1969 instead of Haynsworth's, Russell responded, "There is no doubt in my mind that he would be an improvement on practically every judge now on the Supreme Court, and I shall, of course, be happy to support him vigorously." In keeping with his avoidance of histrionics, Russell did not publicly claim that Douglas had undermined national security or contributed to the social upheaval in the country. He did, however, note that he believed Douglas failed to conform to the judicial ethics canons.[33]

Georgia's junior senator, Herman Talmadge, was more vocal than Russell about Douglas. He claimed that Douglas had led the Court to undermine the military's efforts in Vietnam by opening up conscription to exemptions that Congress had not intended. Although Tom Clark, one of the Court's more conservative justices, had authored *United States v. Seeger,* the first major Vietnam-era decision regarding religious exemption from mandatory military service, Talmadge assigned the blame for it to Douglas. In one instance Talmadge responded to a Georgia state judge who urged him to voice his support for Douglas's removal by agreeing that "Justice Douglas's activities are questionable at best," thereby implying that he would side with Ford.[34]

North Carolina's white population had resisted integration and was often aligned with the Deep South. Yet its senators might have perplexed Ford and Nixon. Samuel Ervin had a reputation for being a brilliant constitutional scholar, and he neither openly gave his support to Ford nor renounced Douglas. By 1970 he challenged the federal government's authority to collect information on US citizens and became an unlikely but fervent ally of antiwar dissenters. Elected to the Senate after a state judicial career, Ervin was a key member of the Judiciary Committee. It is difficult to know how Ervin would have voted on Douglas. However, in late 1969 a North Carolina attorney complied to Ervin that Douglas had stoked racial unrest by calling police practices "anti-Negro" and enclosed a *Playboy* magazine article Douglas authored presaging *Points of Rebellion.* The attorney concluded that Douglas was "apparently a frustrated, embittered old man." Ervin responded, "A justice should avoid participation in activities and decisions, such as the Vietnamese War, which are inevitably presented or implicated in cases that come to the Supreme Court and he should demonstrate a fidelity to the ethics and standards of judicial office."[35]

Had Ervin voted against Douglas's impeachment, it would have constituted a blow to conservatives because he had a history of siding with his fellow Southern Democrats and favoring national security over individual rights. When Senator William Jenner's bill to limit the Court's jurisdiction in national security cases came before the Senate in 1958, Ervin gave a noncommittal response to his constituents. Ervin's position on how to deal with the judiciary was soon to change, but Nixon's backers would not have seen it coming. He informed the University of North Carolina's law professors that he supported some of the aspects of Jenner's bill and opposed others. He also gave the same answer to Roy Wilkins, the NAACP's executive secretary, who likewise opposed the bill. Ervin was consistent in his responses to organizations that wanted him to vote in favor of the bill. When a group of "Christian Citizens" urged him to speak publicly that the Court had weakened the country, and the Southern States Industrial Council argued that the Court had "insulted every member of the House Judiciary Committee," Ervin delayed committing on the vote. However, by August he had voted to get the bill out of committee, but he explained that his reasons for doing so were because he "felt the Supreme Court had far exceeded its proper bounds by acting as a legislative body contrary to the Constitution."[36]

Ervin insisted that his support for Haynsworth and his vote against Fortas in 1968 were based on the two nominees' jurisprudence and not allegations of unethical behavior. "The judicial philosophy of Justice Fortas was the only reason I opposed his nomination and I did not question him at all about his financial dealings during the hearings on his nomination," he informed a law professor. "I do believe that to some extent the accusations against Fortas were motivated by disagreement with his judicial philosophy. I am convinced this is true with Haynsworth." Although Ervin professed that he believed the ethics allegations against Haynsworth and Fortas were exaggerated, he maintained that the Court had taken a central role in undermining law enforcement and national security. To one writer he lamented that the Court had "made it impossible for the states to prevent the peddling of pornography," and he had voted to extend the Subversive Activities Control Board—an executive branch agency charged with detecting and preventing the spread of communist subversion—because of the Court's permissive attitude toward communists gaining federal employment in defense plants. And Ervin charged that the Court had "handcuffed the police against carrying out their duties." Ervin's answer to the Court's shortcomings, however, was not the impeachment of Douglas. Rather, he believed that his proposed bill created minimum requirements for judicial service by requiring a president to convene the chief judges of the courts of appeal and the state supreme courts to recommend candidates.[37]

Then there were Cambodia and Vietnam. One week before Ford called for Douglas's impeachment, Ervin claimed that he had "deplored the war in Vietnam since its inception," but he believed that the United States could not immediately withdraw its forces. He wanted to give Vietnamization a chance to succeed, even though it meant more lives would be lost. On April 27 Bryce Harlow, Nixon's legislative and congressional affairs assistant, notified Ervin that Nixon's popularity had increased to 62 percent in a recent Gallup poll and that the president thanked the senator for his support. When on May 4 a dozen Duke University Medical School professors asked in an open letter whether the Cambodian invasion was a lawful extension of the war, he responded that "it was a realistic attempt to secure American and South Vietnamese soldiers against the hit and run tactics employed by the enemy." Having explained his support for Nixon to the medical school professors, he now found himself questioned for his continued support by the University of North Carolina's psychology department. He explained that because he viewed the Cambodian incursion as temporary and not an extension of the Vietnam War, he had voted against the Cooper–Church Amendment.[38]

While the Deep South, with the exception of Fulbright and Ervin, was reliably anti-Douglas, the Broader South proved disappointing to Nixon and

Ford. In Florida, Democrat Spesard Holland, who had served in the Senate since 1946 and who had signed the Southern Manifesto, drafted a constituent response that merely detailed the procedures involved in the process and emphasized that the House first had to determine whether Ford's allegations were merited. As a result, Holland implied, "a vote commitment on Douglas was not ripe." Holland did not, unlike some of his Southern counterparts, articulate a personal dislike of Douglas, and he added that because the Senate would sit as both "judge and jury" over the accusations, he had to withhold judgment. In June, Holland developed a second draft to respond to anti-Douglas constituents. In this response version, he thanked the writer for his "interest in the impeachment of Justice Douglas."[39]

Although Maryland was a Southern-leaning state, neither of its senators showed an inclination to attack Douglas. Given Joseph Tydings's campaign for judicial reform, he might have been hard-pressed not to have voted on some form of censure against Douglas, but whether he would have supported a trial or a guilty verdict is another matter. While his correspondence is silent on Douglas, it is noteworthy that on July 14, 1970, Tydings issued a press release calling for full financial disclosure across the judicial branch. He lamented that the Court had pulled back from mandating disclosure and that this caused some of the courts of appeal to do the same. "The failure of the Supreme Court to adhere to the reforms is already having ramifications among the lower court judges," Tydings professed. "The judges of the Second Circuit have now asked the Judicial Conference to postpone its directive restricting outside activities of federal judges and requiring annual financial reports from them."[40]

With even more vigor, Tydings's Republican counterpart, Charles McCurdy Mathias, refused to support Douglas's impeachment. In 1968 Mathias narrowly defeated Daniel Brewster, the Democratic Party incumbent, and while Mathias's victory was part of the 1968 Republican wave, he was not Nixon's type of Republican. Mathias had served eight years in the House and supported civil rights, including prohibitions against housing discrimination. Moreover, he had pushed for a quick reduction of forces in Vietnam and opposed any military activity in Laos or Cambodia. When Nixon nominated Carswell, Mathias granted Roy Wilkins a receptive audience to explain why he should vote no. "One would think that somewhere, under some circumstances, there would be an illustration of Judge Carswell's having arrived at the conclusion that racial segregation is wrong and white supremacy is unacceptable," Wilkins wrote to an agreeing Mathias. "No such evidence has turned up and none will be."

In regards to Carswell, Mathias informed his constituents, "None of his decisions seem to belong in the great tradition of Anglo-American jurisprudence in which judges over the years have contributed to the growth and understanding of the law." In a press statement Mathias cited his dissatisfaction with Nixon's refusal to grant him an audience to explain his concerns that Carswell had routinely refused defendants from state criminal trials habeas entry into the federal courts when it was clear that the defendants had been denied their basic rights. It was not until the eve of the vote on Carswell that Mathias was able to meet with John Dean, but by this time it was too late to bring Mathias over to support the nominee. Mathias was on safe ground in opposing Carswell in the sense that he had received 2,803 letters opposing Carswell but only 268 in favor. As in the case of liberal Democrats, in order for Mathias to vote a pro–civil rights justice such as Douglas guilty, there would have to be clear evidence that Douglas had accepted money in exchange for his votes on appeals or that Douglas had consorted with communists.[41]

While West Virginia was not technically a Southern state, some of its voters aligned with the South, and there was a split between the two senators in regard to Douglas. The state had a heavily unionized workforce in the coal mining and manufacturing industries, and Douglas almost always sided with organized labor. Senator Robert Byrd, a onetime member of the Ku Klux Klan, voted against the 1964 Civil Rights Act and 1965 Voting Rights Act, and was not at the time an ally of labor unions. However, his counterpart, Jennings Randolph, voted in favor of both acts and was prounion. Byrd accused Douglas of being "a spokesman for the radical Students for a Democratic Society rather than a guardian of the Constitution." West Virginia's other senator, Jennings Randolph, entered Congress in Roosevelt's first term and had been a loyal New Deal supporter. He also pushed to lower the voting age to eighteen and promised to back an amendment recognizing women's equality. When Ford called for Douglas's impeachment, Randolph remained silent, but Byrd was clearly ready to vote Douglas guilty of some impropriety.[42]

The Midwest

In the Midwest some Senate delegations were aligned on the issue of the Supreme Court and Vietnam, but the positions of the senators were not necessarily reflective of a state's majoritarian political ideology. Although Indiana was a conservative state, its two senators were Democratic Party stalwarts, and neither called for Douglas's removal. Vance Hartke presciently warned against the dangers of a Nixon presidency in late 1967, opposed the Cambodian invasion, and predictably sided with Douglas. So too did Birch Bayh, who had led a successful campaign against Haynsworth and Carswell. Nixon's surrogate, Clark Mollenhoff, engaged in a disinformation campaign against Bayh by trying to highlight that the senator had once been a member of an all-white fraternity, but this only hardened Bayh's stance against Nixon's judicial nominees. Ohio's Republican, William Saxbe, and its Democrat, Stephen Young, voted against Haynsworth. They were split on Carswell, but both men opposed the Cambodian invasion. Neither senator publicly commented abut Douglas, but given that Saxbe later cast aspersions on Ford's efforts, it is unlikely that either he or the more liberal Young would have voted Douglas guilty without compelling evidence of an actual crime. Douglas also had likely allies in both of Wisconsin's senators, William Proxmire and Gaylord Nelson.[43]

Nebraska's two senators took the opposite position on Douglas from their Indiana and Ohio counterparts. Roman Hruska backed Nixon on Cambodia, demanded Fortas's removal, and advocated for Carswell. Carl Curtis sought Douglas's removal in 1969, making it likely he would do so in 1970. In Kansas, Republican senators Robert Dole and James Pearson voted to confirm Haynsworth and Carswell. But they also voted for the Civil Rights Act and Voting Rights Act. It would be harder to find a more conservative national security hawk than Dole. He tried to turn the Cooper–Church Amendment into nothing more than a statement of desire that Nixon proceed with rapidly reducing the numbers of forces in Southeast Asia. He also defended Nixon's actions in Cambodia and hinted that freedom of the press could be limited. Neither Dole nor Pearson made public their views on Douglas, but they had both criticized the Court over its criminal law decisions.[44]

Other Midwestern states saw splits in their senators' approach to the Court. In Michigan, Griffin was a certainty to vote Douglas guilty on some article, but Democrat Philip Hart made it clear that he would protect Douglas against the conservatives. In 1966 Hart defended Douglas against constituent demands that a fourth marriage merited removal. When a constituent complained that Douglas's "morals are disgusting," Hart responded that this was not a basis to remove a sitting justice. Hart had voted against confirming Haynsworth and Carswell, and he opposed the Cambodian invasion. By the middle of April 1970 he suspected that army intelligence officers had surveilled antiwar groups and spied on citizens. Two weeks after Ford called for Douglas's impeachment, Hart insisted to Melvin Laird that a "full explanation" of the Army's Surveillance Target Acquisition and Night Observation office's domestic operations be provided to the Senate. In May and June he answered hundreds of constituents who expressed opposition to the Cambodian invasion by promising he would fight against the administration. In early June he openly accused the administration of destroying free speech by sending "poorly trained troops" to "fire indiscriminately into a crowd" at Kent State University and Jackson State University, and he asked college students to back leaders who safeguarded the right of free speech. This included Douglas.[45]

In Oklahoma, Democrat Fred Harris opposed Ford while Republican Henry Bellmon, who had campaigned for Goldwater in 1964 and worked on Nixon's 1968 presidential campaign, indicated he would vote Douglas guilty on whatever articles the House forwarded. Bellmon voted to confirm Haynsworth and Carswell while Harris opposed both nominees. In South Dakota, Democrat George McGovern was one of the nation's most liberal senators while Karl E. Mundt had long been a conservative anticommunist. Mundt voted for Haynsworth and Carswell, and he supported Nixon's Vietnam and Cambodia policies, while McGovern did not. North Dakota similarly was split between Democrat Quentin Burdick, who voted against Haynsworth and Carswell, and Milton Young, who voted in favor of both nominees. In 1948 Burdick had campaigned for Progressive Party candidate Henry Wallace before becoming a Democrat. In the 1950s Young became a member of the John Birch Society. While Mundt, McGovern, Burdick, and Young were silent on Douglas, it is likely their votes would have been evenly divided.[46]

Both of Minnesota's senators, Eugene McCarthy and Walter Mondale, were liberal Democrats who had been elected by wide margins. In 1958 McCarthy defeated long-serving Republican incumbent Edward Thye by more than 6 percentage points, and in 1964 he breezed to a victory in which he defeated two challengers by over 20 percent of the vote. In 1966 Mondale defeated his Republican challenger by a 7 percentage point margin, and in 1972 he would increase this margin by more than 10 percent. Despite these election victories and the state's unique Democratic Farmer Labor Party, which was in many respects the most liberal part of the national Democratic Party, Minnesota had a large conservative base, as well as an older generation of voters who were appalled at the country's social upheaval. On April 11, 1970, four days before Ford's speech, 185 of the residents of Shevlin, Minnesota, signed a petition demanding McCarthy and Mondale work for Douglas's impeachment. "We support and we urge your support for the impeachment proceedings against Supreme Court Justice William O. Douglas for his on and off bench impertinence," Shevlin's residents implored their congressional delegation. "This we understand is being spearheaded by Representative Louis Wyman of New Hampshire. From what we have read and heard of William O. Douglas's dealings, he has no more right to serve on the Supreme Court than Abe Fortas had."[47]

McCarthy was born in 1916 in Minnesota to parents who had settled in the small town of Watkins, where they worked in the cattle and farming business. First elected to Congress in 1948 and then to the Senate in 1958, McCarthy had solidly liberal credentials. He had denounced Joseph McCarthy and other "red-baiting" conservatives, and had voted for civil rights. By 1965 he was an outspoken opponent of the Vietnam conflict, and in 1968 he had entered the Democratic primaries at the beginning of the campaign and came close to defeating Johnson in New Hampshire. McCarthy went on to best Hubert Humphrey and Robert Kennedy in Wisconsin and Oregon, but ultimately Humphrey became the candidate. Minnesota's junior senator, Mondale, had previously served as the state's attorney general at the youthful age of thirty-two. He was appointed to the Senate in 1964 to serve out Humphrey's term, and in 1966 he was elected to a full term. Along with McCarthy, Mondale was an avid civil rights proponent, and he voted to fund the Great Society. He also backed McCarthy in the 1968 Democratic Party primaries on the basis of ending the war. Like Douglas, Mondale had been accused of enabling socialism in the federal government.[48]

It would be a mistake to assume, simply because Minnesota had a liberal voting base, that McCarthy and Mondale received no pressure from the state's conservative constituents regarding the Court. Indeed, both senators received hundreds of letters from Minnesotans who accused the Court of permitting communism to become normalized in national politics, thereby undermining the social fabric of the country, if not national security. Fifty-nine residents of Le Roy, Minnesota, a town with a population of slightly more than five hundred, sent McCarthy a petition opposing Douglas on this basis. McCarthy responded to the Le Roy petitioners as he did to Shevlin's: "I appreciate your letter concerning the proposal to impeach Justice Douglas," he wrote, before adding, "I do not think there are sufficient grounds for impeachment and I think the whole effort is ill-advised."[49]

One constituent insisted to McCarthy that the Court's liberals had not only "handcuffed" the police but that they also "favored the Communists and their element in our society at every turn." Another claimed that Fortas would permit communists to "work wholesale in the defense industries," and a third urged McCarthy to consider Fortas's defense of Owen Lattimore as a reason to distrust his loyalty to the United States. McCarthy created a form letter to respond to these allegations, but the letter only tepidly supported Johnson's nomination of Fortas and Thornberry. "Both Mr. Fortas and Mr. Thornberry are, I think, adequate choices, and I do not intend to oppose confirmation of their nominations," McCarthy responded.[50]

If McCarthy had been tepid in his support to Fortas and Thornberry, he was much stronger in trying to prevent Nixon's efforts to push the Court into a conservative direction. He was one of only three senators to vote against Burger's nomination, and on this vote he departed from his normal alliance with Mondale. McCarthy worried about the extent to which Nixon would use the Justice Department to intimidate dissenters through wrongful arrests and other unconstitutional actions. To this end, he voiced his support to Douglas after Ford spoke in the House. Although McCarthy did not accuse Ford of malfeasance in seeking Douglas's removal, he would not vote Douglas guilty on the basis of insinuations that the justice had consorted with alleged Mafia men or undermined national security. McCarthy not only opposed the invasion of Cambodia but also believed that Douglas's relationship with Parvin and the CSDI could not be equated to Fortas's misconduct. McCarthy responded to a concerned constituent who asked if any liberals "had guts to save the Court," by saying that he, Mondale, Kennedy, California's Alan Cranston, and New York's Jacob Javits "would stand by Douglas." Earlier Mc-

Carthy also answered another constituent—who accused him of hypocrisy in voting against Haynsworth but remaining silent about Douglas—by writing that Douglas had not committed any impeachable offense.[51]

Mondale informed Minnesotans that he had voted "against Judge Carswell because of his insensitivity to human rights." He also reminded them that he was the first Democrat to call for Fortas's resignation. A month and a half before Ford's speech, Mondale had appeared on *Meet the Press* and argued that Senate's role in judicial nominations had to focus on whether judicial nominees were committed to protecting human rights. Given Douglas's extrajudicial record on human rights, he clearly fell into this category. In June, with Celler's committee underway, Mondale publicly defended *Points of Rebellion,* even though he conceded that anarchists could use the book as an excuse for their activities. "Douglas does not call for the heads of the Establishment, indeed by way of proposed reforms he goes no further than the liberals in the Senate or the House," Mondale explained. "Where he parts with the liberal Congress or elsewhere is in affirming how deep the commitment to individual liberty and justice for all must be if a government is to be made responsive to human needs." Mondale insightfully added that the origin of the attack on Douglas was Attorney General Mitchell, and "it would be a mistake to assume these policies do not represent the views of the Nixon administration."[52]

Senator Harold Hughes, an Iowa Democrat, former truck driver, and recovering alcoholic, voted against both Haynsworth and Carswell and assured his constituents "a careful study of Judge Carswell's record convinced [him] that he did not meet the high standards of judicial temperament and professional competence that Americans have a right to expect of members of the Supreme Court." Hughes told another constituent that Carswell had "promised unswerving loyalty to white supremacy." When several constituents accused Hughes of "falling victim to the heads of labor unions and civil rights organizations" after he voted against Haynsworth, he countered that while a conservative justice would bring balance to the Court, Haynsworth's failure to conform to judicial ethics required a vote against confirmation.[53]

Elected to the Senate in 1968, Hughes promised to curb the CIA, and he sought greater congressional oversight over the government's surveillance of American citizens. In this regard Hughes was a natural ally of Douglas, but some of his constituents accused him of hypocrisy for supporting Douglas and voting against Carswell on the basis of judicial temperament and ethics. "Not only does Douglas fall flat on his face on the score of judicial ethics, he is an open advocate of practices which would ultimately destroy the Court itself," urged an Iowa lawyer. "If Justice Douglas is acceptable to you, then Judge Carswell should pass with flying colors." Unlike senators representing the northeastern and northwestern states, the overwhelming majority of constituent mail Hughes received was pro-Carswell, pro-Haynsworth, and anti-Douglas. Yet one constituent penned that Douglas had been a bulwark against the government committing illegal acts against citizens. Hughes's reply to his constituents was to explain that because he could sit on Douglas's impeachment, he would have to remain silent on his opinions. In reality, unless there was clear evidence of a crime, Hughes would not vote Douglas guilty.[54]

The Industrial North

Of all the regions in the United States, the North's senators were unified as a barrier to Nixon and Ford. Both of Connecticut's senators, Abraham Ribicoff and Thomas Dodd, backed Douglas. Both men voted against Haynsworth and Carswell, and Ribicoff went so far as to call Carswell a racist and likened him to the medieval Danish king, Canute, who ordered the ocean to cease its tidal activities. In response to the Cambodian invasion Ribicoff endorsed the Cooper–Church Amendment as a "means to keep us from making the same mistakes in Cambodia that we made in Vietnam." Dodd's days in the Senate were numbered. Mired in his own scandal, the Senate censured him in 1967, and he lost in the 1970 primary to Joseph Duffy, who in turn lost to Republican Lowell Weicker. Because Weicker had signed a limited resolution calling for the House to investigate Douglas, he might had recused himself from a Senate trial. However, because Weicker had limited his resolution to investigating Douglas for criminal activity, it is unlikely he would have voted Douglas guilty of any impropriety unless there was proof of a crime.[55]

While John J. Williams in Delaware was certain to vote Douglas guilty, he resigned from the Senate on December 31, 1970. Delaware's other senator, Republican James Boggs, did not speak out against Douglas. Neither John Pastore nor Claiborne Pell, Rhode Island's two senators, believed that Ford had damning evidence against Douglas, and both of them concluded that the impeachment was politically motivated. In New York, Democrat Jacob Javits and Republican Charles Goodell voted against Haynsworth and Carswell, and both men opposed the Cambodian invasion. In the midst of the Hard Hat Riot, Javits and Goodell encouraged the Vietnam Veterans Against the War to make their opposition heard. [56]

New Hampshire's Norris Cotton had voted against the 1964 Civil Rights Act but in favor of the Voting Rights Act. As a conservative Republican he was also a consistent supporter of Nixon, and he voted to confirm both Haynsworth and Carswell. Although Cotton maintained his silence on Douglas, when he explained his reasons for voting against Fortas and Thornberry, he insisted that his actions were to prevent the Warren Court's perpetuation. New Hampshire's Democrat, Thomas McIntyre, voted against Haynsworth and Carswell. In contrast to Cotton, McIntyre made it known that he was against impeachment. In Maine, Republican Margaret Chase Smith and Democrat Edmund Muskie voted against confirming Nixon's judicial nominees to the Court and also criticized the Cambodian invasion. Both senators were appalled with the impeachment campaign against Douglas. On May 27 Muskie wrote to a naval officer stationed in Vietnam that he "could not honestly say there are grounds for impeachment." To his constituents who wanted him to vote Douglas guilty, Muskie merely promised to "study the matter carefully."[57]

In addition to Senator Kennedy, who quickly accused Ford of engaging in a baseless political attack, Massachusetts's other senator, Republican Edward Brooke, refused to join with the Southern segregationists or the Midwest's staunch conservatives. Brooke, the Senate's sole African American, responded to one constituent that he would not prejudge the House's investigation into Douglas. Importantly, he had attended the Pacem in Terris II conference and saw nothing remiss in Douglas's foreign policy commentary. Before Ford's April 15 speech, Brooke had resisted intense White House lobbying to vote for Haynsworth and Carswell. In turn, John Dean, Lyn Nofziger, Clark Mollenhoff, and Kenneth E. BeLieu failed to convince Brooke that Haynsworth would preserve civil rights. Brooke reacted to Carswell's nomination by telling his fellow senators that "he searched the record for convincing proof that Judge Carswell's later actions revealed a true dedication to the principles of equal rights under law," but "he searched in vain." Brooke did not spare Nixon in his criticism either, concluding that the president's treatment of the federal judiciary failed his promise of "bringing people together." On top of Brooke's criticisms of Nixon's judicial nominees, he also made it clear to the administration that he supported the Cooper–Church Amendment.[58]

In 1970 the Republican Party dominated Vermont, as it largely had since the Civil War. In 1932 Herbert Hoover won the state over Franklin Roosevelt, and Roosevelt's landslide victory four years later did not result in a Democratic victory in Vermont. Indeed, Vermont and Maine were the only two states to vote for Republican Alf Landon. Vermont's voters' rejection of the New Deal continued through every election until 1964, when Lyndon Johnson barely eked out a victory over Barry Goldwater there, despite Johnson's trouncing Goldwater over the general population. At the time of Ford's speech, Vermont's entire congressional delegation consisted of Republicans. Both of the state's senators had been fixtures in government for more than three decades. Winston Prouty served in the state legislature beginning in 1941 before being elected to the US House of Representatives in 1951, then the Senate in 1959. George Aiken began in the state legislature in 1933 before being elected as lieutenant governor and then governor. In 1941 the state's voters sent him to the Senate. But Aiken was often independent of his party, and he criticized Joseph McCarthy. He was also one of the early senators to openly voice doubts on the wisdom of deploying military forces to Vietnam. Aiken and Prouty voted to confirm Haynsworth, but the two men differed on Carswell. Aiken voted for Carswell while Prouty voted against. However, both men voted in favor of Thurgood Marshall, and in 1970 both men stated their opposition to the Cambodia incursion. Both men refused to take a position on Douglas, and they placed their faith in Celler's committee.[59]

Aiken's constituent letters were equally pro- and anti-Douglas. A navy nurse stationed in Vietnam expressed her concern with the impeachment, to which Aiken replied he was "confident the subcommittee will give fair and impartial consideration to the issues involved." However, he also wrote that he and Prouty had to wait the investigation's findings before giving further comment. Another constituent who worked as a contractor in Vietnam warned that the impeachment of Douglas would alienate youth and worried that the House would consider "irrelevancies" such as Douglas's marriage to a twenty-four-year-old, his opposition to the antiballistic missile weapons system, and criticism of the "CIA and the Pentagon" as a basis for impeachment instead of the fundamental question of whether Douglas had actually accepted money in exchange for issuing decisions. Aiken assured this constituent that Celler's committee would be "fair and impartial," adding that he agreed with the premise that the impeachment could harm the judiciary. A third constituent argued to Aiken that although Douglas's "behavior did not conform to conventional standards of propriety, impeachment was going too far." This time Aiken responded that he had to await the House's findings. When a constituent claimed Douglas was "one of the few sane minds left in the government, whose only crime was to exercise his voice loudly and articulately against interests which exploit all of us and have left us with a horrendous burden of pollution, racism, institutional murder in Vietnam, and dehumanization at home," Aiken assured him that the House Judiciary Committee would be fair to Douglas.[60]

Aiken also heard from citizens as far away as Los Angeles who demanded Douglas's impeachment, including the ever-present William Lurcom, who claimed once more that Douglas was a communist and advocated overthrowing the government. There is no record of Aiken responding to Lurcom. Many of the anti-Douglas letters accused the justice of being un-Christian and communist. "If we are to survive as a nation blessed and protected by God, our highest tribunal must be in accord with the highest tribunal where Christ is on the Throne," urged one writer. When another constituent thanked Aiken for his support to Carswell and asked at the same time for a commitment to impeach Douglas, he responded, "The Democrats know how to play the game and they have the press with them," before detailing the impeachment process. Interestingly, this letter was written one day before Ford spoke.[61]

The West and Southwest

Only a few of the Western senators evidenced a desire to remove Douglas from the Court. In California, Alan Cranston opposed both Haynsworth and Carswell, the invasion of Cambodia, and many of Nixon's other policies. Cranston was a member of the CDSC and an avid environmentalist. He had also come under attack from Nixon over his relationship to a Washington, DC, news station, but this did not dissuade him from calling Ford's campaign a danger to the nation. California's other senator, George Murphy, was a conservative Republican, a former movie actor, and a staunch Nixon ally. He promised Goldwater and Fannin that he would vote Douglas guilty. However, in the midterm elections, liberal Democrat Gene Tunney defeated Murphy, and in all likelihood he would have sided with Douglas. Both of Nevada's senators were silent on Douglas. Both Democrats, Alan Bible and Howard Cannon, voted against Haynsworth, but Bible voted in favor of Carswell. Both men voted for the Civil Rights and Voting Rights acts and opposed the Cambodian invasion. In order for their votes, or Cranston's, to remove Douglas, the investigation would have to prove that the justice committed an actual crime.[62]

With the exception of Goldwater and Fannin, Western state conservatives were circumspect as to how they would vote on Douglas if articles of impeachment came to the upper chamber. Wyoming's Clifford Hansen was a conservative Republican and a friend of Goldwater's. Yet his only comment on the investigation of Douglas was that he had to withhold judgment on the matter. Wallace Bennett was a conservative Republican who had represented Utah since 1951. From the time Ford called for Douglas's impeachment through the end of the summer, Bennett received several constituent letters asking him to support Ford. When in May 1970 a Brigham Young University professor implored him to openly support Ford, he responded that although he believed there were "serious questions as to whether [Douglas] should remain on the Court," it was "critical" for a senator to "not take a position in the matter because in all fairness, not only to Justice Douglas but to our system of government with its separation of powers, doing so would undermine the judiciary." Bennett went on to explain that the Senate had to sit as an impartial jury, and senators who espoused a predetermined opinion would undermine confidence in the government. A month later he told another constituent that he could not agree with the need to impeach Douglas until "all of the facts" came to light. However, Bennett conceded that with the Democrats "in control of the machinery in the House," a vote on Douglas might never occur.[63]

Both of Oregon's senators, Republicans Robert Packwood and Mark Hatfield, not only voted against Haynsworth and Carswell but also condemned the Cambodian invasion and refused to attack Douglas. On September 2 Hatfield lamented the House's rejection of the Cooper–Church Amendment, but he optimistically claimed that "those who favor an uncompromised policy of peace are becoming a decisive political force." To Hatfield, this group included Douglas. This is not to say that Hatfield and Packwood would have voted Douglas not guilty in all circumstances. They might have been willing to do so if evidence of payments in exchange for votes was discovered. But Douglas's connection to Bobby Baker, a foundation's funding from a casino owner, and a sophomoric screed were not enough for them to make an open commitment against Douglas. Neither of Hawaii's two senators, Republican Hiram Fong and Democrat Daniel K. Inouye, showed any inclination to remove Douglas. Alaska's two senators were likewise silent on Douglas, but it would have been unlikely for Mike Gravel, a maverick Democrat, to have voted for impeachment because he had already publicly accused Nixon of usurping the Constitution.[64]

Both of Washington's senators, Henry Jackson and Warren Magnusson, were Democrats and moved to protect Douglas. Elected to the Senate in 1944, Magnusson opposed Haynsworth and Carswell, chiefly on the basis of their anti–civil rights record. Magnusson also considered Carswell's nomination as an "obvious attempt to politically appease the Southern group that supported Nixon." To one constituent, he wrote that Carswell was "incapable of objectively applying the Constitution in cases involving civil rights issues." Magnusson believed that because Nixon had failed to keep his promise to Southerners because of the Senate's refusal to confirm Haynsworth and Carswell, he could show Southerners that he stood with them by having Douglas impeached in the House and prosecuted in the Senate.[65]

Magnusson also opposed the Cambodian invasion, warning that it could collapse the strategic arms limitations talks with the Soviet Union and that "world opinion" would treat the invasion harshly. Like Brock Adams, his Washington counterpart in the House of Representatives, Magnusson suspected that more than retribution for Haynsworth's and Carswell's failed nominations was behind Ford's efforts against Douglas. This did not stop him from assuring his constituents that he believed that sitting justices "must be men of the greatest integrity and honesty and this would be [his] position should impeachment proceedings come to the Senate floor." He answered a constituent who accused Douglas of enabling violence and anarchy, "I think this Court has been at the cutting edge of progressive change and has strengthened and defended our basic bill of rights." He penned to another voter, "It appears to me that many citizens are willing at this time in history to sacrifice our Constitutional liberties for suppression and repression of individual freedoms; with that I strongly disagree."[66]

Henry Jackson likewise opposed Haynsworth and Carswell, and informed his constituents that Nixon had to answer for the escalation of the war by invading Cambodia. Although there is little information in his papers regarding the actual impeachment efforts, on October 30, 1970, he wrote to Douglas, "No one since Brandeis and Holmes has been more dedicated to the Bill of Rights than you," and added, "I am proud of you." Implicit in the letter as well as its timing is that Jackson expected Douglas to prevail over Ford and Nixon.[67]

In New Mexico, Clinton Presba Anderson insisted that Ford had acted out of political motives, not for the good of the nation. A Lyndon Johnson ally who supported civil rights and the Great Society, Anderson voted against Haynsworth and would have voted against Carswell if not absent because of a surgery. Anderson received more constituent mail against both Haynsworth and Carswell then mail favorable to either. On June 16 he expressed to Michigan's Senator Hart that Nixon's actions in Cambodia were not only a breach of his promise to end the war but also a danger to the Constitution. He also made it clear that, absent tangible proof of bribery or some other crime, he would not support Douglas's removal from the Senate.[68]

New Mexico's junior senator, Joseph Montoya, was the only Hispanic in the Senate. He too voted against both of Nixon's nominees, but in 1957 he criticized the Court for overturning the state supreme court regarding the denial of Rudolph Schware to the practice of law. Schware was a veteran of World War II, and he graduated the University of New Mexico's law school. However, after passing the state bar exam, he admitted that before the war he had been a Communist Party member. The New Mexico supreme court upheld the denial on the basis that affiliation with communism at any time in a person's life was proof of bad character. The court determined that the denial of admission to the bar based on political affiliation was a violation of Schware's First Amendment rights. At that time, Montoya informed his constituents that he would seek ways to restrain the Court. Elected to the House in 1956 and the Senate eight years later, he moderated his views on the Court with the passage of time. In 1969 he promised New Mexico's union workers that he would vote against Haynsworth. He also assured a former governor that he did not believe Douglas had committed any wrongdoing.[69]

Neither Idaho's liberal Democrat, Frank Church, who had opposed the military's presence in Vietnam since 1964, nor the state's conservative Republican, Leonard Jordan, who supported Barry Goldwater in 1964 and opposed both the New Deal and Johnson's Great Society, gave any indication they were willing to back Ford. Both men had voted against Haynsworth, and both expressed doubts as to the wisdom of attacking the judiciary. Beyond their party affiliation and views on Vietnam, the politics of both men considerably differed. Jordan did not approve of an activist judiciary, particularly not one that upheld the sweeping federal social and economic programs that both Roosevelt and Johnson had initiated. "One of our foremost traditions is the idea that the true measure of the worth of attainment is the triumph over adversity by self-help and hard work," Jordan urged his constituents. "But, I believe, this great principle is being seriously eroded by the protective programs of the Great Society." Like Goldwater, Jordan argued that individuals were morally weakened by reliance on the federal government, and in turn the government became socialistic.[70]

Jordan believed that the Court had weakened the nation's security, and he promised constituents that he would push Congress to remedy the Court's actions. He agreed with a constituent who argued that the Court was wrong to extend the Constitution's protections to communists, and he promised that he would fight in Congress to control the Communist Party. Yet if all one knew about Jordan was his strident anticommunism and his belief that the Court had enabled communism to survive, then one would assume that he would have also joined with Goldwater, Fannin, and the conservative Southerners to impeach Douglas. On October 1, 1965, he answered a constituent who sought Warren's removal that an impeachment trial would "cause deep repercussions in our judicial and legislative process at a time when we are in a war in Asia." The next year he agreed with another constituent that Douglas's infidelities had brought the judiciary into disrepute, but then lamented that "much has been said as of late about the fact that a man's private life should not be considered when evaluating his public life."[71]

Jordan was also consistent in his defense of constitutional principles, including the right to an independent judiciary. He defended his vote against Haynsworth on the basis of judicial ethics rather than on the judge's jurisprudence. Jordan favored a judge with strict constructionist jurisprudence, but not one who "mixed private business with the work of the court." He also defended senators Williams and Griffin for opposing Haynsworth. "It is important to realize that were it not for Senator Griffin, Abe Fortas would be Chief Justice of the Supreme Court, Judge Warren Burger would have filled the only vacancy, and the vacant seat to which Judge Haynsworth was nominated would not even exist," Jordan argued. When approached by his constituents about his position on Douglas, he remained noncommittal and reminded them that the matter rested with the House. Having earlier informed Idahoans that he did not find Douglas's personal life a basis for impeachment, he now insisted that although *Points of Rebellion* was evidence of Douglas's lack of judgment, it too was not a basis for impeachment. What remained a viable means for impeachment to Jordan was some definitive proof that Douglas had received money or gifts in exchange for his rulings. This was too high a bar for Nixon or Ford to prove.[72]

As to the differences between Jordan and Church: Where Jordan decried the New Deal and Great Society as intrusive socialism, Church advocated for increased federal funds for poverty programs and rural development. Jordan remained mostly silent on Vietnam, though he believed as late as 1970 that a military victory was not only possible but also the only means to achieve peace. To Jordan, antiwar activists were unpatriotic and emblematic of the rise of crime and decline of morality. In this regard he believed that Douglas had failed to set an example expected of a national leader. Church saw a different cause for the spike in crime as well as the decline of morality. To Church, it was the enlargement of the conflict in Vietnam, caused by Johnson's incompetence, if not a series of outright lies, that led to social decay and upheaval. Of course there was another significant difference between the two men. A decade earlier Church had traveled to Asia at Douglas's suggestion, and the two men occasionally communicated with each other. Jordan had no relationship with Douglas.

Even before Ford alleged Douglas had committed misconduct, Church received constituent letters worrying that Douglas was about to be attacked. In 1969 an Idahoan wrote Church, "When the mud starts to boil around Justice Douglas, I urge you to support him. In my opinion his biggest problem is too much courage, which we need." As Celler's committee began to investigate Douglas, Church received letters asking him to hold Douglas to the same standards of accountability as he had held Haynsworth. To one constituent who insisted that Douglas had contributed to the demise of society, Church responded, "Many of the problems which our country faces today, in my view, are largely the result of the tremendous divisions in our society caused by the War in Vietnam." Church went on to remind his constituents that he had opposed military intervention in Vietnam since 1964 and would use his "power as one Senator to bring an end to this conflict and reverse the resulting trends of discord in this country."[73]

Like Jordan, once Ford demanded an investigation, Church publicly presented himself as noncommittal because a Senate trial required the participants not to be predisposed toward a verdict. On May 1 Church approved a draft response to Douglas's detractors and supporters in which he refused to comment on the state of the evidence or Ford's motivations. "Article 1, Section 3 of the Constitution states that, if the House of Representatives votes to undertake impeachment proceedings against Justice Douglas, then the Senators shall act as impartial judges," Church began. "For this reason I am sure you will agree, it would be very improper for me to express an opinion, let alone pass judgment, until the House has voted to impeach and has fully submitted its case to the Senate for a verdict." In May a constituent challenged Church to hold Douglas to the same standards as Carswell and Haynsworth. "If you are for purity in the Supreme Court, why are you not speaking out to rid the Court of Justice Douglas?" the constituent asked. "There isn't any question but he is one of the worst examples of the honor and integrity the high court should exemplify." Church responded by incorporating the form letter rather than make a comparison between the three judges.[74]

Wyoming's senatorial delegation, like Idaho's, was split between the two parties. The majority of the state appears to have been anti-Douglas. The editors of the state's second-largest newspaper, the *Wyoming State Tribune,* supported Ford and accused Douglas's supporters of hypocrisy. Wyoming's Republican senator, Clifford Hansen, was elected in 1966, but he had previously served as governor and had been a rancher by profession. Hansen solidly backed the majority of Nixon's policies, including Vietnamization, and he had close enough ties to the White House to coordinate a defense of the Cambodia invasion to the media. In 1967 he opposed Johnson's order to halt the aerial bombing of North Vietnam, claiming that it would cause the United States to seek a settlement through a position of weakness rather than strength. Hansen's record in regards to the judicial branch indicates that he was likely to support removing Douglas. Early on he had sided with Griffin to oppose Fortas's nomination as chief justice, and he voted for Haynsworth and Carswell. In explaining his opposition to Fortas, he decried the "the dangerous amount of judicial activism under Chief Justice Warren."[75]

Gale McGee, Wyoming's Democratic Party senator, opposed Ford, and in doing so the majority of his constituents. Elected to the Senate by a 1,913-vote margin in 1958 after former president Harry Truman, Lyndon Johnson, and John F. Kennedy came to Wyoming to support his campaign, McGee avidly supported Kennedy's New Frontier, civil rights, and the Great Society. In a similarly close election in which he benefited from the 1964 Johnson landslide, McGee returned to the Senate. McGee's differences with Douglas centered on Vietnam in the sense that McGee was in lockstep with Johnson's foreign and military policies, and he also endorsed Nixon's Vietnamization program. However, McGee voted against Haynsworth and Carswell, and he also voted in favor of the Cooper–Church Amendment.

Most of McGee's correspondents wanted Douglas removed from the Court, and McGee answered with a form letter that expressed his thanks for sharing their views. When a Cheyenne resident insisted that Douglas had "consorted with mafia figures" and "preached rebellion," McGee promised to give the matter his fullest attention if it came before the Senate. Another constituent who sought Douglas's impeachment also advanced an argument for lobbying Nixon to name Attorney General Mitchell to the Court. Again, McGee promised to give Mitchell his consideration, though one could suspect that he found the idea of Mitchell on the Court to be outlandish. In May, McGee showed his disgust with Ford to a constituent who argued that "one need only read Douglas's dissent in *United States v. Dennis,* or his civil rights jurisprudence to understand that without him on the Court, corporate interests could supplant a government of laws." (In *Dennis,* Douglas insisted that persons accused of communism were entitled to the fullest constitutional protections, and the district court judge in that case had denied the defendants these very rights.) McGee responded by assuring the writer that he had full faith in Celler and that Douglas's opponents objected to his liberalism more than anything else. In September, when the House investigation was wrapping up, McGee responded to a constituent by calling the impeachment effort "politically motivated, and retaliation for Haynsworth and Carswell."[76]

The Judiciary Awaits

Added to the hurdles of a Senate trial's ever occurring was that throughout the summer of 1970, some of Douglas's judicial and legal academy allies lobbied members of the upper house to defend him before a trial ever took place. Legal historian Irving Brant called Ford's allegations a farce and claimed to several senators that Ford's standards of proof were nothing more than "a means to bootstrap the prohibition against *ex post facto* rules onto Douglas." Likewise, Benjamin V. Cohen, at one time an influential advisor to Franklin Roosevelt, who publicly defended Douglas's actions in the Rosenberg appeals, lobbied liberal senators to defend Douglas. Brant and Cohen also wrote to judges asking them to support Douglas. In addition to Earl Warren quietly assisting Douglas by helping Paul McCloskey formulate a defense against Ford's allegations in the House, retired justice Tom Clark came to Douglas's defense and argued in a *Harvard Law Review* article that *Points of Rebellion* was not a call for revolution; rather, it "cries out with much truth." On April 19, 1970, Clark appeared on NBC's *Meet the Press* television hour and argued that there was "no reason to impeach Justice Douglas." Thus, instead of Ford successfully cowing the judiciary by threatening Warren from acting on Douglas's behalf, two retired justices came to Douglas's defense. And Clark was a judicial conservative from Texas.[77]

It is true that impeachments are not reviewable in the federal courts. The Constitution's framers wanted to ensure that Congress had the final say in the impeachment process so that the judicial branch could not usurp their decisions. Historically judges refrained from injecting their opinions into the impeachment process, but Ford's effort was an exception to this rule. Brennan was in close contact with Irving Brant, who by this time had published an acclaimed multivolume treatise on James Madison. In late August, Brant filed a legal brief to Celler's committee, arguing that although the post–Civil War impeachment attempt against President Andrew Johnson was a purely political act based on a specious statute, Ford's efforts against Douglas had even less legal merit. Before Brant sent his brief to Celler, Brennan reviewed it and responded to Brant that his argument was "very persuasive." Harold Leventhal and David Bazelon, on the Court of Appeals for the District of Columbia, also made their negative opinions on Ford known by publicly thanking Clark for his review of *Points of Rebellion*.[78]

Douglas received quiet support from Judge Frank Gray in Tennessee and from Roger Traynor on the California supreme court. On the Tenth Circuit, Alfred Murrah wrote Douglas that he would remain in Douglas's corner throughout the investigation. From the Ninth Circuit, Judge Richard Chambers tried to buoy Douglas's spirits by assuring him that the investigation would only yield information on Ford's ulterior motives. Douglas thanked Chambers for his support throughout the investigation but cautioned that while "a rather persistent rumor that the House Committee will be coming out with a report soon," there was a good chance that this rumor was false. Nonetheless, Douglas was determined to stay on the Court until well after his name was cleared.[79]

The most surprising action came from Gerhard Gesell, on the District Court for the District of Columbia. In early October he issued a temporary injunction against the House from publishing the names of sixty-five citizens and organizations that the Internal Security Committee—the successor to the Un-American Activities Committee—had concluded were a threat to national security. Led by Congressman Richard Ichord, one of Missouri's anti-Douglas representatives, the committee's purpose in publishing this list was to prod private organizations into financially starving the persons on the list, as well as enable the government to monitor, and if necessary imprison, them. The American Civil Liberties Union filed for the injunction after learning that the House had never given the persons named any opportunity to confront the allegations against them. Moreover, the sixty-five citizens were quite diverse, including members of the Black Panthers, antiwar leaders, and attorneys such as William Kunstler who defended their causes. On October 28, in a case captioned *Hentoff v. Ichord*, Gesell made his injunction order permanent. Gesell concluded that the publication of the report served no legitimate purpose and was in reality a subterfuge to harass and ultimately diminish the free speech rights and assembly rights of the sixty-five persons. He did not, however, bar individual congressmen from informing the nation of the identities of the sixty-five because to do so would violate the "Speech and Debate Clause." The ruling, then, did not fully protect the sixty-five citizens and organizations, but it provided more than a symbolic protection because if upheld, it prevented Congress from officially informing the nation that it had conclusively determined the persons and organizations were a threat to national security. As a Douglas protégé, Gesell used his authority in a manner that Douglas embraced. By this time several Southerners and conservatives detested Gesell for another reason.[80]

At the time of his appointment to the bench, Gesell was in private practice, but he had a background in military and governmental affairs. After graduating from Yale's law school in 1935, he joined the Securities and Exchange Commission, where he served as an advisor to Douglas. He also served as a counsel to the Democrat majority during a wartime congressional inves-tigation into the attack on Pearl Harbor. From 1941 until his judicial ap-pointment in 1967 Gesell was in private practice in Washington, DC. In 1962 Secretary of Defense McNamara appointed Gesell to chair the President's Committee on Equal Opportunity in the Armed Forces. Shortly afterward he formed a commission to investigate discrimination against African Ameri-can service members and their families. Southern congressmen decried the commission's report and claimed that it was nothing more than a means for the government to force integration in business establishments located near military installations.[81]

The nation's major newspapers and even the *Times* (London) reported on Gesell's order to Congress. Not surprisingly, Gesell was the recipient of angry correspondence accusing him of aiding communists, "when our dear boys are sent to Vietnam." An Ohio resident asked Gesell why he protected people "who intend to overthrow the legal government of the US." On November 3 a South Carolina radio station accused Gesell of inspiring communists. Gesell had support from the legal academy as well as from John Lord O'Brian, a civil rights scholar and former Justice Department attorney who ebulliently, but ultimately wrongly, believed that the decision would become a "landmark." However, O'Brian presciently predicted that Gesell would "face a hostile emo-tional reaction" from Ichord and his allies. Professor Burke Marshal at Yale's law school called the decision "clear and bold." The *Boston Globe* proclaimed Gesell's ruling "a stand for freedom." But the angry letters in Gesell's collec-tion appear to outnumber those who supported him. It appeared for a short time that Gesell would endure the same treatment as his mentor, Douglas.[82]

On December 1, Ichord wrote to his colleagues on the Internal Security Committee that he had scheduled a meeting for the next day so that the committee could consider taking action against Gesell. Ichord also published a letter in the *Kansas City Tribune* defending his committee's actions in inves-tigating the finances of dissenters as well as their attorneys: "If William Kun-stler, lawyer for the Chicago 7 who maintains that he should have the right to burn down an ROTC building states that most of the money to finance the revolution comes from speaking engagements, why should a committee of Congress be denied the right to know how much he is being paid for the privilege of exercising his freedom of speech."[83]

The next day Ichord vented his anger at Gesell to the House for usurping its authority to determine how it would inform the public of its investigation. Shortly after Ichord spoke, Samuel Devine, on Ohio Republican, accused Gesell of "obviously and arrogantly violating the separation of powers between the judiciary and legislative branches of government." John Hunt, a New Jersey Republican, asserted that Gesell had endangered national security, then added that the federal courts had "repeatedly interfered with the due process rights of Congress." Charles Rarick joined in the criticism, claiming that Gesell had been "the author of the infamous and revolutionary report in 1963, which aimed at destroying military effectiveness." Rarick then tried to convince Congress that Gesell's conduct was part and parcel of the military's failure to destroy communism in Vietnam because, like Douglas, Gesell had interfered in the military's affairs. All of these men had worked to impeach Douglas, and now they turned on his protégé. Gesell had his supporters, who not surprisingly opposed Ford and Nixon. In response, Democrats Patsy Mink of Hawaii and Abner Mikva of Illinois opposed the resolution, and they asked their fellow committee members to vote against it "rather than engage in the brinksmanship" proposed in the resolution.[84]

Two days before the House published its report on Douglas, Ichord presented a one-hour speech to the House in which he criticized Gesell for usurping the House's authority. On December 15 the House voted overwhelmingly to pass a resolution that declared a ban on judicial interference with the publication of its reports. This time, Louis Stokes, an Ohio Democrat, implored Congress not to adopt Ichord's proposed resolution. Stokes warned that there was a possibility that the committee would be able to smear "Supreme Court Justices, Cabinet officers, and other distinguished Americans in the Committee's secret files."[85]

While the rancor over Gesell remained confined to the House, it did not escape the Senate's attention, any more than it escaped the *Times* (London), that a district court judge and Douglas protégé had ruled that several anti-Douglas legislators were using their authority to trample the First Amendment rights of citizens, and many of these citizens shared Douglas's belief in the wrongness of the Vietnam conflict as well as the increasing trend of the government to intrude into the everyday lives of citizens for nefarious purposes. No senator came to Ichord's defense in this instance. Moreover, Leventhal and Chief Judge Charles Fahy on the Court of Appeals for the District of Columbia came to Gesell's defense. In the end Gesell avoided serving as a proxy target for Douglas, but the Court of Appeals overturned his ruling. Gesell in fact remained on the bench to oversee some of the Watergate burglar trials. After Ichord's failed assault on Gesell, the House investigation concluded that Douglas had committed no wrongdoing, and it only remained for Congress, and the nation, to receive the report.[86]

No judges spoke publicly against Douglas. Burger kept Nixon informed of how the investigation affected Douglas, and given that Burger supported the Cambodian invasion, it is questionable as to whether he would have tried to convince Nixon to lobby the Ford to stop the investigation. One judge surprisingly backed the administration's efforts to rein in judicial liberals, and may have been quietly siding with the administration over the impeachment campaign. In September, John J. Sirica on the District Court for the District of Columbia thanked Agnew for speaking against antiwar demonstrators, campus administrators, and liberal judges. "I am following with great interest the speeches you are presently making throughout the country, and I believe that the great majority of the American people are with you. Congratulations and please keep up the good work!" Sirica wrote. Three months earlier Sirica had lauded Clark Mollenhoff's contributions to the administration. "I know that you have enjoyed your work in the White House and I feel that you have performed an outstanding service," he told Mollenhoff. At the time few citizens would have had reason to know who Sirica was. By 1974 this would change, as Sirica presided over the trials of the "Watergate Burglars" and issued rulings that ultimately led to Nixon's resignation.[87]

Conclusion

On November 3, 1970, the nation voted in a midterm election that saw the Democratic Party increase its House seats from 243 to 255 and the Republican Party shrink from 192 to 180. All twelve of the Democratic Party's gains came from outside the South. While Ford's demand to impeach Douglas played a role in the election, certainly Cambodia was the biggest issue. For the most part Republican congressmen who backed impeaching Douglas retained their seats. However, there were exceptions. Indiana's Ross Adair, New Mexico's Edward Foreman, and Wisconsin's Henry Schadenberg lost to Democrat opponents. Wyoming's John Schiller Wold, a Republican, retired from Congress to run for governor and was replaced by a Democrat. Congressmen who had demanded a Rules Committee investigation generally did not suffer at the polls. However, Democrat Byron Rogers lost in a primary race to a more liberal candidate, who in turn lost to a conservative Republican. Catherine Dean May also lost her seat to a liberal Democrat. The fact that she had stood up to Ford and denounced the Cambodian invasion was not enough to save her congressional seat. Ford defeated his Democratic challenger, Jean McKee, with almost two thirds of the votes. Joe Waggonner ran unopposed, as did Thomas Abernethy. Louis Wyman and Edward Hutchinson defeated challengers with results similar to Ford's margin of victory. Celler also trounced a Republican opponent, and Carl Albert's ascension to the post of Speaker was all but assured.

On December 3 the Judiciary Committee informed the House

that the investigation had cleared Douglas of significant wrongdoing, but it would be two weeks before it published the report to the House. "Intensive investigation of the Special Subcommittee has not disclosed creditable evidence that would warrant preparation of charges on any acceptable concept of an impeachable offense," the subcommittee concluded. This conclusion largely broke along partisan lines, with Celler, Brooks, and Rogers in agreement. While McCulloch did not believe that impeachment was merited, he noted that his opinion was based on a lack of evidence to "come to a final, fast, hard, conclusion on whether an impeachable offense [had] been committed." Hutchinson dissented from the conclusion, but he too did not call for impeachment. Rather, he complained that because witnesses were not subjected to cross-examination, the investigation was incomplete, and the report should only be considered as merely a second interim report. Ford, Waggonner, and Wyman promised to renew their efforts in the next Congress, though given the addition of Democrats in the House, there was little chance of this occurring.[1]

Douglas understandably did not initially believe that the Judiciary Committee had cleared him because the report had not yet been published. He wrote to Rifkind that although he was pleased that none of the five congressmen had insisted that impeachment was necessary, he fretted that the report was "a political document," which left the possibility open for a further investigation. Moreover, he was certain that "Nixon, Agnew, Mitchell, and Ford put tremendous pressure on McCulloch and Hutchinson to leave the matter open," and he believed that Nixon and Ford would lobby for another investigation. Douglas presciently worried that Nixon and Ford had created a permanent alliance with Southern conservatives, and that they would target other liberal jurists. "I have a feeling that once a person becomes a target of Nixon, he continues to be a target no matter what he does or how many times a jury comes in with a verdict of Not Guilty," Douglas concluded. Whatever else may be said about Douglas's judgment, his characterization of Nixon was historically accurate.[2]

Douglas Cleared and the National Tenor

On December 16 the nation learned that the investigation had determined that Douglas had not performed legal work on behalf of the Parvin Foundation or CSDI. This included a determination that Douglas did not draft or provide input into the foundation's articles of incorporation or provide tax law advice. In terms of the Dominican Republic and Juan Bosch, the investigation concluded that Douglas had not violated the Logan Act or imperiled US foreign policy. Ford's allegations that Douglas had undermined national security, promoted communism, or conducted private foreign policy were also easily disproven, and it should have surprised no one that the subcommittee cleared him of wrongdoing in regards to these particular charges. While the subcommittee did not specifically investigate Parvin, it became clear that he was not a member of the Mafia, even if he had lawful business relations with several members of organized crime.

The subcommittee began its discussion with a brief but largely complimentary biography of Douglas and detailed the political positions of his detractors. "Associate Justice Douglas is noted for his tremendous energy. He has been recognized as one of the workhorses of the Court," the report read, after detailing that Douglas had earned almost $390,000 from his salary—$377,260.19 from his writings and $96,680 from the Parvin Foundation stipend during the period 1960–1969. The report next concluded that in no case in which Douglas sat was there a need for him to be disqualified. This included Allen Ginzburg's various appeals to the Court. Likewise, the investigation concluded that Sherman Skolnick's allegations against Douglas were meritless, and the report added that Skolnick had been uncooperative. In terms of *Points of Rebellion,* the investigation determined that in multiple instances Ford, Wyman, and Waggonner had selectively taken Douglas's words out of context and that it would be improper to recommend that Douglas recuse himself from national security appeals.

The investigation spent considerable space in its conclusion on Hutchinson's allegation that Douglas's efforts to help Kurdish professor Dr. Mustafa Salih Abdulrahman were not a Logan Act violation. Had Douglas championed Kurdish independence without the Nixon administration's permission, he might have run afoul of this never enforced law. However, Douglas used established legal channels, and he conceded to the Immigration and Naturalization Service Commissioner that although he did not personally know Abdulrahman, he believed that the professor's life was in danger if forced to return to Iraq. To this end, the investigation concluded that not only was Douglas innocent of trying to use his office to influence foreign policy, but also his advice to the immigration director—based on his extensive travels to the Middle and Near East—had proved helpful to an important agency determination.[3]

Hutchinson disagreed and insisted that Douglas had violated the Logan Act by using Abdulrahman as a subterfuge for altering the relationship between the United States and Iraq. Although Rifkind ably defended Douglas against this accusation, the State Department's general counsel independently concluded that Douglas had not affected foreign policy. Hutchinson also seemed to ignore the fact that other justices had intervened on behalf of persons awaiting deportation and that Douglas's actions on behalf of Abdulrahman were neither unusual nor unknown to Congress. In 1950, after the Court's determination to uphold a deportation order over Ms. Ellen Knauff, the Czechoslovakian wife of an American soldier, Justice Robert Jackson issued a stay against the deportation and ordered the immigration director to permit Knauff to stay in the United States while she petitioned Congress. The House then passed a specific bill enabling her to remain. While it is true that past practices do not exonerate breaches of judicial ethics, in this instance Hutchinson should have understood that Douglas's act of using a lawful means of redress was hardly a usurpation of executive power. And although the investigation did not rely on Jackson's conduct to clear Douglas, it evidences the spurious nature of Hutchinson's claim.[4]

Although the investigation had concluded that Douglas had not committed any wrongdoing that could result in an impeachment, there remained several matters requiring Douglas's clarification. For instance, in 1968 he had asked Parvin for a loan to purchase two acres of forestland in Washington, but Parvin resisted giving Douglas the loan because it would create the appearance that Douglas was beholden to him. While Douglas secured the loan through the Yakima Federal Savings and Loan Association, this episode revealed Douglas's carelessness in his relationship to Parvin. The final report should have chastened Douglas from his overt political conduct. Ultimately it did not, and in the words of John Dean, the impeachment campaign "created an intractable resolve by Douglas never to resign while Nixon was in office." Douglas would continue to try to stymie the administration's efforts in Vietnam, Cambodia, and Laos, but he was largely unsuccessful in doing so.[5]

By the time the investigation came to an end, the news reporting was minimal in comparison to April 15. The fact that Celler announced the investigation's termination on December 3, but waited until December 16 to have the report published, may have contributed to the lack of front-page reporting. As in the case of the late spring and summer, national and global events overtook the investigation. The *New York Times*'s editors blamed Nixon for starting the impeachment campaign. "It is time for President Nixon and Representative Ford to call a halt to this squalid campaign," the *Times*'s editors concluded. While the *Times* was highly critical of Nixon and Ford, it placed the story in the middle of its newspaper. On television, CBS's Eric Sevareid echoed the *New York Times* and added that Douglas had to cease his political activities. On December 16 Douglas gave a brief statement to ABC News in which he promised to return to the Court to continue his duties, and he asked America's youth to "keep the faith." He also lauded Burger and Blackmun, but he appeared surprised to learn that Sacha Volman may have been in the CIA's employ. Two days later the *Washington Post*'s editors noted that Douglas had not committed any impeachable offense. The *Post*'s editors opined that Douglas's off-bench activities had undermined his credibility. However, they called Ford's efforts "shameless in slandering Douglas" and accused the House of failing "to use the instance as a means for reforming judicial conduct." Although the *Times*'s and *Post*'s editors held a strong belief that Ford and Nixon had acted out of malice, their respective newspapers only minimally reported that the investigation cleared Douglas.[6]

In one respect some of the reporting was more favorable to Ford than to Douglas. Few of the nation's major newspapers cast aspersions on Ford or questioned his motives for demanding impeachment. However, there were several story lines that were not complimentary to Douglas. On December 4 the *Boston Globe* reported that the subcommittee had "cleared" Douglas, but then reported that he had attempted to secure a personal loan from Parvin. While this article was on the *Globe*'s eleventh page and the Calley court-martial was given more prominence, readers were left with the impression that Parvin had been more cautious with his relationship to Douglas than Douglas was toward Parvin. On December 16 the *Wall Street Journal* reported that a settlement had been reached between Denny's restaurants and the major Parvin-Dohrmann shareholders, and that the SEC had determined that Delbert Coleman, along with Edward Torres, had violated antitrust laws. While there was no mention of either Douglas or Parvin, the article had the potential to cause its readers to be reminded of Douglas's association with Parvin.[7]

In a Clark Mollenhoff–authored article, the *Des Moines Register* informed its readers about Douglas's attempt to secure a loan from Parvin as well as the fact that the subcommittee had not questioned witnesses under oath, and that the CIA may have used the CSDI without Douglas's knowledge. Mollenhoff exercised questionable journalistic ethics in failing to inform his readers that he had played an integral role in the impeachment effort. However, he conceded that "presumably there would be nothing illegal about a loan from Parvin whose cash flows from Las Vegas gambling enterprises." Yet even this concession hinted that Douglas had gained money from gambling interests. However, the *Register*'s editors were not in lockstep with Mollenhoff in all matters. They excoriated Richard Ichord for introducing a resolution against Judge Gerhard Gesell. "The House undoubtedly reflects the feelings of many Americans who couldn't care less for the rights of persons called Communists, militants, and revolutionaries," the editors argued. "Equally disturbing is the House's seeming willingness to sanction name-calling, the lazy man's way to instant political wisdom."[8]

On December 16 the *Baltimore Sun*'s top news story reported that Celler's committee had cleared Douglas of wrongdoing, but it headlined its report, "CIA Backing Linked to Trip by Douglas." The *Sun* informed its readers that although the investigation had cleared Douglas, the CIA, without Douglas's knowledge, had infiltrated the CSDI by employing Sacha Volman to obtain intelligence on communist influence in Latin America. The other major stories the *Sun* covered included news that the Food and Drug Administration discovered unhealthy amounts of mercury in canned tuna; that while the economy moved over the $1 trillion mark for the first time, industrial growth had stalled; that the House had weakened the Cooper–Church Amendment; that several state budgets were in crisis; and that Melvin Laird was threatening to resume the bombing campaign in North Vietnam if talks with that government were not fruitful.[9]

The next day the *Sun* reported that Senator Ervin had uncovered the fact that the army had spied on elected officials, and that witnesses in Calley's court-martial testified that atrocities in Vietnam had occurred well before My Lai. On the newspaper's twelfth page, there was a report that Douglas believed Ford's efforts against him were over and impeachment was no longer a possibility. Underneath this article the *Sun* reported that a New York grand jury had indicted Congressman Martin McKneally for tax fraud. While McKneally had not signed any of the resolutions against Douglas, he spoke in support of impeachment in late April. McKneally also had supported Goldwater in 1964, Nixon in 1968, and the Cambodian invasion. In a twist of irony, ABC's evening news program first announced Douglas's exoneration and then McKneally's indictment.[10]

Southern newspapers generally gave little space to the investigation's clearance of Douglas, indicating that even in the most anti–civil rights part of the country, the clamor to impeach Douglas had been overtaken by other events, even if there was disbelief in the conclusion of the House's investigation. The *Atlanta Journal* reported that the subcommittee had "cleared Douglas," but it went on to report that this issue was "still alive." At the same time the *Journal* headlined that a witness in Calley's court-martial testified that the lieutenant "shot the heads off" civilian victims. On December 3, 1970, the Jackson, Mississippi, *Clarion-Ledger* reported that the subcommittee had determined that no basis for impeachment existed. Two weeks later the *Ledger* reiterated its news story on Douglas, but it added that Douglas had been linked to CIA activity in South America. The *Ledger* contained an editorial from conservative James Kilpatrick that the investigation into Douglas was a "whitewash," and it encouraged the incoming Congress to investigate Douglas once more. No counterposition was published by the newspaper. Alabama's *Birmingham News* reported the committee's exoneration of Douglas on its December 16 front page, but it also noted that Ford promised to renew his efforts against Douglas in the next Congress. The next day the newspaper carried an editorial that lamented that Celler's investigation had been "a whitewash."[11]

The *Times* (London) did not report on the investigation, but its reporting on US national security affairs was emblematic of how complex politics had become. In addition to stressing that Nixon's popularity was at its lowest level since entering office, the *Times* headlined that Ervin had discovered that the army had spied on citizens, including Congressman Abner Mikva and Judge Otto Kerner. Additionally, on its December 18 front page, the *Times* informed its readers that the West German government had granted sanctuary to an American military deserter. Deeper in the newspaper was a report that Japanese citizens in Okinawa had destroyed United States Air Force property during a demonstration at an airbase used to launch bombing operations in

Vietnam, Cambodia, and Laos. The *Toronto Globe and Mail* and the *Sydney Morning Herald* carried similar stories, but nothing in regard to Douglas being cleared.[12]

Accusations without Political Liability

Although Ford had blundered in his effort to impeach Douglas, the House Republicans retained him as their leader. He defended Nixon over the Cambodia invasion and led a coalition to defeat the Cooper–Church Amendment. He also benefited from the passage of the Economic Stabilization Act. In fact, Ford suffered little, but when on December 28, 1970, Louis Wyman, William Scott, Joe Waggonner, and Robert Sikes promised to introduce a new resolution against Douglas when the Ninety-Second Congress convened, Ford had enough sense not to strongly advocate for it. Nonetheless, he criticized the investigation as a "whitewash" even before the report's December 16 publication.[13]

Intermittent calls for a new investigation continued until Douglas retired from the Court in November 1975. Georgia's lieutenant governor, Lester Maddox, in a public letter echoing the sentiments of thousands of his state's white citizens, urged Justice Hugo Black to back Ford, and he accused the Court of being responsible for a rise in public violence, pornography, and communism. In 1971 he called for Douglas's removal. Although the investigation had concluded its findings in his favor, Douglas worried that Ford would launch a new campaign against him in the Ninety-Second Congress. To Charles Ares he penned, "Ford's announcement indicates that 1971 is going to be a very arduous and nasty year." Douglas's worries proved to be short-lived. In 1972 Waggonner proudly told his constituents that he would begin a third effort to have Douglas impeached. By this time Waggonner was merely posturing for a lost cause.[14]

It is difficult to assess whether any of Douglas's key detractors suffered any liability. Waggonner and Wyman certainly did not in their lifetimes, and before the 2016 election their political positions were thought to be relics, or perhaps even extinct. In 1979 Ohio Republican John Ashbrook, who argued for Douglas's impeachment, tried to have United States District Court Judge Frank Battisti impeached. To Ashbrook, Battisti's sin was in ordering Cleveland to rapidly desegregate its schools. Ashbrook's resolution never made it to a committee debate, but his district's voters returned him to the House. The Republican Party suffered losses beyond the 1970 election. During the Ninety-Second Congress, Ogden Reid switched party affiliation and became a Democrat, and one year later Donald Riegel followed suit. Although Paul McCloskey waited for over a decade to change party affiliation, in 1972 he challenged Nixon in a short-lived primary campaign for the presidency. All three of these men were disgusted with the impeachment effort and the Cambodian invasion. Nixon's and Ford's actions throughout 1970 contributed to a small exodus of moderates from the Republican Party. This exodus does not seem to have harmed conservatism, but to this day there is an absence of liberal Republicans.

Not only did Nixon avoid a collapse of support from the failure of the anti-Douglas campaign, but also throughout 1971 his popularity rebounded. This rebound occurred in spite of the Court's decision in *New York Times v. Sullivan,* which eviscerated Nixon's attempt to quash freedom of the press and characterized as specious Nixon's argument that presidential secrecy was more important than governmental transparency and basic constitutional rights. A resurgence in popular support enabled Nixon to successfully nominate two conservative justices. In late 1971 Justices Hugo Black and John Harlan retired from the Court; in their place Nixon nominated William Rehnquist and Lewis Powell. Rehnquist's confirmation hearings proved contentious. He was a known conservative, and there was an open question as to whether, while serving as Justice Jackson's clerk in 1953, he had wanted Jackson to dissent in *Brown v. Board of Education.* Rehnquist claimed that his purpose in drafting a dissenting memorandum was to satisfy Jackson's desire to hear both sides of the argument. The Senate knew that before joining the Justice Department, Rehnquist had worked on limiting Hispanic votes in Arizona, and that he had advised Nixon on a variety of national security measures. The same alliance against Haynsworth and Carswell tried to keep Rehnquist from becoming a justice. But he was confirmed by a vote of 68 to 26. The role Rehnquist played in Ford's impeachment campaign against Douglas did not come out during the confirmation hearings.[15]

The Senate easily confirmed Nixon's other nominee, Lewis Powell, by a vote of 89 to 1. Powell was lauded by a number of organizations opposed to Haynsworth, Carswell, and Rehnquist. From a conservative perspective, he also had impeccable national security credentials. In 1969 Nixon appointed

Powell, a World War II veteran, to the Blue Ribbon Panel. This panel was charged with developing recommendations to enhance military readiness after the Vietnam conflict came to an end. There was nothing unusual about a judicial nominee's serving in a government capacity. William Howard Taft served as secretary of war, and other justices had served in cabinet positions, including as secretary of the navy. Interestingly, Powell examined political warfare in military operations. This type of warfare included the use of propaganda to destabilize a government's institutions. Nixon and Laird were provided with copies, and Powell impressed both men.[16]

Powell's reputation for integrity was well deserved. Yet he too engaged in dispensing political advice and making speeches of a political nature. During the late 1970s he frequently corresponded with George H. W. Bush, who had left Congress and served as CIA director under Ford. Powell advised Ford that the United States was being pushed out of East Africa by the Soviet Union because of human rights restraints. In 1986 he spoke at the ABA's annual convention and insisted that lawyers had a duty to educate society about the dangers of communism, and that universities should expand their curricula to include courses on Soviet history and politics for the same purpose. While there may have been merit to Powell's speech, it was reminiscent of Douglas's extrajudicial activities, except that Douglas would not have agreed with Powell's views on the duties of lawyers. Yet Powell gave his talk at a convention and was not paid for it by a foundation.[17]

Nixon, of course, won reelection in 1972 in a landslide over one of Douglas's defenders, Senator George McGovern. As Professor Joshua Glasser surmised in his analysis of McGovern's failed campaign, "It no longer seemed to matter that Nixon had chosen a malignant Spiro Agnew as his vice president and had blundered far worse in his first two Supreme Court nominations." In February 1972 Nixon became the first president to visit the People's Republic of China, and he established a meaningful rapport with Mao Zedong. Vietnamization appeared to have come close to fulfilling its promise, with only 10,000 military forces remaining in South Vietnam, and when South Vietnam came under attack in 1972, Nixon ordered a massive aerial campaign against North Vietnam. Known as Operation Linebacker, heavy bombers targeted Hanoi, and a continuation of the air offense occurred after the election. On January 15, 1973, the North and South Vietnamese governments, along with

Henry Kissinger, signed a peace accord in Paris. Contemporaneously, Nixon met with Soviet premier Leonid Brezhnev, and Americans sensed a deescalation of Cold War tensions. Nixon seemingly achieved his promise of having the United States appear to maintain its military, economic, and diplomatic strength. McGovern, by contrast, was a weak candidate. The most prominent Republican loss in 1972 was Margaret Chase Smith, who had refused to join in the effort to have Douglas removed from the Court.[18]

Even before the investigation concluded, Douglas did not waver from dissenting against the Court's refusal to wade into the legality of the Vietnam conflict. In November 1970 he dissented against the Court's determination that it lacked jurisdiction to determine the Massachusetts governor's challenge to the federal government's authority to conscript the state's citizens and then order them to fight in an undeclared war. The dean of Tufts University's Fletcher School of Government, along with dozens of other academics and lawyers, lauded Douglas's spirited dissent. Early in the next year Random House asked Douglas to write a preface to a book entitled *America's Reign of Terror*. The book focused on the United States between 1917 and 1920, and Douglas penned, "There is a dark ugly streak in all nations. . . . One who reads these pages closely against today's headlines will get clues as to the malady which has affected us." Douglas wrote these words one year to the day after Ford announced his intention to have Douglas impeached.[19]

In March 1972, in *Laird v. Tatum*, Douglas dissented from the Court's determination that a challenge to the Army's surveillance of citizens who opposed the war presented a "political question" outside the Court's jurisdiction. Douglas concluded his dissent by calling the army's program "a cancer on the body politic," adding, "The First Amendment was designed to allow rebellion to remain as our heritage." There were two outstanding features to the decision beyond Douglas's dissent. Rehnquist had played a role at the Justice Department in providing advice over the program, but he did not recuse himself from the case. He sided with the majority's decision that the issue—that is, whether the army's actions curbed the free speech rights of citizens by instilling fear into them—was outside the Court's jurisdiction. However, Rehnquist initially wanted to write that there was nothing unconstitutional about the use of the military to domestically surveil citizens. The second feature of the decision was that Ervin represented one of the parties suing the government. In essence, Ervin and Douglas became of like mind in regard to warning of the dangers of the federal government's use of national security as a reason to curb the rights of minorities.[20]

Although the Paris Accords ended the United States' involvement in the Vietnam War, military operations in Cambodia did not cease. With his election victory in hand, Nixon ordered air strikes into Cambodia in support of Lon Nol's endangered regime. The Khmer Rouge, Cambodia's communist party, was not bound by the accords and had made significant military advances against Lon Nol's government. The Khmer Rouge also began to commit abuses against Cambodia's population on a genocidal scale. On February 9, 1973, air operations once more were undertaken, and continuous bombing occurred until August. The Senate and House passed a new resolution to force an end to the air operations by August 15. Before this termination date, on July 25, Congresswoman Elizabeth Holtzman filed suit in United States District Court in New York and obtained an injunction to prevent further military activities in Cambodia. Two days later the injunction was overturned by the appellate court. In 1972 Holtzman defeated Celler in the Democratic Party primary; she proved to be a strong opponent of both Nixon and Ford.

After the appellate court overturned the injunction, Holtzman filed for a stay against the government with Justice Thurgood Marshall, but Marshall was unwilling to intervene. Holtzman then turned to Douglas, who unsurprisingly issued an order to the government to cease military operations in Cambodia. Once more Douglas received hundreds of letters lauding his stand against Nixon, and once more he created a firestorm both on and off the Court. Marshall was incensed at Douglas's for trumping his decision, and he pointed out errors in Douglas's rationale before concluding that he "was at a loss in attempting to understand any of this." Perhaps Hugo Black and Earl Warren would have sided with Douglas. Certainly Rehnquist and Powell would not. Nor would Burger, Brennan, Marshall, Stewart, Blackmun, or White. Douglas suffered a defeat, as did Holtzman and several military officers who joined in her suit. By this time Nixon's presidency was in jeopardy, though Nixon did not act as though this were the case. In the end eight of the justices overrode Douglas's order. Holtzman later called Douglas's decision remarkable and lauded his courage. She also had harsh words for Ford. In explaining her opposition to his congressional appointment as vice president,

she wrote, "Ford went to the House floor and called for Douglas's impeachment, something that seemed shameful and dishonest to me. Douglas had
done nothing to warrant impeachment except annoy the Republicans by being such a fierce and independent liberal."[21]

Nixon resigned from the presidency on August 9, 1974. Two days earlier,
Senator Barry Goldwater, Senate Minority Leader Hugh Scott, and Congressman John Rhodes had informed Nixon that he had lost conservative support
in Congress and would not survive a Senate trial. Nine months before this
occurred, Spiro Agnew resigned the vice presidency and pled no contest to a
single charge of tax evasion. On December 6, 1973, Congress confirmed Ford
as vice president by a vote of 92 to 3 in the Senate and 387 to 5 in the House.
Congressmen Don Edwards and Jerome Waldie opposed Ford's nomination
on the basis of his impeachment campaign against the Justice. But Carl Albert
did not want a vacancy in the White House, and Ford appeared to be the best
candidate because he disclaimed interest in the presidency and had worked
in a bipartisan manner on other matters. Jack Brooks—who had helped to
clear Douglas—endorsed Ford's ascension to become vice president, as did
several of Douglas's other defenders. Ford, as is well known, became president after Nixon's resignation, then pardoned Nixon. When in 1974 Congress
confirmed Nelson Rockefeller as Ford's vice president, Douglas evidenced a
renewed faith in the executive branch. Rockefeller had taken a nominal role
in the CSDI as late as 1969, a point lost on Nixon and Ford during the impeachment attempt.[22]

On November 12, 1975, Douglas wrote to Ford that he intended to retire
from the Court. Ford responded by expressing his and the country's "great
gratitude" for Douglas's years of public service "matched by few Americans."
Ford went so far as to note his "admiration" for Douglas, and he characterized
his judicial service as "distinguished" and "unequalled in the all the history
of the Court." Whether Ford's response was an expression of a courtesy or
an acknowledgment of error for demanding Douglas's impeachment is difficult to know. To his credit, Ford tried to restore the public's confidence in
the presidency, solve an economic crisis, and project strength to the Soviet
Union, China, and the United States' allies. He did not nominate a conservative to replace Douglas. John Paul Stevens would prove to be an individualist who voted for restraints against government intrusions into the lives of

citizens. When Douglas's staff and clerks wrote of their sadness at Douglas's retirement, Douglas urged them to "keep the faith in the rule of law not only for our own people, but for the people of the world."[23]

The Revived Judicial Attack

Douglas died in 1980. When Burger spoke at his funeral, some of his remarks could have been taken as a rebuke against Ford, Waggonner, Wyman, and the thousands of citizens who had demanded his impeachment. "There was a time when some who differed with him on issues mistakenly described him as an atheist and even questioned his belief in the American system," Burger began. "This shows how terribly wrong—even absurd—perceptions can be." Burger did not mention the impeachment attempt, but he made sure that the audience understood he believed Douglas sincerely felt his decisions on the Court strengthened the United States. After Burger, Clark Clifford spoke and characterized Douglas's life as a long continuous struggle against oppression, with the fundamental principle that government had to be controlled by the governed. Both Burger and Clifford were correct in how Douglas saw himself.[24]

It is difficult to reconcile Ford's presidency and his many other accomplishments with his 1970 campaign against Douglas. In our current time of vitriolic politics, Ford's presidential example of decency and transparency should rightly serve as a beacon for better-natured citizens to enter government, or at least engage in political discourse. Ford, according to Benton Becker, was a "good soldier" who followed Nixon's signal in demanding Douglas's impeachment. There is no reason, despite the lock on Becker's private papers, to believe this is untrue. It might also be the case that Ford did not know the full reasoning of Nixon's grand design against Douglas. Yet it must be recognized that all human beings are fallible: Douglas engaged in extrajudicial activities that evidenced his sincere and realistic worries for democracy, but that nonetheless were ill suited for the judiciary; and Ford made an alliance with bigots in a failed campaign against Douglas. In one respect, the lack of political liability for Ford, in spite of his personal decency, haunts us today.

On March 28, 2006, Justice Antonin Scalia spoke to the University of Freiburg, Switzerland, student body and cast significant doubts on the rights of captured enemy combatants. The speech was nothing less than a mirror of the George W. Bush's administration's legal claims that in the modern conflicts against insurgents, rights embodied in the Geneva conventions are merely a nicety. On the eve of the 2016 election, Justice Ruth Bader Ginsburg called presidential candidate Donald Trump a "faker." Justice Ginsburg apologized for her comment; Justice Scalia disclaimed any wrongdoing. The examples of Justice Rehnquist and Justice Powell should remind us that there is a double standard for judicial conduct. Rehnquist's unwillingness to recuse himself in *Laird v. Tatum,* while conceivably legally defensible for a judge on a court of final appeal, did not prevent his ascension to the post of chief justice. When a judge publicly challenges the national security rationale of the political branches, there is greater chance of being investigated for malfeasance than when a judge openly backs an administration's national security rationale before deciding challenges to that rationale.

The impeachment effort against Douglas failed to resolve whether a constitutional standard exists for impeachment, or whether the standard is what Ford claimed it to be: the agreement by a bare majority of the House of Representatives. Scholars are likely to debate impeachment standards whenever a government officer is subject to significant investigation. The impeachment effort does, however, inform us that current political alignments, particularly in regard to geography, occurred as a part of a battle over civil rights and the meaning of equality, the acceptance of government secrecy, and the use of military forces overseas. The lack of full racial and ethnic equality and a reemergence of nativism in national politics shows that Douglas's battles and the impeachment attempt against him were emblematic of long-term ills.

Then there is President Trump's treatment of the judiciary and his apparent disregard of the rule of law. Perhaps because he has succeeded in defeating less well-financed litigants in the pretrial stages of civil suits, he came to the presidency with an expectation of a servile federal judiciary. After accusing a federal judge of being unable to divest himself from his Hispanic heritage—as though all Hispanics approach life in an identical manner—the electorate placed him in the White House. On several occasions Trump singled out other judges as an alleged danger to national security when they cast doubts on the constitutionality of immigration and entry restrictions. While individual Republican legislators have expressed revulsion about the president's conduct, the party's majority leadership and the majority of its members have responded with silence or obsequious deference. In a time where the rights of disfavored minorities are treated as privileges rather than as part of constitutional rights for all Americans, this silence is empowering to those who would undermine the judiciary with false assertions of being a threat to national security. In analyzing Ford's presidency and postpresidential conduct, one can surmise that he would have fought against the devolution of decency and diminution of respect for the rule of law. Although, as one Douglas biographer has stated in a book title, "he shall not pass this way again," and although no justice has imitated his extrajudicial conduct, the judiciary needs vigorous protection.

Men who accuse others of corruption are often burdened with corrupt designs of their own. This was true not only in regard to Spiro Agnew but also Attorney General John Mitchell, who went to prison after being convicted of tax fraud, and William Wilson, who had to resign from the Justice Department in 1972 after evidence surfaced that he had taken part in gambling and bribery fraud in Texas. Perhaps Mitchell and Wilson believed they had "uncovered" Douglas's alleged frauds by reflecting their own conduct onto the justice. This might be the most charitable explanation for their conduct. But because they had taken part in developing a means to imprison dissenters and had knowledge of the planned Cambodian invasion, it is more likely beyond coincidence that they, and Clark Mollenhoff, were active participants in attempting to remove Douglas for all of the reasons stated: making permanent the Southern strategy, quickly constructing a conservative Court to uphold Nixon's actions, and creating both a news deflection and scapegoat in Douglas to provide political cover for the Cambodian invasion. American democracy is best served by having judges across a jurisprudential philosophy spectrum, including judges with the conscience of Douglas, albeit with greater caution in their extrajudicial lives. Judicial independence, like democracy itself, needs legislative defenders who not only possess the political acumen of Carl Albert, Emanuel Celler, and Thomas "Tip" O'Neill but also the courage of William McCulloch, Paul McCloskey, Edward Brooke, Edith Starrett Green, Patsy Mink, Catherine Dean May, and Florence Dwyer.

NOTES

ABBREVIATIONS USED IN NOTES

BG-ASU   Barry Goldwater Papers, Arizona State University
EW   Earl Warren Papers, Library of Congress
GDA   George D. Aiken Papers, University of Vermont Special Collections
GG-GWU   Gilbert Gude Papers, George Washington University
HLB   Hugo Lafayette Black Papers, Library of Congress
NARG   National Archives and Records Group
PF-ASU   Paul Fannin, Arizona State University
PH-UMich Philip Hart, University of Michigan, Bentley Historical Library
PM   Patsy Mink Papers, Library of Congress
RN-ANF   Richard Nixon Library, Alpha Name Files
RN-PPF   Richard Nixon Library, President's Personal File
SE-UNC   Samuel Ervin Papers, University of North Carolina
WOD   William O. Douglas Papers, Library of Congress

CHAPTER 1. COLD WAR POLITICS AND THE COURT UNDER SIEGE

1   John F. Manley, "The Conservative Coalition in Congress," in *New Perspectives on the House of Representatives,* ed. Robert L. Peabody and Nelson W. Polsby (New York: Rand McNally, 1977), 106; Scott Kaufman, *Ambition, Pragmatism, and Party: A Political Biography of Gerald R. Ford* (Lawrence: University Press of Kansas, 2017), 88–100; Douglas Brinkley, *Gerald R. Ford: The American Presidents Series, the 38th President, 1974–1977* (New York: Times Books, 2007), 135; Robert Mason, *Richard Nixon and the Quest for a New Majority* (Chapel Hill: University of North Carolina Press, 2004), 51–55.

2   David R. Goldfield, *Race Relations and Southern Culture: 1940 to the Present* (Baton Rouge: Louisiana State University Press, 1990), 197; Daily News Digest, Washington Republican Party, October 13, 1970 [Catherine Dean May/3–8].

3   "Republicans Plan Move on Douglas," *Austin American,* April 13, 1970.

4   See, e.g., Laura Kalman, *The Long Reach of the Sixties: LBJ, Nixon, and the Making of the Contemporary Supreme Court* (Oxford: Oxford University Press, 2017), 243–244; Roudebush to Ford, April 10, 1970 [William Lloyd Scott/79].

5   "Sen. Allen Supports Carswell," *Lincoln Star Journal,* March 31, 1970; John Dean, *The Rehnquist Choice: The Untold Story of the Nixon Appointment that Redefined the Supreme Court* (New York: Free Press, 2001), 24–25; William B. Saxbe, *"I've Seen the Elephant": An Autobiography* (Kent, OH: Kent State University Press, 2000), 110–116; Abner J. Mikva and Patti B. Saris, *The American Congress: The First Branch* (New York: Watts Press, 1983), 109; John Ehrlichman, *Witness to Power: The Nixon Years* (New York: Simon & Schuster, 1982), 116.

6   Koch, Petition, April 15, 1970 [Clarence Dickinson Long/51]; *Congressional Record,* April 15, 1970, 3126–3128.

7   Bob Woodward and Scott Armstrong, *The Brethren: Inside the Supreme Court* (New York: Simon & Schuster, 1979).

8   Douglas to Brennan, November 26, 1961 [William J. Brennan/II:109]; Gerald Ford History Project, interview of Benton Becker, June 9, 2009, at Gerald Ford Library; Williams Memorandum, May 22, 1969 [John J. William/40]; Bruce Allen Murphy, *Wild Bill: The Legend and Life of William O. Douglas, America's Most Controversial Supreme Court Justice* (New York: Random House, 2003), 430–434.

9   Benton Becker interview.

10   "Judge Accused of Links with Gamblers," *Sydney Morning Herald,* April 17, 1970; "US Battle to Impeach Judge," *Times* (London), April 17, 1970; "Ford Charges Justice Douglas Was Moonlighter for International Gamblers," *Toronto Globe and Anchor,* April 16, 1970.

11   Henry Kissinger to Richard Nixon, April 26, 1970 [RN-PPF/58]; Justin P. Coffey, *Spiro Agnew and the Rise of the Republican Right* (Santa Barbara, CA: ABC-CLIO, 2015), 109–110; John M. Shaw, *The Cambodian Campaign: The 1970 Offensive and America's Vietnam War* (Lawrence: University Press of Kansas, 2005), 33.

12   Melvin Laird to Nixon, April 27, 1970 [RN-PPF/58]; Andrew L. Johns, *Vietnam's Second Front: Domestic Politics, the Republican Party, and the War* (Lexington: University Press of Kentucky, 2010), 281–284; Walter Isaacson, *Kissinger: A Biography* (New York: Simon & Schuster, 1992), 268–269; Richard Hunt, *Melvin Laird and the Foundation for the Post-Vietnam Military, 1969–1977* (Washington, DC: Department of Defense, Office of the Historian, 2015), 143–152; Richard D. Schulzinger, "Nixon, Congress, and the War in Vietnam," in *Vietnam and the American Political Tradition: The Politics of Dissent,* ed. Randall B. Woods (Cambridge: Cambridge University Press, 2003), 286.

13   Murphy, *Wild Bill,* 366–368.

14   Yanek Mieczkowski, *Gerald Ford and the Challenges of the 1970s* (Lexington: University Press of Kentucky, 2005), 49; David S. Broder, *Behind the Front Page: A Candid Look at How the News Is Made* (New York: Simon & Schuster, 1987), 54.

15   Robert A. Caro, *Master of the Senate: The Years of Lyndon Johnson 3* (New York: Knopf, 2002), 521–524; Richard M. Filipink Jr., *Dwight Eisenhower and American Foreign Policy during the 1960s: An American Lion in Winter* (Lanham, MD: Lexington Books, 2015), 63–65; Blema S. Steinberg, *Shame and Humiliation: Presidential Decision Making on Vietnam* (Montreal: McGill-Queens University Press, 1996), 124–169.

16   Filipink, *Dwight Eisenhower,* 19; Irwin F. Gellman, *The President and the Apprentice: Eisenhower and Nixon, 1952–1961* (New Haven, CT: Yale University Press, 2015), 17.

17   Kalman, *Long Reach,* 209–251.

18   Joseph Aistrup, *The Southern Strategy Revisited: Republican Top-Down Advancement in the South* (Lexington: University Press of Kentucky, 1996), 29–35

19 Eastland to Senator Harry Byrd, October 22, 1957 [James O. Eastland/SI, SS18, 2]; James O. Heath, *To Face Down Dixie: South Carolina's War on the Supreme Court in the Age of Civil Rights* (Baton Rouge: Louisiana State University Press, 2017), 29; statement of Congressman Robert Dole, June 24, 1965 [Robert Dole/V-1].

20 Kerr to Ervin, February 9, 1956 [SE-UNC/12]; V. D. Estes to Ervin, January 30, 1956 [SE-UNC/12]; Chris Myers Asch, *The Senator and the Sharecropper: The Freedom Struggles of James O. Eastland and Fannie Lou Harper* (New York: New Press, 2008), 270.

21 Black to Schneebeli, May 24, 1969 [HLB/211]; "Opinion Ballot," to Gale McGee, November 9, 1966 [Gale McGee].

22 "Opinion Ballot," to Gale McGee; Cabell to colleagues, April 28, 1966 [PM/389].

23 Morse to Douglas, June 29, 1959 [WOD/358]; Morse, speech to the University of Minnesota Law School, February 26, 1969 [WOD/358]; McGee to P. A. Kahle [Gale McGee]; McGee to G. L. Brandon, August 24, 1966 [Gale McGee].

24 Taft to Frank Gates, September 28, 1951 [Robert Taft/169].

25 Kari Frederickson, *The Dixiecrat Revolt and the End of the Solid South, 1932–1968* (Chapel Hill: University of North Carolina Press, 2001), 174–176.

26 Edward M. Pooley to Vinson, May 5, 1952 [Frederick Vinson]; Pooley to Vinson, May 5, 1952 [Frederick Vinson]; Vinson to Pooley, June 11, 1952 [Frederick Vinson].

27 Caro, *Master of the Senate,* 524; Nolan J. Cathal, *Principled Diplomacy: Security and Rights in US Foreign Policy* (Westport, CT: Greenwood Press, 1993), 214–216; *Liberty Lowdown* ("A Confidential Washington Report Supplied Only to Liberty Lobby Pledgers"), no. 81, November 1969; "The Supreme Court and the Communists," Task Force, January 1958 [HLB/24]; Anderson to D. A. Downs, January 30, 1961 [Clinton Presba Anderson/659].

28 Reply by Pennsylvania Supreme Court Justice Michael A. Musmanno to the statement made by Attorney General Herbert Brownell on April 12, 1954, in which he opposed the outlawing of the Communist Party, April 11, 1954 [Emanuel Celler/92].

29 Dan Smoot Report, "Impeaching Earl Warren," January 30, 1961 [HLB/24]; Western Pennsylvania Council for America [HLB/24]; First Christian Church of Central Kentucky, January 1961 [HLB/24]; Arizona Mothers for Earl Warren's Impeachment [HLB/24].

30 Statement of Senator Joseph Montoya, *Congressional Record,* Senate, May 2, 1962, 7599–7607 S.J. Res., 114 (1957); Montoya to Hannett, June 27, 1957 [Joseph Montoya/6].

31 Bruce K. Falk, *The Origins of the Southern Strategy: Two-Party Competition in South Carolina, 1950–1972* (Lanham, MD: Lexington Books, 2001), 118–120.

32 Kevin P. Phillips, *The Emerging Republican Majority* (Princeton, NJ: Princeton University Press, 2015), 266–288.

33 See, e.g., Maarten Zweirs, *Senator James O. Eastland: Mississippi's Jim Crow Democrat* (Baton Rouge: Louisiana State University Press, 2015), 149; Gilbert Fite,

Richard B. Russell Jr., Senator from Georgia (Chapel Hill: University of North Carolina Press, 1991), 333–334.

34 Jack Bass and Marilyn Thomson, *Strom: The Complicated Personal and Political Life of Strom Thurmond* (New York: Public Affairs, 2005), 155–175; Randall Bennett Woods, *J. William Fulbright, Vietnam, and the Search for a Cold War Foreign Policy* (Cambridge: Cambridge University Press, 1995), 12–14.

35 Robert David Thompson, *Ernest Gruening and the American Dissenting Tradition* (Cambridge, MA: Harvard University Press, 1998), 252–253; William C. Gibbons, *The US Government and the Vietnam War: Executive and Legislative Roles and Relationships—Part 2: 1961–1964* (Princeton, NJ: Princeton University Press, 1986), 304–311.

36 See, e.g., Christopher Bassford, *The Spit-Shine Syndrome: Organizational Irrationality in the American Field Army* (Westport, CT: Greenwood Press, 1988), 26–27; David Cortright, *Soldiers in Revolt: GI Resistance during the Vietnam War* (New York: Haymarket Books, 1975), 10–43; Dale R. Herspring, *The Pentagon and the Presidency: Civil Military Relations from FDR to George Bush* (Lawrence: University Press of Kansas, 2005), 198–199.

37 James Lewes, *Protest and Survive: Underground GI Newspapers during the Vietnam War* (Westport, CT: Praeger, 2003), 51–83; Richard Moser, *The New Winter Soldiers: GI and Veteran Dissent during the Vietnam Era* (New Brunswick, NJ: Rutgers University Press, 1996), 48–50.

38 Morris J. MacGregor, *Integration of the Armed Forces, 1940–1965* (Washington, DC: Center for Military Studies, 1981), 578.

39 Roth to Earl Warren, May 28, 1969 [EW/719]; "Douglas Praises Revolutionaries in US Colleges," *New York Times*, April 14, 1969.

40 Black to Cohen, September 11, 1967 [Harry A. Blackmun/23].

41 Douglas to Rockefeller, March 22, 1968 [WOD/367]; Douglas to Horowitz, November 28, 1969 [WOD/341]; Horowitz to Douglas, December 2, 1970 [WOD/341].

42 ulian E. Williams, *The Case against Justice William O. Douglas* (Tulsa, OK: Christian Crusade, 1970), 4–6; H. E. McBride, *Impeach Justice Douglas* (New York: Exposition Press, 1971), 11–26.

43 "Thurman Sensing the News," *Panama City News Herald*, April 23, 1970; Fulton Lewis, "If Reds Are Threat to US, So Are Native Advocates of Sovietism," July 26, 1951 [WOD/207].

44 Powell v. McCormack, 395 US 486 (1969).

CHAPTER 2. THE RISING MEN, THE MUCKRAKERS OF
THE JUDICIARY, AND BELEAGUERED JUDGES

1 Vance Hartke, *The American Crisis in Vietnam* (Indianapolis, IN: Bobbs-Merrill, 1968), 5; Jonathan Bell, *The Liberal State on Trial: The Cold War and American Politics in the Truman Years* (New York: Columbia University Press,

2004), 199–205; Michael A. Cohen, *American Maelstrom: The 1968 Election and the Politics of Division* (Oxford: Oxford University Press, 2016), 56.

2 Joseph E. Lowndes, *From the New Deal to the New Right: Race and the Southern Origins of Modern Conservatism* (New Haven, CT: Yale University Press, 2008), 129.

3 See, e.g., Bruce Allen Murphy, *Fortas: The Rise and Ruin of a Supreme Court Justice* (New York: William Morrow, 1988), 544–577; Laura Kalman, *Abe Fortas: A Biography* (New Haven, CT: Yale University Press, 1990), 359–379; Scherle to Warren, May 6, 1969 [EW/719].

4 Nixon, speech accepting Republican Party's nomination, August 8, 1968, https://www.c-span.org/video/?4022-2/richard-nixon-1968-acceptance-speech.

5 See, e.g., Allen J. Matusow, *Nixon's Economy: Booms, Busts, Dollars, and Votes* (Lawrence: University Press of Kansas, 1998), 2–14; Melvin Small, *The Presidency of Richard Nixon* (Lawrence: University Press of Kansas, 1999), 22–68; Jeffrey Kimball, "The Nixon Doctrine: A Saga of Misunderstanding," *Presidential Series Quarterly* 36, no. 1 (2006): 59–74.

6 Richard M. Nixon, "Asia after Vietnam," *Foreign Affairs* 46 (1967): 111–125.

7 Cohen, *American Maelstrom*, 174–180; John Morton Blum, *Years of Discord: American Politics and Society, 1961–1974* (New York: Norton 1991), 328.

8 Dale van Atta, *With Honor: Melvin Laird in War, Peace, and Politics* (Madison: University of Wisconsin Press, 2008), 1–99.

9 David L. Anderson, *The Columbia Guide to the Vietnam War* (New York: Columbia University Press, 2002), 148–150; Matusow, *Nixon's Economy*, 8.

10 *Hearings before the Select Committee to Study Governmental Operations with Respect to Intelligence Activities of the United States Senate* (Wasington, DC: Government Printing Office, 1976), 2:16–20; "IRS Says Mollenhoff Asked to See Returns Files by Nine Persons," *Wall Street Journal*, April 15, 1970; Stanley Kutler, *The Wars of Watergate: The Last Crisis of Richard Nixon* (New York: Norton, 1990), 119.

11 David Cunningham, *There's Something Happening Here: The New Left, the Klan, and FBI Counterintelligence* (Berkeley: University of California Press, 2004), 33–35; Bryan Burrough, *Days of Rage: America's Radical Underground, the FBI, and the Forgotten Age of Revolutionary Violence* (New York: Penguin, 2015), 131–135.

12 David L. Anderson, "No More Vietnams: Historians Debate the Policy Lessons of the Vietnam War," in *The War That Never Ends: New Perspectives on the Vietnam War*, ed. David L. Anderson and John Ernst (Lexington: University Press of Kentucky, 2007), 28.

13 "Johnson Assailed on Vietnam War by GOP in House: Report Says He Encouraged Red's Miscalculation by '64 Campaign Oratory," *New York Times*, August 25, 1965.

14 Joseph A. Califano, *The Triumph and Tragedy of Lyndon Johnson: The White House Years* (New York: Touchstone, 1992), 29; James N. Cannon, *Time and Chance:*

Gerald Ford's Appointment with History (Ann Arbor: University of Michigan Press, 1998), 76–88; James Cannon, *Gerald R. Ford: An Honorable Life* (Ann Arbor: University of Michigan Press, 2013), 87–88.

15 Kaufman, *Ambition, Pragmatism, and Party,* 1–33.

16 Brinkley, *Gerald R. Ford,* 5–8; Cannon, *Time and Chance,* 51–55.

17 Cannon, *Time and Chance,* 76–88.

18 Jim Newton, *Justice for All: Earl Warren and the Nation He Made* (London: Penguin, 2006), 334; Charles L. Lamb, "Warren Burger," in *The Burger Court: Political and Judicial Profiles,* ed. Charles Lamb and Stephen Halpern (Champaign: University of Illinois Press, 1991), 129–134.

19 See, e.g., Earl Maltz, *The Chief Justiceship of Warren Burger, 1969–1986* (Columbia: University of South Carolina Press, 2003), 8–12; Burger to Nixon, April 30, 1970 [John W. Dean III/23].

20 Burger to Blackmun, September 8, 1960 [Harry A. Blackmun/26].

21 Blackmun to Burger, March 2, 1967 [Harry A. Blackmun/50]; Burger to Blackmun, February 6, 1968 [Harry A. Blackmun/50].

22 Speech of Byrd, July 11, 1969, *Congressional Record,* S7920; Dethmers to Blackmun, June 13, 1969 [Harry A. Blackmun/50]; Register to Blackmun, May 26, 1969 [Harry A. Blackmun/50].

23 "America Challenged Has $3 Million Answer: Justice Douglas' Book Leads to Parvin Foundation which Helps Tell the World of US," *Los Angeles Times,* November 8, 1964; Williams to Warren, October 17, 1966 [EW/352].

24 Longines-Wittnauer with Senator John J. Williams, National Archives and Records Administration, ARC identifier 95861.

25 Carol E. Hoffecker, *Honest John Williams: US Senator from Delaware* (Newark: University of Delaware Press, 2000), 178–219.

26 Robert Caro, *The Passage of Power: The Years of Lyndon Johnson 4* (New York: Vintage, 2002), 282; David W. Reinhard, *The Republican Right since 1945* (Lexington: University Press of Kentucky, 1983), 15; Robert David Johnson, *All the Way with LBJ: The 1964 Presidential Election* (Cambridge: Cambridge University Press, 2009), 28.

27 Caro, *Passage of Power,* 282; Hoffecker, *Honest John Williams,* 181–204.

28 Hoffecker, *Honest John Williams,* 195–205.

29 See, e.g., Kerry Segrave, *Vending Machines: An American Social History* (Jefferson, NC: McFarland, 2002), 1–22; William N. Thompson, *Gambling in America: An Encyclopedia of History, Issues, and Society* (Santa Barbara, CA: ABC-CLIO, 2015), 415; Donald R. Cressey, *Theft of the Nation: The Structure and Operations of Organized Crime in America* (New Brunswick, NJ: Transaction, 2008), 118–122; Peter Reuter, Jonathan Rubenstein, and Simon Wynn, *Racketeering in Legitimate Industries: Two Case Studies* (Washington, DC: Department of Justice, 1983), 1–24.

30 Hoffecker, *Honest John Williams,* 178–195; Francis Ralph Valeo, *Mike Mansfield,*

Majority Leader: A Different Kind of Senate (New York: M. E. Sharpe, 1999), 79–80; Johnson, *All the Way,* 26.

31 Williams to Warren, October 17, 1966 [EW/352]; Warren to Williams, October 31, 1966 [EW/352]; "Ethics and the Supreme Court," *Los Angeles Times,* October 19, 1966 [EW/352].

32 Warren to Williams, draft response, October 31, 1966 [EW/352]; Douglas to Warren, October 24, 1966 [EW/UPA-R/7].

33 Gossett to John J. Williams, May 28, 1969 [William Gossett/11]; William Gossett to Benton Gates, June 6, 1969 [William Gossett/11].

34 Williams, Notes: "Call from Clark Mollenhoff from the West Coast This Morning," October 28, 1969 [John J. Williams/38]; Mollenhoff to Williams, October 27, 1969 [John J. Williams/38]; Clark R. Mollenhoff, *Strike Force: Organized Crime and the Government* (Englewood Cliffs, NJ: Prentice-Hall, 1972); Bayh to Eastland, December 20, 1970 [James O. Eastland/SI, SS18, 1]; Bayh to Anderson, October 8, 1969 [Clinton Presba Anderson/381].

35 Evan Thomas, *Robert Kennedy: His Life* (New York: Simon & Schuster, 2000), 72; Jack Anderson, *Peace, War, and Politics: An Eyewitness Account* (New York: Forge Books, 1999), 83–85.

36 Anderson, *Peace, War, and Politics,* 265.

37 Donald Ritchie, *Reporting from Washington: The History of the Washington Press Corps* (Oxford: Oxford University Press, 2006), 223–226; see "House Unit Finds No Grounds to Impeach Justice Douglas," *Des Moines Register,* December 3, 1970.

38 Jack Brooks to Celler, July 6, 1962 [NARG 233, Box 5.1]; Celler to Brooks, July 10, 1962 [NARG 233, Box 5.1]; "Federal Courts: Judicial Councils," *ABA Journal,* March 1955, 51–52; In re. Reapplication of Grimes, 494 P.2d 635 (OK 1971).

39 "US Judge Stephen Chandler, 89; Often Feuded with His Colleagues," *New York Times,* April 29, 1989.

40 In re. Harlan Grimes, 364 US 654 (CA 10, 1966); Joshua E. Kastenberg, "The Right to an Independent Judiciary and Avoidance of Constitutional Conflict: The Burger Court's Flawed Reasoning in *Chandler v. Judicial Council of the Tenth Circuit* and Its Unfortunate Legacy," *St. Mary's Journal of Legal Malpractice and Ethics* 8 (2017): 91–101.

41 E. J. Albright to Williams, January 7, 1966 [John J. Williams/40]; Albright to Williams, January 5, 1966 [John J. Williams/40].

42 "Campbell Resigns Foundation," *Chicago Tribune,* January 10, 1967; Campbell to Ashmore, October 20, 1966 [EW/352].

43 Statement of John Ashbrook, *Congressional Record,* May 19, 1969, 12983; "Judge Said He Quit Post Foundation, Campbell 'Never Got a Nickel,'" *Chicago Tribune,* January 3, 1967; "Sherman Skolnick, 1930–2006: Even Before Blogs, Activist Had a Scoop on Government," *Chicago Tribune,* May 23, 2006; "Parvin Fund: Hood Front or Scholar Spur," *Chicago Daily News,* June 3, 1969, 6–7.

44 Skolnick v. Board of Commissioners of Cook County et al., 389 US 26 (1967);

Campbell to Attorney General Robert Jackson, June 19, 1939 [Robert H. Jackson/10].

45 Ervin to Clinton Presba Anderson, September 25, 1968 [Clinton Presba Anderson/734]; Douglas to US Maritime Commission, March 20, 1946 [WOD/255].

46 Murphy, *Fortas,* 441–462; Kalman, *Abe Fortas,* 337–339.

47 Robert Griffin to James Leckander, March 21, 1967; Griffin to Jessie Schade, March 21, 1967 [Robert Griffin/69]; Joseph Crespino, *Strom Thurmond's America* (New York: Macmillan, 2012), 207–230.

48 William Lambert, "The Stock Manipulator," *Life Magazine,* May 9, 1969, 33–37; Mitchell to Hoover, June 5, 1969 [J. Edgar Hoover Files, University Press of America/15].

49 Murphy, *Fortas,* 560–561.

50 Williams to Warren, May 6, 1969 [EW/719]; Douglas to Brennan, August 5, 1968 [WOD/501]; Leventhal to Fortas, December 15, 1969 [Harold Leventhal/3]; Walter Mondale, speech, June 1970 [Walter Mondale/153.L.8.8.F].

51 See, e.g., The Lawyer's Washington (column), "In Book and on Boards," *ABA Journal,* September 1972, 964–967.

52 Blackmun to Howard Burchell, May 29, 1969 [Harry A. Blackmun/50].

53 Hugo Black to John Frank, September 8, 1969 [HLB/33]; Hawkins v. North Carolina Dental Society, 355 F.2d 718 (CA 4, 1966); Coppedge v. Franklin County Board of Education, 384 F.2d 410 (CA 4, 1968); Griffin v. Board of Supervisors of Prince Edward County, 322 F.2d 322 (CA 4, 1963); Dillard v. School Board of the City of Charlottesville, 308 F.2d 290 (CA 4, 1962).

54 Griffen v. County School Board, 363 F.2d 206 (CA 4, 1966).

55 Eaton v. Board of Managers of James Walker Memorial Hospital, 261 F.2d 521 (CA 4, 1958); Simkins v. Moses Cone Memorial Hospital, 323 F.2d 959 (CA 4, 1963).

56 Eaton v. Grubbs, 329 F.2d 210 (CA 4, 1964).

57 "William J. Eaton, Haynsworth Had $450,000 Stock Linked to Suit," *Washington Post,* August 24, 1969.

58 Darlington Mfg. Co. v. National Labor Relations Board, 325 F.2d 682 (CA 4, 1963); Textile Workers Union v. Darlington Mfg. Co., 380 US 263 (1965).

59 Frank Mankiewicz and Tom Braden, "Haynsworth Was in Clear Violation of Canons of Ethics for Ten Years," *Los Angeles Times,* 1969.

60 Rehnquist to Hruska, September 26, 1969 [John W. Dean III/23]; Mollenhoff to Senator Montoya, October 8, 1969 [Joseph Montoya/178]; Statement of Mr. Dole, May 5, 1970 [RB-RDC/111].

61 Remarks of Hon Robert P. Griffin, "Individual Views," November 20, 1969 [Robert Griffin/235].

62 Charles McCurdy Mathias, statement of Charles McCurdy Mathias, April 8, 1970 [Charles McCurdy Mathias Jr./Series 1.1, Box 53]; Clarence Mitchell to Edward Brooke, April 21, 1970 [Edward William Brooke/187].

63 Haldeman to Nofziger, April 4, 1970 [Haldeman, RN-ANF/63]; Higby to Nofziger, April 7, 1970 [Haldeman, RN-ANF/63].

64 Kutler, *Wars of Watergate,* 149; Kalman, *Long Reach,* 245–261.

65 On Hooker's friendship with Douglas, see Douglas to Justice Harold Burton, October 4, 1945 [WOD/255]; Edith Allen to Hooker, June 20, 1949 [WOD/258]; "Mistrial Ordered in Hoffa Jury Case," *New York Times,* September 15, 1964; "Politics," *Nashville Tennessean,* January 28, 1970; "Chicken and Tennessee Politics," *New York Times,* January 27, 1970.

66 "A Question of Ethics," *Wall Street Journal,* October 20, 1970; Harry Phillips to *Wall Street Journal* editors, December 23, 1970.

67 Burger, "Memorandum to the Conference," July 21, 1970 [HLB/428]; Black to Burger, July 22, 1970 [HLB/428]; Black to chief of Washington Bureau, *Los Angeles Times,* July 27, 1970 [HLB/428]; Douglas, "Memorandum for the Court, Re. Recommendation of the Judicial Conference," October 1969 [WOD/594] "Most Warren Colleagues Rebuff Him on Ethics Code," *New York Times,* June 18, 1969; proposed resolution presented by Walter Ely, Judge of the United States Court of Appeals for the Ninth Circuit, July 1969 [WOD/594]; Douglas, "Memorandum for the Court, Re.: Recommendation of the Judicial Conference," October 1969 [WOD/594].

68 Marshall to Reverand Alfred Shands, May 3, 1968 [Thurgood Marshall/32]; see Joshua E. Kastenberg, "Chief Justice William Howard Taft's Conception of Judicial Integrity: The Legal History of *Tumey v. Ohio,*" *Cleveland State Law Review* 65 (2017): 317–378.

69 Wyzanski to Warren, June 20, 1969 [EW/720].

70 Beck to Latham R. Reed, October 10, 1934 [James Beck/5].

71 Administrative Office of the United States Courts, William E. Foley to the Supreme Court, January 23, 1970 [WOD/594], Administrative Office of the United States Courts, press release and report, January 26, 1970 [WOD/594].

72 Douglas to the Justices, 1970 [WOD/594]; "The ABA Will Inquire into Douglas," *Akron Beacon Journal,* May 25, 1969.

73 S.J. Res., 194, July 23, 1968; S. 1097, February 25, 1969; Ervin to Paul Wright, March 5, 1969 [SE-UNC/159].

74 S.1516 sec. 377, Non-judicial Activities of Supreme Court Justices and Other Federal Judges: Hearings before the Subcommittee on Separation of Powers of the Senate Committee on the Judiciary, 91st Cong. 327 (1969); Tydings to E. Barrett Prettyman, April 9, 1969 [Elijah Barrett Prettyman/8].

75 Black to Tydings, February 21, 1966 [HLB/53]; Black to Tydings, March 12, 1968 [HLB/53]; Tydings, address to Catholic University, November 6, 1969 [HLB/415]; Black to Carswell, May 2, 1969 [HLB/21]; Carl McGowan to Bazelon, October 23, 1969; N. J. Paulson to Bazelon, October 21, 1969; Tydings to Bazelon, October 17, 1969; Bazelon to "all judges," October 22, 1969 [Harold Leventhal/173].

76 MacGregor, press release, May 15, 1969 [Clark MacGregor]; MacGregor to Warren, May 17, 1969 [EW/719].

77 Statement by the Hon. Robert Taft Jr., "On the Resignation of Supreme Court Abe Fortas," May 15, 1969 [Robert A. Taft Junior/44-f4]; HR 11109, 91st Cong. 1st Sess, at (a). See also Taft to Emanuel Celler, May 26, 1969 [Robert A. Taft Junior/44-f5].

78 Taft to Celler, November 4, 1969 [Robert A. Taft Junior/44-f5]; Celler to Taft, November 7, 1969 [Robert A. Taft Junior/44-f5]; Taft to Professor C. M. Hulley, December 5, 1969 [Robert A. Taft Junior/44-f5]; "Ford Hints Move to Oust Douglas: Says Any Standard Applied to Haynsworth Should be Used for Present Court," *New York Times,* November 7, 1969; "Contempt of Court," *New York Times,* November 11, 1969; "Rep. Ford Says He Pushes Study of Justice Douglas," *New York Times,* November 22, 1970; Spencer Rich, "Ford Eyes Ousting Douglas," *Washington Post,* November 8, 1969; Royce Brier, "Douglas Hostage for Haynsworth," *San Francisco Chronicle,* November 19, 1969.

79 Ervin to Warren, August 29, 1969; Warren to Ervin, September 24, 1969; Ervin, opening statement to the Subcommittee on the Separation of Powers, April 7, 1970; Warren to Ervin, April 27, 1970 [EW/719].

80 Brennan to Warren, March 14, 1968 [William J. Brennan/I:168]; "The ABA Will Inquire into Douglas," *Akron Beacon Journal,* May 25, 1969.

81 Statement of Assistant Attorney General William Rehnquist before the Subcommittee, September 25, 1969 [John W. Dean III/56]; "Publisher Free Despite Conviction," *Pittsburg Press,* April 1, 1970; Fannin to Churchill, July 30, 1969 [PF-ASU/247].

82 Kalman, *Long Reach,* 183–184.

83 "Justice Murtagh's Home Target of Three Bombs," *New York Times,* February 22, 1970.

84 Burger to Black, March 20, 1970 [HLB/416]; Burger to Black, March 24, 1970 [HLB/416]; Douglas to the Conference, May 24, 1970 [HLB/416]; Burger to Douglas, March 24, 1970 [HLB/416]; Black, Memorandum to the Conference, March 30, 1070 [HLB/416].

CHAPTER 3. DOUGLAS, EXTRAJUDICIAL ACTIVITIES,
AND THE VIETNAM CONFLICT

1 Statement of the Honorable Dean Acheson before the Senate Committee on the Judiciary, Subcommittee on the Separation of Powers, July 16, 1969 [John Marshall Harlan/479]. Acheson's statements were printed in the *American Bar Association Journal* 55 (1969).

2 William O. Douglas, *The Court Years* (New York: Random House, 1980), 180–188; Usborne to Douglas, July 18, 1957 [WOD/1712]; Sir O. Franks to Rt. Hon. Selwyn Lloyd October 9, 1956 [Selwyn Lloyd/371, 16410].

3 Donovan to Edith Waters and Douglas, March 20, 1945 [WOD/667]; F. Eberstadt

to Douglas, August 20, 1945; Forrestal to Douglas, November 24, 1946; Douglas to Forrestal, November 29, 1945 [WOD/328].

4 Mary Ann Dzuback, *Robert M. Hutchins: Portrait of an Educator* (Chicago: University of Chicago Press, 1991), 252; Milton Stanford Mayer, *Robert Maynard Hutchins: A Memoir* (Berkeley: University of California Press, 1993), 74.

5 Johnson to Douglas, December 2, 1964 [NARG 233/90—AP File]; Hutchins to Douglas, November 16, 1966 [NARG 233/90—AP File]; Noah Feldman, *Scorpions: The Battles and Triumphs of FDR's Great Supreme Court Justices* (New York: Twelve Books, 2010), 60–68; Harry Ashmore, *Mission to Hanoi: A Chronicle of Double-Dealing in High Places* (New York: Putnam, 1968).

6 James L. Moses, "An Interesting Game of Poker: Franklin D. Roosevelt, William O. Douglas, and the 1944 Vice Presidential Nomination," in *Franklin D. Roosevelt and the Transformation of Supreme Court,* ed. Steven K. Shaw, William D. Pederson, and Frank J. Williams (London: Taylor & Francis, 2004), 2:133–146; Murphy, *Wild Bill,* 284.

7 See, e.g., *Strange Lands and Friendly People* (New York: Harper, 1951); *Beyond the High Himalayas* (New York: Doubleday, 1952); *North From Malaya: Adventure on Five Fronts* (New York: Doubleday, 1953); *Alamanac of Liberty* (New York: Doubleday, 1954); *Russian Journey* (New York: Doubleday, 1956); *We the Judges: Studies in American and Indian Constitutional Law from Marshall to Mukhejera* (New York: Doubleday, 1956); *Right of the People* (New York: Doubleday, 1958); *America Challenged* (New York: Doubleday, 1960).

8 Michael Janeway, *The Fall of the House of Roosevelt: Brokers of Ideas and Power from FDR to LBJ* (New York: Columbia University Press, 2004), 3–12.

9 See, e.g., Vern Countryman, *The Judicial Record of Justice William O. Douglas* (Cambridge, MA: Harvard University Press, 1974), 170–174; Marjorie Heins, *Priests of Our Democracy: The Supreme Court, Academic Freedom, and the Anticommunist Purge* (New York: New York University Press, 2013), 141–81

10 Michal Belknap, *The Supreme Court under Earl Warren* (Columbia: University of South Carolina Press, 2005), 244–249.

11 Douglas, December 30, 1947, address given at the Hotel Stevens, Chicago, IL [Wiley Rutledge/166]; "Justice Criticizes US Policy," *New York Times,* May 31, 1964.

12 On Truman's offer to Douglas to be secretary of the Interior, see Douglas to Truman, February 23, 1946, and Truman to Douglas, February 25, 1946 [WOD/380]. On Truman's suggestion as Douglas for vice president, see Truman to Douglas, August 9, 1948 [WOD/380]. On the matter of China, see Truman to Douglas, September 13, 1951 [WOD/380]; "Recognize Peiping, Justice Urges US," *New York Times,* September 1, 1951.

13 On the matter of China, see Truman to Douglas, September 13, 1951 [WOD/380]; "Recognize Peiping, Justice Urges US," *New York Times,* September 1, 1951.

14 Truman to Douglas, September 13, 1951 [WOD/380]; "Recognize Peiping, Justice Urges US," *New York Times,* September 1, 1951.

15 Douglas to Truman, September 25, 1951 [WOD/380].

16 *Congressional Record,* June 29, 1953, 7586.

17 William O. Douglas, "The Power of Righteousness," *New Republic,* April 27, 1952, https://newrepublic.com/; Douglas to Donovan, March 27, 1951 [WOD/260].

18 Douglas to Colonel Roger Seely, March 28, 1951; Douglas to Shabazz, March 28, 1951; Douglas to Shabazz, March 27, 1951 [WOD/260].

19 Douglas to Jack E. Finks, March 16, 1951 [WOD/260].

20 "Douglas Says US Should Aid Iranian Land Reform," *New York Times,* January 12, 1953.

21 Arthur M. Schlesinger, *Robert Kennedy and His Times* (New York: Houghton Mifflin), 122–128.

22 Campbell to Douglas, April 17, 1963 [WOD/1725]; program for the US visit of Masauku Chipembere [WOD/1725].

23 In 1952 alone, Douglas authored the following articles for *Look Magazine:* "The Man Who Saved the Philippines from Red Conquest," "Jungle Treachery in Malaya," "Revolution in Burma," "Indo-China Near Disaster," and "The Choice in Korea."

24 On Buttinger, liberal intellectuals, and the American Friends of Vietnam, see Joseph G. Morgan, *The Vietnam Lobby: The American Friends of Vietnam, 1955–1975* (Chapel Hill: University of North Carolina Press, 1997), 8–10.

25 Oral history interview with William O. Douglas by John F. Stewart, November 9, 1967 [WOD/594]; Diem to Douglas, November 19, 1953 [WOD/1731]; Diem to Douglas, April 13, 1957 [WOD/1731]; Diem to Douglas, July 11, 1954 [WOD/1731]; Douglas to Ambassador Tran Van Chuong, April 19, 1957 [WOD/1731]; Douglas to Diem, October 8, 1954 [WOD/1731].

26 Douglas to Wesley Fishel, May 20, 1965 [WOD/527]; statement by the American Friends of Vietnam; Fishel to Douglas, 1965 [WOD/527]; Adeline Corradi to Douglas, May 21, 1965 [WOD/527]; "Douglas for Settlement in Viet Nam," *Orlando Evening Star,* November 4, 1965.

27 Kutler, *Wars of Watergate,* 17.

28 Simon Hall, *Peace and Freedom: The Civil Rights and Anti-war Movements in the 1960s* (Philadelphia: University of Pennsylvania Press, 2005), 10.

29 Sellers v. Laird, 395 US 950 (1968). [Douglas, Warren, and Marshall's dissent from the denial of certiorari.]

30 George C. Herring, *America's Longest War: The United States and Vietnam, 1950–1975,* 4th ed. (New York: McGraw-Hill, 2001), 182; Blum, *Years of Discord,* 260–291; Peter Felton, "Yankee, Go Home and Take Me with You: Lyndon Johnson and the Dominican Republic," in *Beyond Vietnam: The Foreign Policies of Lyndon Johnson,* ed. H. W. Brands (College Station: Texas A&M Press, 1997), 61–97; George O. Flynn, *Louis B. Hershey: Mr. Selective Service* (Chapel Hill: University of North Carolina Press, 1985) 235; See particularly *In Pursuit of Equity: Who Serves When Not All Serve?,* Report of the National Advisory Commission

on Selective Service (Washington, DC: Government Printing Office, 1967). The 291-page document, the result of an official government inquiry, concluded that inequities existed within the Selective Service, particularly in terms of race. The Court, during Warren Burger's early tenure, would cite this report in Parisi v. Davidson, 405 US 34 (1972) and Gillette v. United States, 401 US 437 (1971).

31 See, e.g., Allen J. Matusow, The *Unraveling of America: A History of Liberalism in the 1960s* (Athens: University of Georgia Press, 1990), 391–396; David F. Schmitz, *The Tet Offensive: Politics, War, and Public Opinion* (Lanham, MD: Rowman & Littlefield, 2005), 59–145; Robert Dallek, *Flawed Giant: Lyndon Johnson and His Times, 1961–1973* (Oxford: Oxford University Press, 1999) 501–511.

32 Douglas to Hugh B. O'Neill, July 27, 1968 [WOD/527].

33 Douglas to Hutchins, June 9, 1966 [NARG 233/90—AP File]; Hutchins to Douglas, November 16, 1966 [NARG 233/90—AP File]; Ashmore, *Mission to Hanoi*, 3–4.

34 Douglas to Banerjee, March 4, 1968 [WOD/307]; Banerjee to Douglas, August 28, 1968 [WOD/307]; Douglas to Ernest Goldstein, February 29, 1968 [WOD/1732]; Douglas to Clark Clifford, February 29, 1968 [WOD/1732]; Douglas to Clifford, February 25, 1968 [WOD/316]; Clifford to Douglas, February 3, 1968 [WOD/316].

35 Douglas, speech, May 30, 1967 [WOD/583]; revised program, Pacem in Terris, May 30, 1970 [WOD/583].

36 Revised program, Pacem in Terris, May 30, 1970.

37 See, e.g., American Association for the United Nations to Douglas, November 9, 1967 [WOD/1427]; William H. Reeves to Douglas, November 24, 1967 [WOD/1421]; Professor Leonard Matchinger, November 21, 1967 [WOD/1421]; Robert Sitnaff to Douglas, November 8, 1967 [WOD/1421]; States Army Surveillance of Dissidents, "Report on the Fort Hood Three" (United States Army Surveillance Records, University Press of America, 2005), 16.

38 Winters v. United States, 281 F.Supp 289 (ED NY, 1968). On Dooling, see Leslie Bennetts, "Judge John Dooling Jr., 72, Dies; Made Ruling on Abortion Funds," *New York Times*, January 13, 1981. Winters v. United States, 390 F.2d 879 (CA 2, 1968).

39 Morse v. Boswell, 289 F.Supp 812 (DC MD 1968); Winters v. United States, 89 S.Ct 57 (1068); McArthur v. Clifford, 402 F.2d 58 (CA 4, 1968); Haynsworth to Winter and Butzner, August 13, 1968 [Clement Furman Haynsworth/17]; Butzner to Boreman, September 30, 1968 [Simon Sobeloff/195]; Winter to Butzner, October 8, 1968 [Simon Sobeloff/195]; Bryan to Butzner, October 9, 1968 [Simon Sobeloff/195]; McArthur v. Clifford, 393 US 1002 (1968).

40 Sobeloff to Haynsworth, September 26, 1968 [Clement Furman Haynsworth/17]; Haynsworth to Sobeloff, September 24, 1968 [Clement Furman Haynsworth/17].

41 "Judicial Shop Around," *Washington Post*, September 16, 1968; McArthur v. Clifford 393 US 1002 (1968).

42 Morse to Douglas, September 12, 1968 [WOD/1441].
43 Drifka v. Brainard, 89 S.Ct 934; In re. Drifka v. Brainard, undated draft, 1968 [WOD/1440].
44 See, e.g., "Dr. Levy Gets Three Years at Hard Labor" and "Army Ousts Foe of Viet War," *Chicago Tribune*, 1967.
45 Adam Fairclough, *Race and Democracy: The Civil Rights Struggle in Louisiana, 1915–1972* (Athens: University of Georgia Press, 1999), 81; Frank J. Smist, *Congress Oversees the US Intelligence Community, 1947–1989* (Knoxville: University of Tennessee Press, 1994), 6–7; Hebert to Burger, August 8, 1969 [HLB/59]. On the Levy court-martial, see Robert N. Strassfield, "The Vietnam War on Trial: The Court-Martial of Howard W. Levy," *Wisconsin Law Review* (1994): 839–963; Joshua E. Kastenberg, *Shaping Military Law: Governing a Constitutional Military* (London: Ashgate, 2013), 98; Parker v. Levy, 417 US 733 (1974).
46 Hebert to Burger, August 8, 1969 [HLB/59]. This letter is contained in a memorandum from Charles Morgan, Levy's attorney, to Senator Sam J. Ervin, and forwarded to Justice Black. Hebert to Warren, September 19, 1968 [HLB/59]; Hebert to Warren, January 24, 1969 [HLB/69]; HR 922 in vol. 4, pt. 74, of Associate Justice William O. Douglas, "Final Report, Pursuant to H. Res. 93," United States Congress House Committee on the Judiciary, Special Subcommittee on H. Res. 920 (1970).
47 Ben B. Blackburn to Mr. C. Leonard Meeker, chief of legal section, Department of State, September 25, 1967 [Edward Hutchings, Gerald Ford Library/14]; See, e.g., Talmadge to Ms. Jeanette Butler, July 2, 1970 [Herman Talmadge/157]; Talmadge to Mrs. David Kennerson, July 2, 1970 [Herman Talmadge/157].
48 395 US 258 (1969).
49 Joshua E. Kastenberg, "Cause and Effect: The Origins and Impact of Justice William O. Douglas's Anti-military Ideology from World War II to *O'Callahan v. Parker*," *Thomas Cooley Law Review* 26 (2009): 163–170.
50 Kastenberg, "Cause and Effect."
51 See Noyd v. McNamara, 267 F.Supp 701 (1967); Noyd v. Bond, 402 F.2dd 441 (CA 10, 1969); Noyd v. Bond, 395 US 683 (1969); "Dale E. Noyd, Air Force Captain and Vietnam War Foe," *Seattle Times*, January 28, 2007; "Dale E. Noyd: Air Force Captain Became Conscientious Objector," *Los Angeles Times*, January 30, 2007.
52 Thomas C. Grey to Marshall, March 2, 1970 [Thurgood Marshall/56]; Black to Burger, February 27, 1970 [Thurgood Marshall/56].
53 William O. Douglas, *Points of Rebellion* (New York: Random House, 1969).
54 Douglas, *Points of Rebellion*, 37–41; See, e.g., Sidney Hook, in "Forum: *Points of Rebellion*," *Brooklyn Law Review* 37 (1970): 16–21.
55 The letters are contained in Douglas's collection at the Library of Congress in Box 1045. See especially Patrice Leach, June 5, 1970; Stanley Heisler to Douglas, January 5, 1971 [WOD/1045]; Kean constituent letter model, March 13, 1970 [Florence Dwyer-Kean University]; Hart to J. E. Taylor, June 9, 1970 [Phillip Hart, Bently Historical Library/189].

56 Hay Aull to Edward Hunter, May 28, 1970, Aull to E. A. Dominianni, August 7, 1970; Aull to Jacob E. R. Pfohl, August 7, 1970. What appears to have occurred is that Muskie first used the quote in in 1969 and Douglas cribbed it from Muskie. See Aull to Alexander Sacks, May 14, 1970; Terry Watts to Aull, August 27, 1970 [WOD/1045].

57 Scott, press release, April 15, 1970 [William Lloyd Scott/79]; Scott to N. Frey, March 19, 1970 [William Lloyd Scott/79]; Byrd, press release, June 30, 1971 [Robert C. Byrd/141].

58 May to Scott, March 16, 1970 [William Lloyd Scott/79].

59 "Industries Felt Ruler of W.Va.: Justice's Book Sparks Criticism," *Herald Dispatch*, March 17, 1970; United States Anti-communist Congress (Wilson C. Lucom, president) to Gude, March 11, 1970 [GG-GWU/56]; Daniel Seligman, "Revolution, Rant, and Justice Douglas," *Life Magazine*, May 1, 1970 [HLB/59]; "Judicial Shop-Around," *Washington Post*, September 16, 1968, "Justice Douglas Says Revolution May Be Only Honorable Reply to Oppression," *New York Times*, February 1, 1970; "Justice Douglas Has Forfeited His Right to Sit on the Court," *Orlando Sentinel*, February 10, 1970; "All Wet Mr. Justice," *Greensboro Daily News*," February 5, 1970.

60 Church to Josephine Yearian, April 2, 1970 [Frank Church/S 34 B1 f-2]; Unknown to Douglas, April 28, 1970 [WOD/358].

61 Douglas to Tom O. Griessemer, January 25, 1947 [WOD/256].

62 James F. Simon, *The Center Holds: The Power Struggle inside the Rehnquist Court* (New York: Simon & Schuster, 1995), 102; Alan Balboni, *Beyond the Mafia: Italian Americans and the Development of Organized Crime* (Reno: University of Nevada Press, 1996), 62; "Sidney Korshak, 88, Dies; Fabled Fixer for the Chicago Mob," *New York Times*, January 22, 1996.

63 "Mobster Lansky Tied to Parvin Hotel Deal in Vegas," *Milwaukee Journal*, October 22, 1969.

64 Parvin to Douglas, July 25, 1960; Parvin to Douglas, August 7, 1960 [WOD/610]; "Douglas Honored," *Princeton Alumni Weekly* 65 (February 23, 1976): 6; Howard Ball, *Of Power and Right: Hugo Black, William O. Douglas, and America's Constitutional Revolution* (Oxford: Oxford University Press, 1992), 303.

65 Douglas, *Court Years*, 363.

66 Parvin to Douglas, January 23, 1961 [WOD/610]; Parvin to Douglas, January 13, 1961 [WOD/610]; Parvin to Douglas, October 31, 1960 [WOD/610].

67 Douglas to Parvin, December 21, 1960; Wiley to Parvin, December 17, 1960; Price to Douglas, November 23, 1960; Campbell to Mindlin, October 17, 1960; William C. Campbell to Douglas, October 17, 1960 [WOD/610].

68 Douglas to Parvin, January 17, 1961 [WOD/610]; Douglas, draft press release, January 17, 1960.

69 Bryce Harlow to Nixon, November 27, 1968 [John J. Williams/5].

70 In re. case #47914 State v. Parvin and Seigel; "Mobster Lansky Tied to Parvin Hotel Deal," *Milwaukee Journal*, October 29, 1969; Sibert to Ashmore, December 8, 1969 [WOD/612].

71 "Denny's Trims Bid for Parvin: $62.9 Million Cut Off Companies Take Merger Actions," *New York Times*, July 11, 1969; "Court Settles Action by Denny's against Parvin Holders," *Wall Street Journal*, December 16, 1970.
72 Douglas's letter to Parvin Sharpens Court Controversy, *Los Angeles Times*, May 27, 1969; "Unjudicial Behavior," *New York Times*, May 27, 1969.
73 Buchanan to Haldeman, December 9, 1970 [John W. Dean III/43]; Thrower to Kennedy, Setpember 22, 1969; Buchanan to Nixon, September 26, 1969; Ehrlichman to Nixon, October 1, 1969 [John W. Dean III/23].
74 F. S. Schmidt, district director, IRS, to Parvin Foundation, April 14, 1969; Agger to Douglas, April 19, 1968; Agger to Douglas, March 31, 1969; Agger to Douglas, April 17, 1969; Douglas to Agger, April 29, 1970 [WOD/613].]
75 Joseph L. Tulchin, "US Relations with Latin America," in *Lyndon Johnson Confronts the World: American Foreign Policy, 1963–1968*, ed. Warren I. Cohen and Nancy Bernkopf Tucker (Cambridge: Cambridge University Press, 1995), 233–236; Stephen G. Rabe, *Eisenhower and Latin America: The Foreign Policy of Anticommunism* (Chapel Hill: University of North Carolina Press, 1988), 15; Stephen G. Rabe, "The Caribbean Triangle: Bettencourt, Castro, and Trujillo and US Foreign Policy, 1958–1963," in *Empire and Revolution: The United States and the Third World since 1945*, ed. Peter L. Hahn and Mary Ann Hess (Columbus: Ohio State University Press, 2001), 52.
76 Jonathan Colman, *The Foreign Policy of Lyndon B. Johnson: The United States and the World, 1963–1969* (Edinburgh: Edinburgh University Press, 2011), 173–175.
77 Bosch to Douglas, January 23, 1963 [WOD/614]; Douglas to Ashmore, November 9, 1963 [WOD/286].
78 H. W. Brands, *The Wages of Globalism: Lyndon Johnson and the Limits of American Power* (Oxford: Oxford University Press, 1995), 50–54; Stephen G. Rabe, "Controlling Revolutions: Latin America, the Alliance for Progress, and Cold War Anticommunism," in *Kennedy's Quest for Victory: American Foreign Policy, 1961–1963*, ed. Thomas G. Patterson (Oxford: Oxford University Press, 1989), 108–115; Mark Eric Williams, *Understanding US–Latin American Relations: Theory and History* (New York: Routledge, 2011), 163; Dallek, *Flawed Giant*, 262–263.
79 Helms to Celler, July 15, 1970 [Gerald Ford/14].
80 Volman to Douglas, April 16, 1963, 137 [Final Report]; Helms to Celler, July 15, 1970 [Gerald Ford/14]; Bosch to Douglas, Januay 31, 1963; Douglas to Parvin, January 31, 1963 [WOD/614]; Parvin to Douglas, February 4, 1963 [WOD/614]; Parvin to Douglas, June 23, 1963; Douglas to Martin, June 29, 1963 [WOD/614]; Karen Paget, *Patriotic Betrayal: The Inside Story of the CIA's Secret Campaign to Enroll American Students in the Crusade against Communism* (New Haven, CT: Yale University Press, 2015), 394; Jerome Adams, *Liberators, Patriots, and Leaders of Latin America* (Jefferson, NC: McFarland, 1991), 171.
81 Douglas to Bosch, February 1, 1963 [WOD/1712]; "Edward Lamb is Dead at 84, Millionaire and Labor Lawyer," *New York Times*, March 25, 1987.

82 Lamb disbarment amicus [Robert H. Jackson/Box 82]; Jackson to William S. Daley, June 7, 1938 [Robert H. Jackson/Box 82]; Chesley Manley, "Jackson Fights Disbarment of CIO Attorney: Solicitor General Backs Ohio Lawyer," *Chicago Daily Tribune,* June 23, 1938, 11.
83 Text of address of Vice President Richard Nixon before the 38th National Convention of the American Legion [Stanley Forman Reed].
84 Thurmond, statement of Strom Thurmond on the Senate Floor, referencing Supreme Court reservist call-up stay by Justice Douglas, September 30, 1968.
85 Address by Senator Strom Thurmond to Twentieth Century Reformation Freedom Rally, Robert Lee Gardiner Memorial Stadium, Cape May, New Jersey, June 13, 1969; statement by Senator Strom Thurmond on the Senate Floor, reference Justice Douglas, CIA Agent, June 9, 1969; excerpts of remarks by Senator Strom Thurmond to Trunk n Tusk Club Dinner, Grand Ballroom, Del Webb's Townhouse, Phoenix, Arizona, June 20, 1969.
86 Clark Mollenhoff notes, March 2, 1970 [Clark Mollenhoff/16].
87 "He'll Offer Impeachment Resolution," *Des Moines Register,* June 8, 1969
88 Douglas to Ares, February 6, 1970 [WOD/1117]; Douglas to Horowitz, April 15, 1970 [WOD/297].
89 Douglas to the Conference, 1969 [WOD/594]; Victor Mindlin to John Martin, May 13, 1969 [WOD/612]; Douglas to Harry Ashmore, November 26, 1969 [WOD/612]; "Congress Asks for Fortas' Resignation," *Arizona Republic,* May 6, 1969.
90 Douglas to Parvin, October 23, 1969 [WOD/316]; WOD to Clifford, November 19, 1969 [WOD/316]; WOD to Clifford, December 31, 1969 [WOD/316].
91 Douglas to Clifford, April 16, 1970 [WOD/316].
92 Murphy, *Wild Bill,* 430–434.

CHAPTER 4. FORD'S ATTACK ON DOUGLAS BEGINS
1 "Critics of Douglas Ponder Impeachment Moves," *Las Vegas Sun,* April 13, 1970; Herbert L. Thompson to White House Staff, April 10, 1917 [Spiro Agnew/Series III, SS V, Box 18].
2 "Agnew Says Unqualified Swept into Colleges on Wave of New Socialism," *Clarion Ledger,* April 15, 1970.
3 HR 926, April 20, 1970; Douglas to Ramsey Clark, May 7, 1970 [WOD/588]; Haley to George R. Barth, March 4, 1970 [James A. Haley/78]; Haley to R. E. Hess, March 20, 1970 [James A. Haley/78].
4 Pennsylvania v. Nelson, 350 US 497 (1956); Robert Lichtman, *The Supreme Court and McCarthy-Era Repression: One Hundred Decisions* (Champaign: University of Illinois Press, 2012), 88–90; "Louis C. Wyman: Served 5 Terms in House," *New York Times,* May 9, 2002; Wyman to Philbrick, June 24, 1958 [Herbert Philbrick/213].
5 Remarks by Representative Gerald Ford, Republican Leader, prepared for delivery

on the Floor of the United States House of Representatives on April 15, 1970, 116th Proceedings and Debates of the 91st Congress, 2d Sess., *Congressional Record,* No. 60, 1.

6   See, e.g., Ginzburg v. United States, 383 US 463 (1966). Although Doulas joined in Black's dissent, he also separately dissented. See Ginzburg v. United States, 383 US at 482 [Douglas J., dissenting]

7   Goldwater v. Ginzburg, 414 F.2d 324, 342 (CA 2, 1969), cert. denied, 396 US 1049 (1970). See also, e.g., "Court Allows Goldwater Judgment to Stand," *New York Times,* January 27, 1970.

8   *Congressional Record,* April 15, 1970, H 3115.

9   Remarks by Representative Gerald Ford, Republican Leader.

10 Sergio Lalli, "Howard Hughes in Las Vegas," in *The Players: The Men Who Made Las Vegas,* ed. Jack Sheehan (Reno: University of Nevada Press, 1997), 133–139.

11 Memorandum of Investigation, August 21, 1970 [NARG 233/88—AP File].

12 Alexander Charns, *Cloak and Gavel: FBI Wiretaps, Bugs, Informers, and the Supreme Court* (Champaign: University of Illinois Press, 1992), 67; Robert Dallek, *Lone Star Rising: Lyndon Johnson and His Times, 1908–1960* (Oxford: Oxford University Press, 1991), 477; Neil MacNeil and Richard A. Baker, *The American Senate: An Insider's History* (Oxford: Oxford University Press, 2013), 36–37.

13 Charns, *Cloak and Gavel,* 115.

14 Charns, *Cloak and Gavel,* 115.

15 Charns, *Cloak and Gavel,* 115. Perhaps this was because the first Pacem in Terris conference occurred in New York in 1965, but since the conference was held in full public view, it seems not to have caused concern to Johnson's administration.

16 Charns, *Cloak and Gavel,* 115.

17 *Congressional Record,* April 16, 1970, H 3119.

18 Remarks by Representative Joseph D. Waggonner, for delivery on the Floor of the United States House of Representatives on April 15, 1970, 116th Proceedings and Debates of the 91st Congress, 2d Sess., *Congressional Record,* No. 60, 8. This resolution was also, by coincidence, numbered as 920, but to avoid confusion, the number is not listed in the text. See David W. Childs, "Congressman Joe D. Waggoner: A Study in Political Influence," *North Louisiana Historical Association* 13 (1982): 119–130. In 1976 Waggonner was arrested for soliciting a prostitute. See Ronald Kessler, *Inside Congress: The Shocking Scandals, Corruption, and Abuse of Power Behind the Scenes on Capitol Hill* (New York: Pocket Books, 1997), 21. On Waggonner and Rhodesia, see Anthony Lake, *The "Tar Baby" Option: American Policy in Southern Rhodesia* (New York: Columbia University Press, 1976), 116–117.

19 Uphaus v. Wyman, 360 US 72 (1959).

20 Virginia Foster Durr, *Freedom Writer: Virginia Foster Durr—Letters from the Civil Rights Years,* ed. Patricia Sullivan (Athens: University of Georgia Press, 2003), 157 Sweezy v. New Hampshire, 354 US 234 (1957); Arthur J. Sabin, *In Calmer Times:*

The Supreme Court and Red Monday (Philadelphia: University of Pennsylvania Press, 1999), 156; DeGregory v. New Hampshire, 383 US 825 (1966); Brennan to Douglas, March 24, 1966 [WOD/1368]; Fortas to Douglas, March 21, 1966 [WOD/1368]. M. J. Heale, *McCarthy's Americans: Red Scare Politics in State and Nation, 1935–1965* (Athens: University of Georgia Press, 1988), 264.

21   Speech of Hon. Louis C. Wyman in the House of Representatives, April 15, 1970.

22   *Congressional Record,* April 16, 1970, H 3246. On Bennett, see Kevin Kruse, *One Nation Under God: How Corporate America Invented Christian America* (New York: Basic Books, 2015), 121.

23   Ray E. Boomhower, *Robert Kennedy and the 1968 Indiana Primary* (Bloomington: Indiana University Press, 2008), 130; Edith Green, Memorandum, April 1970 [Edith Green/188]; Belcher to W. F. Lefeber, April 24, 1970 [Page Belcher/154].

24   Laurel Leff, *Buried by the "Times": The Holocaust and America's Most Important Newspaper* (Cambridge: Cambridge University Press, 2005), 1–34; Herbert J. Gans, *What's News: A Study of "CBS Evening News," "NBC Nightly News," "Newsweek," and "Time"* (Chicago: Northwestern University Press, 2004), 1–24.

25   "Political Reprisal," *Wall Street Journal,* April 15, 1970.

26   "Hundreds of Bodies of Vietnamese Seen in Cambodian River," *New York Times,* April 16, 1970; See, e.g., "Hopes Rise for Safe Landing by Apollo in Pacific Today," *Times* (London), April 17, 1970; "Apollo Rocket Burn Sets Home Course," *Atlanta Journal Constitution,* April 16, 1970; "US Ambassador Recalled in Wake of Demand," *Chicago Tribune,* April 18, 1970; "Jordanian Mob Burns US Embassy Library," *Atlanta Journal Constitution,* April 16, 1970.

27   "Debate Opens on Possible Impeachment Move against Douglas," *Boston Globe,* April 16, 1970.

28   "Files Move to Impeach Douglas," *Des Moines Register,* April 16, 1970; editorial, *Des Moines Register,* April 17, 1970.

29   "The Campaign to Get Justice Douglas," *Cincinnati Enquirer,* April 16, 1970; James Reston, "Justice Douglas Put on the Spot by GOP Heads," *Cincinnati Enquirer,* April 16, 1970; James Reston, "Douglas, the Court, and Politics," *Atlanta Journal Constitution,* April 16, 1970; "Douglas Impeachment Move Introduced," *Atlanta Journal Constitution,* April 16, 1970; "Resolution to Impeach Douglas Filed," *Detroit Free Press,* April 16, 1970; "Ford's Attack Won't Get Douglas Off Supreme Court," *Detroit Free Press,* April 16, 1970; "Unfit for His Post," *Arizona Republic,* April 16, 1970.

30   "Apollo 13 Heads toward the Moon," *Philadelphia Inquirer,* April 12, 1970; "Agnew Attacks Douglas, Asks Exemption," *Philadelphia Inquirer,* April 12, 1970; "I Was Pressured to Vote for Carswell," *Philadelphia Inquirer,* April 12, 1970; "Power Failure Cancels Landing, Apollo Fires in Return Course," *Philadelphia Inquirer,* April 14, 1970; "Russian A-Sub Reported Sunk Off Spain's Coast," *Philadelphia Inquirer,* April 14, 1970; "4 Viet Cong Rockets Miss US Embassy," "Nixon's Popularity Drops over Fears on Laos," *Philadelphia Inquirer,* April 14, 1970; "Israeli

Plains Raid 20 Miles from Cairo," *Philadelphia Inquirer,* April 14, 1970; "Rep Ford Leads Move to Investigate Justice Douglas's Off-Bench Activities," *Philadelphia Inquirer,* April 14, 1970.

31 "Crippled Apollo 13 Circles Moon, Starts 3 Day Trip Back to Earth," *Philadelphia Inquirer,* April 15, 1970; "Pennsylvania Legislature Considers Bill," *Philadelphia Inquirer,* April 15, 1970; "Blackmun Moderate on Civil Rights," *Philadelphia Inquirer,* April 15, 1970; "US Envoy Heckled by Swedish Crowd," *Philadelphia Inquirer,* April 15, 1970.

32 "Apollo Back on Path to Earth after Rocket Corrects Course," *Philadelphia Inquirer,* April 16, 1970; "Enemy Slays 25 Americans in Viet Action," *Philadelphia Inquirer,* April 16, 1970; "House Quizzes 6 Army Men on My Lai," *Philadelphia Inquirer,* April 16, 1970; "Blackmun's Worth, Rulings Described to Senator Eastland," *Philadelphia Inquirer,* April 16, 1970; "Douglas Impeachment Grows," *Philadelphia Inquirer,* April 16, 1970.

33 "Mitchell Asks Halt to Court Criticism," *Philadelphia Inquirer,* May 2, 1970; Mitchell to Editors, *Grand Rapids Press,* June 1, 1970 [Edward Hutchinson L/56]; "Mitchell's Warning," *Grand Rapids Press,* May 6, 1970; "US Plans Attack in N. Vietnam; Laid Warns of New Raids," *Philadelphia Inquirer,* May 3, 1970; "Declare War or Withdraw, Senators Urge," *Philadelphia Inquirer,* May 3, 1970; "Soviets Denounce Cambodian Drive as Aggression," *Philadelphia Inquirer,* May 3, 1970; "Egypt, Israel Use Guns in 3 Hour Duel," *Philadelphia Inquirer,* May 3, 1970; "Firebombs Damage ROTC Foyers at Princeton," *Philadelphia Inquirer,* May 3, 1970; "Troops Push Students Back to Campus after Protest," *Philadelphia Inquirer,* May 4, 1970; "65% of Draftees in N. California Evade Army Service," *Philadelphia Inquirer,* May 4, 1970; "Senate Unit Approves Blackmun, 17–0," *Philadelphia Inquirer,* May 6, 1970; "4 Students Shot to Death By Troops at Kent State," *Philadelphia Inquirer,* May 5, 1970; "Nixon Usurps War Powers, Senators Say," *Philadelphia Inquirer,* May 6, 1970.

34 "Ford Planning Broad Attack on Douglas in House Today," *News and Courier,* April 15, 1970; "Justice Douglas's Behavior Questioned by Ford," *News and Courier,* April 16, 1970; "Douglas Accused of Vague Ties to Gamblers," *Birmingham News,* April 16, 1970; editorial, "Douglas May Retire," *Birmingham News,* April 17, 1970; editorial, *News and Courier,* April 17, 1970; "Remove Justice Douglas, a Suspected Cancer in Our Body of States," May 22, 1970.

35 "Spong Will Vote against Carswell, Explains Stand," *Richmond Times Dispatch,* April 7; "Next: Confirmation" (editorial), *Richmond Times Dispatch,* April 8; "Investigating Douglas" (editorial), *Richmond Times Dispatch,* April 15, 1970.

36 "Douglas Removal Motion Introduced," *Clarion Ledger,* April 16, 1970; "Douglas Attack Growing," *Clarion Ledger,* April 17, 1970; "Arabs Fire US Office in Jordan," *Clarion Ledger,* April 17, 1970; "Anti-Douglas Move Gains: GOP Leaders Back Bipartisan Look at Justice," *New Orleans Times Picayune,* April 15, 1970; "Douglas Case Issue Looms: Charges against Douglas May Affect Fall Vote," *New Orleans Times Picayune,* April 18, 1970.

37 "Move Again to Oust US Judge," *Times of India,* April 16, 1970; "Carswell Crisis Marked Three US Leaders," *New Zealand Herald,* April 16, 1970; "Impeachment Moves against Judge," *New Zealand Herald,* April 16, 1970; "Further Bitter Wrangle over Supreme Court," *New Zealand Herald,* April 17, 1970.

38 "Attempt to Impeach US Judge," *Glasgow Herald,* April 15, 1970; "US Battle to Impeach Judge," *Times* (London), April 17, 1970; "Violence Erupts in United States after War Protests," *Times* (London), April 17, 1970.

39 "Ford Charges Justice Douglas Was Moonlighter for International Gamblers," *Toronto Globe and Anchor,* April 16, 1970; "Judge Accused of Links with Gamblers," *Sydney Morning Herald,* April 17, 1970.

40 J. Robert Schaetzel to Acheson, April 28, 1970 [Dean Acheson].

41 Shaw, *Cambodian Campaign,* 25–27.

42 Kissinger to Nixon, April 26, 1970 [RN-PPF/58]; Isaacson, *Kissinger,* 268–269; John Hart Ely, *War and Responsibility: Constitutional Lessons of Vietnam and Its Aftermath* (Princeton, NJ: Princeton University Press, 1993), 99–103; Douglas Kinnard, *The Secretary of Defense* (Lexington: University Press of Kentucky, 1980), 135.

43 Hunt, *Melvin Laird,* 152–153.

44 Peter N. Carroll, *It Seemed Like Nothing Happened: America in the 1970s* (New Brunswick, NJ: Rutgers University Press, 2003), 13–14; Gibbons to Eunice Shields, November 18, 1968 [Sam Gibbons/45]; press release, May 15, 1970; press release, May 15, 1970; press release, August 15, 1970.

45 Andrew E. Hunt, *The Turning: An American History of Vietnam Veterans against the War* (New York: New York University Press, 1999), 39–42; Louis Liebovich, *Richard Nixon, Watergate, and the Press: A Historical Perspective* (Westport, CT: Praeger, 2003), 25–28.

46 "New Clash Erupts at Ohio State University," *New York Times,* May 1, 1970; "Key Unit Opposes Sending Aid to Cambodia," *New York Times,* April 28, 1970; Kenton Clymer, *The United States and Cambodia, 1969–200: A Troubled Relationship* (New York: Routledge, 2004), 31; petition, April 29, 1970 [PM/512]; Harrington to Colleagues, April 30, 1970 [PM/512]; O'Tiernan to Colleagues, April 29, 1930 [PM/512]; Rosenthal to Colleagues, April 30, 1970 [PM/512]; Koch, news release, May 7, 1970 [PM/512].

47 "The Nation," *New York Times,* April 26, 1970.

48 Dean Kotlowski, *Nixon's Civil Rights: Politics, Principle, and Policy* (Cambridge, MA: Harvard University Press, 2001), 78; James L. Sundquist, *The Decline and Resurgence of Congress* (Washington, DC: Brookings Institution Press, 1981), 374; Randolph Hoehle, *Race and the Origins of American Neoliberalism* (New York: Routledge, 2015), 198; Ari Berman, *Give Us the Ballot: The Modern Struggle for Voting Rights in America* (New York: Farrar, Straus and Giroux, 2015), 83.

49 Donald R. Wolfensberger, *Congress and the People: The Deliberative Democracy on Trial* (Baltimore, MD: Johns Hopkins University Press, 2000), 93.

50 Martin F. Nolan, "The Man Who Could Push Richard Over the Edge," *New York*

Magazine, December 24, 1973; O'Neil to John E. Thayer, June 17, 1970 [Thomas O'Ncill/44]; Statement by Chairman William M. Colmer, House Rules Committee, Regarding Impeachment Proceedings against William O. Douglas, April 24, 1970; "Inquiry on Supreme Court Justice Is Given Backing," *New Orleans Times-Picayune,* April 17, 1970.

51 Drew Pearson, *Washington Merry-Go-Round: The Drew Pearson Diaries, 1960–1969* (Washington, DC: Potomac Books, 2015), 44; "Celler Will Head Panel on Douglas," *New York Times,* April 22, 1970; Michael Belknap, *Federal Law and Southern Order: Racial Violence and Constitutional Conflict in the Post-Brown South* (Athens: University of Georgia Press, 2011), 221.

52 Release for news, Edward Hutchinson, April 21, 1970 [Gerald Ford/14]; Howard W. Fogt to Hutchinson, May 19, 1970 [Gerald Ford/14]; Belknap, *Federal Law and Southern Order,* 221; "Administration Presses GOP to Bar Voting Rights Extension," *New York Times,* December 11, 1969; Carl Albert, *Little Giant: The Life and Times of Speaker Carl Albert* (Norman: University of Oklahoma Press, 1990), 278; Foley to Dave Driver, April 27, 1970 [Thomas Foley/673].

53 Webb to McCulloch, November 23, 1969; McCulloch to Webb, December 1, 1969 [William McCulloch/29-14]; "Undersigned" to McCulloch, April 9, 1970; William O'Neill to McCulloch, April 24, 1970 [William McCulloch/29-14].

54 HR 922.

55 Scott to Celler, May 5, 1970 [William Lloyd Scott/79]; William C. Gibbons, *The US Government and the Vietnam War: Executive and Legislative Roles and Relationships, Part 1: 1945–1960* (Princeton, NJ: Princeton University Press, 1985) 95; Timothy Zick, "The First Amendment in Transborder Perspective: Toward a More Cosmopolitan Orientation," *Boston College Law Review* 52 (2011): 941, 960; United States v. Peace Information Center, 971 F.Supp 255 (DC Dist. Col., 1951); Jamie L. Whitten to Celler, May 11, 1970 [NARG 233/88—AP File]; Watkins Moorman Abbitt to Celler, May 11, 1970 [NARG 233/88—AP File]; Detlev F. Vagts, "The Logan Act: Paper Tiger or Sleeping Giant?," *American Journal of International Law* 60 (1966): 268, 270.

56 Ford to Celler, July 29, 1970 [NARG 233/88—AP File].

57 Falk, April 16, 1970 [WOD/1118]; Falk to Douglas, July 6, 1970 [WOD/1118]; Bernard Jacob, August 17, 1970 [WOD/1120]; Douglas to Hans Linde, December 4, 1970 [WOD/1120].

58 Douglas to Ares, April 15, 1970 [WOD/1117]; Wallace Caldwell to Douglas, April 17, 1970 [WOD/589]; Mauricio A. Molina to Douglas, April 17, 1970 [WOD/589]; Alice Roeder to Douglas, April 14, 1970 [WOD/588]; Thomas C. Minnerick to Douglas, April 17, 1970 [WOD/589]; Stanley Heiser to Douglas, April 13, 1970 [WOD/589].

59 Rodell to Douglas, December 29, 1969 [WOD/368]; Rodell to *New York Times,* April 15, 1970 [WOD/368]; Rodell, "Letter to the Editor," *New York Times,* April 21, 1970; Rodell to Douglas, April 28, 1970 [WOD/368]; Rodell to Douglas,

August 7, 1970 [WOD/638]; Rodell to Douglas, August 7, 1970 [WOD/638]; Douglas to Rifkind, April 18, 1970 [WOD/298].

60 Fogt to Celler, May 11, 1970 [Gerald Ford/18].

61 Douglas to Celler, April 27, 1970; Statement of the Honorable Simon Rifkind before the Senate Committee on the Judiciary, Subcommittee on the Separation of Powers, July 15, 1969 [John Marshal Harlan/479]; Douglas to Rifkind, April 18, 1970 [WOD/297].

62 Douglas to Governor Brown, November 13, 1969 [WOD/1118]; Douglas, *Court Years,* 363; Douglas to Clark, April 29, 1970 [WOD/297].

63 Douglas to Millie, May 6, 1970 [WOD/297]; Douglas to Rifkind, April 19, 1970 [WOD/297].

64 Celler to Parvin, May 7, 1970; Ball to Celler, May 12, 1970; Ball to Celler, June 11, 1970 [NARG 233/88—AP File].

65 Final Report, 323.

66 Report, 48.

67 Report, 48.

68 Rifkind to Celler, May 18, 1970 [NARG 233/88—AP File].

69 Rifkind to Celler, May 18, 1970 [NARG 233/88—AP File].

70 Rifkind to Celler, May 18, 1970 [NARG 233/88—AP File].

71 Wyman to Celler, May 6, 1970 [NARG 233/88—AP File]; Ford to Celler, May 20, 1970 [NARG 233/88—AP File]; Ford to Celler, July 29, 1970 [NARG 233/88—AP File].

72 Nixon to Celler, May 13, 1970; Celler to Nixon, May 21, 1970; Nixon to Celler June 2, 1970 [NARG 233/88—AP File].

73 Douglas to Clark, April 30, 1970 [WOD/588]; Douglas to Clark, May 5, 1970; [WOD/588]; Columbia Broadcasting System v. Loews, 356 US 43 (1958); United States v. Southwestern Cable Corporation, 392 US 157 (1968).

74 Douglas to Clark, May 5, 1970; [WOD/588].

75 National City Bank v. Republic of China, 348 US 356 (1955).

76 Douglas to Clark, May 7, 1970 [WOD/588].

77 Douglas to Clark, May 22, 1970 [WOD/315]; Douglas to Clark, May 7, 1970 [WOD/588].

78 Douglas to Clark, July 27, 1970 [WOD/588].

79 John Ehrlichman, Conference notes for April 16, 1970 [John Ehrlichman, RN-ANF/1]; Higby to Macgruder, April 14, 1970 [Haldeman, RN-ANF/63].

80 Haldeman to Nofziger, May 6, 1970 [Haldeman, RN-ANF/63].

81 Bud Krogh to William Rehnquist, May 27, 1970 [Egil "Bud" Krogh, RN-ANF/2]; Bud Krogh to Larry Higby, June 19, 1970 [Egil "Bud" Krogh, RN-ANF/1]; citing to Rehnquist, Administratively Confidential Memorandum for the Honorable Egil Krogh, Bud Krogh to Ehrlichman, June 1, 1970 [Egil "Bud" Krogh, RN-ANF/1].

82 "Mitchell Warns of Danger in Attacks on High Court," *New York Times,* May 2, 1970.

83 "Mitchell's Warning," *Grand Rapids Free Press,* May 6, 1970; Ford to Mitchell, May 20, 1970; Mitchell to Editorial Staff, *Grand Rapids Free Press,* June 1, 1960 [Gerald Ford Library/18].
84 Nofiziger to Haldeman, May 5, 1970 [Haldeman, RN-ANF/63].

CHAPTER 5. THE HOUSE OF REPRESENTATIVES RESPONDS
TO FORD AND THE CAMBODIAN INVASION
1 Roy Taylor, news release, April 16, 1970 [Roy A. Taylor/72]; O'Neal to Mrs. Eugene C. Black, April 17, 1970 [Maston O'Neal/43]; HR 924.
2 Matusow, *Nixon's Economy,* 2–3.
3 See, e.g., Goldfield, *Race Relations,* 197; Frank B. Atkinson, *The Dynamic Dominion: Realignment and the Rise of Two-Party Competition in Virginia, 1945–1980* (Lanham, MD: Rowman & Littlefield, 2006), 192; Gary May, *Bending toward Justice: The Voting Rights Act and the Transformation of American Democracy* (New York: Basic Books, 2006). Votes on the Civil Rights Act are available online (https:/www.govtrack.us/congress/votes/89-1965/h87).
4 Mink to Annette J. McWilliams, May 9, 1969 [PM/385]; UPI-111, Statement of Paul McCloskey, May 8, 1970 [Clarence Dickinson Long/31].
5 "Speaker: Where Do You Draw the Ethical Lines?," *New York Times,* January 18, 1970; "McCormack Says He Will Not Seek New House Term," *New York Times,* March 21, 1970.
6 "Albert on the Spot in House's Controversy over Douglas," *Oklahoman,* April 16, 1970; Albert, *Little Giant,* 277–367; Albert to Mrs. Floyd Diller, March 13, 1970 [Carl Albert/120]
7 "McCormack Says He Will Not Seek New House Term," *New York Times,* March 21, 1970; "House Democrats to Pick Leader," *New York Times,* January 18, 1971; Albert to Charles Duffy, June 1, 1970 [Carl Albert/145]; Bevill to Albert, May 21, 1970 [Carl Albert/145].
8 R. Odom to Albert, May 1, 1970 [Carl Albert/120]; Norman Bayless to Albert, April 17, 1970 [Carl Albert/120]; Lorrin Anderson, April 14, 1970; Draft Response [Carl Albert/120]; Albert to Genie Cockerman, May 8, 1970; Albert to Rena Wyatt, May 18, 1970; Albert to Dr. I. C. Gunning, May 1, 1970; Albert to Clyde Madden, May 1, 1970.
9 Daniel J. Sargent, *A Superpower Transformed: The Remaking of American Foreign Relations in the 1970s* (Oxford: Oxford University Press, 2015), 53–52.
10 "Nixon Sends Combat Troops to Cambodia to Drive Communists from Staging Zone," *New York Times,* May 1, 1970; "US Troops Flown in for Panther Rally: New Haven Braces for Protest by 20,000," *New York Times,* May, 1970; "New Clash Erupts at Ohio State University," *New York Times,* May 1, 1970; "Court Bars Police Tie-up: PBA Ponders Its Reply," *New York Times,* May 1, 1970; "Friends of Miss Kopechne Said They Were Told She Was Safe," *New York Times,* May 1, 1970; "Key Congressmen Briefed: Reaction Called Favorable," *New York Times,* May 1, 1970;

"Mitchell Warns of Danger in Attacks on High Court," *New York Times,* May 2, 1970.

11 Tim Spofford, *Lynch Street: The May 1970 Shootings at Jackson State College* (Kent, OH: Kent State University Press, 1988), 24–50; Jeffrey Bloodworth, *Losing the Center: The Decline of American Liberalism, 1968–1992* (Lexington: University Press of Kentucky, 2013), 29.

12 Douglas, *Points of Rebellion,* 7–10.

13 James L. Merriner, *Mr. Chairman: Power in Dan Rostenkowski's America* (Carbondale: Southern Illinois University Press, 1999), 107–114; Daniel Rostenkowski to Messrs John C. Blaszak and Lawrence A. Choate, April 11, 1968 [Daniel Rostenkowski/I:371 f-4]; Gorski to DR, August 19, 1969 [Daniel Rostenkowski/I:127 f-11]; DR to Mr. Martin Gorski, September 3, 1969 [Daniel Rostenkowski/I:127 f-4].

14 DR to Martin C. Gorski, April 17, 1970 [Daniel Rostenkowski/I:127 f-11]; DR to Mr. Bruce Gauber, June 22, 1970 [Daniel Rostenkowski/I:371 f-8]; DR to Mr. Frank Kalisz, November 25, 1969 [Daniel Rostenkowski/I:127 f-5].

15 William Keller, *The Liberals and J. Edgar Hoover: The Rise and Fall of a Domestic Intelligence State* (Princeton, NJ: Princeton University Press, 1989), 133.

16 Griffiths to Mr. and Mrs. O. Mielke, August 10, 1970 [Martha Wright Griffiths/43]; Griffiths to Mr. and Mrs. M.B. Williston, May 18, 1970 [Martha Wright Griffiths/43]; Griffiths to Mr. and Mrs. Gabriel Des Hannais, June 30, 1970 [Martha Wright Griffiths/43]; Douglas to Rooney, October 30, 1970 [WOD/298].

17 Cohelan to Richard E. Jay, April 28, 1970 [Jeffery Cohelan/66]; Jay to Ford, April 20, 1970 [Jeffery Cohelan/66]; Cohelan to Laurence Dosser, April 22, 1970 [Jeffery Cohelan/66]; W. J. Rorabaugh, *Berkeley at War: The 1960s* (Oxford: Oxford University Press, 1989), 98–100.

18 Geoffrey Kabaservice, *Rule and Ruin: The Downfall of Moderation and the Destruction of the Republican Party, from Eisenhower to the Tea Party* (Oxford: Oxford University Press, 2012), 342.

19 Paul McCloskey to Gude, May 4, 1970 [GG-GWU/322].

20 Statement of McCloskey in 116th Proceedings and Debates of the 91st Congress, Second Session, April 21, 1970.

21 Statement of McCloskey in 116th Proceedings and Debates of the 91st Congress, Second Session, April 21, 1970; Cohelan to Richard E. Jay, April 28, 1970 [Jeffery Cohelan/66].

22 Statement of McCloskey in 116th Proceedings and Debates of the 91st Congress, 1st Sess., *Congressional Record,* April 21, 1970; McCloskey to Warren, June 24, 1970 [EW/352]; Douglas to Warren, June 27, 1870 [EW/352]; Paul N. McCloskey to Celler, August 18, 1970 [NARG 233/88—AP File]; see Johns, *Vietnam's Second Front,* 280–282; Richard Reeves, "The Case of Gerald Ford," *New York Magazine,* October 13, 1971; "Anti-Douglas Move Gains: GOP Leaders Back Bipartisan Look at Justice," *New Orleans Times-Picayune,* April 15, 1970.

23   McCloskey to Reid, May 4, 1970 [Ogden Rogers Reid/212]; Reid, notes, May–June [Ogden Rogers Reid/212]; Schulzinger, "Nixon, Congress," 287–289.
24   Davis to Mr. J. C. Kay, December 2, 1969 [John W. Davis/44].
25   Goldwater Memo—March 24, 1970 [BG-ASU/AF-15]; William Macomber to Gibbons, April 10, 1968 [Sam Gibbons/40].
26   Heath, *To Face Down Dixie*, 232–233.
27   Patrick J. Manney, "Hale Boggs: The Southerner as National Democrat," in *Masters of the House: Southern Leadership over Two Decades,* ed. Roger Davidson (Westview, CT: Westview Press, 1998).
28   Griffin to Corliss, May 13, 1970 [John Stennis/2, F-36]; Jamie L. Whitten to Celler, May 11, 1970, [John Stennis/2, F-36]. On Boggs and Albert, see John McCormack, Carl Albert, and Hale Boggs, Joint Letter to Congress, June 14, 1965 [Carl Albert/89].
29   Abernethy to J. M. Thomas, July 23, 1956 [Thomas Abernethy/144]; press release, July 9, 1956 [Thomas Abernethy/144]; Abernethy to J. K. Kitchell, June 12, 1968 [Thomas Abernethy/144]] Abernethy to William Ross, January 25, 1968 [Thomas Abernethy/144].
30   Abernethy to Carolyn Ellis, May 5, 1970 [Thomas Abernethy/144]; Abernethy to J. C. Mullins, June 2, 1969.
31   Davis, press statement, April 24, 1970 [John W. Davis/44]; Davis to Morgan McNeel, April 20, 1970 [John W. Davis/80].
32   O'Neal to Mr. and Mrs. Edwin Scull, July 26, 1966 [Maston O'Neal/20].
33   O'Neal to Mr. Jack Wingate, April 23, 1970 [Maston O'Neal/43]; O'Neal to Mrs. Eugene C. Black, April 17, 1970 [Maston O'Neal/43].
34   Nichols to Mrs. Milton Rose, May 5, 1970 [William Nichols]; Ms. Milton Rose to Nichols, May 1, 1970 [William Nichols].
35   Kalman, *Long Reach,* 255–267.
36   Clarence Long, press release, April 29, 1970 [Clarence Dickinson Long/31]; Clarence Long, press release, April 30, 1970 [Clarence Dickinson Long/31].
37   Fulton Lewis, press transcript, *The Top of the News with Fulton Lewis III* (Fulton, MO, 1970), 12:92; Democratic Study Group Fact Sheet, February 11, 1969 [Democratic Study Group/I:4]; Durward Hall, "An Invitation to Rebellion," February 17, 1970 [Durward Hall Papers].
38   "Ford Sounds Call to Probe Douglas," *St. Petersburg Times,* April 16, 1970; Haley to Pickering, February 20, 1970 [James A. Haley/78]; Haley to Dellet, February 20, 1970 [James A. Haley/78]; Haley to R. F. Greene, February 26, 1970 [James A. Haley/78]; Haley to Lagerborg, March 10, 1970 [James A. Haley/78]; Haley to McKean, April 22, 1970; Haley to Weymon Bryd, April 27, 1970 [James A. Haley/78].
39   Hon Louis Frey, April 8, 1970, *Congressional Record,* E2942; Frey, draft letter to constituents, April 16, 1970 [Louis Frey/6]; Frey Footnotes, April 20, 1970 [Louis Frey/6]; Frey Footnotes, February 1, 1970 [Louis Frey/6].
40   Gibbons to C. A. Hollingsworth, December 29, 1967 [Samuel Gibbons/41];

Gibbons to Ed Blackburn, June 6, 1968 [Sam Gibbons/40]; William MacOmber to Gibbons, April 10, 1968 [Sam Gibbons/40]; Gibbons to C. A. Hollingsworth, December 29, 1967 [Sam Gibbons/41]; Gibbons to Ernestine Siegel, December 18, 1967 [Sam Gibbons/41]; Gibbons to Ronald Farneth, November 22, 1967 [Sam Gibbons/41]; press release, May 15, 1970; press release, Gibbons to Eunice Shields, November 18, 1968 [Sam Gibbons/45].

41 Press release, May 15, 1970; press release, May 21, 1970; press release, June 24, 1970; press release, August 15, 1970 [Sam Gibbons/49].

42 Pepper to Celler, 1970 [NARG 233/89—AP File].

43 Edwin O. Cartright to Teague, May 20, 1969 [Olin Teague]; Teague to Cartright, May 27, 1969 [Olin Teague]; Teague to Joe Faulk, March 25, 1970 [Olin Teague]; Teague to R. R. Pyle, April 17, 1950 [Olin Teague]; Teague to Harry Erwin, April 29, 1970 [Olin Teague], August 20, 1970; Teague to Capps, September 1, 1970 [Olin Teague].

44 "Nineteen Texans Opposed to Cooper Church Plan," *Corpus Christi Caller,* July 10, 1970; J. Brooks Flippen, *Speaker Jim Wright: Power Scandal, and the Birth of Modern Politics* (Austin: University of Texas Press, 2018), 200–208; *Congressional Record,* April 15, 1970, H 3121.

45 Brock Adams, statement of April 15, 1970 [Brock Adams/96]; "If Douglas Were a Nominee," *Seattle Times,* April 13, 1970; Adams to Ms. Sayuri Okawara, May 12, 1970 [Brock Adams/29].

46 William Mullins to Adams, April 20, 1970 [Brock Adams/29]; Mr. and Ms. Garver to Adams, April 18, 1970 [Brock Adams/29]; Francis Blake to Adams, April 22, 1970 [Brock Adams/29]; W. Martens to Adams, April 16, 1970 [Brock Adams/29]; Adams to Arthur Gifford, May 5, 1970.

47 On Green, see Matthew Andrew Wasniewski, *Women in Congress: 1917–2006* (Washington, DC: Government Printing Office, 2006), 353–355; Green to Reggie Robertson, May 13, 1970 [Edith Green/188].

48 Green to D. A. Dirks, June 16, 1970 [Edith Green/188]; Reggie Robinson to Green, April 16, 1970; Stephen Lins to Green and Ford, April 16, 1970 [Edith Green/188]; Raymond Harlow to Green, May 20, 1970 [Edith Green/188]; Green to Raymond Harlow, May 12, 1970 [Edith Green/188].

49 Mink to Mrs. Bruce, July 26, 1966 [PM/389]; Alice Berman (American Association of University Women) to Mink, February 2, 1970 [PM/388]; Peter Bryce Gilreath to Mink, February 1, 1970 [PM/388]; Richard Harris (New Yorker) to Mink, February 9, 1971 [PM/388]; Mink to Nilda Gonzales, May 5, 1970 [PM/389].

50 Julian Zelizer, *On Capitol Hill: The Struggle to Reform Congress and Its Consequences, 1948–2000* (Cambridge: Cambridge University Press, 2004), 36–37; Sean J. Savage, *JFK, LBJ, and the Democratic Party* (New York: State University of New York Press, 2004), 94–95.

51 "Bolling Takes Douglas' Side," *Kansas City Star,* April 16, 1970; "Area Hand in Douglas Case," *Kansas City Star,* April 24, 1970.

52 Charlotte Millham to Bolling, April 21, 1970; S. C. Masters to Bolling, March 30,

1970; Bada Sawyer to Bolling, April 17, 1970; Eugene Eisalt to Bolling, April 18, 1970; I.. R. Duggan to Bolling, April 17, 1970 [Richard Bolling/76-20]. For an example of Bolling's responses, see Bolling to James Gill, April 28, 1970 [Richard Bolling/76-20].

53 Dwyer, form letter, May 4, 1970 [Florence Dwyer]; Dwyer, form letter, May 5, 1970 [Florence Dwyer].

54 May to David Burt, May 11, 1970; May to Stan Lebens, July 9, 1970 [Catherine Dean May/3–8].

55 Karen Foerstel, *Biographical Dictionary of Congressional Women* (Westport, CT: Greenwood Press, 1992), 118–120.

56 James S. Fleming, *Window on Congress: A Congressional Biography of Barber B. Conable Jr.* (New York: University of Rochester Press, 2004), 73.

57 Michael K. Honey, *Going Down Jericho Road: The Memphis Strike, Martin Luther King's Last Campaign* (New York: Norton, 2007), 181; Belcher to W. Lefeber, April 24, 1970 [Page Belcher/154]; Belcher to James Holder, May 26, 1969 [Page Belcher/154].

58 HR 1802, June 2, 1969; William C. Cramer, news release, June 2, 1969 [William Lloyd Scott/41].

59 John J. Rhodes to Mr. Joseph Worm, July 11, 1968 [John James Rhodes/203]; Rhodes to Cecilia Schultz, September 9, 1968 [John James Rhodes/203]; John J. Rhodes to Paul J. Martin, February 4, 1969 [John James Rhodes/252]; Rhodes to Phil Hutchins, February 3, 1970 [John James Rhodes/203]; Rhodes to Maude Fairchild, March 16, 1970 [John James Rhodes/203]; Rhodes to Phil Hutchins, February 3, 1970 [John James Rhodes/203]; Rhodes to Maude Fairchild, March 16, 1970 [John James Rhodes/203].

60 Rhodes to Mr. Randle King, June 4, 1969 [John James Rhodes/252]; Rhodes to Mr. Dominic, Corey, June 4, 1969 [John James Rhodes/252]; Rhodes to George L. Read, February 17, 1970 [John James Rhodes/252].

61 Rhodes to Dean Charles E. Ares, University of Arizona School of Law, May 20, 1970 [John James Rhodes/252]; Ares to Rhodes, May 20, 1970 [John James Rhodes/252].

62 Lake, *"Tar Baby" Option,* 116–117; House Resolution 23 (1961).

63 "Head 'Em Off at the Pass," *Fresno Bee,* January 5, 1970; Clausen to Mr. Hogan, August 27, 1968 [Don Clausen]; "Impeach Douglas?," report by Burt Talcott, April 16, 1970 [William Lloyd Scott/79].

64 Dellenback to More Tonkin, January 26, 1971 [WOD/590]; "John R. Dellenback, 84, Former Oregon Republican Congressman," *New York Times,* December 11, 2002; Doris Weatherford, *Woman's Almanac* (Westport, CT: Greenwood Press, 2002), 301; Dellenback to Moe Tonkin, January 27, 1971 [WOD/590].

65 Mrs. Griffin to Pelly, April 12, 1970; Pelley to Ms. Griffin, April 16, 1970; Pelly to George Barmuta, April 20, 1970; Pelly to Claire Gorsline, April 20, 1970 [Thomas Pelly/23].

66 Pelly to Carol Olson, April 21, 1970, Pelly to Sally Dunbar, April 22, 1970; Larry Venable to Pelly, April 12, 1970; Pelly to Larry Venable, April 24, 1970; Pelly to David Driver, April 24, 1970; Pelly to Henri Duvall, April 24, 1970 [Thomas Pelly/23].

67 Gude, Form Letter to Constituents, 1967 [GG-GWU/15]; Gude to Constituents, April 15, 1970 [GG-GWU/47]; Gude to Jane Farbger, August 8, 1969 [GG-GWU/47].

68 Potter to Gude, May 7, 1969 [GG-GWU/47]; Draft Letter to Constituents (May 1970) [GG-GWU/15]; Veterans of Foreign Wars, Howard County Post (Eric Ford) to Gude, May 23, 1970 [GG-GWU/15]; American Legion to Gude, May 5, 1970 [GG-GWU/15].

69 Gude to Tellock, May 21, 1970 [GG-GWU/57]; Gude to Robert Melville, June 4, 1970 [GG-GWU/57]; Douglas to Gude, June 10, 1970 [WOD/297].

70 Ball to Celler, June 11, 1970; First Report by the Special Subcommittee on H. Res 920 of the Committee of the Judiciary, House of Representatives, Ninety-First Congress Pursuant to H. Res 93, June 20, 1970 (1970).

71 Ford to Celler, July 29, 1970 [Gerald Ford/R-12].

72 Ford to Celler, July 29, 1970 [Gerald Ford/R-12].

73 Ford to Celler, July 29, 1970 [Gerald Ford/R-12].

74 "Charge Whitewash on Justice Douglas," *Des Moines Register,* August 4, 1970.

75 Waggonner to Celler, August 1, 1970 [NARG 233/88—AP File]; Becker, oral interview [Gerald Ford/1].

76 Wolfson to Rifkind, November 19, 1973; Wolfson to Associated Press, November 21, 1973; Wolfson to Rifkind, October 20, 1970; Wolfson to Rifkind, September 14, 1970; Rifkind to Wolfson, October 9, 1970; Rifkind to Wolfson, October 7, 1970; Becker to Wolfson, September 3, 1970; Wolfson, Confidential Memorandum, September 10, 1970; Wolfson to William Bittman, September 14, 1970 [WOD/590].

77 Aull to Waggonner, August 10, 1970 [WOD/297]; N.B. to Douglas, August 4, 1970 [WOD/297]; "Douglas Lists $20,568 Income from His Off-Bench Activities," *New York Times,* August 5, 1970.

78 Wyman to Colmer, August 12, 1970; Colmer to Celler, August 14, 1970. RG [NARG 233/88—AP File].

79 Nixon to Celler, May 13, 1970 [NARG 233/88—AP File]; Nixon to Celler, June 2, 1970 [NARG 233/88—AP File].

80 Mitchell to Celler, June 29, 1970; Mitchell to Celler, August 17; Fay Aull to Douglas, September 9, 1970 [WOD/657].

81 Confidential Memorandum, Points Made by Justice Douglas, November 15, 1955; Mathew Baird to Deputy Director, CIA, March 22, 1957 [CIA–Freedom of Information Act Release].

82 Celler to Helms, June 22, 1970; Helms to Celler, July 15, 1970; Larry Houston, Memorandum for Record, July 10, 1970; Larry Houston, Memorandum for Record, July 6, 1970.

83 Houston to Helms, July 17, 1970; Houston, Memorandum for Record [conversation with Ford], July 20, 1970.
84 Helms to Celler, August 10, 1970 [NARG 233/89—AP File].
85 Final Report, 68–69; Nevada Gaming Control Board search of investigations into Parvin and Douglas [NARG 233/88—AP File].
86 Ford to Celler, August 5, 1970 [NARG 233/89—AP File]; Ford, *Congressional Record,* August 6, 1970 H 7933.
87 Ford to Celler, August 5, 1970 [NARG 233/89—AP File]; McCloskey to Celler, August 18, 1970.
88 Memorandum, August 5 [NA RGNARG 233/89—AP File].
89 Memorandum, August 5 [NA RGNARG 233/89—AP File].
90 McCloskey to Celler, August 18, 1970 [HR 920].
91 Rifkind, second memorandum, August 18 [HR 920].
92 Rifkind, second memorandum, August 18 [HR 920].
93 William Telley, *October Crisis, 1970: An Insider's View* (Alberta: University of Alberta Press, 2007), 83–85.

CHAPTER 6. A LONG SUMMER OF DISCORD:
THE SENATE AWAITS THE HOUSE

1 Black to Rodell, June 5, 1970 [HLB/47]; Rodell to Black, June 1, 1970 [HLB/47]; Black to Rodell, May 13, 1970 [HLB/43]; Luke A. Nichter, *Richard Nixon and Europe: The Reshaping of the Postwar Atlantic World* (Cambridge: Cambridge University Press, 2015), 6–24.
2 See Michael Gerhardt, *The Federal Impeachment Process: A Constitutional and Historical Analysis* (Chicago: University of Chicago Press, 2000), 38.
3 Gerhardt, *Federal Impeachment Process,* 38.
4 William C. Berman, *William Fulbright and the Vietnam War: The Dissent of a Political Realist* (Kent, OH: Kent State University Press, 1988), 32–40.
5 On Republican moderates and Nixon, see Kabaservice, *Rule and Ruin,* 293–346.
6 Joseph A. Fry, *Debating Vietnam: Fulbright, Stennis, and Their Senate Hearings* (Lanham, MD: Rowman & Littlefield, 2006), 156–160; Cooper and Church to Anderson, May 22, 1970 [Clinton Presba Anderson/368]; "The Legal Basis for the US Role in Conflict in Cambodia," *New York Times,* May 1, 1970.
7 Louis Baldwin, *Honorable Politician: Mike Mansfield of Montana* (Missoula, MT: Mountain Publishing, 1979), 13–18; Valeo, *Mike Mansfield,* 124; Seth Jacobs, *America's Miracle Man in Vietnam: Ngo Diem, Religion Race, and US Intervention in Southeast Asia* (Durham, NC: Duke University Press, 2004), 41.
8 Everett L. Schapsmeir, *Dirksen of Illinois: Senatorial Statesman* (Urbana: University of Illinois Press, 1985), 31–112; Dirksen, draft letter, 1969; Dirksen, draft letter, September 1966 [Everett Dirksen/2142].
9 Senate, draft memo, February 6, 1970 [Hugh Scott/32].
10 Scott, form letter, February 1970 [Hugh Scott/32]; Scott to Clarence Mitchell,

January 28, 1970 [Hugh Scott/68]; Scott to Roy Wilkins, January 29, 1970 [Hugh Scott/68]; Scott to Dr. Ralph Abernathy, January 29, 1970 [Hugh Scott/68].

11   Statement of Robert Griffin, April 15, 1975 [Robert Griffin/292].

12   "The Dog Owners Who Give Their Pets LSC," *San Francisco Chronicle,* August 4, 1970; "Impatience over Probe of Douglas," *San Francisco Chronicle,* August 4, 1970; "Critics of Douglas Call Inquiry a Whitewash and Travesty," *New York Times,* August 4, 1970; "President Refers to Manson as Guilty: Later Denis Intent to Speculate," *Washington Post,* August 4, 1970; "Douglas Whitewash Charged," *Washington Post,* August 4, 1970.

13   "Huge Caseload, Small Staff Slow Supreme Court Work," *Baltimore Sun,* July 20, 1970; "Guerillas Tell Arab Chiefs to Reject Peace Proposals," *Baltimore Sun,* July 21, 1970; "Nixon Plans Veto if Trade Quotas Exceed his Goals," *Baltimore Sun,* July 21, 1970; "5 Justices Offer Data on Income," *Baltimore Sun,* August 4, 1970; "Douglas Foes Say Panle Is Dragging Its Feet," *Baltimore Sun,* August 4, 1970.

14   "Report on Douglas Kept Under Wraps," *Chicago Tribune,* July 21, 1970; "Kidnapped Girl Found Slain," "Nixon Sees Upturn in Economy, but No Cut in Taxes," "Florida Bandit Slays Two Women," and "Charge Whitewash on Justice Douglas," *Des Moines Register,* August 4, 1970; "Income Divulged by 5 of 9 on US Supreme Court," August 4, 1970; "US Hits Hamburger Chain for Deceptive Ad Contest," *Detroit Free Press,* July 21, 1970; "Does Nixon's Blunder Hint at Attitude on System?," *Detroit Free Press,* August 5, 1970.

15   "Whitewash of Douglas Is Charged: Celler Says It's Not True," *Richmond Times Dispatch,* August 4, 1970; "Douglas Lists Off-Bench Earnings," *Richmond Times Dispatch,* August 5, 1970; "Waggonner Calls Probe of Douglas a Travesty," *Shreveport Times,* August 4, 1970; "Stalling in Douglas Impeachment Proceeding Hints of Whitewash," *Clarion Ledger,* July 20, 1970; "Five Justices File Reports on Income," *Clarion Ledger,* August 5, 1970.

16   Hoyt to Douglas, August 15, 1970 [WOD/321].

17   Goldwater Memo—January 27, 1970 [BG-ASU/AF-15]; Goldwater Memo—March 24, 1970 [BG-ASU/AF-15]; Nina M. Moore, *Governing Race: Policy, Process, and the Politics of Race* (Westport, CT: Praeger, 2002), 64.

18   Goldwater Memo—August 6, 1970 [BG-ASU/AF-15].

19   Nixon to Goldwater, August 17, 1970 [BG-ASU/AF-15].

20   Form letter on Cambodia, May 22, 1970 [BG-ASU/IV-251].

21   Goldwater to Richard Addison, January 22, 1970 [BG-ASU/III-189].

22   Goldwater to William Huesler, March 24, 1970 [BG-ASU/IV-252]; Goldwater to Roy Rainwater, April 9, 1970 [BG-ASU/IV-252]; Mr. Dean Wright to Goldwater, April 16, 1970 [BG-ASU/IV-251]; Goldwater to Wright, April 27, 1970 [BG-ASU/IV-251]; Goldwater to Harry Everingham, March 3, 1970 [BG-ASU/III-189]; Ervin to Goldwater, May 11, 1970 [BG-ASU/AF-6].

23   Goldwater to Ms. Jean Okamura, May 14, 1970 [BG-ASU/IV-252]; Goldwater to John Scates, May 16, 1970 [BG-ASU/IV-252].

24 Fannin to Mr. Lisle McKim, August 31, 1966 [PF-ASU/82]; "Paul J. Fannin, 94, Who Served in Top Elected Offices in Arizona," *New York Times,* January 17, 2002.

25 Fannin to Harry Anderson (form letter), July 11, 1966 [PF-ASU/85]; Fannin to Henry Klopfar, July 21, 1966 [PF-ASU/85].

26 Fannin to Ms. Beaton, July 27, 1966 [PF-ASU/82]; Fannin to Ms. Ralph Coggins, July 25, 1966 [PF-ASU/82]; Fannin to Mrs. D. Hopson, July 25, 1966 [PF-ASU/82]; Fannin to Mr. Churchill, July 30, 1969 [PF-ASU/247]; Fannin to Arthur Fossland, June 23, 1969 [PF-ASU/247].

27 Joseph A. Fry, *The American South and the Vietnam War: Belligerence, Protest, and Agony in Dixie* (Lexington: University Press of Kentucky, 2015), 269–271; Fannin to Helen Anderson, May 20, 1970 [PF-ASU/246]; Fannin to Mr. Wallace Broberg, May 14, 1970 [PF-ASU/246]; Fannin to Lee Scott, May 19, 1970 [PF-ASU/246].

28 Gary Stone, *Elites for Peace: The Senate and the Vietnam War, 1964–1968* (Knoxville: University of Tennessee Press, 2007), 55–58; James C. Olson, *Stuart Symington: A Life* (Columbia: University of Missouri Press, 2003), 380; James Giglio, *Call Me Tom: The Life of Thomas F. Eagleton* (Columbia: University of Missouri Press, 2011).

29 Patricia Cox, *Ralph W. Yarborough: The People's Senator* (Austin: University of Texas Press, 2001), 240–249; Asch, *The Senator and the Sharecropper,* 265.

30 Zweirs, *Senator James O. Eastland,* 120–123; Asch, *The Senator and the Sharecropper,* 269–270; Bayh to Eastland, December 20, 1970 [James O. Eastland/SI SS18, 1]; Lake, *"Tar Baby" Option,* 143.

31 Fry, *Debating Vietnam,* 3–6; Michael Scott Downs, "Advise and Consent: John Stennis and the Vietnam War, 1954–1973," *Journal of Mississippi History* 55 (1993): 87–114.

32 Stennis to J. L. Schwartz, March 16, 1970, 24 [John Stennis/2, F-36]; Stennis to Lieutenant J. M. Pearson, May 25, 1970 [John Stennis/2, F-36]; Stennis to Willie Simmons, July 30, 1970 [John Stennis/2, F-36].

33 A. Armstrong Smith (state senator) to Russell, July 9, 1968 [Richard Russell/XV-316]; Russell to Hon. Lamar Sizemore, November 25, 1969 [Richard Russell/36]; Fite, *Richard B. Russell Jr.,* 246–248; Sally Russell, *Richard Brevard Russell: A Life of Consequence* (Macon, GA: Mercer University Press, 2011), 261, 262.

34 Talmadge to David Kennerson, July 2, 1970 [Herman Talmadge/157]; Talmadge to Hon. G. O. Terrell, October 22, 1970 [Herman Talmadge/157].

35 R. A. Whittaker to Ervin, December 22, 1970 [SE-UNC/221]; Ervin to Whittaker, January 31, 1970 [SE-UNC/221].

36 Henry P. Brandis to Ervin, June 3, 1958 [SE-UNC/29]; Wilkins to Ervin, June 6, 1958 [SE-UNC/29]; Ina Reid to Ervin, July 18, 1956; Southern States Industrial Council to Ervin, March 7, 1958 [SE-UNC/29]; Ervin to Edward D. Stennis, August 6, 1958 [SE-UNC/29].

37 Ervin to Richard Williams, November 6, 1969 [SE-UNC/221]; Ervin to Grace Matthews, May 26, 1969 [SE-UNC/129].

38 Ervin to Perci L. Foy, April 8, 1970 [SE-UNC/212]; Harlow to Ervin, April 27, 1970 [SE-UNC/212]; Ervin to Robert Watterson, May 4, 1970 [SE-UNC/212]; Ervin to Francis J. Kane, July 2, 1970 [SE-UNC/212].

39 Holland to Pat Marotta, April 21, 1970; Holland to L. Manookian, August 14, 1970 [Spessard Holland].

40 Tydings, press report, July 14, 1970 [Joseph Tydings/VI B 30].

41 Speech of Mathias, February 17, 1970; Nixon to Senator William Saxbe, March 3, 1970; Charles Mathias to John Dean, April 1, 1970; Charles Mathias, Memorandum, April 1, 1970; Statement of Charles Mathias, April 8, 1970 [Charles Mc-Curdy Mathias Jr./121].

42 Individual Views of Mr. Byrd of West Virginia, April 1, 1970 [Robert Byrd/141].

43 Saxbe, *I've Seen the Elephant*, 110–116; Bill Christofferson, *The Man from Clear Lake: Earth Day Founder Senator Gaylord Nelson* (Madison: University of Wisconsin Press, 2004), 345–347.

44 "The Douglas Retainer," speech by Carl Curtis, May 20, 1969 [Carl Curtis/70]; "The Current Controversy Involving Associate Justice Douglas," speech by Carl Curtis, June 5, 1969 [Carl Curtis/70]; statement of Mr. Dole, May 12, 1970 [Robert Dole/111]; statement of Mr. Dole, November 10, 1969 [Robert Dole/111].

45 Michael O'Brien, *Philip Hart: Conscience of the Senate* (Lansing: Michigan State University Press, 1995), 122–134; Hart to Alex Blotsky, April 20, 1970 [PH-UMich/73]; Hart to Melvin Laird, April 28, 1970 [PH-UMich/75]; Edna Lennon to Hart, July 20, 1960 [PH-UMich/161]; Hart to Lennon, July 22, 1966 [PH-UMich/161]; Hart to Charles Ross, May 25, 1970 [PH-UMich/187]; Hart to Mary Mikkelson, May 28, 1970 [PH-UMich/187]; Hart to Mayor Cecil Phillips, May 25, 1970 [PH-UMich/187]; Hart to Dr. Eduardo Rivera, May 25, 1970 [PH-UMich/187]; Hart to Roseanne Letvin, June 9, 1970 [PH-UMich/187].

46 Stone, *Elites for Peace.*

47 Petition, dated April 11, 1970 [Eugene McCarthy/153.K.18.6.F].

48 Steven M. Gillan, *The Democrat's Dilemma: Walter F. Mondale and the Liberal Legacy* (New York: Columbia University Press, 1992), 128–136.

49 Muriel Dokken, Iron Range Labor Assembly secretary, to McCarthy, May 19, 1970 [Eugene McCarthy/255-145.E.6.8.F].

50 J. F. Woodrin to McCarthy, September 3, 1986 [Eugene McCarthy/225]; Darrell Blackwell to McCarthy, September 12, 1968 [Eugene McCarthy/225].

51 McCarthy to Mary Beth Nelson, July 17, 1969; Mary Beth Nelson to McCarthy, June 23, 1969 [Eugene McCarthy/225]; McCarthy to Lannan, May 22, 1969. Lanan also wrote, "Until more information of a clear and precise nature is brought to the front concerning Douglas, I am asking all due influence and power to make sure that a thorough investigation and study of the situation takes place so that all information will be available." See R. L. Heunisch to McCarthy, November 23, 1969 [Eugene McCarthy/225].

52 Mondale, draft letter February 1970: [Walter Mondale/153.L.8.8.F], Mondale, speech, June 8, 1970 [Walter Mondale/153.L.8.8]; Solon Simmons, *The Eclipse of*

American Equality: Arguing Equality on "Meet the Press" (Stanford, CA: Stanford University Press, 2013), 173–174; Walter F. Mondale, *The Accountability of Power: Toward a Responsible Presidency* (New York: McKay, 1975), 116.

53 Ross Guyer to Hughes, November 25, 1969 [Harold Hughes/S25].

54 Statement by Harold Hughes in Opposition to the Nomination of Judge G. Harrold Carswell as a Justice of the US Supreme Court, February 16, 1970 [Harold Hughes/ S25]; Hughes to William Fulton, April 10, 1970 [Harold Hughes/S25]; Hughes to D. E. Willard, April 14, 1970 [Harold Hughes/S25]; M. R. Shaw to Hughes, February 21, 1970 [Harold Hughes/S26].

55 Ribicoff, statement of March 23, 1970 [Abe Ribicoff/122]; Ribicoff, press release for May 11, 1970. [Abe Ribicoff/123].

56 Rhodri Jeffreys-Jones, *Peace Now: American Society and the Ending of the Vietnam War* (New Haven, CT: Yale University Press, 1999), 200–210.

57 Hunt, *Turning*, 44; William Bundy, *A Tangled Web: The Making of Foreign Policy in the Nixon Presidency* (New York: Hill & Wang, 1998), 387; Belknap, *Supreme Court under Earl Warren*, 286; Muskie to Steven Norden, May 27, 1970 [Edmund Muskie/172]; Muskie to George Blanchette, May 18, 1970 [Edmund Muskie/172].

58 Brooke to Richard Elwinger, May 13, 1970 [Edward William Brooke/207]; Kenneth E. BeLieu, Dept Ass't to the President, to Brooke, October 1, 1969 [Edward William Brooke/444 f-5]; Lyn Nofziger, Dept Ass't to Nixon to Brooke, October 6, 1969 [Edward William Brooke/443 f-1]; Clark Mollenhoff to Brooke, October 16, 1969 [Edward William Brooke/443 f-1]; *Congressional Record,* S 2384, February 25, 1970; Brooke to Nixon, May 11, 1970 [Edward William Brooke/187].

59 See, e.g., Samuel B. Hand, *The Star That Set: The Vermont Republican Party* (Lanham, MD: Lexington Books, 2003), 280–283; James M. Jeffords, *An Independent Man: Adventures of a Public Servant* (Simon & Schuster, 2003), 64–66; Stone, *Elites for Peace*, 71.

60 Aiken to Carolyn McAnnich, May 5, 1970 [GDA/C 19-2 F-8]; Baker to Aiken, April 20, 1970 [GDA/C 19-2 F-8]; Aiken to Baker, April 27, 1970; [GDA/C 19-2 F-8]; Harold Frost to Aiken, April 20, 1970 [GDA/C 19-2 F-8]; Aiken to Frost, April 22, 1970 [GDA/C 19-2 F-8]; Bill Anderson to Aiken, April 18, 1970 [GDA/C 19-2 F-8].

61 William Lurcom to Aiken, March 11, 1970 [GDA/C 19-2 F-8]; George Blanchette, to Aiken, April 24, 1970 [GDA/C 19-2 F-8]; Aiken to William Murray, April 14, 1970 [GDA/C 19-2 F-8]; G. Earl Carlson to Aiken, April 25, 1970 [GDA/C 19-2 F-8].

62 Kabaservice, *Rule and Ruin*, 293–346; Fannin to Frank Stelling, June 18, 1969 [PF-ASU/247].

63 Dr. Darrell Moses to Wallace Bennett, May 8, 1970 [Wallace Bennett]; Bennett to Darrell Moses, May 13, 1970; [Wallace Bennett]; Dalvin J. Williams to Bennett, May 27, 1970 [Wallace Bennett]; Bennett to Williams, June 5, 1970 [Wallace Bennett].

64 Senator Mark O. Hatfield (R-OR) news release, March 26, 1970]] [Hugh Scott/68]; Mark Hatfield to Hart, September 2, 1970 [PH-UMich/74].
65 Magnusson, press release, February 20, 1970 [Warren Magnusson/229].
66 Magnusson to J. Sempter, May 7, 1970 [Warren Magnusson/91]; Magnusson, press release May 5, 1970 [Warren Magnusson/91]; Magnusson to Glenn E. Brown, April 28, 1970; Magnusson to Elmer Jacks, May 19, 1970 [Warren Magnusson/91].
67 Jackson, form letter, January 1, 1971; Jackson to Douglas, October 30, 1970 [Henry Jackson/11].
68 Anderson to Coklin, June 1, 1970 [Clinton Presba Anderson/381]; Anderson to Hart, June 16, 1970 [Clinton Presba Anderson/368].
69 Montoya to Joseph Saunders, June 24, 1957 [Joseph Montoya/6]; Montoya to C. J. Mosely [Joseph Montoya/178].
70 Jordan to Carl Herendeen, July 26, 1966 [Len Jordan/152]; Jordan to Dr. Harry T. Phillips, December 3, 1965 [Len Jordan/152].
71 Jordan to Mrs. Wanda Hoskins, November 24, 1966 [Len Jordan/152]; Jordan to Jack Gerard, October 1, 1965 [Len Jordan/152]; Jordan to Raymon L. Smith, August 30, 1966 [Len Jordan/152].
72 Jordan to Dean Rodgers, November 20, 1969 [Len Jordan/152]; Jordan to Clyde Schoonover, November 25, 1970 [Len Jordan/152]; Jordan to J. E. Cratty, April 20, 1970 [Len Jordan/152].
73 Church to Mr. and Ms. Bob Montgomery, May 8, 1970 [Frank Church/S 34 B1 f-2]; Roy E. Williams to Church, June 19, 1969 [Frank Church/S 34 B1 f-2].
74 Church, draft letter, May 1970 [Frank Church/S 34 B1 f-2]; D. W. Burnett to Frank Church, May 20, 1970 [Frank Church/S 34 B1 f-2]; Church to Burnett, June 26, 1970 [Frank Church/S 34 B1 f-2].
75 William M. Hammond, *Public Affairs: The Military and the Media, 1962–1968* (Washington, DC: Center of Military History, United States Army, 1990), 479; Johns, *Vietnam's Second Front,* 138; Benjamin Wittes, *Confirmation Wars: Preserving the Independent Courts in Angry Times* (Lanham, MD: Rowman & Littlefield, 2014), 55; "And Why Not Impeach Douglas," *Wyoming State Tribune,* April 21, 1970.
76 Shirley Garrett to Ford and McGee, April 23, 1970 [Gale McGee]; McGee to Garrett, April 29, 1970 [Gale McGee]; Jean Scheider to McGee, April 28, 1970 [Gale McGee]; Deborah Stafford to McGee, May 23 [Gale McGee], 1970; McGee to Saryua Okawara, Septe 18, 1970 [Gale McGee]
77 Brant to Brennan, October 1, 1970 [William J. Brennan/II:12]; Douglas to Cohen, June 30, 1953 [Benjamin V. Cohen/8]; Cohen to Douglas, April 22, 1970 [Benjamin V. Cohen/8Tom C. Clark, review of *Points of Rebellion* by William O. Douglas, *Harvard Law Review* 83 (1970): 1931–1933; Tom Clark and Ramsay Clark, *Meet the Press* transcript [Lawrence Spivak/245].
78 Brennan to Brant, October 14, 1970 [William J. Brennan/II:146]. Interestingly,

this memorandum is located in a file marked "Subcommittee on Improvements in Judicial Machinery, Committee on the Judiciary, US Senate." As a result, a scholar researching Brennan's views on judicial ethics will find correspondence with Brant, as well as Senator Joseph Tydings of Maryl and Tom Clark to Harold Leventhal, April 21, 1970 [Harold Leventhal/3]; Brant to Douglas, July 21, 1970 [WOD/313].

79 Murrah to Douglas, May 29, 1970 [WOD/313]; Douglas to Chambers, November 28, 1970 [WOD/298].

80 Hentoff v. Ichord, 318 F.Supp 1175 (DDC 1970); Report of Inquiry Concerning Speaker's Honoraria at Colleges and Universities by the Committee on Internal Security, December 14, 1970, 91st Cong, 2d Sess.

81 *Congressional Record,* December 2, 1969, H 11060.

82 "Judge Loses Civil Liberties Battle," *Times* (London), December 16, 1970; see "A Judge Bars US From Publishing Lists of Radicals: Limits Congressional Power and Defends the Rights of 65 Campus Speakers," *New York Times,* October 29, 1970; "Judge Curbs Speaker Blacklist," *Daily Oklahoman,* October 29, 1970. On the letters, see, e.g., J. C. Foriel to Gesell, October 29, 1970 [Gerhard Gesell/49]; Ed Berry to Gesell, October 29, 1970 [Gerhard Gesell/49]; "Your Right to Know—Suppressed," WDIX, November 3, 1970; O'Brien to Gesell, November 10, 1970 [Gerhard Gesell/49]; Professor Lori Rhinelander to Gesell, October 29, 1970 [Gerhard Gesell/49]; "A Stand for Freedom," *Boston Globe,* November 6, 1970.

83 Ichord to Leron Hill, December 1, 1970 [Richard Ichord/R-48]; Ichord to Colleagues, December 1, 1970 [PM/378].

84 *Congressional Record,* December 2, 1969, H11060; Mikva to Colleagues, December 10, 1970 [PM/378].

85 Stokes to Colleagues, December 10, 1970 [PM/378].

86 Leventhal to Fahy, 1970 [Charles Fahy/68].

87 Sirica to Agnew, September 18, 1970 [John J. Sirica/5].

CHAPTER 7. CONCLUSION

1 Ricard L. Lyons, "No Grounds to Impeach Justice Douglas Found," *Washington Post,* December 4, 1970.

2 Douglas to Rifkind, December 4, 1970 [WOD/298].

3 Douglas to Hon. Raymond Farrell, Commissioner INS, February 6, 1970 [Edward Hutchinson/56]. Final Report, 68–69.

4 United States ex. rel. Knauff v. Shaughnessy, 338 US 537 (1950). Testimony before the House of Representatives Subcommittee on the Judiciary, Monday, April 3, 1950; Knauff to Frankfurter, December 16, 1951; Frankfurter to Knauff, December 19, 1951 [Felix Frankfurter, Library of Congress/43]; Jackson to Knauff, December 19, 1951 [Robert H. Jackson/164]. See Testimony before the House of Representatives Subcommittee on the Judiciary, Monday, April 3, 1950; Knauff to Frankfurter, December 16, 1951; Frankfurter to Knauff, December 19, 1951

[Felix Frankfurter, Harvard/43]; Jackson to Knauff, December 19, 1951 [Robert H. Jackson/164]; Hutchinson to Raymond Farrell, Commissioner INS, February 6, 1970 [Edward Hutchinson/56]; Final Report, 68–69; Fay Aull to Douglas, September 8, 1970 [WOD/657].

5   Douglas to Gerald Stern, December 4, 1970 [WOD/298]; Dean, *Rehnquist Choice*, 26.
6   "The Campaign against Justice Douglas," *New York Times*, December 16, 1970; "The Committee Report on Justice Douglas," *Washington Post*, December 18, 1970.
7   "Court Settles Action by Denny's against Parvin Holders," *Wall Street Journal*, December 16, 1970; "Loan Bid by Douglas Revealed," *Boston Globe*, December 4, 1970.
8   "Douglas Bid for Parvin Loan Told," *Des Moines Register*, December 4, 1970.
9   "CIA Backing Linked to Trip by Douglas," *Baltimore Sun*, December 16, 1970; "Nixon Helps Usher in 1 Trillion Economy," "Cooper–Church Bid Softened," *Baltimore Sun*, December 16, 1970; "Excessive Mercury Found in Canned Tuna," *Baltimore Sun*, December 16, 1970.
10 "Army Said to Spy on Illinois Officials," *Baltimore Sun*, December 17, 1970; "Witness in Calley Case Tells of Atrocities Before My Lai," *Baltimore Sun*, December 17, 1970.
11 "Douglas Tells Young People: Keep Faith, Fight through Law," *Birmingham News*, December 16, 1970; "Pattern of Impeccability Prescribed for Justices," *Birmingham News*, April 17, 1970; "Ex-GI: Calley Shot Heads Off," *Atlanta Journal*, December 4, 1970; "Panel OKs Douglas, but Issue Alive," *Atlanta Journal*, December 4, 1970; "Douglas Is Cleared by Panel," *Clarion Ledger*, December 3, 1970; "House Probe Report Links Douglas with CIA Activity," *Clarion Ledger*, December 16, 1970; "A Conservative View," *Clarion Ledger*, December 16, 1970.
12 "W. German Refuge for Negro Deserter," *Times* (London), December 18, 1970; "Sgt. James Henry Grant Deserted and Sought Asylum in Germany after Receiving Orders for Vietnam. A Bavarian Court Granted Him Asylum," *Times* (London), December 18, 1970; "Congress Is Told Army Spied on Officials," *Times* (London), December 18, 1970; "Mr. Nixon Sees Popularity Fall to Lowest Point," *Times* (London), December 18, 1970; "Okinawa Rioters Invade US Base," *Times* (London), December 18, 1970.
13 Wyman to Congress, December 28, 1970 [Clarence Dickinson Long/31].
14 Douglas to Ares, December 7, 1971 [WOD/1117]; Lester Maddox to Black, September 15, 1970 [HLB/39]; Waggonner to Henry J. Lacquer, August 4, 1972 [Joseph Waggonner/19].
15 Leadership Conference on Civil Rights, Statement, November 15, 1971 [Joseph Rauh/39]; Rauh to Eastland, November 22, 1971 [Joseph Rauh/39].
16 Powell to John Shenefield, June 21, 1970 [Lewis Powell]; Powell to Laird, June 26, 1970 [Lewis Powell]; Powell to Nixon, June 26, 1970 [Lewis Powell].
17 Powell to Bush, March 4, 1978; Bush Commencement Speech, August 13, 1977

[Lewis Powell]; Bush to Powell, September 20, 1977; Powell, speech draft, 1986 [Lewis Powell].

18 Laird v. Tatum, 408 US 1 (1972).

19 Robert Stewart to Douglas, November 10, 1970 [WOD/889]; Eugene Sarver to Douglas, November 2, 1970 [WOD/889]; John C. Hilsinki to Douglas, November 23, 1970 [WOD 889]; Massachusetts v. Laird, 400 US 886 (1970); Douglas to Janet Finnie, April 12, 1971 [WOD/889]; Roberta Strauss Feuerlicht, *America's Reign of Terror, World War I, the Red Scare, and the Palmer Raids* (New York: Random House, 1971).

20 Laird v. Tatum, 408 US 1 (1972).

21 Marshal to the Conference, August 8, 1973 [WOD/1639]; Douglas, Order to Vacate Stay, August 3, 1973 [WOD/1639]; Elizabeth Holtzman, *Who Said It Would Be Easy? One Woman's Life in the Political Arena* (New York: Arcade, 1996), 57–73.

22 Douglas to Rockefeller, December 20, 1974 [WOD/374]; Douglas to Rockefeller, December 19, 1969 [WOD/374].

23 Ford to Douglas, November 12, 1975 [WOD/1760]; Douglas to Clerks, November 14, 1975 [WOD/1760].

24 Warren Burger, Funeral remarks in tribute to Justice William O. Douglas, October 16, 1970. Clark Clifford, funeral remarks in tribute to Justice William O. Douglas, October 16, 1970 [WOD/1768].

BIBLIOGRAPHY

PRIMARY SOURCES

American Heritage Center, University of Wyoming
    Gale McGee
Arizona State University
    Paul Fannin
    Barry Goldwater
    John James Rhodes
Auburn University
    William Nichols
Bates University
    Edmund Muskie
Boise State University
    Frank Church
    Len Jordan
Boston College
    Thomas "Tip" O'Neill
Brigham Young University
    Wallace Bennett
Carl Albert Center, University of Oklahoma
    Carl Albert
    Page Belcher
    Jeffery Cohelan
Central Michigan University
    Robert Griffin
Clemson University
    Strom Thurmond
Everett Dirksen Papers, Dirksen Center
    Everett Dirksen
Florida Southern College
    James A. Haley
George Mason University
    William Lloyd Scott
George Washington University
    Gilbert Gude
Gerald Ford Library, Ann Arbor, Michigan
    Gerald Ford
    Edward Hutchinson
Harvard University
    Felix Frankfurter

Herbert Hoover Institution at Stanford University
    John Ehrlichman
Herbert Hoover Library
    Clark Mollenhoff
Humboldt State University
    Don Clausen
Johns Hopkins University
    Clarence Dickinson Long
    Charles McCurdy Mathias Jr.
Kean University
    Florence Dwyer
Library of Congress
    Clinton Presba Anderson
    Hugo Lafayette Black
    William J. Brennan
    Edward William Brooke
    Emanuel Celler
    Benjamin V. Cohen
    Democratic Study Group
    William O. Douglas
    Charles Fahy
    Felix Frankfurter
    Gerhard Gesell
    Clement Furman Haynsworth
    Robert H. Jackson
    Harold Leventhal
    Thurgood Marshall
    Patsy Mink
    Herbert Philbrick
    Elijah Barrett Prettyman
    Joseph Rauh
    Abe Ribicoff
    Wiley Rutledge
    John J. Sirica
    Simon Sobeloff
    Lawrence Spivak
    Robert Taft
    Robert Taft Jr.
    Earl Warren
Loyola University of Chicago
    Daniel Rostenkowski
Minnesota Historical Society
    Hubert Humphrey

Clark MacGregor
Eugene McCarthy
Walter Mondale
Mississippi State University
John Stennis
Missouri Historical Society
Durward Gorham Hall
Richard Ichord
National Archives, Foreign Office, Great Britain
Selwyn Lloyd
National Archives and Records Administration
Report on HR 920
Nebraska Historical Society
Carl Curtis
Ohio State University
William McCulloch
Princeton University
James Beck
John Marshall Harlan
Richard Nixon Library, Yorba Linda, California
John Dean
John Ehrlichman
Robert Haldeman
Egil "Bud" Krogh
Shepherd University, Robert C. Byrd Center
Robert C. Byrd
Texas A&M University
Olin Teague
University of Central Florida
Louis Frey
University of Delaware
John J. Williams
University of Florida
Spessard Holland
University of Georgia
John W. Davis
Maston O'Neal
Richard Russell
Herman Talmadge
University of Iowa
Harold Hughes
University of Kansas
Robert Dole

University of Kentucky
    Stanley Forman Reed
University of Louisiana, Monroe
    Joseph Waggonner
University of Maryland
    Spiro Agnew
    Joseph Tydings
University of Michigan, Bentley Historical Library
    Martha Wright Griffiths
    Philip Hart
University of Mississippi
    Thomas Abernethy
    James O. Eastland
University of Missouri
    Richard Bolling
University of New Mexico
    Joseph Montoya
University of North Carolina, Ashville
    Roy A. Taylor
University of North Carolina, Chapel Hill
    Samuel Ervin
University of Oregon
    Edith Green
University of South Florida
    Sam Gibbons
University of Vermont
    George Aiken
University of Virginia
    Hugh Scott
University of Washington
    Brock Adams
    Henry "Scoop" Jackson
    Warren Magnusson
    Thomas Pelly
Washington and Lee School of Law
    Lewis Powell
Washington State University
    Thomas Foley
    Catherine Dean May
Yale University
    Dean Acheson
    Ogden Rogers Reid

NEWSPAPERS
Arizona Republic
Atlanta Journal
Austin American
Baltimore Sun
Birmingham Daily News
Boston Globe
Charleston News and Courier
Cincinnati Enquirer
Clarion Ledger
Des Moines Register
Detroit Free Press
Glasgow Herald
Las Vegas Sun
Los Angeles Times
New Orleans Times Picayune
New York Times
New Zealand Times
Orlando Sentinel
Philadelphia Inquirer
Pittsburgh Press
Richmond Times Dispatch
Rolla Daily News
San Francisco Chronicle
Seattle Times
Shreveport Times
St. Petersburg Times
Sydney Tribune
Times of India
Times of London
Toronto Globe and Mail
Wall Street Journal
Washington Post

REFERENCES
Adams, Jerome. *Liberators, Patriots, and Leaders of Latin America.* Jefferson, NC: Mc-Farland, 1991.
Aistrup, Joseph A. *The Southern Strategy Revisited: Republican Top-Down Advancement in the South.* Lexington: University Press of Kentucky, 1996.
Albert, Carl. *Little Giant: The Life and Times of Speaker Carl Albert.* Norman: University of Oklahoma Press, 1990.

Anderson, David L. *The Columbia Guide to the Vietnam War.* New York: Columbia University Press, 2002.

———. "No More Vietnams: Historians Debate the Policy Lessons of the Vietnam War." In *The War That Never Ends: New Perspectives on the Vietnam War,* edited by David L. Anderson and John Ernst. Lexington: University Press of Kentucky, 2007.

Anderson, Jack. *Peace, War, and Politics: An Eyewitness Account.* New York: Forge Books, 1999.

Asch, Chris Myers. *The Senator and the Sharecropper: The Freedom Struggles of James O. Eastland and Fannie Lou Harper.* New York: New Press, 2008.

Ashmore, Harry. *Mission to Hanoi: A Chronicle of Double-Dealing in High Places.* New York: Putnam, 1968.

Atkinson, Frank B. *The Dynamic Dominion: Realignment and the Rise of Two-Party Competition in Virginia, 1945–1980.* Lanham, MD: Rowman & Littlefield, 2006.

Balboni, Alan. *Beyond the Mafia: Italian Americans and the Development of Organized Crime.* Reno: University of Nevada Press, 1996.

Baldwin, Louis. *Honorable Politician: Mike Mansfield of Montana.* Missoula, MT: Mountain Publishing, 1979.

Ball, Howard. *Of Power and Right: Hugo Black, William O Douglas, and America's Constitutional Revolution.* Oxford: Oxford University Press, 1992.

Bass, Jack, and Marylyn Thomson. *Strom: The Complicated Personal and Political Life of Strom Thurmond.* New York: Public Affairs, 2005.

Bassford, Christopher. *The Spit-Shine Syndrome: Organizational Irrationality in the American Field Army.* Westport, CT: Greenwood Press, 1988.

Belknap, Michael. *Federal Law and Southern Order: Racial Violence and Constitutional Conflict in the Post-Brown South.* Athens: University of Georgia Press, 2011.

———. *The Supreme Court under Earl Warren.* Columbia: University of South Carolina Press, 2005.

Bell, Jonathan. *The Liberal State on Trial: The Cold War and American Politics in the Truman Years.* New York: Columbia University Press, 2004.

Berman, Ari. *Give Us the Ballot: The Modern Struggle for Voting Rights in America.* New York: Farrar, Straus and Giroux, 2015.

Berman, William C. *William Fulbright and the Vietnam War: The Dissent of a Political Realist.* Kent, OH: Kent State University Press, 1988.

Bloodworth, Jeffrey. *Losing the Center: The Decline of American Liberalism, 1968–1992.* Lexington: University Press of Kentucky, 2013.

Blum, John Norton. *Years of Discord: American Politics and Society, 1961–1974.* New York: Norton, 1991.

Boomhower, Ray E. *Robert Kennedy and the 1968 Indiana Primary.* Bloomington: Indiana University Press, 2008.

Brands, H. W. *The Wages of Globalism: Lyndon Johnson and the Limits of American Power.* Oxford: Oxford University Press, 1995.

Brinkley, Douglas. *Gerald R. Ford: The American Presidents Series, the 38th President, 1974–1977*. New York: Times Books, 2007.

Broder, David S. *Behind the Front Page: A Candid Look at How the News Is Made*. New York: Simon & Schuster, 1987.

Bundy, William. *A Tangled Web: The Making of Foreign Policy in the Nixon Presidency.* New York: Hill & Wang, 1998.

Burrough, Bryan. *Days of Rage: America's Radical Undergreround, the FBI, and the Forgotten Age of Revolutionary Violence:* New York: Penguin, 2015.

Califano, Joseph A. *The Triumph and Tragedy of Lyndon Johnson: The White House Years.* New York: Touchstone, 1992.

Cannon, James. *Gerald R. Ford: An Honorable Life.* Ann Arbor: University of Michigan Press, 2013.

Cannon, Joseph. *Time and Chance: Gerald Ford's Appointment with History.* Ann Arbor: University of Michigan Press, 1998.

Caro, Robert A. *Master of the Senate: The Years of Lyndon Johnson 3.* New York: Knopf, 2002.

———. *The Passage of Power: The Years of Lyndon Johnson 4.* New York: Vintage, 2002.

Carroll, Peter N. *It Seemed Like Nothing Happened: America in the 1970s.* New Brunswick, NJ: Rutgers University Press, 2003.

Cathal, Nolan J. *Principled Diplomacy: Security and Rights in US Foreign Policy.* Westport, CT: Greenwood Press, 1993.

Charns, Alexander. *Cloak and Gavel: FBI Wiretaps, Bugs, Informers, and the Supreme Court.* Champaign: University of Illinois Press, 1992.

Childs, David W. "Congressman Joe D. Waggoner: A Study in Political Influence." *North Louisiana Historical Association* 13 (1982): 119–130.

Christofferson, Bill. *The Man from Clear Lake: Earth Day Founder Senator Gaylord Nelson.* Madison: University of Wisconsin Press, 2004.

Clark, Tom C. Review of *Points of Rebellion* by William O. Douglas. *Harvard Law Review* 83 (1970): 1931–1933.

Clymer, Kenton. *The United States and Cambodia, 1969–200: A Troubled Relationship.* New York: Routledge, 2004.

Coffey, Justin P. *Spiro Agnew and the Rise of the Republican Right.* Santa Barbara, CA: ABC-CLIO, 2015.

Cohen, Michael A. *American Maelstrom: The 1968 Election and the Politics of Division.* Oxford: Oxford University Press, 2016.

Colman, Jonathan. *The Foreign Policy of Lyndon B. Johnson: The United States and the World, 1963–1969.* Edinburgh: Edinburgh University Press, 2011.

Cortright, David. *Soldiers in Revolt: GI Resistance during the Vietnam War.* New York: Haymarket Books, 1975.

Countryman, Vern. *The Judicial Record of Justice William O. Douglas.* Cambridge, MA: Harvard University Press, 1974.

Cox, Patricia. *Ralph W. Yarborough: The People's Senator*. Austin: University of Texas Press, 2001.

Crespino, Joseph. *Strom Thurmond's America*. New York: Macmillan, 2012.

Cressey, Donald R. *Theft of the Nation: The Structure and Operations of Organized Crime in America*. New Brunswick, NJ: Transaction, 2008.

Cunningham, Stanley. *There's Something Happening Here: The New Left, the Klan, and FBI Counterintelligence*. Berkeley: University of California Press, 2004.

Dallek, Robert. *Flawed Giant: Lyndon Johnson and His Times, 1961–1973*. Oxford: Oxford University Press, 1999.

———. *Lone Star Rising: Lyndon Johnson and His Times, 1908–1960*. Oxford: Oxford University Press, 1991.

Dean, John. *The Rehnquist Choice: The Untold Story of the Nixon Appointment that Redefined the Supreme Court*. New York: Free Press, 2001.

Douglas, William O. *The Court Years, 1939–1975: The Autobiography of William O. Douglas*. New York: Random House, 1980.

———. *Points of Rebellion*. New York: Random House, 1969.

Downs, Michael Scott. "Advise and Consent: John Stennis and the Vietnam War, 1954–1973." *Journal of Mississippi History* 55 (1993): 87–114.

Durr, Virginia Foster. *Freedom Writer: Virginia Foster Durr—Letters from the Civil Rights Years*. Edited by Patricia Sullivan. Athens: University of Georgia Press, 2003.

Dzuback, Mary Ann. *Robert M. Hutchins: Portrait of an Educator*. Chicago: University of Chicago Press, 1991.

Ehrlichman, John. *Witness to Power: The Nixon Years*. New York: Simon & Schuster, 1982.

Ely, John Hart. *War and Responsibility: Constitutional Lessons of Vietnam and Its Aftermath*. Princeton, NJ: Princeton University Press, 1993.

Fairclough, Adam. *Race and Democracy: The Civil Rights Struggle in Louisiana, 1915–1972*. Athens: University of Georgia Press, 1999.

Falk, Bruce K. *The Origins of the Southern Strategy: Two-Party Competition in South Carolina, 1950–1972*. Lanham, MD: Lexington Books, 2001.

Feldman, Noah. *Scorpions: The Battles and Triumphs of FDR's Great Supreme Court Justices*. New York: Twelve Books, 2010.

Felton, Peter. "Yankee, Go Home and Take Me with You: Lyndon Johnson and the Dominican Republic." In *Beyond Vietnam: The Foreign Policies of Lyndon Johnson*, edited by H. W. Brands. College Station: Texas A&M University Press, 1997.

Feuerlicht, Roberta Strauss. *America's Reign of Terror, World War I, the Red Scare, and the Palmer Raids*. New York: Random House, 1971.

Filipink, Richard M., Jr. *Dwight Eisenhower and American Foreign Policy during the 1960s: An American Lion in Winter*. Lanham, MD: Lexington Books, 2015.

Fite, Gilbert. *Richard B. Russell Jr., Senator from Georgia*. Chapel Hill: University of North Carolina Press, 1991.

Fleming, James S. *Window on Congress: A Congressional Biography of Barber B. Conable Jr.* New York: University of Rochester Press, 2004.

Flippen, J. Brooks. *Speaker Jim Wright: Power Scandal, and the Birth of Modern Politics.* Austin: University of Texas Press, 2018.

Flynn, George O. *Louis B. Hershey: Mr. Selective Service.* Chapel Hill: University of North Carolina Press, 1985.

Foerstel, Karen. *Biographical Dictionary of Congressional Women.* Westport, CT: Greenwood Press, 1992.

Frederickson, Kari. *The Dixiecrat Revolt and the End of the Solid South, 1932–1968.* Chapel Hill: University of North Carolina Press, 2001.

Fry, Joseph A. *The American South and the Vietnam War: Belligerence, Protest, and Agony in Dixie.* Lexington: University Press of Kentucky, 2015.

———. *Debating Vietnam: Fulbright, Stennis, and Their Senate Hearings.* Lanham, MD: Rowman & Littlefield, 2006.

Gans, Herbert J. *Deciding What's News: A Study of "CBS Evening News," "NBC Nightly News," "Newsweek," and "Time."* Chicago: Northwestern University Press, 2004.

Gellman, Irwin F. *The President and the Apprentice: Eisenhower and Nixon, 1952–1961.* New Haven, CT: Yale University Press, 2015.

Gerhardt, Michael. *The Federal Impeachment Process: A Constitutional and Historical Analysis.* Chicago: University of Chicago Press, 2000.

Gibbons, William Conrad. *The US Government and the Vietnam War: Executive and Legislative Roles and Relationships, Part 1: 1945–1960.* Princeton, NJ: Princeton University Press, 1985.

———. *The US Government and the Vietnam War: Executive and Legislative Roles and Relationships, Part 2: 1961–1964.* Princeton, NJ: Princeton University Press, 1986.

Giglio, James. *Call Me Tom: The Life of Thomas F. Eagleton.* Columbia: University of Missouri Press, 2011.

Gillan, Steven M. *The Democrat's Dilemma: Walter F. Mondale and the Liberal Legacy.* New York: Columbia University Press, 1992.

Goldfield, David R. *Race Relations and Southern Culture: 1940 to the Present.* Baton Rouge: Louisiana State University Press, 1990.

Hall, Simon. *Peace and Freedom: The Civil Rights and Anti-war Movements in the 1960s.* Philadelphia: University of Pennsylvania Press, 2005.

Hammond, William M. *Public Affairs: The Military and the Media, 1962–1968.* Washington, DC: Center of Military History, United States Army, 1990. https://history.army.mil/html/books/091/91-13/CMH_Pub_91-13-B.pdf.

Hand, Samuel B. *The Star That Set: The Vermont Republican Party.* Lanham, MD: Lexington Books, 2003.

Hartke, Vance. *The American Crisis in Vietnam.* Indianapolis, IN: Bobbs-Merrill, 1968.

Heale, M. J. *McCarthy's Americans: Red Scare Politics in State and Nation, 1935–1965.* Athens: University of Georgia Press, 1988.

Hearings before the Select Committee to Study Governmental Operations with Respect to Intelligence Activities of the United States Senate. Volume 2. Washington, DC: Government Printing Office, 1976.

Heath, James O. *To Face Down Dixie: South Carolina's War on the Supreme Court in the Age of Civil Rights*. Baton Rouge: Louisiana State University Press, 2017.

Heins, Marjorie. *Priests of Our Democracy: The Supreme Court, Academic Freedom, and the Anti-communist Purge*. New York: New York University Press, 2013.

Herring, George C. *America's Longest War: The United States and Vietnam, 1950–1975*. 4th ed. New York: McGraw-Hill, 2001.

Herspring, Dale R. *The Pentagon and the Presidency: Civil Military Relations from FDR to George Bush*. Lawrence: University Press of Kansas, 2005.

Hoehle, Randolph. *Race and the Origins of American Neoliberalism*. New York: Routledge, 2015.

Hoffecker, Carol E. *Honest John Williams: US Senator from Delaware*. Newark: University of Delaware Press, 2000.

Holtzman, Elizabeth. *Who Said It Would Be Easy? One Woman's Life in the Political Arena*. New York: Arcade, 1996.

Honey, Michael K. *Going Down Jericho Road: The Memphis Strike, Martin Luther King's Last Campaign*. New York: Norton, 2007.

Hook, Sidney. "Forum: *Points of Rebellion*." *Brooklyn Law Review* 37 (1970): 16–21.

Hunt, Andrew E. *The Turning: An American History of Vietnam Veterans against the War*. New York: New York University Press, 1999.

Hunt, Richard. *Melvin Laird and the Foundation for the Post-Vietnam Military, 1969–1977*. Washington, DC: Department of Defense, Office of the Historian, 2015.

Isaacson, Walter. *Kissinger: A Biography*. New York: Simon & Schuster, 1992.

Jacobs, Seth. *America's Miracle Man in Vietnam: Ngo Diem, Religion Race, and US Intervention in Southeast Asia*. Durham, NC: Duke University Press, 2004.

Janeway, Michael. *The Fall of the House of Roosevelt: Brokers of Ideas and Power from FDR to LBJ*. New York: Columbia University Press, 2004.

Jeffords, James M. *An Independent Man: Adventures of a Public Servant*. Simon & Schuster, 2003.

Jeffreys-Jones, Rhodri. *Peace Now: American Society and the Ending of the Vietnam War*. New Haven, CT: Yale University Press, 1999.

Johns, Andrew L. *Vietnam's Second Front: Domestic Politics, the Republican Party, and the War*. Lexington: University Press of Kentucky, 2010.

Johnson, Robert David. *All the Way with LBJ: The 1964 Presidential Election*. Cambridge: Cambridge University Press, 2009.

Kabaservice, Geoffrey. *Rule and Ruin: The Downfall of Moderation and the Destruction of the Republican Party, from Eisenhower to the Tea Party*. Oxford: Oxford University Press, 2012.

Kalman, Laura. *Abe Fortas: A Biography*. New Haven, CT: Yale University Press, 1990.

————. *The Long Reach of the Sixties: LBJ, Nixon, and the Making of the Contemporary Supreme Court.* Oxford: Oxford University Press, 2017.

Kastenberg, Joshua E. "Cause and Effect: The Origins and Impact of Justice William O. Douglas's Anti-military Ideology from World War II to *O'Callahan v. Parker.*" *Thomas Cooley Law Review* 26 (2009): 163–170.

————. "Chief Justice William Howard Taft's Conception of Judicial Integrity: The Legal History of *Tumey v. Ohio.*" *Cleveland State Law Review* 65 (2017): 317–378.

————. "The Right to an Independent Judiciary and Avoidance of Constitutional Conflict: The Burger Court's Flawed Reasoning in *Chandler v. Judicial Council of the Tenth Circuit* and Its Unfortunate Legacy." *St. Mary's Journal of Legal Malpractice and Ethics* 8 (2017): 91–101.

————. *Shaping Military Law: Governing a Constitutional Military.* London: Ashgate, 2013.

Kaufman, Scott. *Ambition, Pragmatism, and Party: A Political Biography of Gerald R. Ford.* Lawrence: University Press of Kansas, 2017.

Keller, William. *The Liberals and J. Edgar Hoover: The Rise and Fall of a Domestic Intelligence State.* Princeton, NJ: Princeton University Press, 1989.

Kessler, Ronald. *Inside Congress: The Shocking Scandals, Corruption, and Abuse of Power Behind the Scenes on Capitol Hill.* New York: Pocket Books, 1997.

Kimball, Jeffrey. "The Nixon Doctrine: A Saga of Misunderstanding." *Presidential Series Quarterly* 36, no. 1 (2006): 59–74.

Kinnard, Douglas. *The Secretary of Defense.* Lexington: University Press of Kentucky, 1980.

Kotlowski, Dean. *Nixon's Civil Rights: Politics, Principle, and Policy.* Cambridge, MA: Harvard University Press, 2001.

Kruse, Kevin. *One Nation Under God: How Corporate America Invented Christian America.* New York: Basic Books, 2015.

Kutler, Stanley. *The Wars of Watergate: The Last Crisis of Richard Nixon.* New York: Norton, 1990.

Lake, Anthony. *The "Tar Baby" Option: American Policy in Southern Rhodesia.* New York: Columbia University Press, 1976.

Lalli, Sergio. "Howard Hughes in Las Vegas." In *The Players: The Men Who Made Las Vegas,* edited by Jack Sheehan. Reno: University of Nevada Press, 1997.

Lamb, Charles L. "Warren Burger." In *The Burger Court: Political and Judicial Profiles,* edited by Charles Lamb and Stephen Halpern. Champaign: University of Illinois Press, 1991.

Leff, Laurel. *Buried by the "Times": The Holocaust and America's Most Important Newspaper.* Cambridge: Cambridge University Press, 2005.

Lewes, James. *Protest and Survive: Underground GI Newspapers during the Vietnam War.* Westport, CT: Praeger, 2003.

Lewis, Fulton. *The Top of the News with Fulton Lewis III.* Fulton, MO, 1970.

Lichtman, Robert. *The Supreme Court and McCarthy-Era Repression: One Hundred Decisions.* Champaign: University of Illinois Press, 2012.

Liebovich, Louis. *Richard Nixon, Watergate, and the Press: A Historical Perspective.* Westport, CT: Praeger, 2003.

Lowndes, Joseph E. *From the New Deal to the New Right: Race and the Southern Origins of Modern Conservatism.* New Haven, CT: Yale University Press, 2008.

MacGregor, Morris J. *Integration of the Armed Forces, 1940–1965.* Washington, DC: Center for Military Studies, 1981.

MacNeil, Neil, and Richard A. Baker. *The American Senate: An Insider's History.* Oxford: Oxford University Press, 2013.

Maltz, Earl. *The Chief Justiceship of Warren Burger, 1969–1986.* Columbia: University of South Carolina Press, 2003.

Manley, John F. "The Conservative Coalition in Congress." In *New Perspectives on the House of Representatives,* edited by Robert L. Peabody and Nelson W. Polsby. New York: Rand McNally, 1977.

Manney, Patrick J. "Hale Boggs: The Southerner as National Democrat." In *Masters of the House: Southern Leadership over Two Decades,* edited by Roger Davidson. Westview, CT: Westview Press, 1998.

Mason, Robert. *Richard Nixon and the Quest for a New Majority.* Chapel Hill: University of North Carolina Press, 2004.

Matusow, Allen J. *Nixon's Economy: Booms, Busts, Dollars, and Votes.* Lawrence: University Press of Kansas, 1998.

———. *The Unraveling of America: A History of Liberalism in the 1960s.* Athens: University of Georgia Press, 1990.

May, Gary. *Bending toward Justice: The Voting Rights Act and the Transformation of American Democracy.* New York: Basic Books, 2006.

Mayer, Milton Stanford. *Robert Maynard Hutchins: A Memoir.* Berkeley: University of California Press, 1993.

McBride, H. E. *Impeach Justice Douglas.* New York: Exposition Press, 1971.

Merriner, James L. *Mr. Chairman: Power in Dan Rostenkowski's America.* Carbondale: Southern Illinois University Press, 1999.

Mieczkowski, Yanek. *Gerald Ford and the Challenges of the 1970s.* Lexington: University Press of Kentucky, 2005.

Mikva, Abner J., and Patti B. Saris. *The American Congress: The First Branch.* New York: Watts Press, 1983.

Mollenhoff, Clark R. *Strike Force: Organized Crime and the Government.* Englewood Cliffs, NJ: Prentice-Hall, 1972.

Mondale, Walter F. *The Accountability of Power: Toward a Responsible Presidency.* New York: McKay, 1975.

Moore, Nina M. *Governing Race: Policy, Process, and the Politics of Race.* Westport, CT: Praeger, 2002.

Morgan, Joseph G. *The Vietnam Lobby: The American Friends of Vietnam, 1955–1975.* Chapel Hill: University of North Carolina Press, 1997.

Moser, Richard. *The New Winter Soldiers: GI and Veteran Dissent during the Vietnam Era.* New Brunswick, NJ: Rutgers University Press, 1996.

Moses, James L. "An Interesting Game of Poker: Franklin D. Roosevelt, William O. Douglas, and the 1944 Vice Presidential Nomination." In *Franklin D. Roosevelt and the Transformation of Supreme Court,* volume 2, edited by Steven K. Shaw, William D. Pederson, and Frank J. Williams. London: Taylor & Francis, 2004.

Murphy, Bruce Allen. *Fortas: The Rise and Ruin of a Supreme Court Justice.* New York: William Morrow, 1988.

———. *Wild Bill: The Legend and Life of William O. Douglas, America's Most Controversial Supreme Court Justice.* New York: Random House, 2003.

Newton, Jim. *Justice for All: Earl Warren and the Nation He Made.* London: Penguin, 2006.

Nichter, Luke A. *Richard Nixon and Europe: The Reshaping of the Postwar Atlantic World.* Cambridge: Cambridge University Press, 2015.

Nixon, Richard M. "Asia after Vietnam." *Foreign Affairs* 46 (1967): 111–125.

Nonjudicial Activities of Supreme Court Justices and Other Federal Judges: Hearings before the Subcommittee on Separation of Powers of the Senate Committee on the Judiciary. 91st Cong. 327 (1969).

O'Brien, Michael. *Philip Hart: Conscience of the Senate.* Lansing: Michigan State University Press, 1995.

Olson, James C. *Stuart Symington: A Life.* Columbia: University of Missouri Press, 2003.

Paget, Karen. *Patriotic Betrayal: The Inside Story of the CIA's Secret Campaign to Enroll American Students in the Crusade against Communism.* New Haven, CT: Yale University Press, 2015.

Pearson, Drew. *Washington Merry-Go-Round: The Drew Pearson Diaries, 1960–1969.* Washington, DC: Potomac Books, 2015.

Phillips, Kevin P. *The Emerging Republican Majority.* Princeton, NJ: Princeton University Press, 2015.

Rabe, Stephen G. "The Caribbean Triangle: Bettencourt, Castro, and Trujillo and US Foreign Policy, 1958–1963." In *Empire and Revolution: The United States and the Third World since 1945,* edited by Peter L. Hahn and Mary Ann Hess. Columbus: Ohio State University Press, 2001.

———. "Controlling Revolutions: Latin America, the Alliance for Progress, and Cold War Anti-communism." In *Kennedy's Quest for Victory: American Foreign Policy, 1961–1963,* edited by Thomas G. Patterson. Oxford: Oxford University Press, 1989.

———. *Eisenhower and Latin America: The Foreign Policy of Anti-Communism.* Chapel Hill: University of North Carolina Press, 1988.

Reinhard, David W. *The Republican Right since 1945.* Lexington: University Press of Kentucky, 1983.

Reuter, Peter, Jonathan Rubenstein, and Simon Wynn. *Racketeering in Legitimate Industries: Two Case Studies.* Washington, DC: Department of Justice, 1983.

Ritchie, Donald. *Reporting from Washington: The History of the Washington Press Corps.* Oxford: Oxford University Press, 2006.

Rorabaugh, W. J. *Berkeley at War: The 1960s.* Oxford: Oxford University Press, 1989.

Russell, Sally. *Richard Brevard Russell: A Life of Consequence.* Macon, GA: Mercer University Press, 2011.

Sabin, Arthur J. *In Calmer Times: The Supreme Court and Red Monday.* Philadelphia: University of Pennsylvania Press, 1999.

Sargent, Daniel J. *A Superpower Transformed: The Remaking of American Foreign Relations in the 1970s.* Oxford: Oxford University Press, 2015.

Savage, Sean J. *JFK, LBJ, and the Democratic Party.* New York: State University of New York Press, 2004.

Saxbe, William B. *"I've Seen the Elephant": An Autobiography.* Kent, OH: Kent State University Press, 2000.

Schapsmeir, Everett L. *Dirksen of Illinois: Senatorial Statesman.* Urbana: University of Illinois Press, 1985.

Schlesinger, Arthur M. *Robert Kennedy and His Times.* New York: Houghton Mifflin.

Schmitz, David F. *The Tet Offensive: Politics, War, and Public Opinion.* Lanham, MD: Rowman & Littlefield, 2005.

Schulzinger, Richard D. "Nixon, Congress, and the War in Vietnam." In *Vietnam and the American Political Tradition: The Politics of Dissent,* edited by Randall B. Woods. Cambridge: Cambridge University Press, 2003.

Segrave, Kerry. *Vending Machines: An American Social History.* Jefferson, NC: McFarland, 2002.

Shaw, John M. *The Cambodian Campaign: The 1970 Offensive and America's Vietnam War.* Lawrence: University Press of Kansas, 2005.

Simmons, Solon. *The Eclipse of American Equality: Arguing Equality on "Meet the Press."* Stanford, CA: Stanford University Press, 2013.

Simon, James F. *The Center Holds: The Power Struggle inside the Rehnquist Court.* New York: Simon & Schuster, 1995.

Small, Melvin. *The Presidency of Richard Nixon.* Lawrence: University Press of Kansas, 1999.

Smist, Frank J. *Congress Oversees the US Intelligence Community, 1947–1989.* Knoxville: University of Tennessee Press, 1994.

Spofford, Tim. *Lynch Street: The May 1970 Shootings at Jackson State College.* Kent, OH: Kent State University Press, 1988.

Steinberg, Blema S. *Shame and Humiliation: Presidential Decision Making on Vietnam.* Montreal: McGill-Queens University Press, 1996.

Stone, Gary. *Elites for Peace: The Senate and the Vietnam War, 1964–1968.* Knoxville: University of Tennessee Press, 2007.

Strassfield, Robert N. "The Vietnam War on Trial: The Court-Martial of Howard W. Levy." *Wisconsin Law Review* (1994): 839–963.

Sundquist, James L. *The Decline and Resurgence of Congress.* Washington, DC: Brookings Institution Press, 1981.

Telley, William. *October Crisis, 1970: An Insider's View.* Alberta: University of Alberta Press, 2007.

Thomas, Evan. *Robert Kennedy: His Life.* New York: Simon & Schuster, 2000.

Thompson, Robert David. *Ernest Gruening and the American Dissenting Tradition.* Cambridge, MA: Harvard University Press, 1998.

Thompson, William N. *Gambling in America: An Encyclopedia of History, Issues, and Society.* Santa Barbara, CA: ABC-CLIO, 2015.

Tulchin, Joseph L. "US Relations with Latin America." In *Lyndon Johnson Confronts the World: American Foreign Policy, 1963–1968,* edited by Warren I. Cohen and Nancy Bernkopf Tucker. Cambridge: Cambridge University Press, 1995.

Vagts, Detlev F. "The Logan Act: Paper Tiger or Sleeping Giant?" *American Journal of International Law* 60 (1966): 268–302.

Valeo, Francis Ralph. *Mike Mansfield, Majority Leader: A Different Kind of Senate.* New York: M. E. Sharpe, 1999.

Van Atta, Dale. *With Honor: Melvin Laird in War, Peace, and Politics.* Madison: University of Wisconsin Press, 2008.

Wasniewski, Matthew Andrew. *Women in Congress: 1917–2006.* Washington, DC: Government Printing Office, 2006.

Weatherford, Doris. *Woman's Almanac.* Westport, CT: Greenwood Press, 2002.

Williams, Julian E. *The Case against Justice William O. Douglas.* Tulsa, OK: Christian Crusade, 1970.

Williams, Mark Eric. *Understanding US–Latin American Relations: Theory and History.* New York: Routledge, 2011.

Wittes, Benjamin. *Confirmation Wars: Preserving the Independent Courts in Angry Times.* Lanham, MD: Rowman & Littlefield, 2014.

Wolfensberger, Donald R. *Congress and the People: The Deliberative Democracy on Trial.* Baltimore, MD: Johns Hopkins University Press, 2000.

Woods, Randall Bennett. *J. William Fulbright, Vietnam, and the Search for a Cold War Foreign Policy.* Cambridge: Cambridge University Press, 1995.

Woodward, Bob, and Scott Armstrong. *The Brethren: Inside the Supreme Court* (New York: Simon & Schuster, 1979.

Zelizer, Julian. *On Capitol Hill: The Struggle to Reform Congress and Its Consequences, 1948–2000.* Cambridge: Cambridge University Press, 2004.

Zick, Timothy. "The First Amendment in Transborder Perspective: Toward a More Cosmopolitan Orientation." *Boston College Law Review* 52 (2011): 941–1025.

Zweirs, Maarten. *Senator James O. Eastland: Mississippi's Jim Crow Democrat.* Baton Rouge: Louisiana State University Press, 2015.

INDEX

Abernethy, Thomas, 2, 14, 158, 169, 170, 243
Acheson, Dean, 69, 129
Adams, Brock, 177–178, 232
Agger, Carol, 52, 102–103, 117, 147
Agnew, Spiro, 58, 111–112, 210, 242, 244, 255, 258
Albert, Carl, 115–116, 121, 135–137, 157–159, 162, 169, 172, 176, 180, 243, 255, 258
Alderman v. United States, 67
American Friends of Vietnam, 80–81, 84
Arizona Republic, 125
Ashbrook, John, 23, 48, 156, 183, 250, 265
Ashmore, Harry, 42, 47, 71–72, 109
Atlanta Journal, 124, 170, 249
Aull, Fay, 94
Avant Garde (magazine), 66, 151

Baker, Howard, 202
Baker, Robert, 5, 39–44, 57, 100, 108, 117, 118, 144–146, 148, 232
Baker v. Carr, 13, 47
Baltimore Sun, 203, 248
Becker, Benton, 6, 108, 191–192
Bellmon, Henry, 223
Black, Fred, 41
Black, Hugo, 14, 18, 23, 47, 53, 63–65, 67, 73, 77, 92, 110, 114, 147, 150, 162, 172, 251
    supports William O. Douglas against Ford, 200, 250
Blackburn, Benjamin, 90, 170
Blackmun, Harry A., 8, 36–37, 53, 57–60, 120, 126–129, 147, 198, 247
Black Panthers, 67, 116, 160, 239
Bolling, Richard, 177, 179–181
Bosch, Juan, 103–105, 109–110, 118
    and alleged Mafia ties, 118
    and Douglas, 118, 129, 138, 144–145, 148, 245

Boston Globe, 124, 208, 240, 247
Brandeis, Louis, 50, 61, 72, 149, 233
Brant, Irving, 238
Brennan, Peter J., 163
Brennan, William J., 6, 23, 37, 49, 66–67, 92, 238, 254
Brooke, Edward, 203, 228–239, 258
Brooks, Jack, 45, 135–137, 244, 255
Brown, Edmund G., 143
Brown, H. Rapp, 175
Brownell, Herbert, 11, 36, 169
Brown v. Board of Education, 13, 19–20, 53, 120, 134, 210, 216–217, 251
Burger, Warren, 29, 35–37, 58, 60, 120, 128, 146–147, 234, 254
    and Douglas, 109, 247, 256
    and judicial reform efforts, 60–62, 68, 89, 95, 113, 208, 210, 225
    and role in the House investigation, 242
Buttinger, Joseph, 80
Byrd, Harry, 20
Byrd, Robert C., 4, 13, 37, 94, 221
Byrnes, James, 150

Cabell, Earle, 15
Cambodia, war in, 7, 31–33, 110, 123–124, 126, 130–134, 160–161, 192, 199
    congressional opposition to invasion, 203–205
    Ford's knowledge of Nixon's secret invasion plans, 8–9
    1970, invasion of, 4, 8–10, 112
    Nixon's secretiveness prior to invasion, 31
    Operation Menu, 8–9
Campbell, William J., 47–49, 71, 147, 205
    and Douglas's opinion of, 71, 79, 99, 151
    investigation of, 49, 144

Carswell, G. Harrold, 3–5, 7, 16, 58, 90, 125–129, 141, 152, 170, 174, 179, 181, 203–206, 213,215–216, 220–223, 226–236
Case, Clifford, 57, 203–204
Celler, Emanuel, 14, 45, 54, 65, 77, 121, 136, 163, 170, 175–176, 182–185, 202, 208–209, 235
  and friendship with Douglas, 80
  and friendship with William McCulloch, 136–137
  and investigation of Abe Fortas, 54
  and 1954 investigation of Douglas, 77
  and 1970 leadership of the investigation of Douglas, 121–124, 133, 135–136, 138, 140–145, 148–151, 153, 159, 170–176, 189–199, 226, 243
  and rebuke to Douglas, 101
Center for the Study of Democratic Institutions (CSDI), 71–72, 84, 104–107, 119, 138, 143, 145, 148, 195, 225, 245–248, 255
Central Intelligence Agency, 25, 32, 48, 78, 84, 92, 105, 108, 149, 175, 193, 226, 229, 247–248, 250
  Douglas's work with, 78
  and investigation of Douglas, 149, 193–196, 249
  and Sasha Volman, 105
Chandler, Stephen, 45–48
Chicago Daily News, 47–48
Chicago Tribune, 8, 48, 95, 106, 208
China, People's Republic of, 30, 70, 75–77, 106, 130–131, 204–205, 255
  Douglas supports recognition of, 75–77, 106, 138
Christopher, Warren, 139, 142–143
Church, Frank, 79, 95, 131, 204, 233, 235
Churchill, Winston, 78
Cincinnati Enquirer, 125
Clarion-Ledger, 128, 209, 249
Clark, Joseph, 23
Clark, Ramsey, 51, 110, 142–143, 149–151, 196
Clark, Tom, 69, 217, 238

Clausen, Don, 186–187
Clifford, Clark, 73, 84–85, 109–110, 142, 196, 256
Cohelan, Jeffrey, 164
Cohen, Benjamin V., 23, 238
Colmer, William, 134–135, 149, 158, 169–170, 192–194
Conyers, John, 5
Cooper, John Sherman, 16, 57, 71, 131, 203–204, 215
Cooper–Church Amendment, 203–205, 211–214, 219, 222, 227, 229, 231, 237, 248, 250
Cooper v. Aaron, 13
Countryman, Vern, 142
Cramer, William, 3, 173, 183–184

Darlington Manufacturing Co. v. NLRB, 71
Dean, John, 5, 221, 228, 243, 246
DeGregory v. Attorney General, 121
Dennis v. United States, 25, 237
Des Moines Register, 7, 43, 108, 124, 209, 248
Detroit Free Press, 125, 153, 209
Dickinson, William, 15, 171
Diem, Ngo Dinh, 80–81, 205
Dirksen, Everett, 34, 48, 51, 76, 104, 205, 221–222, 206
Dominican Republic, 103–105, 109
Donovan, William, 70, 78, 194
Douglas, William O., 1–3, 9, 12, 15–16, 22, 25–26, 33–36, 44–45, 60–62, 66–68, 69–70, 72–73, 79, 148–154, 250–254
  and Abe Fortas, 49–51, 53
  and Albert Parvin, 6–7, 9, 25, 71, 96, 101, 138, 144–145, 165, 176, 225, 244
  America Challenged, 73, 97–90, 102
  argues to recognize China, 75–76
  assists Kurdish professor Salih Abdulrahim, 139, 245–246
  and Central Intelligence Agency generally, 78–80
  and Earl Warren, 22, 41–43, 47, 74, 88, 152, 238
  Ford, opinion of, 140
  and Harry A. Blackmun, 247

and Harry Truman, 76
and Hugo Black, 23, 200, 250
impeachment, prior calls for, 2–4, 77
and intelligence work with the Central
    Intelligence Agency regarding Iran,
    78–79, 194
and intelligence work with the Central
    Intelligence Agency regarding the
    Soviet Union, 194
and intelligence work with the Office
    of Strategic Services, 70, 194
Iran, travels to, 77–78
and Juan Bosch, 118, 129, 138,
    144–145, 148, 245
Look Magazine, 79, 80, 151
and Lyndon Johnson, 9, 69, 71, 72, 93,
    119
and Mohammad Mossadegh, 77–79
Nixon, opinion of, 23–24, 66, 70, 107
Nixon's opinion of, 3–5, 35, 108, 192
Parvin Foundation, 32, 47, 71,
    101–106, 108, 128, 138, 147–148,
    185, 225, 244–246
and Perendu Kumar Banerjee, 84
Points of Rebellion, 92–96, 112, 115–
    116, 125, 133, 137–140, 143–147,
    151, 170–173, 181, 184–186, 190,
    214, 216, 218, 226, 235, 238, 245
pornography, association with, 9
and Ralph Ginzburg, 149–150
as Roosevelt's advisor, 72–73
Roosevelt considered for vice
    president, 73
Vietnam War, 20, 69, 70–73, 80, 86–93,
    108–110, 115
and Warren Burger, 109, 247, 256
"We Have Become Victims of the
    Military Mind," 79, 97, 99
and William Brennan, 6, 52, 238
Dwyer, Florence, 93, 156, 181–183, 258
Dykema, Gossett, Spencer, Goodnow, and
    Trigg Law Firm, 196

Eastland, James O., 13–14, 18, 20, 43, 202
Eaton v. Grubs, 55
Edwards, Donald, 132, 255

Edwards, Edwin, 168
Edwards, William, 5, 171
Ehrlichman, John, 5, 152, 165
Einstein, Albert, 36, 96
Eisenhower, Dwight, 11, 13–16, 20, 31, 36,
    43, 70, 79, 81, 99, 103, 120, 136, 160,
    169, 211, 216
Ervin, Samuel, 13, 20, 49, 62, 212,
    216–219, 248–249, 253–254
and efforts at judicial ethics reform,
    62–63, 65
Evergreen magazine, 115, 137, 147, 151, 190

Fahy, Charles, 242
Fannin, Paul, 66, 108, 213–214, 230–231,
    234
Federal Bureau of Investigation, 18, 25, 41,
    44, 96, 136, 149, 187, 193, 209
Ford, Gerald, 1, 8, 33, 37, 47, 50, 53, 57,
    78, 94, 96–98, 110–112, 137–139,
    143–145, 152–153, 162, 164, 166,
    178–180, 185, 198, 205–207, 210,
    217, 219–220, 225, 227, 231, 233,
    238, 239, 243–245, 247, 250
Albert Parvin, accusations against, 93–94
alliance with Southern Democrats
    and segregationists, 3, 19, 133–134,
    155–156, 167, 169–172
and Carl Albert, 158–159
and civil rights, 1
Douglas, accusations against, 1–5,
    9–10, 20, 23, 31, 39, 41, 44, 53, 71,
    83, 103–106, 111–120
Douglas's opinion of, 140
Emanuel Celler, complaints against,
    148, 159, 190–193, 196
as House minority leader, 1, 11–12
and judicial reform efforts, 65
and Lyndon Johnson, 1
and Melvin Laird, 31
motives to have Douglas impeached,
    4–5, 9, 19–21, 24–26, 31, 33
newspaper characterization of attack
    on Douglas, 123–130
Nixon and secret planning for invasion
    of Cambodia, 9, 33, 35–36

Ford, Gerald, *continued*
  as president, 10–11
  support from Christian Evangelical
    organizations to impeach Douglas,
    141–142
Fortas, Abe, 3, 9, 12, 28–29, 40, 42, 49–58,
    61, 63–64, 69, 73, 107, 110, 118,
    143, 169, 184, 186, 214, 217–219,
    224–227
Frankfurter, Felix, 16, 18, 50, 69, 73, 77,
    146, 150, 169
Frey, Louis, 174
Fulbright, William, 20–21, 71, 132,
    202–203, 215, 219

Gesell, Gerhard, 22, 82, 172–173, 240–242
  and armed forces integration, 82–83
  issues injunction against the House
    Internal Security Committee,
    239–240
Gibbons, Samuel, 131–132, 174–175
Ginsburg, Ruth, 36, 257
Ginzburg, Ralph, 44, 66, 149–150
Ginzburg v. United States, 66
Glasgow Herald, 129
Goldwater, Barry, 2, 10, 13, 30, 44, 52, 66,
    97, 107–108, 168, 184–186, 207,
    210–215, 229–230, 234, 249, 255
Gore, Albert, 21, 203
Gray, Frank, 59, 193, 238
Green, Edith, 79, 122, 177–179, 258
Grimes, Harlan, 45, 47
Gross, Harold R., 2, 7, 165–167
Gude, Gilbert, 165–166, 188–189
Gutknecht v. United States, 170

Haldeman, H. R., 58, 152, 154, 167
Haley, James, 112–113, 173–174
Hall, Durward Gorham, 172, 180
Halleck, Charles, 1, 33, 186
Hansen, Clifford, 231, 236
"Hard Hats," 156, 159, 161–164, 228
Harding, Warren G., 6, 61
Harlan, John, 114, 120, 251
Harlow, Bryce, 99–100, 219
Harris, Fred, 223

Haynsworth, Clement, 3–4, 12, 16, 43,
    53–58, 60, 63, 88, 115, 125–128,
    132, 141, 147, 150, 152, 162, 167,
    170, 177, 181, 203, 205–207, 210,
    213, 215–219, 222, 226–231
Hebert, F. Edward, 89–90, 168
Heckler, Margaret, 156, 181–182
Helms, Richard, 32, 194–195
Holland, Spessard, 220–221
Hooker, John J., 59–60
HR 920, 121, 137–139, 158–159, 161, 165,
    168, 171–173, 176, 183, 186, 190
Hughes, Charles Evans, 42, 110, 150
Hughes, Harold, 226–227
Hughes, Howard, 100, 116, 148
Hull, William R., 172, 180
Humphrey, Hubert, 11, 19, 28, 50, 71,
    118–119, 179, 224
Hutchins, Robert, 71–73, 84, 98, 120
Hutchinson, Edward, 136, 138–139,
    243–246
Horowitz, Charles, 23, 100, 110
Huston, Charles, 32
Huston Plan, 32, 132

Ichord, Richard, 172–174, 188, 239–242,
    248
Internal Revenue Service (IRS), 32, 38, 40,
    52, 96, 101–102, 107, 118, 147, 149,
    189, 193, 196
Internal Security Committee, House,
    239–241
Iran, 77–78, 90, 194

Jackson, Henry, 232–223
Jackson, Robert, 48, 73, 106, 246, 251
Jacobs, Andrew, 121–122, 158
John Birch Society, 16–17, 95, 178, 183,
    186, 239
Johnson, Lyndon, 1, 5, 10, 11–12, 14, 19,
    20, 27, 33, 39, 40–41, 43, 48, 50,
    103–104, 117–118, 135–136, 142–
    143, 157, 162, 168, 176, 180, 182,
    205, 211, 215, 217, 225, 229, 233
  and Abe Fortas, 50–52
  disparaged Gerald Ford, 1–2

opinions of Douglas on, 9, 69, 71, 72, 93, 119
and the Vietnam War, 21, 28, 30–33, 69, 71, 76, 81, 84, 130, 235, 237
Jordan, Lem, 233–236

Kennedy, Edward, 7, 124, 206–207, 225, 228
Kennedy, John F., 1, 10, 20–22, 29, 59, 69, 70, 81, 98, 103–104, 118, 134–135, 142, 146, 148, 168, 178, 180, 211, 237
Kennedy, Joseph, 43, 72
Kennedy, Robert, 21, 44, 56, 79, 122, 194
Kent State University, 127, 161, 223
Kissinger, Henry, 8, 10, 31, 130–131, 253
Kleindeinst, Richard, 58, 147
Koch, Edward, 5, 132–133, 172

Laird, Melvin, 8–9, 31, 33, 131, 211, 223, 248, 252
Laird v. Tatum, 253, 257
Lansky, Meyer, 17, 97, 100, 116, 120, 191
Leventhal, Harold, 52, 62, 238, 242
Levinson, Edward, 41, 96, 100, 117, 144–145, 191, 195
Liberty Lobby, 17
Long, Clarence Dickinson, 157, 172
Look Magazine, 79–80, 151
Los Angeles Times, 7, 8, 37, 41, 42, 57, 60, 95, 100–101, 107, 208

MacGregor, Clark, 23, 64 109
Mafia, 7, 17, 96, 102, 109, 118, 176, 237, 245
  allegations of Douglas's connection to, 7, 109, 116, 237
  allegations of Parvin's connection to, 41, 96–98, 100, 176, 225, 245
Mansfield, Michael, 81, 131, 204
Marshall, Thurgood, 14, 60, 92, 150, 184, 205, 217, 229, 254
Mathias, Charles, 58, 203, 220–221
May, Catherine Dean, 94, 156, 181, 187, 258
McArthur v. Clifford, 87
McCarthy, Eugene, 21, 36, 223–225

McCarthy, Joseph, 11, 15–16, 38, 52, 93, 112, 229
McClellan, John, 20, 41, 43
McCloskey, Paul, 34, 157, 164–167, 182, 186, 197, 238, 251, 258
McCormack, John, 104, 115, 122, 134–135, 152, 157–158, 162, 172–173, 175
McCullogh, William, 14, 136–138, 142, 159, 193, 244, 258
McGovern, George, 23, 204, 223, 252
McGowan, Carl, 52, 242
Minh, Ho Chi, 71, 84–85, 119, 138
Mink, Patsy, 5, 132, 157, 177, 179, 184, 258
Miranda v. Arizona, 28–29, 213
Mitchell, John, 5–6, 31, 52–53, 57, 66, 110, 117, 152–154, 180, 193–194, 205, 226, 237, 244, 258
Mollenhoff, Clark, 7, 32, 42–47, 57, 100, 108–109, 117, 124, 139, 152, 222, 228, 242, 248, 258
Mondale, Walter, 52, 223–227
Morse, Wayne, 15, 21, 95, 110, 142
Morse, Wylie, 191
Morse v. Boswell, 87–88
Muskie, Edwin, 80, 93–94, 228

National City Bank v. Republic of China, 150
New York Times, 8, 23, 34, 39, 59, 92, 95, 101, 123–124, 131–132, 140, 151, 153, 158, 160, 192, 208, 247, 251
New Zealand Herald, 128
Nixon, Richard, 1, 6, 14, 16, 25, 27, 29, 38, 47, 49, 51, 72, 76, 88, 93, 99–103, 110–118, 123, 125–127, 130, 136, 145, 149, 157, 160, 177, 179, 184, 187, 191–194, 208, 210–212, 215, 221–222, 225–226, 229, 245–247
  anti-communism, 11
  antipathy for William O. Douglas, 3–5, 35, 108, 192
  beginning of presidency, 29–31
  Cambodia, invasion of, 8–9, 129–133, 161–166, 172, 199, 219
  and Clark Mollenhoff, 7, 43–45
  Congress's attempts to limit power, 203–226

Nixon, Richard, *continued*
    Douglas's opinion of, 23–24, 66, 70, 107
    Henry Kissinger, secrecy with, 31
    impeachment and resignation of, 12,
        255
    political attacks on opponents, 27, 70
    political attacks on the federal
        judiciary, 27–28, 52–59
    shaping a conservative court, 4, 7–8, 67
    and Southern strategy, 2, 19
    threatens Earl Warren, 152–153
    Vietnamization policy, 31–33
    and Warren Burger, 35
Nofziger, Lyn, 58, 152, 154, 228

O'Callahan v. Parker, 90–92, 121
Office of Strategic Services, 70, 194
O'Neal, Maston Emmett, 155, 170–172
O'Neill, Thomas "Tip," 5, 135
Orlando Sentinel, 95

Parvin, Albert, 5, 32, 38, 41, 101–106,
        116–117, 125, 189–192, 195–196,
        205, 248
    accusations of connection to organized
        crime, 10, 41–43, 96–99
    connection to Douglas, 6–7, 9, 25, 71,
        96, 101, 138, 144–145, 165, 176,
        225, 244
    IRS audit, 107–109, 147
    Parvin-Dorhman Corporation,
        100–102, 108, 117, 158, 189, 190,
        192, 247
    Parvin Foundation, 32, 47, 71,
        101–106, 108, 128, 138, 147–148,
        185, 225, 244–246
    Securities and Exchange Commission
        investigation of, 158
    and Speaker of the House John
        McCormack, 158
Philadelphia Inquirer, 8, 125
Points of Rebellion, 92–96, 110, 115–115,
        125, 133, 137, 140, 145–147, 151,
        170, 172, 176, 181, 184–186, 190,
        214, 218, 226, 235, 238
Powell, Adam Clayton, 79

Powell, Lewis, 251–252, 257
Powell v. McCormack, 25, 37
Princeton University, 42, 61, 97, 98, 127
Pye, Christopher, 32

Rayburn, Samuel, 134–135, 157, 176, 180
Reagan, Ronald, 16, 216
Rehnquist, William, 57, 66, 147, 153, 251,
    253–254, 257
Reid, Ogden Rogers, 167
Rhodes, James, 102, 132
Rhodes, John Jacob, 184–185, 255
Rhodesia, 119, 168, 175, 185, 200,
    212–213, 215
Richmond Times-Dispatch, 127, 209
Riegle, Don, 165–166, 251
Rifkind, Simon, 109–110, 142–149, 192,
    196–198, 244, 246
Rockefeller, Nelson, 16, 23, 30–31, 73, 186,
    188, 255
Rodell, Fredrick, 35, 140–141, 200
Rogers, Byron, 134, 135–136, 243–244
Rogers, Paul G., 173
Rogers, William, 31, 131, 157
Romney, George, 16, 50, 71
Roosevelt, Eleanor, 16
Roosevelt, Franklin D., 1, 23, 45, 50,
    61–62, 70, 72, 75, 80, 93, 95, 106,
    142, 169, 175, 183, 229, 234, 238
    advised by Douglas, 72–73
    considered Douglas as a vice
        presidential candidate in 1944, 73
Rostenkowski, Dan, 162–164
Rules Committee, House, 112, 127,
    133–135, 149, 155, 169, 171, 174,
    176, 182, 185, 192–193, 243
Rusk, Dean, 84
Russell, Richard, 9, 16, 20, 40, 217

Scherle, William, 29, 184
Schneebeli, Herman, 14
Scott, Hugh, 16, 131, 133, 206, 210, 255
Scott, William Lloyd, 3, 94, 138, 156, 183,
    250
Seattle Times, 177, 208
Selective Service, 82–84, 90, 170

Sensing, Thurman, 24–25
Sirica, John J., 242
Skolnick, Sherman, 47–49, 71, 144–145, 152, 205, 245
Smith, Howard K., 135
Smith, Ian, 168–169, 185–186, 215
Smith, Margaret Chase, 16, 57, 228, 253
Smith, Ralph Tyler, 205–206
Sobeloff, Simon, 13, 52, 55–56, 87
Southern Manifesto, 19–20, 89, 109, 134, 156, 168–169, 171–176, 203, 215–216, 220
Southern strategy, 19, 53, 112–113, 167, 258
Soviet Union, 24, 70, 77–79, 126, 138, 194, 199–200, 232, 252, 255
Stennis, John, 9, 20, 216
Stewart, Potter, 6, 86, 114, 120, 147, 254
St. Petersburg Times, 173
Sydney Morning Herald, 8, 129, 250

Taft, Robert, 14, 16, 38
Taft, Robert, Jr., 35, 64–65, 102, 113
Taft, William Howard, 61–62, 208, 252
Teague, Olin, 176
Teamsters Union, 7, 43, 59, 127
Terry v. Ohio, 66
Thurmond, Strom, 2, 16, 19–20, 52, 107–109, 128, 202, 207, 210, 214
Times (of London), 8, 129, 249
Times of India, 128
Times Picayune, 135
Truman, Harry S., 10–11, 16, 20, 22, 30, 38, 50, 69, 73–78, 84, 93, 98, 142, 211, 237
rebuke of Douglas, 76
Tydings, Joseph, 63–65, 220

Un-American Activities Committee, House, 11, 172, 188, 239
United States v. Robel, 174

Vietnam, war in, 7–9, 16, 20–24, 30, 50, 52, 67, 85, 107, 123–126, 130–137, 157–160, 164, 169, 173, 175–177, 202–207, 220, 227–233, 240, 246, 248–250, 252–254
Douglas's assistance to Diem, 80–81

Douglas's criticism of, 20, 69, 70–73, 80, 86–93, 108–110, 115
election issue in 1968, 28
Nixon's policies, 29, 30–33, 182–183, 188, 212–214, 218–219, 223, 237
US population in opposition to, 27, 83
Vinson, Frederick, 16–17, 36, 50, 150

Waggonner, Joe, 119–120, 139, 148–149, 155, 158, 168, 170–171, 181, 191–192, 195, 208–209, 243, 245, 250, 252, 256
Waldie, Jerome, 132, 255
Warren, Earl, 6, 28–29, 37, 48–49, 51–52, 66, 95, 127, 134, 150, 153, 168, 207, 210, 213, 228, 236
accusations of sympathy for communism, 17–19
and Douglas, 22, 41–43, 47, 74, 88, 152, 238
efforts at judicial reform, 60–63, 65
Nixon administration's threats against, 152
Southern Democrat view of, 13, 217
Warren Commission, 1, 33, 110
Whalen, Charles, 166
White, Byron, 91, 140
Wiley, John Cooper, 98
Williams, John J., 6–7, 37–38, 52, 204, 207, 234
and interest in the Douglas-Parvin relationship, 38–49, 100, 108
and opposition to Clement Haynsworth, 58
and Sherman Skolnick, 144
Wilson, William, 5–8, 52–54, 144, 191, 194, 258
Wyman, Louis, 112–113, 120–121, 128, 135, 137, 139, 148, 170–172, 176, 181, 191–193, 196, 224, 243, 245, 250, 256

Yencopal, Albert, 94

Ziegler, Ronald, 124–125